And the Russians Stayed

And the Russians Stayed

THE SOVIETIZATION OF CUBA
A Personal Portrait by Néstor T. Carbonell

William Morrow and Company, Inc.
New York

Library of Congress Cataloging-in-Publication Data

Carbonell, Néstor T.
    And the Russians stayed : the Sovietization of Cuba : a personal
portrait / by Néstor T. Carbonell.
        p.   cm.
    ISBN 0-688-07213-5
    1. Cuba—Politics and government—1959–   2. Cuba—Politics and government—1933–1959. 3. Carbonell, Néstor T. 4. Russians—Cuba—History—20th century. 5. Communism—Cuba—History—20th century. 6. Military assitance, Russian—Cuba—History—20th century. 7. Counterrevolutions—Cuba—History—20th century. 8. Cuba—Relations—Soviet Union. 9. Soviet Union—Relations—Cuba. 10. Cuba—Foreign relations—1959–   I. Title.
F1788.C2566   1989
972.91'064—dc19   88-38565

Printed in the United States of America   CIP

First Edition

1 2 3 4 5 6 7 8 9 10

BOOK DESIGN BY NICOLA MAZZELLA

To Rosa, with love

Acknowledgments

It is impossible to thank individually all the many people who encouraged and helped me put together this book, which for years remained in its conceptual stage, brewing in my mind. But I would like to express my deep appreciation to the following:

Pat Hass, a talented writer, who introduced me to the heady world of publishing and assisted in structuring the outline.

Leona Schecter, my ebullient and resourceful literary agent, and her husband, the distinguished author Jerrold Schecter, who gave me valuable advice and backing throughout the arduous process.

Bruce Lee, my perceptive editor, and his able staff, who sharpened my focus, kindled my faith, and steered the project to completion.

José Miró Torra and Ascensión C. Pérez (Nena), who gave me access to the personal files of the former president of the Cuban Revolutionary Council (in exile), the late Dr. José Miró Cardona, and authorized me to disclose, at my sole discretion, unknown facts about the Bay of Pigs, the Missile Crisis, and the Cuban exiles' secret entente with Washington.

Ernesto Aragón, Dr. Miró Cardona's executive assistant and interpreter, who shared with me his notes and recollections of the private meetings with President John F. Kennedy, Attorney General Robert Kennedy, and other U.S. government officials.

The Honorable Mauricio Solaún, former U.S. ambassador to Nicaragua, who shed new light on the circumstances that led to the Sandinistas' rise to power in Managua and to the Soviet-Cuban penetration in Central America.

All those who took the time to read or skim through the manuscript, and gave me the benefit of their insights and observations, including: Former President Richard M. Nixon, General Brent Scowcroft, Dr. Zbigniew Brzezinski, Ambassador Jeane Kirkpatrick, Ambassador Armando Valladares, Dr. Carlos Márquez Sterling, Dr. Manuel Antonio de Varona, Ambassador Guillermo Belt, Dr. Luis Botifoll, Mr. Jorge Mas Canosa, Dr. Luis E. Aguilar, and Dr. José Manuel Hernández. Although in most cases I heeded their counsel and followed their recommendations, I am solely responsible for any errors of fact or judgment found in the book.

My dear friends, Allie and Lee Hanley, who were always there when I needed them, with creative solutions and unflagging endorsement.

And finally, of course, I would like to thank my entire family, without whose understanding, patience, and collaboration this book could not have been written. When the project was but a nebulous concept, both of my grandfathers illuminated my thoughts and spurred me on to undertake the task. My parents, so emotionally attached to our country of birth and the cause of freedom, were a tremendous source of information and sound advice. And my cousins Ofelia and Eduardo Arango, Ramón Puig, and Humberto Cortina, who played a prominent role in the Cuban resistance movement, broke their discreet silence and recounted their daunting experiences.

At home, I found what all fledgling authors yearn for: reassurance and tranquility. My daughter, Rosa María, and my sons, Néstor Gastón and José Manuel, who during many a weekend became my captive audience and critiqued the drafts, exuded optimism, and urged me to pursue the journey. And my wife, Rosa, with whom I shared the dreams and frustrations of writing, gave me the zeal, support, and inspiration to overcome the obstacles and scale the heights.

Contents

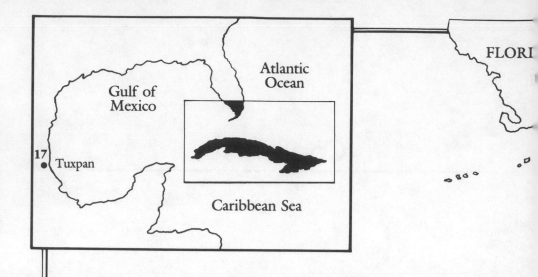

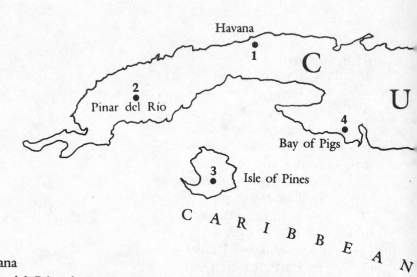

1. Havana

2. Pinar del Río—large percentage of Moncada recruits came from here

3. Isle of Pines (now Isle of Youth), Castro and company imprisoned here, 1953–1955

4. Bay of Pigs (or Playa Girón), April 17, 1961, exiles' invasion

5. Santa Clara, capital of Las Villas province—conquest climaxes Che's campaign

6. Escambray Mountains—non-Castro guerrillas in 1958/site of anti-Castro guerrillas, 1960–1965

7. Bayamo—simultaneous rebel attack on barracks, July 26, 1953

8. *Granma* landing—Los Cayuelos, December 2, 1956

9. Alegría de Pío battlefield—first Castro defeat

10. La Plata—Fidel's headquarters atop Sierra Maestra

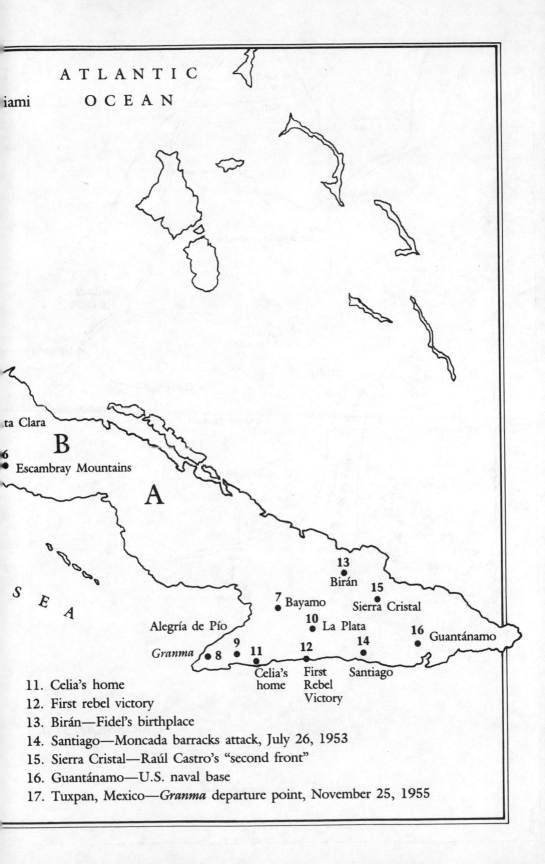

ATLANTIC

OCEAN

iami

ta Clara

B

6
● Escambray Mountains

A

S E A

13
● Birán

7 Bayamo
●

15
● Sierra Cristal

Alegría de Pío

10
● La Plata

16
● Guantánamo

Granma

9
●

11
●

12
●

14
●

8
●

Celia's
home

First
Rebel
Victory

Santiago

11. Celia's home
12. First rebel victory
13. Birán—Fidel's birthplace
14. Santiago—Moncada barracks attack, July 26, 1953
15. Sierra Cristal—Raúl Castro's "second front"
16. Guantánamo—U.S. naval base
17. Tuxpan, Mexico—*Granma* departure point, November 25, 1955

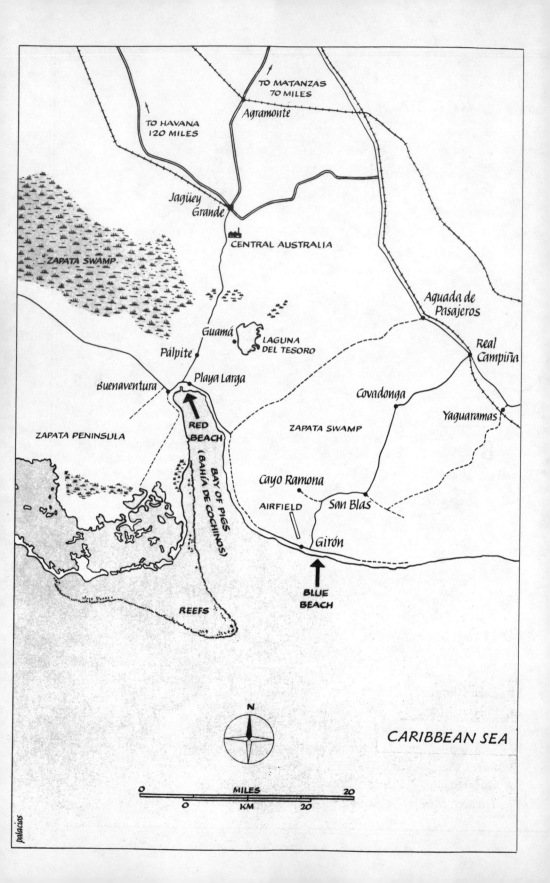

Introduction

Columbus was enchanted by the natural splendor of Cuba. Shortly after discovering the island in October 1492, he sent off a letter to King Ferdinand and Queen Isabella of Spain:

> I have been so overwhelmed at the sight of so much beauty that I have not known how to relate it. The multitude of palm trees of various forms, the highest and most beautiful I have ever seen, and an infinity of other tall and green trees, the birds in rich plumage, and the verdure of the fields render this country, most serene princes, of such marvelous beauty that it surpasses all others in charms and graces as the day does the night in luster.

Nearly five hundred years later, Cuba cast the same spell on me. She dazzled me with her wide and splendid skies, her hills, her white beaches, and the myriad blues of her seas; her scented flowers, her valleys, her gentle breezes, and the exuberance of her trees. But above all, she enthralled me with her sun, a most brilliant sun, that brought warmth and color to the island and liveliness to her people. That is how I still remember Cuba: bathed in the sunlight that inspired my youth, vivid in my thoughts, glowing in my dreams.

My Cuban roots are deep and strong. I am attached to the island not only because I was born and raised there, but also because of my family's involvement in her independence and politi-

13

cal struggles, her economic and social development, and her manifold cultural pursuits.

On my father's side of the family, the patriarch and legendary figure was Néstor Leonelo Carbonell, who participated in the first Cuban war of independence, known as the Ten Years War (1868–1878). He fought against the superior forces of Spain, and also against epidemic fevers which almost consumed him. He escaped from seventeen ambushes and withstood the terrible blow of the death of his wife and four children, who were stricken down with smallpox.

Following the inconclusive war, Néstor Leonelo rebuilt his life, remarried, and emigrated with his family to Tampa, Florida. There he founded a school, wrote in newspapers and magazines, and organized the patriotic Club Ignacio Agramonte to rekindle the flame of rebellion against Spanish colonial rule. Under the auspices of that club, Néstor Leonelo invited Cuba's foremost hero, poet, and visionary, José Martí, to address the large exile community in Tampa. It was a momentous occasion, for it was then and there that Martí delivered his two most famous speeches, which electrified the Cubans and laid the groundwork for the final liberation war.

Roused by Martí's oratory and by Néstor Leonelo's example, my grandfather José Manuel joined the insurgency at age fifteen. Following independence, he undertook diplomatic assignments, cultivated poetry and oratory, and emerged as one of the leaders of the intellectual movement in Cuba. My father also chose public service. Very young, he gave up the practice of law and entered politics, which became the breath of his life.

On my mother's side, the most prominent figure was José Manuel Cortina. Born into a middle-class family of agriculturists, he worked during his early youth as a *lector de tabaquería*—a reader who regaled tobacco workers with selections of poetry, novels, essays, and the daily news. This experience, coupled with the leadership role he played in the university and the Liberal Party, spawned his mastery of oratory (he later became the "tribune of the republic"), and broadened his interests in life, from law and business to Parliament and diplomacy.

Given this family background, it was not surprising for me to engage in public affairs even before graduating from law school. That was the expectation, the unwritten rule at home: to be involved, regardless of risks and blunders—and we had our share of both. Community interests, political affiliations, social and humanitarian projects—each one of us was free to choose. But inhibition or aloofness was hardly an option. With privileges, we were told, go responsibilities.

What was not anticipated or foreseen was that we would be blocked from pursuing these endeavors and forced to leave our homeland by a totalitarian regime that accepted no compromise and allowed no dissent. Uprooted and dispersed, we continued to be involved, but in areas that were new to most of us: intelligence activities, propaganda, agitation, diplomatic intrigue, and paramilitary operations.

This book narrates my experiences and those of other members of my family and close friends, in the underground, within the exile community, in Washington, D.C., and in Latin American capitals, inside Castro's *gulag,* and before the firing squad. It spans thirty years, beginning on the fateful dawn of January 1, 1959, with the fall of Batista, but includes relevant episodes of Cuban Colonial and Republican history. It covers the secret anti-Castro Cuban-American alliance, the Bay of Pigs, the OAS response, the Missile Crisis, the continued Soviet military buildup in Cuba, and Castro Communist subversion from the Horn of Africa to the Caribbean Basin, and recounts some previously untold stories. It assesses the current situation, both inside Cuba and among the émigrés, and offers a perspective of the future.

This memoir does not purport to have the detachment and intellectual rigor of academia. After all, during most of this process I was an advocate and not a scholar. But having preserved copious notes taken during this turbulent period, I have tried to impart to the narrative the freshness of a witness and the immediacy of a protagonist. And having studied at length the causes and ramifications of the struggle, I have augmented mere description of the pivotal events with insights into the three critical factors that shaped them—the "Three Cs": the Cuban People, Castro, and the Compelling Geography.

CHAPTER 1

The Fateful Dawn

It was 4:00 A.M. when the phone rang on January 1, 1959. A colleague of my father's who was connected with the Batista regime called to advise us that the dictator and his family and intimate friends had fled Cuba on the presidential plane. Our informant was reliable. The message, though astonishing, was believable. It did not contain the elaborate adornments of fabrication. It carried the sober, unaffected ring of truth.

A few weeks before, rumors had circulated that Batista was preparing to abandon the island because the army was unwilling to fight the rebels. The government countered these rumors, and others that spelled disaster, by announcing a major offensive involving the call to active duty of a feared former chief of police, General Eleuterio Pedraza, and the deployment of fresh troops and guns on an armored train. This last-minute effort to regain the initiative proved fruitless and gave added momentum to the anti-Batista conspiracies that had already reached the highest levels of the army. Frightened, Batista stealthily prepared his exit. On December 31 he invited members of his cabinet, senior military officers, and close friends to celebrate the advent of the new year at army headquarters at Camp Columbia. Following the traditional toasts, he shocked his guests with the news that he was resigning and leaving the country immediately. Batista's decision was final; the stampede began.

After confirming the report of the flight, I awoke my maternal grandparents, José Manuel and María Josefa C. Cortina. My father, my mother, and I had moved in with them in mid-1958 after leasing our house to the Argentine ambassador, Julio Amoedo. We wanted to be close to the Cortinas, considering their advanced age and the proximity of their turn-of-the-century villa to Cuba's nerve center of urban revolutionary activities, the University of Havana. The villa and its residents had always been respected and protected, even in periods of turmoil. This time, however, no one could predict what would happen. We were not only facing the fall of a government; we were also exposed to the possible collapse of the republic. Many thoughts crossed our minds as we caucused in the early morning hours of January 1. Would there be a total vacuum of authority? Would the winds of anarchy lacerate the country, already beset by hatred and violence? Cortina was reluctant to leave the house, but we finally persuaded him to spend a day or two at a hotel in the residential area of Miramar. From there, we would gauge developments and determine what to do.

As we drove through the city that morning, not a single policeman could be seen. Youngsters wearing the red-and-black armbands of Castro's 26th of July Movement were taking over public buildings and broadcasting stations. Looters, like hungry birds of prey, were preparing to plunge into the homes of Batista supporters who had left Cuba or sought diplomatic asylum. Members of the underground were flaunting their guns and shooting at real or imaginary pockets of resistance. Drivers were honking their horns, and housewives were unfurling their flags. The news of Batista's flight had rapidly spread, and one could feel the first waves of excitement and jubilation.

Shortly after arriving at the hotel, we were informed that the acting chief of staff of the armed forces, General Eulogio Cantillo, wanted to see my grandfather and a few other elder statesmen at the presidential palace. Cantillo was seeking support and advice to ensure an orderly transition. The message did not totally surprise us, since Cortina had been called upon in various stages of the republic to help resolve major national crises. Although he had retired from politics in the 1940s after serving as senator, foreign minister, and president of the coordinating committee of the 1940 Constitutional Assembly, he remained alert and retained his prestige. His commanding presence—he was six feet tall, and had wavy black hair and a thick mustache—his broad culture, and his eloquence enhanced his impact as a mediator.

Cortina's mission—his last one in Cuba—was futile. He met

at my uncle Humberto's house in Miramar with some of the other notables, including the former constitutional vice-presidents of Cuba Raúl de Cárdenas (my wife-to-be's grandfather) and Gustavo Cuervo Rubio, and the learned jurist Alberto Blanco. They reviewed the changing situation and then drove to the presidential palace. There they were greeted by Cantillo and Dr. Carlos Manuel Piedra, the eldest Supreme Court justice, who was trying to form a provisional government as mandated by the Constitution in the absence of the President and other designated leaders.

Cortina and most of his companions argued that prompt and decisive action was essential to restore authority, but Judge Piedra opted to wait for the arrival of the other justices before taking the oath of office and integrating a cabinet of national unity acceptable to Castro. The justices never came. Instead they rejected the constitutional succession under Judge Piedra and solemnly declared that the triumphant revolution was fountain of legitimacy, source of law. Denied by his own colleagues the support necessary to salvage the rudderless ship of state, Piedra quietly left the presidential palace and went home. Meanwhile, Castro spurned the proposed constitutional transition, accused Cantillo of treason for having reneged on an alleged secret accord with Fidel, and gave orders to arrest him and have him executed. Thanks to the personal intervention of the American and Brazilian ambassadors, Cantillo's life was spared, but he was sentenced to fifteen years' imprisonment.

When my grandfather returned from the presidential palace to my uncle's house, his face was grim. The family gathered around him, as we usually did in times of peril and anxiety. He told us about the belated attempt to find a constitutional solution and said he regretted not having done more in the past to avert this crisis. He then added with a tone of sadness: "Seven years of corrupt dictatorship have gravely weakened the fabric of the republic and sapped its political and moral defenses. This is like a case of severe immune breakdown: Cuba lacks the vital antibodies to protect itself. It has fallen into the hands of Castro, and there is nothing solid in sight to limit his power or contain his influence. Who knows what the future will bring?"

We listened attentively to Cortina, but not all of the family shared his apocalyptic views. Some of my cousins were fascinated with the romance of the revolution and harbored no fears. Early signs were encouraging: the outbreak of violence was not as widespread as expected. Feeling more at ease, we drove back home on January 2 and stared at the television set. Castro and his followers had descended from the mountains in the far-eastern province of Oriente and were commencing their triumphal march to the capital. They carried rosaries, medallions, and scapulars and displayed impressive dark beards. It was like a procession of prophets, heralding the beginning of a new era. The Batista nightmare was over. Throughout Cuba, crowds celebrated in the streets and awaited the arrival of the revolutionary hero with placards that read "Thank you, Fidel," and "This is your home." With the Cubans' penchant for providential men and heroic deeds, the masses anointed him savior.

Castro basked in adoration. He moved slowly across the island, stopping in every town, seemingly oblivious of the exigencies of government. That was just an act. Castro had already taken the reins of power, was involved in every important decision, and only awaited the execution of the general strike he had decreed to force the resignation of all remaining officials and pave the way for absolute rule.

I did not fully understand why Castro was insisting on a national strike that would only cause more unrest and retard his ascendancy. It seemed illogical and unnecessary. The Batista regime had already disintegrated; Castro had emerged as the undisputed leader, and there were no real obstacles impeding the fulfillment of the revolutionary goals. What escaped me then was that from Castro's perspective, leadership alone was not enough. It was necessary to eliminate or neutralize all vestiges of authority predating the revolution, including the remnants of Cuba's standing army. It was essential to grab unlimited power without any strings attached to the past or any links compromising the future.

By moving swiftly and boldly, Castro was able to establish the primacy of his 26th of July Movement and the Rebel Army, to the exclusion of the other parties and groups that had participated in the struggle against Batista. It was a masterly coup that mirrored Lenin's "All the power to the Soviets"—except that Castro cunningly concealed his true intentions until the end of 1961, when he publicly confessed his Marxist-Leninist design.

By the time Castro reached Havana on January 8, two of his key aides, Camilo Cienfuegos and Che Guevara, were in complete control of army headquarters at Camp Columbia and of La Cabaña fortress. The last hope of a countervailing force within the army had vanished when Colonel Ramón Barquín and other prestigious military officers resigned their posts. They had been imprisoned by Batista following an aborted conspiracy in 1956, and had assumed command of the armed forces when they were freed on January 1. Their prestige, however, was not enough to withstand the overwhelming influence of Castro. On January 3, they turned over their command to the representatives of the revolutionary paladin, who promised to respect all those who had honored their uniform and now abided by the dictates of the new government.

Only the leaders of the Student Directorate occupying the University of Havana posed a potential challenge to Castro's power. With a single, eloquent speech to the masses gathered at Camp Columbia (and a follow-up appearance on television), he removed the threat and disarmed the students. He made an impassioned plea for national unity; he promised to turn the garrisons into schools ("Arms for what?" he rhetorically asked); and he pledged democracy and justice for all. And as he intoned an ode to harmony and peace, a white dove glided over the podium and perched on his shoulder. This favorable omen capped Castro's charismatic performance. The crowds, delirious with joy, gave him a thunderous ovation. Many of those who had opposed him, myself included, publicly praised his statesmanlike address and cautiously extended a vote of confidence.

With his canny knowledge of Cuban psychology, Castro spiced his dramatic renditions with touches of down-to-earth humor. During his first public rally, he paused after an eloquent flourish, turned to the popular cowboy-hatted Rebel Army Major Camilo Cienfuegos, and playfully asked him with an impish smile: "Am I doing well, Camilo?" This ingenious remark, which soon became a slogan, humanized *El Líder Máximo* and earned him the coveted accolade for success in Cuba: *simpático*. Very few perceptive observers saw in his engaging smile the elastic mask of a consummate actor.

At that time, I was a twenty-three-year-old bachelor working as an attorney at the law firm founded by Cortina. I had graduated from Villanova University in Havana in 1957, and had subsequently attended Harvard Graduate School of Law, where I earned a LL.M. degree. As well as practicing law, I had begun to write newspaper articles on national and international topics. Consistent with my family background and personal vocation, I was getting involved in public affairs.

As a young boy I had been exposed to the exhilaration and challenges of politics. My father, an ebullient personality who during the period 1940–1952 served as speaker of the House of Representatives and senator, took me to public rallies and encouraged me to listen to spirited debates on national issues. My mother, more subdued and reflective, also encouraged my interest in current events and imparted a sense of mission. She worried about the enervating influence of the sun-and-fun world that surrounded me. Preparing me perhaps for dark days ahead, she often repeated this poetic nugget of wisdom: "It's easy enough to smile when life flows like a song; but the man worthwhile is the man who smiles when everything goes dead wrong."

Both of my grandfathers took a keen interest in broadening my education. Cortina enlightened me with discussions about democracy, oratory, and international affairs. And my paternal grandfather, José Manuel Carbonell, who served as president of the Cuban Academy of Arts and Letters and ambassador to Brazil and Mexico, regaled me with poetry and stories of my ancestors' involvement in the wars of independence.

Given this heritage, and my growing devotion to country, culture, and freedom, I decided not to be a bystander in the tumultuous process that started on January 1, 1959. I would have preferred more time to mature before entering the public arena, but the revolution was not going to wait for me. It had taken off, and none of the senior members of my family was in a position to play a meaningful role. My grandfathers, too old to crusade on their own, were shunned by the apostles of the new regime, who were determined to sever all ties with the institutions and personages of the past. And my father, as a prominent politician who had taken a stand against both Batista and Castro, was also ostracized.

I felt that my turn had come to share the burden of civic responsibilities. To gain perspective, I delved into history and reviewed the French and Russian revolutions. I studied the laws that were being enacted by the new government and discussed them at length with my family. The Cuban phenomenon became the focus of my attention, the center of my life. Everything else, including my profession, social activities, and personal hobbies, was pushed into the background. I was fascinated by the popularity and audacity of the new leaders. But I also was concerned. I wasn't quite sure where they were heading.

The announcement of the first revolutionary government was generally well received. Manuel Urrutia, an independent judge who had bravely upheld democratic ideals during the Batista regime, was sworn in as Provisional President of Cuba. José Miró Cardona, a highly respected university professor of criminal law who steadfastly opposed the dictatorship, was named Prime Minister. Roberto Agramonte, another distinguished professor and presidential candidate in 1952, was appointed Foreign Minister. Rufo López Fresquet, a free-market economist and tax expert, became Finance Minister. The cabinet also included several young members of the 26th of July Movement who were close to Castro, such as Armando Hart, Minister of Education; Faustino Pérez, Minister of Recovery of Embezzled Property; and Augusto Martínez Sánchez, Minister of Defense.

None of the cabinet ministers was an avowed, card-carrying Communist. This allayed initial fears of radicalism. Few realized, however, that the minister without portfolio in charge of drafting new legislation, Osvaldo Dorticós, had been an active member of the Socialist Popular (Communist) Party. Despite his capitalistic habits as commodore of the aristocratic Cienfuegos Yacht Club, he never really renounced his Marxist vows. In just six months, following the partial restructuring of this Kerensky-type government, Fidel appointed Dorticós Provisional President to accelerate the Communist takeover of Cuba. As to Castro himself, he initially held no cabinet post, but he ruled behind the scene as secretary general of the 26th of July Movement and commander-in-chief of the Rebel Army.

The 1940 Constitution, which had been the rallying point during the struggle against Batista, was not fully reinstated as promised. The revolutionary government explained that amendments were necessary to punish Batista's "war criminals" and collaborators. A major campaign was launched to magnify the horrors of the dictatorship. Morbid details of murders and tortures were published everyday. Batista's "twenty thousand dead"—a deliberate exaggeration—became the justification for wholesale persecution and intimidation. Castro whipped up the crowds to a frenzy. He held them spellbound with his towering figure, magnetic personality, theatrical gestures, and endless oratory.

Castro's charisma was greatly enhanced by his skillful use of power. He was most effective when he launched scathing attacks against the "enemies of the people." First on the list were Batista's henchmen, whom Castro accused of genocide. The crowds, enraged by the horrendous crimes, demanded retribution, even vengeance. "To the firing wall!" became a public outcry. Castro obliged. He instituted kangaroo-court proceedings to legitimize summary executions. Hundreds were shot in the first few weeks. The masses asked for more.

Faced with growing criticism from responsible quarters, Castro proceeded to stage a major war trial in public. He wanted to prove to the world the integrity of revolutionary justice. The principal defendant was former Major Jesús Sosa Blanco, accused of committing many crimes under Batista in the province of Oriente. The site chosen was the huge sports coliseum in Havana. It could seat thousands of spectators and journalists. I decided to attend.

What I saw and heard at the trial was shocking. The inebriated crowd, craving for blood, constantly interrupted the proceedings, yelling "Assassin!" and "Bandit!" and "Thug!" The members of the tribunal, watching impassively, hardly examined the witnesses before handing down the death penalty. And the cynical defendant, smiling with scorn, defied the mobs and termed the entire spectacle "a Roman circus." Despite the apparent guilt of Sosa Blanco, world public opinion reacted very negatively. This was not surprising, for what was presented by the government as a model of fairness was nothing more than a masquerade of justice.

After Sosa Blanco was put to death, the executions continued, but with less fanfare. Then came the "case of the airmen." Forty-four members of Batista's air force, accused of war crimes, were brought to trial. The revolutionary tribunal was headed by Major Félix Peña, who had fought with Castro in the Sierra Maestra. The defense argued persuasively that the accused pilots had not killed civilians, but had dropped their bombs on unpopulated areas. To mislead Batista, they concocted reports of massacres which had never occurred. The tribunal found that the evidence presented by the prosecutor was insufficient to prove the pilots' guilt, and proceeded to acquit them.

Infuriated by the outcome of the trial, Castro ordered the court not to release the pilots, announced on television that the acquittal had been an error, and called for a retrial. Without relying on any new set of facts or evidence, the second tribunal swiftly convicted and sentenced the airmen—most of them to thirty years' imprisonment. Castro declared: "Revolutionary justice is based not on legal precepts, but on moral conviction. . . ." The defense counsel was dismissed from his post and disappeared; several witnesses who had testified for the airmen were arrested, and the president of the first tribunal, Major Peña, who had acquitted the pilots, was found dead in his car with a .45 bullet in his heart.[1]

While this was going on, my family, among many others, started to feel the effects of the revolutionary storm that was lashing the island. My uncle Manolo Cortina, a career foreign service officer who had held a high post at the Foreign Ministry, was compelled to leave Cuba despite his solid record of humanitarian actions which had saved the lives of many revolutionaries. On his departure, the authorities froze his bank account. The freeze was subsequently extended to include one of the accounts of my grandfather Cortina, because of an alleged confusion of names. Moreover, my father and all those who had taken the electoral challenge during the Batista government instead of marching to the revolutionary drummer were stripped of their political prerogatives and banned from public life for thirty years.

The succession of unexpected blows continued. I was not to be spared. My turn came when the government passed Law No. 11, which declared null and void all university degrees issued during the final stages of the struggle against Batista, while the University of Havana remained closed. The rationale was that youngsters who continued to study and graduated from other universities should not be better off than those who joined the ranks of the revolution and took up arms.

I was stunned by the punitive nature of this law, which in one sweep invalidated my five years of legal studies at the University of Villanova in Cuba and barred me from practicing my profession. I could not understand the reasoning behind this arbitrary measure. It had no legal foundation or moral justification, The fact that many of us studied during the rebellion did not necessarily imply insensitivity or neglect of our patriotic duties. It certainly constituted no crime.

Not expecting the government on its own to revoke or amend the law, I met with several professionals who shared my fate. We decided to denounce the measure and assert our rights. We marshaled our arguments, developed our brief, and mapped out a comprehensive campaign that encompassed possible legal actions, press statements, television debates, appeals from bar associations, professors, and student leaders, and rallies at the University of Villanova.

Despite the strength of our case and the support we had garnered, the government remained adamant and started to counterattack. Hard pressed for additional backing, we went to see Archbishop Enrique Pérez Serantes, a husky and powerful church leader who had saved Castro's life in 1953 after the aborted attack on the Moncada barracks. He listened to our plea and promised to help, but urged us not to exacerbate the situation with vitriolic attacks. He said: "The revolutionaries are bound to make mistakes, but they are generally well-intentioned. Be patient and have faith in Fidel."

A few days after our meeting with the archbishop, the government revoked the law. To save face, our degrees were suspended, but only for a few months. We could soon resume our professional activities. The regime had felt the pressure of public opinion and backed down. This seemed to signal an opportunity for a civilized dialogue. I thought of Msgr. Pérez Serantes and his unwavering faith in the revolution. Perhaps he was right after all.

The excesses of the Castro regime were generally accepted as the inevitable price of revolution. Many felt that the errors of inexperience were more than offset by the freshness of candor. The new rulers were ostensibly intent on eradicating corruption. They had created an invigorating climate with their populist style and colorful rallies. And they had generated widespread support by lowering rents by 50 percent, reducing the prices of meat, medicine, electricity, and telephone services, and raising the salaries of employees. With more money to spend and adequate supplies of goods not yet depleted by the government, the people went on a consumer binge and cheered.

In this early period of euphoria, however, not all was applause and adulation. Independent newspapers often carried words of caution and exercised constructive criticism. The prestigious journalist Humberto Medrano, for one, summarized the existing concerns in an editorial addressed to Castro which ended with the following dictum from Saint-Just, the "archangel" of the French Revolution: "The stones have been cut for the edifice of liberty. You can build with them a temple or a tomb."

Castro was angered by this and other editorials. He resented admonitions, and, spurred by the inflammatory climate created by his able propagandists, he fulminated against those who dared criticize or question his revolutionary decrees. Notwithstanding these disturbing tendencies, I was somewhat encouraged by the outcome of the university-degree incident, and decided to test the waters myself.

On March 8, 1959, I published an article titled "The New Republic" in Cuba's oldest newspaper, *Diario de la Marina,* headed by the courageous José Ignacio Rivero. It was divided into three sections: "The Rule of Law," "The 1940 Constitution as a Revolutionary Program," and "The People: Guardian of Their Freedom." The article was not intended to be controversial. It simply enunciated fundamental principles of democracy and pointed out what happens when governments violate or ignore them. It stressed the urgent need to restore the rule of law, and stated: "Life in a community, if not regulated by law, ineluctably leads to anarchy or to transitory governments of force. Citizens without the guaranty of law, duly established and enforced, are but miserable helots who have no rights or freedom. Rulers without the restraint of law become corrupt and often turn into real monsters obsessed by greed and a frantic quest for power."

The article also asserted that the key objective of the revolution against Batista had been the reinstatement of the 1940 Constitution, which was sufficiently broad and flexible to allow major socioeconomic reforms compatible with democracy and free enterprise. And it concluded by urging the Cuban people to play a more active role in public affairs in order to check the excesses of the revolutionary government and avoid further eclipses of liberty.

I never thought that Castro would have the time or the interest to read my article, which was not prominently displayed. I certainly did not expect an answer. In a speech delivered on March 13, 1959, he indirectly retorted as follows: "Some have started to write advising me that I am going too fast and urging caution. . . . They often refer to the law; but which law—the old law or the new law? Because there are two types of laws: those of the past made by vested interests and those of the present which we are going to make. We shall abide by the law, but the revolutionary law. . . . For the old law no respect; for the new law all our respect."

Castro then alluded to the point I had made concerning the full reinstatement of the 1940 Constitution. "Those of us who have defended the Constitution can speak about it," he postulated. "But of which Constitution? Of that which embodies the interests of the country. It is appropriate to state here that the revolutionary Council of Ministers, representing the large majority of the people, has the constitutional power of the republic at this time, and if an article of the Constitution becomes inoperative [or] too old, the revolutionary Council of Ministers . . . shall transform, modify, change, or substitute that constitutional provision."[2]

The implications of Castro's pronouncements were clear to me. Since he controlled the Council of Ministers (particularly after succeeding Dr. Miró Cardona as Prime Minister) and was purging the courts and modifying or suspending many of the constitutional guarantees, his political power was virtually boundless. To tighten his grip further, he later created broadly defined counterrevolutionary crimes which enabled the government to imprison and even execute those who were deemed enemies of the revolution.

An example of blatant arbitrariness to stifle dissent was the case of my former classmate Enrique Llaca Orbiz. After writing several articles criticizing Castro's economic policies, Enrique was accused of conspiring against the government and arrested. His able lawyer, Dr. Francisco Lorié Bertot, secured a writ of habeas corpus and obtained his release. As Enrique was leaving the courthouse with his young bride, he was again arrested on newly fabricated charges and whisked away by the secret police. The independent press denounced this travesty of law and turned it into a *cause célèbre*. Facing considerable pressure, Castro reluctantly set Llaca free but instructed the Ministry of Justice to proceed against the judges who had released him in the first place. A Supreme Court magistrate who was asked to investigate the case absolved the judges and declared that "only tyrants and despots abhor and disavow habeas corpus. . . ."[3] Castro confirmed this axiom by ultimately purging, arresting, or exiling all of the recalcitrant judges and suppressing the right of habeas corpus.

I was very much concerned over these developments. Political repression was certainly not a new phenomenon in Cuba. We had in the past endured, and ousted, oppressing dictators and mesmerizing *caudillos*. But Fidel Castro was different. He was a new breed of demagogue with a greater capacity for domination. And his style and techniques were also different. The numbing staccato of his slogans, the catchy simplicity of his dialectics, the awesome regimentation of his rallies, and the subversive hatred of his tirades—they did not have the familiar ring of a local dictatorship. They had exotic and disquieting totalitarian overtones.

CHAPTER 2
The Genesis

As the revolutionary process unfolded, the discussions at home centered on Castro. Who is he really and what is his background? How was he able to seize unlimited power? Does he have a master plan, or is he wavering and improvising without any set course or preconceived design? Is he totally in charge, or is he being led or influenced by others? We knew of Castro's record of violence since his university years, and of his intransigence and insatiable ego. We also were aware of the radicalism of some of his colleagues. But we didn't have too much information on Fidel himself: his family heritage, proclivities, and ideological tendencies or commitments. It took time for the data to surface and shed some light on Castro and on the extraordinary circumstances that led to his ascent. It was all so puzzling and astounding—even to those close to the scene.

Perhaps the most perceptive analysis of Castro's complex personality was published in Miami, in 1961, by Dr. Oscar Sagredo Acebal, former president of the Cuban Society of Psychoanalysis and of the Cuban Society of Psychotherapy, and member of the American Psychiatric Association. History seems to have validated his diagnostic observations, which at the time were not read or believed by many.

In his article, written shortly after leaving Havana, Dr. Sagredo refers to a joke that circulated in Cuba in late 1959. A group of psychiatrists had been asked to analyze Fidel Castro. After listening to him on radio, watching him carefully on television, and interviewing him personally, the psychiatrists reached the following conclusion: "When he is mad he is paranoiac; when he is lucid he is a Communist."

According to Dr. Sagredo, Castro is not psychotic, but his personality reflects serious abnormalities. Like all paranoids, he has delusions of being persecuted or attacked, and believes himself superior to the rest of the world (a sign of megalomania). The cult of personality he fosters, the many titles he collects, even the two watches he used to carry—they all point to basic insecurity. Without the reassurance of applause, Dr. Sagredo points out, Castro does not shine as a speaker. When confronted by unexpected face-to-face challenges (such as the Spanish ambassador's irate rebuttal before TV cameras in early 1960), Castro turns pale and starts to stutter.[1]

Dirtiness, Dr. Sagredo reminds us, has been one of Castro's hallmarks. During his school days he was called *bola de churre*— "greaseball." Habitual dirtiness is generally a symptom of severance from or aggression toward the outside world. In Castro's case it signifies breaking of ties with family, culture, values, and society at large.

Dr. Sagredo also affirms that Castro has two faces as expressions of his personality: the soiled, tired, bearded face with an alert and distrustful look, like that of an animal that expects an attack; and the placid, boyish-looking face with an aura of candor and idealism that projects charisma. Castro's two distinct facial expressions, in the opinion of the renowned psychiatrist, reflect lack of integration of personality caused by defective identification with his father and mother.

Born in 1926, in Birán, on the eastern tip of the island, Fidel was the son of Angel Castro and his second wife, Lina, who used to perform domestic services at the Castro estate. Angel was a rugged Spaniard from Galicia who came to Cuba and fought against the Cuban patriots and the United States during the Spanish-American War. Given this background, Fidel was considered an outsider in Cuban society during his formative school years. He inherited his father's rancor toward the United States, which probably stemmed from Spain's defeat during the Spanish-American War and from Angel's traumatic experience with the United Fruit Company. As revealed by the noted historian Hugh Thomas, Angel was reportedly accused of systematic theft as a checker of sugar, but the charge was never pressed.[2]

Castro's family life was characterized by dissension and violence. No strong bonds united his father's nine children (including two from the first marriage). Angel was authoritarian at home and often clashed with his sons. There were explosions of anger and bursts of restlessness. He became a wealthy landlord, relying not only on hard work, but on chicanery and force to filch title deeds and encroach on his neighbors' farms.

Fidel's rebelliousness and desire to attract attention arose early in life. At school he once barricaded the classroom and roused his fellow students to resist punishment for not having memorized a poem.[3] When he was only thirteen, under the influence of a radical tutor, he attempted to organize a strike of his father's own plantation workers. These and other incidents prompted his parents to keep him in boarding school under strict discipline. His mother, the patient and resourceful Lina, was full of advice and saw in Fidel's pugnacious temperament and loquacity the makings of a successful lawyer. Angel was not so confident, but he readily agreed to pay the costs of an elitist education for his son.

Fidel first went to La Salle school, run by the Christian brothers, in Santiago de Cuba, and then to the Jesuit Colegio Dolores. In 1942 he was sent to Belén, Havana's leading Jesuit educational institution, which attracted the sons of many of Cuba's prominent families. There Fidel displayed an exceptional memory (not always matched by creativity) and outstanding skills in mountaineering and intercollegiate sports. Determined to excel in basketball, which was not his forte, he practiced day and night until he became the best player. Coach Campuzano's pronouncement that Fidel lacked poise and balance for track did not dishearten him. He trained for the 800-meter competition, won the race despite his unconventional style, and was named Belén's best all-around athlete for the year 1943–1944.

Fidel also excelled in debates, with his silver tongue and fertile mind. According to several classmates, he read avidly and recited excerpts from the political manifestos and speeches of famous tyrants and *caudillos,* including José Antonio Primo de Rivera (founder of Spanish Falangism), Perón, Hitler, Mussolini, and Lenin. Shakespeare also captured his imagination. Rafael Esténger, a distinguished Cuban author, heard Fidel years later declaim by heart passages from Macbeth describing crimes.

Fidel was very competitive at school and eager to gain recognition and leadership at any cost. When he was about fifteen, he bet that he could ride his bicycle at full speed into a stone or concrete pillar. He achieved his goal but remained unconscious for several days. Despite his exhibitionistic and occasionally bizarre conduct, Fidel made an impression on his classmates and teachers. The Belén yearbook for 1945 predicted that his life would be filled with "brilliant pages," and added that "the actor in him will not be lacking."[4]

After graduating from Belén in 1945, Fidel enrolled in the University of Havana to study law. He did not concentrate, however, on academic excellence, but on power politics and terrorist activities. Unable to muster the votes necessary to rise through the ranks of student organizations, Castro joined one of the existing action groups called the Insurrectional and Revolutionary Union. As a member of this ruthless organization, he received his "baptism of fire," which indelibly marked him for life. He was implicated in the murder of his rival, the president of the Federation of University Students, Manolo Castro (no relation to Fidel), and of Sergeant Fernández Carral of the university police. He also was accused of shooting Leonel Gómez, another rival student. Owing to insufficient evidence and a measure of threats and clout, Castro was released shortly after his detentions.

During most of Castro's five-year university stint, violence reigned rampant in Havana. Armed groups proliferated, seeking patronage, subsidies, and political influence. The constitutional President of Cuba during the period 1944–1948, Dr. Ramón Grau San Martín, decided not to confront them, but to let them fight each other. And fight they did, using the University of Havana as a haven. Back in the early 1930s the University Student Directorate had surged as the heroic vanguard of the revolution against the oppressive regime of General Gerardo Machado, the fifth President of Cuba. But the idealism of the 1930s waned and "revolutions" turned into a lucrative business that provided easy access to government funds and power. And the university became an incubator of violence, seemingly devoid of ideological content. The Communists, however, who generally thrive in this climate, did not remain passive. They availed themselves of prevailing corruption and discord to plant their seeds and spread their gospel. Their primary target was not the hungry stomachs of the poor and the unemployed, but the febrile minds of the students and the intellectuals.

One of those who fell under their spell was Fidel Castro. He developed at the university a close relationship with the Juventud Socialista—the official youth organization of the Cuban Communist Party, headed by Flavio Bravo, Lionel Soto, and Alfredo

Guevara. Fidel himself acknowledged in his startling speech of December 1, 1961, that these university liaisons played an important role in the formation of his Marxist-Leninist creed. But he did not allude to the secret contacts he reportedly had with the Soviet clandestine apparatus that then existed in Cuba: the Bashirov net.

The roots of the apparatus can be traced to a German friend of Karl Marx, George Weeth, who was expelled from his native country and settled in Santiago de Cuba until his death in 1854. He propagated the Marxist ideology and predicted that Cuba would mark the turning point for social change in the Americas. One of his disciples, the epicurean Pablo Lafargue, who came from an affluent Cuban family, studied in Paris and married Marx's daughter, Laura. Lafargue's closest friend, Carlos Baliño, kept the Marxist flame alive through the early stages of the republic and founded the Cuban Communist Party in 1925 under the stewardship of the fiery student leader Julio Antonio Mella.

The Cuban Communist Party promptly joined the Comintern, represented by Moscow's *éminence grise*, the Pole Aaron Simkovich, alias Fabio Grobart. The mysterious Grobart embarked on a long-term mission to build in Cuba a Communist forward base for proselytism, espionage, and subversion. The turmoil that followed the overthrow of the Machado dictatorship in 1933 enabled Grobart and his followers to make significant inroads. The Cuban Communist Party penetrated many labor unions and, waving the red flag, started to form soviets in major production centers. Washington, which had refused to recognize the provisional government that emerged, dispatched to Cuba an impressive naval force to evacuate American citizens should the situation deteriorate. This proved to be unnecessary. The Provisional President resigned, and after several interim governments controlled by a sergeant who had risen on the crest of a populist movement, Fulgencio Batista, the nation ended the revolutionary cycle and adopted a progressive constitution in 1940.

Batista, who was then elected President of the Republic with the support of the Communist Party, gave cabinet posts to two distinguished Party leaders. One of them, Carlos Rafael Rodríguez, is Castro's current Vice Prime Minister. The appointment of Communist ministers, for the first time in the Americas, did not stir much opposition, since the Soviets had already joined forces with the Allies in the global war against the Fascist powers. Moreover, the Communist leaders invited by Batista had an aura of

intellectual brilliance and civility which placed them above conspiratorial suspicions.

Discerning an opportunity to increase its influence, the Cuban Communist Party (later called Socialist Popular Party) launched
a major drive and gained control of the labor federation. And the
Soviets, eager to penetrate the Western Hemisphere, promptly
deployed resources into Cuba when Batista established diplomatic
relations with the USSR in April 1943. Russia's emissary, Ambassador Maxim Litvinov, and his successor, the wily Andrei Gromyko, proceeded to strengthen the island's subversive apparatus
with a staff of from 150 to 200 persons. Spruille Braden, then U.S.
ambassador to Cuba, who described Gromyko as having "the
coldest eye I have ever seen in a human being," sounded his
warnings in Washington about the growing Communist infiltration
in the Caribbean.[5]

Among the Soviet officers who came to Cuba was G. W.
Bashirov, who during the Spanish Civil War had acted as an agent
to recruit young Spaniards for the various Soviet apparatuses.
Fluent in Spanish, Bashirov was ideally suited for his new assignment: the formation of groups of youths, intellectuals, and artists
who would be kept apart from the Communist Party to carry out
Soviet instructions without arousing suspicions.

According to Salvador Díaz-Versón, director of Cuban military intelligence during the government of Dr. Carlos Prío Socar-
rás (deposed by Batista in 1952), Bashirov did not live at the Soviet
embassy building, but in a private residence at 6 Second Street in
Miramar. During the mid-1940s, states Díaz-Versón, "young Cubans, who had already entered the service of the Soviet Union
and were in receipt of monthly stipends to cover their expenses,
began to visit Bashirov's house." Among the twenty persons
monitored by Díaz-Versón were the geographer Antonio Núñez
Jiménez, the ballet dancer Alicia Alonso, and the student Fidel
Castro. When Batista severed relations with the USSR in 1952,
the Soviet connection was maintained through Mexico.[6]

During the years prior to Castro's rise to power, Díaz-Versón,
who served as president of the Inter-American Organization of
Anti-Communist Newspapermen, built up a private archive "which
comprised 250,000 cards of Latin American Communists and 943
personal records." The dossier on Fidel Castro, No. A-943, reportedly ran to 269 pages and contained incriminating photographs, an intercepted letter Fidel wrote in 1948 to a Cuban comrade
then in Czechoslovakia, and the photostat of a false passport used

by Castro to travel to Mexico in 1952 under the alias Federico Castillo Ramírez. Díaz-Versón was not able to produce this dossier to substantiate his startling allegations. On January 26, 1959, less than a month after Castro took power, he ordered the raid of Díaz-Versón's offices and the seizure of the files. The records compiled by Batista's intelligence services ran the same fate.

There is still no consensus on Castro's Communist background and early Soviet ties. His former university classmate and brother-in-law, Rafael Díaz Balart, testified before a U.S. Senate subcommittee that Fidel as a youngster was a member of the Soviet Union's Third International for Latin America, but not a regular card holder of the Cuban Communist Party.[7] Juan Vivés, a former officer of Castro's secret service who defected several years ago, asserted that Fidel was a Soviet mole recruited in 1947 by the leaders of the "Caribe" clandestine organization, Fabio Grobart and Vittorio Vidali.[8] Most historians and pundits, however, still deny Castro's Soviet connection, even his Communist militancy, prior to 1959–1960. They point to Fidel's opportunistic allegiances, egotistical behavior, and erratic course to dismiss the theory of deception. And yet, in retrospect, after allowing for historical coincidences, there is a pattern in his unstable conduct; there is direction in his meandering path.

In 1947, Castro joined the ill-fated Cayo Confites expedition against the Dominican dictator Rafael Leónidas Trujillo. The operation, supported and financed by the Grau San Martín government, consisted of some twelve hundred Cubans, Dominicans, Guatemalans, and Venezuelans who formed what was later called the Caribbean Legion. This force, infiltrated but not controlled by the Communists, was backed by an armada of two ships, twelve to fourteen planes, artillery, bazookas, and hundreds of rifles and machine guns.

The expedition was never launched. The plans were leaked to the press, and President Grau had to abort the operation under pressure from Washington. The expeditionary force at Cayo Confites was surrounded by the Cuban army and navy, and forced to surrender. All but Castro. He jumped with his gun overboard, swam ashore, and escaped.

The following year, 1948, Castro took part in an attempt to sabotage the Ninth International Conference of American States at Bogotá and overthrow the government of Colombia. According to the reports of the intelligence services of Colombia,[9] the Soviet Union feared that the Bogotá conference would bolster the burgeoning regional alliance and ban communism from the Americas. Determined to prevent this through a chain of destabilizing events known as the Bogotazo, the Soviets did not rely solely on the divided Colombian Communist Party. They deployed foreign agents and enlisted the support of Latin American leaders, like Rómulo Betancourt from Venezuela and Juan Domingo Perón from Argentina, who were keen on taking a stand against "American imperialism" and British "colonial" vestiges in Latin America (the Falkland Islands, or Malvinas). Among the foreign Communist agents identified in Bogotá by the chief of security was "the Cuban Fidel Castro."

The student delegation from Havana, headed by Enrique Ovares, had been invited by Perón's representatives to attend an international student congress in Bogotá. Ovares was aware of the anti-imperialist bent of the congress, but he did not know that it would be linked with one of the bloodiest political riots in the history of Latin America. Castro reportedly flew from Caracas carrying a letter of recommendation from Rómulo Betancourt. Declining to stay with Ovares and his fellow student Alfredo Guevara at a boardinghouse in Bogotá, Fidel chose the more comfortable Claridge Hotel as his living quarters and operational base. Ovares, who was arrested by Castro in 1959 and remained in prison for seven years, recently recounted his Colombian experiences to me. Enrique does not believe that the then immature Castro played a leading role in the Bogotazo. "But not because of lack of interest," affirmed Ovares. "Fidel craved limelight and armed action—and he got his share."

In a May 1958 interview by Jules Dubois, Castro acknowledged that he had attended the Bogotá student congress and joined a crowd marching on a police station. He denied, however, any sinister motive. "I did what every student in Colombia did," he said. "I joined the people. . . . I tried, insofar as it was possible, to avoid the fire-bombings and vandalism that caused that rebellion to fail. . . . My conduct could not have been more disinterested or altruistic. . . . Is that a good reason for thinking me a possible Communist? I have never been, nor am I now a Communist." [10]

Colombian police records and witness reports tell us a different story, however. They indicate that Fidel distributed subversive leaflets printed in Havana, and gave a lecture to Communist activists on the techniques of the coup d'état. The intelligence reports also point out that Castro carried several photographs of

Jorge Eliécer Gaitán, the popular leader of the Colombian Liberal Party, whose mysterious murder touched off the April 9 riots. Fidel met separately with Gaitán and his reputed killer, Juan Roa Sierra, shortly before the assassination, and was spotted near the scene of the crime in the company of well-known Communists.

As soon as Gaitán was shot dead, Roa Sierra, a twenty-five-year-old-drifter, was killed before he could speak. He was grabbed by a mob and kicked and beaten until his body was but a piece of shapeless flesh, unrecognizable. A voice was heard then: "To the palace! Let the bosses see the barbarian assassin hired by the government!" In a matter of minutes, thousands of leaflets were distributed in the streets of Bogotá accusing President Ospina Pérez and his administration of ordering Gaitán's murder and warning the people not to believe the official lie that the Communists were implicated in the monstrous crime. Then, with synchronized discipline, teams of activists distributed arms, incited the masses to loot, burn and destroy, and unleashed a bacchanalia of blood.

Radical students and labor union leaders promptly took over radio stations in Bogotá and urged the people to revolt against the government, the conference, and Yankee imperialism. One of those who reportedly spoke over the radio that day was Fidel Castro. William D. Pawley, former U.S. ambassador to Brazil and Peru, who had been asked by Secretary of State George C. Marshall to organize the conference, testified before a Senate committee as follows: "The day that this happened General Marshall was at our house. . . . Walter Donnelly, then ambassador to Venezuela . . . , was also with us, and when General Marshall left, Walter and I started down to the headquarters in our car and on the radio I heard a voice say: 'This is Fidel Castro from Cuba. This is a Communist revolution. The President has been killed, all of the military establishments are now in our hands. The Navy has capitulated to us, and this revolution has been a success.' "[11]

Castro's statement, while untrue, was not all that wild. The revolution had gathered momentum and could have swept the government had not President Ospina Pérez joined forces with the Liberal Party and doggedly resisted the palace siege until army reinforcements arrived from the interior. "Better a President dead than a President fugitive" was his battle cry. It took four days to quash the riots and restore law and order. On April 13 the police went to the Claridge Hotel in Bogotá to arrest Castro and his colleague Rafael del Pino, who also had participated in the riots. The Cubans, however, had already left the country in a cargo plane;

the flight was arranged by the head of the Cuban delegation to the inter-American conference. The hotel manager informed one of the detectives that "on the night of the 9th, they [Castro and his colleague] had arrived with rifles or shotguns and revolvers and with a good haul of loot which they were hardly able to cram in their valises." The manager added that in the last two days of their stay in the hotel, Fidel was so preoccupied and nervous that he even begged the hotel manager to hide them in a secret place.

The detectives reportedly found "a booklet . . . with a photograph of the two Cubans, identifying them as first-grade agents of the Third Front of the USSR in South America." (The term "Third Front," in the vocabulary of International Communism, denoted political and revolutionary actions aimed at disrupting the foreign policies of the United States and undermining Free World alliances. The Bogotazo seemed to fall into that category.)

Another piece of incriminating evidence that was found was a letter sent to Fidel by his fiancée and future wife, Mirtha Díaz Balart. The letter, reportedly intercepted by the Colombian police, was primarily amorous, but contained a revealing statement: "I remember that you told me you were going to Bogotá to start a revolution." [12]

The police findings on the Bogotazo were assailed by radical members of Colombia's opposition, who accused Ospina Pérez's administration of using phantoms and scapegoats to generate anti-Communist hysteria. Relying on a report issued by Scotland Yard's chief, several reputable historians and journalists have denied that the riots were part of a carefully planned Soviet operation and asserted that Gaitán's presumed assassin, Roa Sierra, was a psychopath who acted alone, incensed by the Liberal leader's refusal to see him.

As to Fidel Castro, the pundits believed that he was not following Communist instructions, and that his participation in the uprising—more brag than fact—was driven by his unquenchable lust for notoriety. [13]

Whatever his links and the extent of his involvement, Castro emerged unscathed from this grievous episode that left some three thousand dead on the streets of Colombia. He escaped punishment and avoided severely damaging condemnation. Well-known journalists and biographers of Castro downplayed his guilt and attributed his adventurous excesses to the "exuberance of youth."

Meanwhile, in Cuba, elections were held in 1948, and the candidate of the Auténtico Party, Dr. Carlos Prío, became President. During his term of office, Prío created such vital institutions as the National Bank of Cuba, the Agricultural and Industrial Development Bank, and the Tribunal of the Exchequer. As deputy leader of the majority party in the Senate, my father supported these initiatives and helped to build consensus. Prío also enacted progressive social legislation and enabled moderate labor union leaders to assume control of the Cuban Confederation of Workers, which had previously fallen into the hands of the Communists. A true democrat, like his predecessor Grau, Prío irradiated cordiality even under attack, and allowed unrestrained political freedom.

Prío, however, did not curb corruption, which again reached scandalous proportions. The festering problem of corruption—faced by other Latin American countries as well—is deeply rooted in history. In colonial times, underpaid Spanish officials who were sent to Cuba, usually for a short period, viewed their assignments as an ideal opportunity for personal enrichment. Not having a strong attachment to the island, these functionaries sought a quick financial return regardless of the means. Civil service thus became a bountiful harvest. Corrupt practices included patronage, sinecures, illicit commissions or fees, and outright embezzlement. Some of these techniques were refined during the period 1906–1909 by U.S. intervenors, who skillfully dispensed favors in exchange for political support. To deal with the mercurial Cubans, they took advantage of the prevailing venality. Subsequent Cuban governments shared the spoils of electoral victory with some of the vocal members of the opposition and the press, who became beneficiaries of the system and were thereby conveniently neutralized.

To oppose these degenerative practices, Eduardo Chibás, a former Auténtico leader, organized his own Ortodoxo Party and mounted a virulent radio campaign. His slogan was "Dignity against money," and his symbol was a broom to sweep corruption. In his weekly radio broadcasts, which earned incredibly high ratings, he challenged, censored, and attacked like an implacable Cato. Few in government were spared. Then one day he made a mistake. He accused the honest and combative Minister of Education, Aureliano Sánchez Arango, of embezzling funds and investing them in Guatemala. Pressed publicly to present the evidence, Chibás was unable to do so. His offensive was blunted, and he lost credibility; he shot himself at the end of one of his radio transmissions. His tragic death was a national loss.

Chibás had indeed voiced the feelings of the majority of the

Cuban people, who wanted to put an end to corruption. But in his denouncements, he went too far. He cauterized with the hot iron that burns tissues, and in doing so, destroyed reputations on hearsay, undermined institutions, and further weakened the republic. When in March of 1952—less than two months before general elections—Batista perpetrated his infamous coup, the demoralized government was unable to respond, and the strongest opposition leader, Chibás, was not there to forestall the assault and prevent the crime.

Two years before the coup, Castro became a member of Chibás's Ortodoxo Party, which embraced a wide spectrum of ideological tendencies. Castro joined the most radical section, the leftist wing. The official Communist Party had deliberately reduced its affiliates from 126,000 in 1949 to less than 60,000 in order to infiltrate other parties, especially the Ortodoxo.[14] But Chibás, who was unabashedly anti-Communist, kept the extremists at bay. Fidel, personally, did not carry much weight within the Ortodoxo hierarchy. Chibás and other leaders considered him a radical "gangster" and distrusted him. During the 1952 electoral campaign, with Chibás gone, Castro tried to run for Congress. Batista's coup crushed his political ambitions but opened a theater of operations more attuned to his personality and experience—one in which he had no equal: direct action, propaganda, agitation, and revolutionary violence.

Batista lost no time consolidating his regime. Determined to improve his image, he shunned his uniform and avoided being photographed with the military. He established a "consultative council" (in addition to the cabinet), which included various prominent politicians, intellectuals, and businessmen. He implemented a major public works program, stimulated the economy, and attempted to balance draconian repression with periods of unrestrained freedom. He became a part-time dictator with a democratic complex: too arbitrary to win popularity, yet too irresolute to preserve stability; too imperious and greedy to negotiate a settlement for peace, yet too erratic and complacent to snuff out the early brushfires of war.

The contradictory policies adopted by Bastista after the coup did not placate the leaders of the opposition. They demanded the full reinstatement of the 1940 Constitution, the resignation of Batista, and the formation of a neutral government that would hold free elections. The rejection by Batista of these conditions prompted the heads of the two main opposition parties—Auténtico and Ortodoxo—to subscribe in June 1953 to the so-called Montreal Pact designed to coordinate efforts to topple the dictator. Castro, who had vehemently argued for a broader coalition involving the Communists, was not invited to attend.[15] He lacked the standing, the constituency, indeed the power to play a national role. Intent on seizing the initiative and gaining visibility before others struck, Fidel launched the attacks on the Moncada and Bayamo barracks in Oriente on July 26, 1953.

With a combined force of some 150 men, the attackers were to gain entrance by surprise, subdue the barracks, and distribute arms to other activists, who would capture Santiago and Bayamo with lightning raids. The date chosen was propitious because it coincided with the carnival of Santiago. Many soldiers were expected to attend the public dances of the carnival on the evening of July 25 and sleep profoundly the following morning. Executional errors, however, alerted the soldiers and foiled the attack. Outnumbered eight to one, Castro, who led the Moncada assault, decided to retire without regrouping his men. Many of those left behind were slaughtered.

The operation was a military disaster, but turned out to be a psychological victory and propaganda feat for Castro. At the behest of the rector of Santiago University and the archbishop of Santiago de Cuba, Batista spared Castro's life and allowed him to defend himself before a civil court. Fidel proclaimed his goal of restoring democracy and justice; he embraced the dignifying doctrine of Cuba's national hero, José Martí; he outlined a program of educational, housing, and agrarian reforms within the framework of the 1940 Constitution; he denounced the savagery of the army's repression and vowed to continue to struggle for freedom until the end. Showing no repentance or regret, he concluded his peroration with a defiant cry: "Sentence me, no matter; history will absolve me." The court sentenced him and twenty-nine companions to imprisonment. Fidel himself received fifteen years, but, amnestied by Batista, he actually served less than two.

During the Moncada attack, the most prominent members of the old guard of the Cuban Communist Party had gathered in Santiago, not far from the barracks, ostensibly to celebrate the birthday of their leader Blas Roca. (Blas, however, came from Manzanillo, not Santiago, and was not known to indulge in the capitalistic rituals of birthday celebrations.) Arrested by the police, they repudiated the assault as a "putschist" method peculiar to bourgeois factions, and were acquitted. Another disturbing development was the discovery of subversive materials, including a book on Lenin, among the attackers' possessions. Castro was quick to explain: "Yes, that was our book, and anyone who does not read those books is an ignoramus." Other efforts made by Batista's police to establish a Marxist-Leninist link also proved futile. The rank-and-file raiders were, in the main, modest workers without any defined political ideology or affiliation. It was not generally known at the time that their leaders were Communist sympathizers who had formed the nucleus of a revolutionary movement around Chibás's Ortodoxo Party. The movement was to be named "26th of July" after the date of the Moncada attack.

The militant members of that nucleus were impassioned students of Lenin and other Soviet revolutionaries, and were training in the art of subversion. Some of them, like Haydée Santamaría, Ramiro Valdés, Pedro Miret, and Juan Almeida, were to play a major role in the revolutionary struggle against Batista and in the Castro regime. A late addition to the Moncada conspiracy was Fidel's younger brother, Raúl, who had just returned from Vienna, Bucharest, and Prague and had officially joined the Communist Youth Movement in Havana. On arrival, the police found in Raúl's possession a large amount of Marxist propaganda, banners, and badges acquired behind the Iron Curtain. Raúl was arrested, but, through political influence, was released in time to participate in the assault.

The Moncada operation was a turning point in the struggle against Batista. If it was designed to create conditions in which the army would retaliate against the attackers with a brutality that would shock and polarize the nation, the operation certainly achieved its objective. My father and I, among others, felt its impact. As a former senator ousted by Batista at the time of the 1952 coup, my father opposed the regime but was not involved in any insurrectionary plot. He had always rejected violence as a method of settling political disputes. On the day of the assault, he was vacationing with my mother, my sister, Marta, and me at the beach resort of Varadero along with hundreds of families who were attending the third crew regatta of the season. It was a festive occasion marked by cheers, toasts, and embraces. The news of the assault, however, jolted us all.

As I drove to a friend's villa that evening—following the traditional post-regatta celebrations—I was ambushed by eight heavily armed policemen. At gunpoint they forced me to locate my father. They arrested him and took him to military headquarters in Havana for questioning. When he arrived in a van along with other political prisoners, a large group of irate soldiers surrounded them. They were seething with wrath, having heard that some of the Castro assailants had murdered convalescing soldiers at the Moncada hospital. Suddenly, a lieutenant who emerged from the group pointed at my father and shouted: "There is Carbonell—one of the intellectual authors of the Moncada massacre!" My father was stunned. He wanted to ignore the damning accusation, but he could not remain quiet lest his silence be perceived by the agitated crowd as admission of guilt. He quickly retorted, raising his voice: "That is a lie! I oppose the hatred and violence that bloodies the country. I seek peace with freedom and dignity for *all* Cubans." My father didn't wait for a response; he kept on walking—his muscles tense and his eyes ablaze. Impressed by his bravado, the soldiers let him through. He was interrogated for several hours, warned not to conspire against the government, and subsequently released.

Following this chilling experience, my father reflected on the gravity of the situation. He realized that it was necessary to end Batista's illegitimate rule. That, for him, was not at issue. The question, however, was *how* to do it without setting off the traumatic convulsions of a civil war and its unpredictable aftermath.

CHAPTER 3
Rise to Power

While in prison, Castro organized seminars to teach his comrades mathematics, grammar, history, and political ideology. He received more than a hundred books by diverse authors—from Victor Hugo to José Martí; from José Ingenieros to Max Weber.[1] But what he enjoyed most was the works of Marx and Lenin. In one of his private letters he wrote: "After breaking my head on Kant for a good while, Marx seems easier to me than saying an Our Father. He, like Lenin, had a terrific appetite for polemic, and I really enjoy myself and laugh as I read them. They were implacable and terrifying to their enemies. Two real revolutionary prototypes."[2]

In another letter Fidel extolled Robespierre, whom he called "an idealist and an honorable man. . . . A few months of terror was necessary to end a terror that had lasted centuries." Castro affirmed, "Cuba needs many Robespierres."[3] Fidel himself, however, was spared from the horrors of tyranny. Except for a period of solitary confinement, prison for him was hardly an ordeal. He wrote: "Now I'm going to eat: spaghetti with squid, Italian bonbons for dessert, fresh coffee—then an H Upmann 4 [cigar]. Don't you envy me? They all take care of me. . . . They never listen, and I'm always fighting with them so they won't send me anything. When I take a sun bath in my shorts in the morning and feel the sea air, it's as if I'm on a beach, then in a small restaurant. People are going to think I'm on vacation. What would Marx think of such a revolutionary?"[4]

Following the November 1954 rigged elections, designed to legitimize Batista's de facto rule, public opinion clamored for a general amnesty that would encompass all political prisoners, including Castro. Feeling sufficiently secure to make a magnanimous gesture, Batista consented to a pardon that set Castro free only twenty-two months after the Moncada assault. Fidel immediately regained the limelight, but did not receive the support he was expecting. Without openly breaking his ties with the Ortodoxo Party, he laid the groundwork for his 26th of July Movement and left for Mexico in mid-1955. Having divorced his wife, he harbored only one thought, one obsession: revolution.

The mood of the country, however, was not yet ripe for insurrection. Batista had relaxed government repression and allowed his opponents to vent their spleen. The Cuban economy was healthy: both national income and national output were up 7 percent over 1954. Construction was booming, and tourism reached an all-time high. Plans were under way to build even more luxurious hotels to cater to visitors and investors, including, alas, unscrupulous promoters of gambling and licentiousness.

Despite the debilitating influence of a carefree environment, Havana thrived, with a strong entrepreneurial class and a growing intellectual and artistic community that was considered one of the most sophisticated in Latin America. During the early stages of the republic, Havana had attracted such international stars as Sarah Bernhardt, Ignace Paderewski, Anna Pavlova, and Enrico Caruso. In the '50s it lured Maurice Chevalier, Edith Piaf, Nat King Cole, and Katyna Ranieri. Politically, however, the nation had suffered a major setback with Batista's coup, which had derailed Cuba's fragile democratic process, painstakingly maintained during the period 1940–1952. But the great majority of the population was tired of violence and yearned for a civilized settlement.

Most of the Cuban exiled leaders, including former President Carlos Prío, had availed themselves of Batista's amnesty and returned to the island in 1955. The major opposition groups coalesced under the aegis of the Society of Friends of the Republic, headed by the venerable Cosme de la Torriente, a veteran of the War of Independence and a distinguished diplomat who had presided over the League of Nations in Geneva. Multitudinous rallies were held to press for a democratic opening, but as the speakers called for free elections, boisterous radicals drowned them out, chanting, "Revolution, revolution, revolution!" They were largely

Castro followers trying to block any attempt to reach an electoral solution.

In order to avoid a dangerous stalemate, Torriente met privately with Batista and agreed on the ground rules for serious negotiations between the representatives of the government and of the nonviolent opposition. These negotiations, known as the Civic Dialogue, were conducted during the first quarter of 1956. Fearing that they could lead to a peaceful accord, Castro blasted off a diatribe entitled "Against Everyone." Unfortunately, Batista offered only the stalling device of a constitutional assembly, and the opposition demanded again his immediate resignation followed by general elections. True to their Spanish heritage, Cuban leaders from both sides took extreme positions and rejected compromise as humiliating weakness.

The failure of the Civic Dialogue brought about renewed violence. In April 1956 the government thwarted an army conspiracy led by Colonel Ramón Barquín and fended off an attack on the Goicuría barracks in Matanzas. In October, members of the Student Revolutionary Directorate killed the chief of military intelligence. In retaliation, the police penetrated the sanctuary of the Haitian embassy and killed several of the refugees. During the attack, Batista's chief of police was shot dead. The outlook was bleak. The bloody pendulum of terror and counterterror had been unleashed.

Meanwhile, in Mexico, Castro was feverishly trying to organize an expedition against Batista. He established a training base at the Santa Rosa farm, some twenty miles from Mexico City. There, under strict military discipline, recruits received guerrilla training and political indoctrination. Fidel controlled all expenditures and retained the recruits' passports. The chief military instructor was the leftist Alberto Bayo, a former colonel of the Spanish army who had sided with the Spanish Republic during the civil war and had gained considerable experience in guerrilla warfare. Among the trainees present were Raúl Castro, several other Moncada veterans, and Ernesto "Che" Guevara, a colorful Argentine medical graduate, age twenty-six, who had been involved with the Argentine Communist Youth organization in his country. While in Guatemala, he vigorously opposed the CIA-backed overthrow of Communist-leaning President Jacobo Arbenz and had to flee the country. A sharp, cold-blooded tactician, Guevara would soon become one of the leaders of the Cuban revolution, supplementing Castro's penetrating insight and balancing his impetuousness.

In June 1956, the Mexican police raided the Santa Rosa farm and another hideout, where they found large quantities of arms, Marxist books, and subversive materials. Twenty of the revolutionaries, including the Castro brothers and Guevara, were arrested and kept in jail for over a month. Thanks to Castro's powerful allies in Mexico—the Cuban Communist leader Lázaro Peña, Mexico's radical labor strongman Lombardo Toledano, and the former leftist President of Mexico Lázaro Cárdenas—the militant revolutionaries were released and not deported.

Castro publicly rejected the charges of being a Communist. Attributing them to Batista, Fidel lashed back, saying that the Cuban dictator had no moral right to speak, since he had been "the presidential candidate of the Communist Party in the elections of 1940." To launch the expedition, Castro accepted financial support from old politicos he despised. "There will be time afterward" he had written, "to crush all the cockroaches together."[5] He coordinated the operation with members of the 26th of July underground and of the Communist Party who secretly visited him in Mexico, but he did not heed their advice to postpone the landing.[6] He was determined to fulfill his public pledge: "Free or martyrs in 1956." On November 25, Castro and eighty-one of his companions sailed from Tuxpan on the yacht *Granma*, and a week later they landed at Los Colorados beach, on the southwestern coast of the province of Oriente, facing the imposing Sierra Maestra cordillera.

The operation was a debacle. Castro's plan had been to synchronize the landing with a revolt in Santiago, which was to be followed by a general strike to topple the regime. The landing was delayed because of bad weather; the Santiago uprising crippled the city for a few hours but dwindled away, and the revolutionary strike never materialized. Lacking coordination and support, the rebels were decimated by government troops and aircraft spewing fragmentation bombs. But Castro, yet again, managed to survive. Batista unwittingly helped him.

When Batista was informed of the landing, he was attending an intimate social gathering at his Prime Minister's residence. Showing no apprehension or concern, he dismissed Castro's operation as a "local adventure without importance" and continued his canasta game.[7] After several hours of enjoyable distraction, he reviewed the situation with his military chiefs and agreed to dispatch five hundred soldiers to attack the rebels. Following the initial encounters, just when the troops were about to corner the few scattered survivors, Batista ordered a cease-fire. He told the befuddled army officers: "Let them climb the Sierra Maestra, for there nobody can live."[8] This fateful decision enabled Castro and his twenty or so remaining companions to regroup and hide in the thickly forested mountains of the Sierra with the aid of Crescencio Pérez, a fugitive farmer who awaited them.

Government spokesmen declared that Castro had been killed in combat. For a while it seemed that the adventure was over. Then came a string of propaganda coups which gave a shot of life to the foundering rebel cause: the interviews and articles published by Herbert Matthews from the *New York Times* and Jules Dubois from the *Chicago Tribune,* and the documentary on Castro staged by CBS-TV with Ed Sullivan as interviewer. Castro was portrayed as "the most remarkable and romantic figure to arise in Cuba since José Martí," as the "Robin Hood of the Sierra Maestra," and as a great leader "in the real American spirit of George Washington."

The publicity campaign gave Castro international prominence, respectability, and support at a time when he most needed them. Matthews was tricked into inflating Castro's insignificant force, was awed by Fidel's overpowering personality, and gave the American people the assurance, reiterated over and over again, that "there is no Communism to speak of in Fidel Castro's 26th of July Movement." Given the extraordinary prestige and influence of the *New York Times,* Matthews was not too presumptuous in asserting that his articles "literally altered the course of Cuban history."[9]

Holed up in the mountains with scarce human resources, Castro's guerrilla actions were sporadic and limited during most of 1957. Anti-Batista feelings were definitely growing, but the revolution lacked a well-structured urban apparatus to engage in fundraising activities, logistics, sabotage, and paramilitary action. To address this urgent need, Civic Resistance was formed in Santiago, in early 1957, and subsequently rolled out to the rest of the island. With strong backing, primarily from middle- and upper-class professionals, the insurgency started to gain impetus.

Castro tried to monopolize urban support, given the scant peasant solidarity, and opposed any act of rebellion that could upstage him, including the March 1957 assault on the presidential palace. This daring commando-type action was carried out by some fifty revolutionaries, mostly from the Student Directorate, along with a thirty-three-year-old Spanish exile who had been in both the French Resistance and the U.S. Army. Shooting their way into the palace, they entered Batista's office on the second floor and might have reached his private suite, where he was getting dressed, had the second wave of the attack arrived as planned. Thirty-five rebels and five members of the palace guard were killed.

In a related clash with the police that day, the president of the Federation of University Students, José Antonio Echevarría, was shot dead. Cuba lost a promising idealist, with strong moral and democratic convictions, who was emerging as a potential Castro rival. The next morning, the distinguished Ortodoxo ex-Senator Pelayo Cuervo was found murdered, and several weeks later, four of the surviving student leaders of the palace raid were assassinated by the police. Another terrible blow was the murder in July 1957 of Frank País, the young and fiery hero of the 26th of July underground, who had shown the courage and foresight not only to fight Batista, but also to stand up to the autocratic Fidel.[10]

After these and other setbacks, like the ill-fated Corinthia expedition financed by former President Prío, Castro remained the only living symbol of armed resistance on the island. He had gained credibility with his successful attack on the El Uvero military post with some 120 guerrillas, but he was still viewed with apprehension, if not distrust, by major sectors of the population. To improve his image and broaden his constituency, at a time when eight opposition groups were trying to negotiate a peaceful and democratic settlement with Batista's Interparliamentary Committee, Castro met in the Sierra Maestra with two prestigious Cuban leaders: Raúl Chibás, brother of the founder of the Ortodoxo Party, and Felipe Pazos, former president of the National Bank of Cuba. They drafted and signed a moderate manifesto intended to serve as the platform for a Civic Revolutionary Front that would embrace all the opposition movements. The manifesto promised free elections in one year, under the umbrella of the 1940 Constitution, and contained no xenophobic or extremist prescriptions.

Castro did not reveal then, or at any time during the insurrection, the real tenets of his totalitarian revolution. Had he done so, Fidel later confessed with unprecedented cynicism, "We would not have been able to descend from the Pico Turquino [the highest peak in the Sierra Maestra] to the plain." Castro knew full well that most Cubans were not yearning for a radical change. Economic and social conditions were not fueling agitation. That is why the peasants did not swarm into Fidel's camp and the workers did not back his call for a general strike as late as April

1958. Dictatorship and corruption were the main causes of the unrest. Despite high rates of unemployment and glaring inequities between urban and rural areas that had to be corrected, Cuba's per capita income in 1958 was considerably higher than Japan's and almost equal to Italy's. Among Latin American republics, Cuba ranked third in both GNP per capita and percentage of literates, second in consumption of calories per capita, and first in the number of both television stations and sets per thousand population. Moreover, Cuba was rapidly bridging social differences with a talented and energetic middle class that represented almost a third of the population. The myth of Cuba's underdevelopment as the root cause of communism was to be challenged by none other than Aníbal Escalante, a Cuban Communist luminary—at least until he was purged by Castro. Escalante said:

> In reality, Cuba was not one of the countries with the lowest standard of living of the masses in America, but, on the contrary, one of those with the highest standard of living, and it was here where the first great patriotic, democratic, and socialist revolution of the continent burst forth and where the imperialist chain was first broken. If the historical development had been dictated by the false axiom expressed above, the revolution should have been first produced in Haiti, Colombia, or even Chile, countries of greater poverty for the masses than the Cuba of 1952 or 1958.[11]

Apart from deception, Castro and his followers effectively employed sabotage and terrorism to provoke bloody reprisals by the government and thereby create a climate of insurgency. They also availed themselves of the natural barriers of the Sierra Maestra, of the army's inexperience in guerrilla warfare, and, above all, of pervading corruption. In the early stages of the insurrection, when it would have been relatively easy to quell the Castro guerrillas, the Batista regime had no determination—indeed, no incentive—to do so. The maintenance of a state of war was a convenient device to suspend constitutional guarantees and divert emergency funds to the private purses of the government and military cliques.

Castro exploited the ensuing demoralization. What he couldn't gain in battle he won with money, which eventually came in large quantities from industrialists who feared the revolutionaries or wished to gain their favor; from upper-, middle- and lower-middle-class supporters of the 26th of July Movement; from public collections in the United States and several Latin American countries; and sub rosa from international Communist front organizations. Bribes were sometimes more effective than bullets to induce disheartened army officers and soldiers to refrain from fighting or to switch camps. These enticements enabled the columns of Che Guevera and Camilo Cienfuegos to descend from the Sierra Maestra in August 1958, traverse some three hundred miles of level territory with hardly any opposition, and open a new front in the mountains that lie in the central province of Las Villas. Bribes were also used by the rebels to obtain the spectacular surrender of a government armored train laden with arms.[12]

Another factor that helped Castro was the fragmentation and relative inefficacy of the rest of the opposition. Those who favored free elections, like my father, were blocked by Batista's obduracy and the unrealistic demands of some of his adversaries. Those who abstained eventually became passive spectators of the unfolding drama. And those who backed the insurrection generally remained in exile, except for a few leaders like former Prime Minister Manuel Antonio de Varona, who led an unsuccessful revolt in Cienfuegos in September 1957 and had to seek diplomatic asylum. Most of the ostracized politicians thought they could wage war from Miami and control or temper Castro by inviting him to join a united front under their directorate. They failed to realize that in the course of revolutions, leaders in absentia are no match for agitators or warriors in the trenches.

As opposition against Batista grew, Castro gained popularity. He was able to galvanize and magnetically attract anti-Batista feelings. His very effective propaganda apparatus, particularly the clandestine Radio Rebelde, which started operating in February 1958, served to magnify the battles and glorify *El Líder Máximo*. Reports of Communist influence were mostly rejected as a Batista ploy to discredit the revolution. Its supporters only thought of toppling the dictator. Many who disliked Castro or distrusted him were not overly concerned. "Nothing could be worse than Batista," the saying went. And fears of a Marxist-Leninist takeover were dismissed as farfetched or ridiculous, given the Cubans' ardent individualism and passion for freedom, and the United States' proximity and geopolitical interests.

These views were poignantly expressed by former President Prío at a private meeting held in late 1956 with Dr. Carlos Márquez Sterling, leader of the electoral faction of the Ortodoxo Party and former president of the 1940 Constitutional Assembly. Márquez Sterling argued that it would be better for the democratic opposition to take Batista's electoral challenge, even with limited guarantees, than to back an insurrection that could play into the hands of Castro and his radical colleagues. Prío responded that, given Batista's intransigence and unbridled ambition, there was no alternative to the overthrow of his regime. To achieve that objective, Prío added, we needed the support of all the opposition leaders, including Castro. When Márquez Sterling underscored the possible danger of Communist infiltration through Castro, Prío responded that he did not see that as a real threat. "In any case," he added, "the United States would not tolerate it." "What if they do?" prodded Márquez Sterling. "Then we're screwed," retorted Prío.[13]

In early 1958, Castro stepped up his guerrilla activities and sent his brother Raúl to open another front at Sierra Cristal, also in the province of Oriente. Still, the rebels had a combined force of no more than three hundred guerrillas in the mountains—by no means a threat even to an unmotivated army of 35,000 soldiers. What started to tilt the balance in Castro's favor was the massive military aid he received from abroad during the first half of 1958. Several pilots flying a Cessna 99, a Beechcraft, and a Lockheed PB-2 Lodestar repeatedly took off from an abandoned airfield in Florida to transport arms to Castro in the Sierra Maestra. More than twenty such missions were successfully completed.[14] Military shipments came also from Mexico, Venezuela, and Costa Rica. The most important one originated in Punta Arenas, Costa Rica, and included about ten tons of machine guns, rifles, mortars, bullets, and dynamite.

Castro also benefited from U.S. government support. In his recent biography of Castro, Tad Szulc disclosed that between October or November of 1957 and the middle of 1958, Robert D. Wiecha, a CIA case officer attached to the U.S. consulate general in Santiago de Cuba, delivered no less than $50,000 to a half-dozen or more key members of the 26th of July movement.[15] According to a Cuban underground leader, the equipment required to install Castro's most effective weapon, Radio Rebelde, was secretly brought into the country thanks to the personal intervention of Park F. Wollam, then U.S. consul in Santiago.[16] And as reported by Paul D. Bethel, press attaché to the American embassy in Havana at the time, the embassy harbored an American pilot, Charles Hormel, involved in airlifting arms to Castro in the Sierra Maestra. Having either run out of gas or experienced mechanical failure, the pilot crashed his plane in Guantánamo Bay. U.S. naval personnel rescued him and spirited him off to Havana, where embassy officials healed his wounds and arranged his exit.[17]

Washington had already concluded that Batista's end was only a matter of time. At least that was the impression given by the State Department officials of the "Fourth Floor" who were instrumental in shaping U.S. policy toward Cuba: Roy R. Rubottom, Assistant Secretary of State for Latin American Affairs, and William Wieland, director of the Office of Caribbean and Mexican Affairs. They were vocal in their dislike of Batista, but were not too active in fostering or supporting an alternative to Castro, even though both reportedly had been in Bogotá during the 1948 Communist-inspired riots and presumably knew of Castro's involvement. Manifesting an anti-Batista bent, U.S. federal and state agencies eased the enforcement of neutrality laws with respect to Cuba. Although former President Prío was indicted in February 1958 for aiding and abetting Cuban insurrection from Florida, Castro representatives in Miami were able to pursue their revolutionary activities, including collection of funds and smuggling of arms, without major interference.

The U.S. ambassador to Havana, Earl E. T. Smith, believed that "Cuba was torn in a struggle between a Rightist, corrupt dictator who was friendly to the United States, and a would-be Leftist dictator, who could be a Communist." He was alarmed at the Marxist-Leninist inclinations of some of the leaders of the 26th of July Movement and reported to the Department of State in March 1958 that Radio Moscow had made shortwave broadcasts supporting the Castro revolutionaries.[18] In an effort to find a solution to the Batista-Castro predicament, Ambassador Smith repeatedly asked Washington for authorization to support the mediation of the Cuban bishops and professional institutions aimed at forming a cabinet of national unity that would ensure free elections and pave the way for Batista's orderly departure. The State Department, which contended that Smith was too soft on Batista,[19] refused to lend its weight to those efforts, alleging that such a stand would be tantamount to intervention. And yet, in March 1958, pressed by mounting pro-Castro propaganda, the United States ordered an embargo on arms to Batista.

No action by Castro could have so shaken the Cuban dictator. The embargo meant much more than a denial of some two thousand Garand rifles, twenty armored cars and fifteen training planes. It signaled the withdrawal of U.S. support to the Batista government and provided a tremendous psychological uplift to Castro's followers.

Batista tried to rally his forces during the summer of 1958 following Castro's failed attempt to cripple the country with a general strike. The commander in charge of the operation, General Eulogio Cantillo, deployed eleven batallions to encircle and crush the guerrillas in the Sierra Maestra. Half of the soldiers, however, had just been recruited and lacked military training. Most of them did not want to fight. Cantillo reported an extraordinarily high number of self-inflicted wounds, capitulations and betrayals. Among the military equipment and supplies captured by the insurgents were the government's communications trailer and campaign codes. This enabled Castro to anticipate the army's moves at the peak of their operation.[20]

Determined to turn the tide, the government halfheartedly pursued the summer offensive. Thereupon, Raúl Castro, purportedly without Fidel's knowledge, decided to carry out a bold operation that would paralyze and embarrass the Batista regime: the kidnapping of fifty North Americans, including twenty-seven marines and sailors captured aboard a bus on their way back to the naval base at Guantánamo. Negotiations drifted for almost one month, forcing Batista to suspend bombing and strafing operations and avoid all military activities in the area. The rebels had achieved their objective. Batista's offensive lost momentum and waned; government morale collapsed; the end was near.

The conciliatory efforts made by the church and professional institutions earlier in the year came to naught. Castro rebuffed the peace overtures, and Batista again suspended the constitutional guarantees. Deeply troubled by the civil strife that was tearing apart the fabric of the republic, Dr. Márquez Sterling invited my father and other moderate leaders to form a new political party (the Free People's Party), rally those who rejected both Batista and Castro, and press the government to grant minimum safeguards for general elections. This was a desperate, last-minute attempt, perceived by some as divisive and naive, to break the impasse that had set the country on a blind collision course.

Alarming signs loomed on the horizon. The three next-to-the-top commanders of the insurrection appointed by Castro were Communist agents or sympathizers: Raúl Castro, Che Guevara, and Camilo Cienfuegos. The most vocal of the three, Guevara, had unequivocally expressed his views in a private letter sent to an underground chief on December 15, 1957. He wrote, "I belong, because of my ideological background, to that group which believes that the solution of the world's problems lies behind the Iron Curtain, and I understand this movement as one of the many provoked by the desire of the bourgeoisie to free itself from the economic chains of imperialism."[21]

Another telling development was the appearance in the Sierra Maestra and Sierra del Escambray of prominent members of the Communist Party, like Carlos Rafael Rodríguez, Antonio Núñez Jiménez, and Félix Torres. They had tactically distanced themselves from Castro in the early phases of the insurrection, but by mid-1958 they started to trickle into the mountains and wield their influence. Prior to their arrival, Raúl Castro had discreetly established Marxist indoctrination centers to teach selected officers ideological formation along with other aspects of education.

Still, Fidel remained the dominant force in the Sierra Maestra, perched high above all ideological factions. To counter invidious rumors of a radical tilt, he ratified his professed democratic and anti-Communist goals in an article carried in the February 1958 issue of *Coronet* magazine. On the subject of private and foreign investments, he went so far as to say: "I personally have come to feel that nationalization is, at best, a cumbersome instrument. It does not seem to make the state any stronger, yet it weakens private enterprise . . . ; foreign investments will always be welcome and secure here."

The Soviet Union was extremely cautious during the insurgency, and kept a low profile. Few reports pointed to any direct Moscow intrusion or support. The London-based *Intelligence Digest,* however, did state in December 1957 that Russian submarines had twice surfaced off Cuba and discharged munitions for Castro forces.[22] In July 1959, Castro's former chief of the air force, Major Pedro Luis Díaz Lanz, testified before a U.S. Senate subcommittee that a Soviet submarine had delivered modern arms to Raúl Castro on the northern shore of Oriente. Admiral Arleigh Burke seemed to give some credence to these reports when he disclosed in late 1959 that unidentified submarines had been lurking in Cuban waters.

Single-minded in their intent to overthrow Batista, the Cuban groups integrating the belligerent opposition continued to dismiss the danger of extremism and of possible Soviet encroachment. They were heartened by Castro's willingness to sign in mid-1958 the so-called Caracas Pact, which theoretically bound him to a constitutional, free-enterprise platform. Skeptical of the sincerity of Castro's commitment, Dr. Márquez Sterling, my father, and several other political figures decided not to join the warring front and to pursue an independent electoral course under the banner of the newly constituted Free People's Party. Former President Ramón Grau San Martín, backed by a faction of the Auténtico Party, did likewise. The government had called for general elections in June 1958 (they actually were held in November), and Batista agreed not to run. This could lead to a peaceful solution, these groups felt, if only Batista would not rig the elections to impose his own candidate.

Determined to convince Batista not to close this last window of opportunity, my father and two other former senators, Dr. Antonio Martínez Fraga and Dr. José A. Casabuena, went to see him in August at his private farm. Their relationship with Batista, although strained since the coup, went back many years and enabled them to engage in frank and open discussions. The delegation carried a memorandum drafted by my grandfather Cortina invoking historical precedents. It urged Batista to ponder the example set by an earlier Cuban President, General Mario G. Menocal, who averted an all-out civil war, after a second stormy term in office, by relinquishing power through an electoral entente with one of the opposition parties. Looking Batista straight in the eyes, my father said: "The people expect a genuine government change which your candidate, with all due respect, could not possibly provide." A Márquez Sterling victory through fair and honest elections, my father contended, was the best, perhaps the only guarantee the nation and Batista himself really had to avoid endless persecutions and the possible breakdown of the republic. "Change cannot be avoided and should not be delayed," my father stressed. "It will come, for sure, with ballots or with bullets."

The discussion went on for more than three hours. Batista was attentive and cordial, but rather defensive at first. He pointed to the intransigence of the belligerent opposition and to the efforts he had made to reach a peaceful accord. He acknowledged, however, the seriousness of the crisis, agreed to press on with elections, and promised to reflect on the cogent points made by my father and his colleagues. Although he was not explicit on the central issue of restoring constitutional guarantees and facilitating a real government change, he did say that he viewed Dr. Márquez Sterling and his associates as honorable adversaries with whom he could reach an understanding in the interest of the nation. The meeting ended without clear assurances, but with a small ray of hope.

Castro's reaction to the electoral campaign was more violent than expected—such was his fear of a constitutional solution that would deny him omnipotent rule. He turned down the offer of a government of national unity under Márquez Sterling, even against the firm commitment that the latter would shorten his mandate, if he won, and hold new elections within two years after taking office. Determined to thwart the electoral process and accelerate Batista's fall, Castro primed his followers for total war.

I well remember those perilous days. Having just returned from Harvard University, I started campaigning with my father, who was running for senator in Matanzas province. The situation was tense and frightening. We vigorously opposed Batista and therefore incurred the wrath of hard-line supporters of his regime. We also rejected the Castro-controlled insurgency and were exposed to rebel attacks. As the campaign started to unfold, Castro mounted a major offensive. The guerrillas burned sugar crops and blew up factories, public buildings, and bridges. They also bombed political offices and attempted to assassinate several candidates, including Márquez Sterling. Some were ambushed and killed pursuant to Castro's Revolutionary Law No. 2, which called for capital punishment for all those running for public office.

The rebels' terroristic onslaught achieved its paralyzing objective. Large segments of the population refrained from participating in the campaign and stayed home. Batista, for his part, made no serious effort to build confidence; instead he foiled the last opportunity for a peaceful and democratic solution by manipulating the results of the elections in favor of his own candidate, Dr. Andrés Rivero Agüero. Batista had thus validated Castro's claim: the entire process was a sham. War seemed then the only alternative left, and it rapidly spread to the central province of Las Villas.

Meanwhile, in Washington, an intelligence section of the State Department prepared an "Estimate Regarding the Communist Danger in Cuba." According to Ambassador Smith, this confidential report acknowledged that the 26th of July Movement was susceptible to Communist exploitation and conceded the existence of Communist infiltration and control of the revolutionary movement, the degree of which was still undetermined.[23] Alarmed by the foreboding implications of the report and irked by Batista's unwillingness to yield power to a neutral caretaker government, as privately proposed by former Ambassador William D. Pawley, Washington decided to act.[24] On December 14, 1958, Assistant Secretary Roy Rubottom instructed Ambassador Smith to inform Batista that the United States would not support his government nor that of his successor, and that it would be advisable for him to leave Cuba.

Batista interpreted the message as a U.S. ultimatum. While General Cantillo, at Batista's behest, commenced secret negotiations with Castro, and while other senior army officers pursued their own plots, Batista furtively prepared his escape. Castro then had no more than three thousand guerrillas, yet his force seemed invincible in the face of a demoralized army with stampeding chiefs. Washington did not cause the collapse; it just cast the die and sealed the regime's fate.[25]

According to Ambassador Smith, "When the timing was propitious and opportunities were available for a solution without Batista or Castro, our Department of State refused to lend its support. The refusal was based on the grounds that the U.S. would be accused of intervening in the internal affairs of Cuba. Yet, eventually, the State Department did advise Batista that the time had come for him to absent himself from his country. This was positive intervention on behalf of Castro."[26] Five former U.S. ambassadors, who also were familiar with the Cuban situation, basically concurred under oath.

Like a modern Caesar, hero of daunting battles shrouded in myth, Castro began his march on Havana. The Cubans, who collectively tend to oscillate between the extremes of submission and rebellion, bowed unconditionally to his command. And the United States, eager to skirt confrontation, recognized his government even before it was duly constituted. Castro seemed larger than life. Master of the present, he started to rewrite the past and shape the future. Many believed what he was saying; few discerned what he was doing. Most celebrated the precipitate fall of a native dictatorship without noticing the ominous rise of an alien tyranny.

CHAPTER 4

Laying the Groundwork

During its first one hundred days, the Castro regime rocked the island with whirlwind intensity. It purged tainted or potentially dangerous government and army officials, reorganized departments, occupied properties, froze bank accounts, suspended or revoked contracts, abrogated laws—in short, drastically changed the institutional landscape of the country. Nothing seemed solid enough to withstand the revolutionary turmoil. But during this initial period of sweeping reforms, the new rulers did not exceed the limits of political control; nor did they seem to cross the point of no return. Perhaps, we thought, they would take a more pragmatic approach to social and economic matters. After all, Castro himself had repeatedly rejected the "extremes of both capitalism and communism." That was the hope that flickered at home, where relatives and friends gathered around the television set to listen to Castro's midnight utterances—a few hours before they became law.

By April 1959, reports of creeping communism started to alarm us. Independent analysts, however, dismissed these allegations on the strength of compelling arguments. The revolution had socialistic inclinations, they generally conceded, but it was not following a rigid totalitarian pattern. The 26th of July Movement had thwarted the initial attempts of the Marxists to infiltrate the labor unions, and the government-controlled newspaper *Revolución* had taken exception to policy statements carried by the Communist daily *Hoy*. Admittedly, the independent press was under attack,

59

but journalists could criticize the Castro regime and even expound on the Communist peril. Private sectors of the economy were under pressure, and some businesses had been taken over by the government. However, no systematic, frontal attack had yet been mounted against private property and free enterprise. Elections were postponed, allegedly because the revolution had other more pressing priorities. But this did not give rise to widespread protests. The people seemed happy with Castro's mass rallies, billed as a spontaneous form of direct democracy.

Most of the analysts acknowledged that there were radical factions within the government, represented primarily by Che Guevara and Raúl Castro; but they were quick to point out that the deciding factor, the key player, continued to be Fidel. He was viewed as a magnetic leader hungry for power, not as a militant activist or a disciplined zealot. If threatened, he would sweep away the Communists, we were told. Fidel was indignant at the U.S. government for having helped Batista, and he effectively fueled anti-American feelings. However, analysts believed that he would not break with Washington. He might become the Cuban Nasser, but he would never bow to Moscow.

The arguments put forth by the analysts were cogent, in our opinion, but somewhat naive. They seemed to overlook the totalitarian propensity of the regime and to rule out the possibility of deception. We were particularly uneasy about certain developments that had been brought to our attention by friends connected with the Castro regime. Upon arriving in Havana in early January, Che Guevara instructed one of his aides to seize all the records kept by Cuba's anti-Communist police (BRAC). Captain José Castaño, the competent deputy director of BRAC, who had worked closely with U.S. and Western European intelligence agencies, was arrested and shot. None of the charges lodged against him was verified, so a rape allegation was fabricated. He was condemned and executed before foreign embassies could intervene in his behalf.

Another disturbing sign was the quiet return to Havana, shortly after Castro's triumph, of several prominent leaders of the international Communist movement. Among them was Lázaro Peña, a Cuban labor chief who had been in Prague, and Moscow's *éminence grise,* the unfathomable Fabio Grobart. As noted earlier, Grobart had frequently operated in Cuba, laying the foundations of the Kremlin's clandestine apparatus in the Caribbean. His return marked a new Red offensive—this time, we were told, with the blessing of the Cuban government. This was confirmed years later by Juan Vivés, Castro's G-2 defector, who wrote: "On March 3, 1959, at the offices Che had at La Cabaña [fortress], Fidel Castro held a private meeting with Fabio Grobart, the Comintern's secret envoy to Cuba since 1927. . . . This truly secret conference went on from 2:45 to 5:30 in the morning. I recall the date and time because that day I was on duty and I recorded all those details on the registry. The next morning, Che tore the page with the annotations and told me not to make any comments."[1] Vivés reported that following this meeting five Cuban Communist leaders left for the Soviet Union and Red China on a secret government mission.[2]

We also heard alarming rumors of a Soviet-Cuban connection through Mexico, which turned out to be true. As early as July 1959, Captain Manuel Villafaña, who at the time was Cuba's air attaché in Mexico, was asked to greet Major Ramiro Valdés, chief of Cuban intelligence (G-2), and to escort him from the airport to the Soviet embassy in that city. Valdés arrived at the embassy with his suitcase and stayed overnight—such was his close relationship with the Soviet ambassador, Vladimir Bazikin. A few weeks later, following Valdés's second sojourn at the Soviet embassy, the Russian air attaché told Villafaña that he had instructions from his government to exchange intelligence information with him. Villafaña refused and later defected to the United States and joined the Bay of Pigs Brigade.[3]

Yet another disquieting development was the high profile and growing influence of the Socialist Popular (Communist) Party in Cuba. None of the old parties, not even those that had supported the revolution against Batista, was permitted to function as a political organization. The sole exception was the Communist Party, which started to indoctrinate 26th of July cadres and to operate as a sort of shadow government in connivance with Castro. Moreover, a large number of Marxist operatives from other Latin American countries came to Cuba in early 1959. Some of them were assigned to government posts, others to the armed forces.

An additional source of concern was the anti-Yankee invectives that colored most of the revolutionary statements after the rise of Castro. The tirades had become so frequent and strident that José Figueres, a former President of Costa Rica, a strong supporter of Castro, and no lackey of Washington, urged the Cubans at a large rally held in Havana on March 22, 1959, to embrace the cause of democracy and stand with the United States and the West in the event of war. To the astonishment of many of us who were watching the rally on television, the then labor leader of the revolution, David Salvador, pulled the microphone away from Figueres and shouted that under no circumstances would Cuba support the United States in a new war. Fidel subsequently echoed this line, accused Figueres of being a false friend, and affirmed that U.S. corporations in their greed had killed many more Cubans than had the dictatorship of Batista.

On April 8, 1959, a regional meeting of American ambassadors was held in El Salvador. The press reported that Cuba was to be the focal point of the conference. Most of my relatives and I assumed that the U.S. ambassadors and Department of State officials would discuss intelligence data pointing to increased Communist penetration in Cuba. We also thought they would agree on a policy of "carrot and stick"—a policy that would offer economic assistance to build a new Cuba under a democratic system, but that would also warn Castro that the United States would not tolerate the establishment of a Marxist-Leninist regime in contravention of existing inter-American treaties. We were wrong. The ambassadors did not review intelligence data; they disagreed on their approach to Cuba and issued a bland statement that satisfied no one.

At the Conference of El Salvador, Philip Bonsal, the urbane newly appointed U.S. ambassador to Cuba, clashed with Robert Hill, U.S. ambassador to Mexico, and with Whiting Willauer, U.S. ambassador to Costa Rica. Hill and Willauer called for a strong stance against Castro. They believed that the Cuban leader was turning the strategic island into a Communist base and that the United States should disclose the evidence available and take appropriate action in conjunction with the Organization of American States. Bonsal, on the other hand, urged continuance of a hopeful and watchful wait-and-see policy. As Hill testified before the U.S. Senate Judiciary Subcommittee, Bonsal stressed that

Castro was in power; that he had tremendous popular support . . . and that we ought to go slow in dealing with him . . . despite the fact that he was constantly insulting the U.S. and our President . . . Bonsal felt that eventually Castro would see the light and return to the family of Latin American nations. He said Cuba needed a revolution and Cuba would then start to prosper and make its contribution to the Latin American family. . . . The Ambassador pointed out that of course Castro had

Communistic associates. However, he made it clear that Castro made the decisions. . . .[4]

The feedback we got indicated that Bonsal, champion of the policy of patience and forbearance, had prevailed in that pivotal conference. At home we discussed the serious implications of such policy. We feared that Washington's passiveness, far from taming Castro, would exacerbate the radicalism of his regime. Friends who were also tracking developments, however, were not as pessimistic. They informed us that during Castro's announced visit to Washington starting April 15 (the week after the El Salvador conference), his ministers would commence negotiations with the United States to obtain economic assistance. The negotiations, we were told, would necessarily lead to a compromise between the two governments which would help ease tensions.

Castro went to Washington with a full-fledged economic team: Rufo López Fresquet, Minister of Finance; Felipe Pazos, president of the National Bank; and Regino Boti, Minister of the Economy. They were prepared to discuss economic aid programs and to submit supporting documentation for the loans they required. However, just before leaving Havana and during their stay in Washington, Castro instructed them not to request or accept any financial support.

Two years later, in exile, López Fresquet disclosed what happened.

> When I accompanied Fidel to this country in April 1959, the Prime Minister warned me as we left Havana not to take up Cuban economic matters with the authorities, bankers, or investors of the North. At various times during the trip, he repeated the warning. That is why, when I visited the then Secretary of the Treasury, Robert B. Anderson, I did not respond to the American official's indications that the United States was favorably disposed toward aiding our country. Also for this reason, during our stay in Washington, when I exchanged views with Assistant Secretary of State for Latin American Affairs Roy Rubottom, I feigned polite aloofness to his concrete statement that the U.S. Government wished to know how and in what form it could cooperate with the Cuban Government in the solution of the most pressing economic needs.[5]

Felipe Pazos went through the same experience at the International Monetary Fund.

Several explanations were given to us for Castro's decision: nationalistic pride, anger at not having been received by President Eisenhower, unwillingness to compromise his principles. The fact is that Washington was prepared to assist Cuba, and Castro blocked all discussions. According to López Fresquet, Fidel did not want American aid in the slightest. "He wanted to be able to say, afterward, that the United States had not helped Cuba."

Castro's game plan also became clear to a distinguished Cuban lawyer and businessman, Dr. Luis Botifoll, who met with Fidel during his brief stay in New York. In the course of their private discussion at Fidel's hotel suite, the latter received a telephone call from his brother, Raúl, in Havana. Botifoll heard Fidel assure Raúl that, press reports notwithstanding, no U.S. financial assistance had been requested by the Cuban delegation and none would be accepted. He also told his brother, who was urging him to make a radical pronouncement during the May 1 labor day parade in Havana, that he (Fidel) was not yet in a position to do so. For that reason, Fidel decided to absent himself from the parade and asked his Minister of the Economy, in Botifoll's presence, to make the arrangements necessary for Fidel to attend an inter-American conference that was to be held in Buenos Aires in late April. Botifoll left the meeting convinced that there were no fundamental ideological differences between the Castro brothers, but that Fidel called the shots with a virtuoso's sense of timing.[6]

While in the United States, Castro tried to improve his image, which was somewhat tarnished by the continued summary executions in Cuba and by persistent charges of extremism. He reiterated that he was not a Communist and that the color of the revolution was olive green, like the Cuban palm trees. He was eloquent at Harvard and charismatic on television, and he enthralled most of his interlocutors. Vice-President Nixon was a notable exception. He wrote: "I was convinced Castro was either incredibly naive about Communism or under Communist discipline and that we would have to treat him and deal with him accordingly."[7] It took months for this thought to permeate thick layers of disbelief in the official corridors of Washington.

Meanwhile in Cuba we were awaiting with trepidation the touted Agrarian Reform Law. I expected it to be a watershed in the path of the revolution. It would determine, beyond words, whether the Castro regime was irretrievably bound to a totalitarian design. I harbored hopes of moderation, but they were crushed by the law that was promulgated on May 17. It was preceded by a well-orchestrated government campaign that roused the peasants—the *guajiros*—leading them to believe that they would receive the land they tilled. The campaign also created the impression that all large sugar cane and tobacco growers, as well as cattle ranchers, were exploiters of the people and had no right to the land they owned. This "guilt by association" paralyzed or weakened the resolve of agribusinessmen, and prompted some of them to appease the government with spectacular donations before the enactment of the law.

Finally, the campaign built emotional support among workers, employees, and professionals through incessant propaganda that declared the agrarian reform to be the "salvation of Cuba." Those who opposed it—even partially—were viewed as counterrevolutionaries or traitors. Infectious slogans dulled critical reason and made people forget that despite prevailing inequities and shortcomings, Cuba had achieved one of the highest levels of socioeconomic development in Latin America. Agricultural reforms were undoubtedly needed, but within the framework of the progressive 1940 Constitution.

That is what Fidel Castro had promised when he was fighting in the Sierra Maestra. The revolutionary agrarian reform that was drafted in November 1958 generally conformed to the constitutional charter. However, the May 1959 law exceeded even the worst fears of radicalism. It was written by several Marxists, including Antonio Núñez Jiménez, a well-known geographer and speleologist who had always aligned himself with the Socialist Popular Party. The law proscribed estates larger than 1,000 acres (3,300 acres in special cases), even if they were cultivated. Land over those limits was to be expropriated. Compensation would be based on the assessed value of the land for tax purposes, which in most cases was ridiculously low. The stipulated payments (which never materialized) were to be made in twenty-year bonds, bearing an annual interest of 4½ percent. The expropriated land would be used primarily to form state cooperatives. Distribution of individual holdings, which was the focal point of the Sierra Maestra draft, was deemphasized in the law and represented only a small part of the program.

The law was to be interpreted and executed by the newly created Agrarian Reform Institute (INRA). INRA had such broad political, fiscal, financial, and even judicial powers that it was a kind of parallel government of its own. Castro appropriately became its president. The law applied directly to about 40 percent of the total land in farms, but nothing prevented INRA from engulfing the rest. As we would soon find out, the precedents had been established and the momentum had been created to do just that.

Within the agricultural sectors of Cuba, the law gave rise to conflicting tactical approaches. Some of the affected landowners wished to keep a low profile, thinking that the legislation had plenty of loopholes and grayish areas to work out private deals with INRA. Others believed that low-key negotiations with the government were the best avenue to revise the most stringent provisions of the law. Still others felt that only a strong, coordinated, and vocal stance, involving the industrialists, businessmen, and independent media, would force the government to listen and agree to drastic changes.

Not even the Catholic Church maintained a consistent, unified position on this issue. Msgr. Evelio Díaz spoke of the Agrarian Reform Law as fundamentally just, whereas Msgr. Pérez Serantes, who had initially praised the law as "necessary and humane," later echoed suspicions that "the authors of the law and the Communists had been drinking of the same spring." Independent analysts also offered varied interpretations. Those who focused on isolated articles of the law did not seem too preoccupied. They indicated, for instance, that the rates of interest on the Cuban bonds were higher than those established under MacArthur's reform in Japan, and the time of repayment was shorter than under the Formosa reform. However, pundits who studied the Cuban Agrarian Reform Law as a whole and analyzed its far-reaching encroachment on private enterprise warned of grave dislocations leading to unbridled collectivism.

I was deeply worried as I saw a confused and disjointed nation inexorably falling into a radical trap. Few realized that the announced agrarian reform was not really an economic and social program, but a political device to install totalitarianism in Cuba. And those who knew lacked the power or the will to influence and the constituency to lead. The hour was late—perhaps too late—to stem the tide. For months, Cuba had been relentlessly subjected to a plethora of revolutionary techniques designed to divide and conquer: class struggle, anesthetizing propaganda, and diffuse terror. Pulled apart and weakened during this process, the nation seemed unwilling or unable to confront the government and avert a complete takeover.

Under these circumstances, the director of the Cuban Cattlemen's Association urgently convened a national assembly on May 24, 1959, to review the Agrarian Reform Law and agree on a common course of action. For several years before the rise of Castro, my grandfather Cortina had presided over the association. He was reasonably pleased with the progress made by this important sector of the economy. Heads of cattle had increased to almost six million in 1958, with large ranches accounting for not more than 15 percent. The quality of Cuban cattle had significantly improved with crosses of Holstein, Jersey Brown Swiss, and Santa Gertrudes. Cattle fairs were major events that stirred competition and stimulated national pride, since the cattle industry was fundamentally in Cuban hands. Meat consumption per capita had reached one of the highest levels in Latin America (surpassed only by Argentina and Uruguay), and Cuba had commenced to export high-quality meat to the United States.

My grandfather was ill and could not attend the extraordinary assembly, so he asked me to represent him and proceed as I saw fit. I arrived a few minutes before the start of the meeting. The auditorium was packed. Groups swarming the halls conversed in hushed tones and concealed their emotions. Few smiles lightened the gravity of the environment. One could feel the tension that precedes momentous deliberations.

I sat in the back of the room not sure whether I could or should address the assembly. My doubts did not stem from lack of preparation. I had carefully studied the law, reviewed historical precedents, and drawn my own conclusions. The questions that assaulted me were of a different nature. Would a combative speech such as the one I had in mind be allowed by this gathering of sturdy and individualistic ranchers, who, for the most part, did not know who I was? If so, would it have any meaningful impact on the various groups of cattlemen, including the wishful thinkers who did not want to face up to reality and take a stand? Finally, would such a critical speech attract the attention of government officials and expose my family and me to harassment or arrest?

After listening to the first few speakers, I was no longer inhibited by doubts. The cattlemen's analyses seemed to lack relevance and depth. They meandered through the written text of the Agrarian Reform Law without considering its full scope and intent. They reviewed their rights under the law without analyzing the myriad restrictions that nullified them. They discussed the extension of land they could keep without realizing that the central issue was not acreage, but private property and individual free-

dom. I rose to speak. I carried no prepared statement or notes—
just mental distillations of my studies and the audacity of youth.
Unable to determine how much time I would have to review the
law, I went straight into the heart of the matter.

"I address this historic assembly," I said, controlling my ner-
vousness, "conscious of the critical moment facing Cuba. We are
not discussing here today isolated issues of small or large cattlemen; we are not defending personal or group interests. What we
are debating is the economic and political future of our country. I
do not come, therefore, to protect acres of land more or less. I
come to uphold a principle: private property. To support a system: free enterprise. To defend a regime: representative democracy. I do not come to oppose a constructive and harmonious
agrarian reform that would benefit Cuba; I come to combat a dis-
ruptive and punitive agrarian reform that will devastate the island.
I do not come to obstruct the agricultural and industrial development of our country; I come to challenge, from its very base, the
ominous Agrarian Reform Law because it is confiscatory, de-
structive, totalitarian, and unjust!"

The assembly greeted my opening remarks with prolonged
applause. Heartened by the response, I proceeded to analyze all
of the unconstitutional features of the law and pointed out what I
thought it would trigger: massive expropriations without compensation; parceling of land without regard to productivity; repudiation of contracts and annulment of existing rights; creation of
agricultural communes without issuance of title or recognition of
private ownership; establishment of a gigantic state agency (INRA)
with total control over major segments of the economy and over
the lives of farmers and rural workers. The description of that
agency must have struck a very sensitive chord. The audience
clapped vehemently when I said: "I see in INRA a monstrous
political, economic, and social superstructure. I see in INRA a
state within the state. I see in INRA the INRI of the Cubans!"

Toward the end of my impromptu remarks (excerpts of which
were preserved), I stated that if the legislation was not substantially modified, we could no longer speak of private property in
Cuba, for it would have been deprived of its main attributes. Large
and medium-size farms and ranches would disappear, only to be
replaced by the most absorbent, inefficient, and despotic of all
latifundia: the latifundia of the state. Small landed possessions
would be allowed to remain in private hands, but only as temporary concessions, revocable by whim of omnipotent authority. The

end result of such radical transformation would not be the redistribution of wealth, but the dissemination of misery, the generation of hunger, and the proscription of freedom.

I concluded my speech with the following exhortation:

"Cattlemen of Cuba, I urge you to join forces with other economic sectors to defend the democratic principles and liberal traditions that this law would destroy. I urge you to oppose the law as a crime against the nation and to denounce the dislocations and convulsions that it would provoke.

"Cattlemen of Cuba, stand up and be counted, for if you do not rise, you will be crushed by the uncontainable avalanche of state interventionism!"

When I finished my peroration, the cattlemen were on their feet applauding wildly. Belligerent shouts were heard, including "Down with Communism!" and "March on the presidential palace!" I had to address the assembly again to explain that I was not inciting them to revolt (clearly premature), but to exercise their rights in concert with other private sector organizations and civic institutions. A prominent cattleman, fearful of confronting the government, tried to discredit me by rejecting what he called the "precipitate conclusions of an impetuous and irresponsible youngster, who must have just finished reading the *Psychology of the Masses* of Gustave Le Bon!" These barbs did not require a response on my part. I received the unwavering support of several cattlemen, including the respected Camagüey patriarch Justo Lamar Roura, who said: "The vehemence of youth in this case came to us with the insight of talent, the magic of eloquence, and the integrity of patriotism. We welcome the courageous and enlightened leadership of Carbonell."

I was invited to join a special committee of the association which had been asked to mount a public relations campaign against the law, in coordination with other economic institutions. At the request of the committee, I drafted a statement of principles extracted from my speech. It elicited a broad consensus and became a democratic manifesto. Armando Caíñas Milanés, president of the Cattlemen's Association, became the unofficial leader of the emerging private-sector movement. He declared on television that the Agrarian Reform Law was even more radical than the program outlined by the Communists in 1956. Ricardo R. Sardiña, a spokesman for the Sugar Cane Growers Association, also denounced the totalitarian features of the law. The Sugar Mill Owners Association argued that the law would have "grave economic repercussions," since sugar cane could not be adequately prepared for harvest if the large landholdings were broken up. Even the tobacco growers in Pinar del Río, who did not seem to be significantly affected by the law, protested vigorously. I recall that one of them, an old, dignified farmer, dismissed threats of reprisal and said with gloom: "They [the government] can take away the farm I own. That will not silence me. I don't need land to live. I just need a grave to die."

Despite the conflicting interests and tactical differences that separated the economic sectors, some of them started to coalesce into an informal free-enterprise confederation. They attempted to conduct serious negotiations with the government, but Castro precluded the dialogue, accusing the critics of the Agrarian Reform Law of treason—of being preoccupied with their "vested interests." He also declared that not a comma of the law would be changed. The U.S. government did not fare any better. Even though it acknowledged that Cuba had the right to expropriate foreign property and that land reform was a step toward social progress, Washington received no satisfactory answer to its request for "prompt, adequate, and effective compensation."

Castro's intransigence soon led to the first major conspiracy against his regime, known as the "cattlemen's plot." It was initiated by Armando Caíñas Milanés and other ranchers, by a former congressman and Minister of Labor, Arturo Hernández Tellaheche, and by a group of young professionals. Among them was my cousin Eduardo Arango. A twenty-eight-year-old bachelor, athletically built and debonair, Eddy had become very concerned over the Communist trend of the Castro regime. Not expecting any peaceful, democratic overtures, he gave up his busy social and professional life and discreetly joined the conspiracy. On several occasions he invited me to participate, but I declined because I did not think that the climate was ripe for a rebellion. I also felt uneasy about the reported involvement of disgruntled Rebel Army officers. For all I knew, they could be agents provocateurs planted by Castro to mislead and destroy the opposition.

My instincts were unfortunately correct. The conspiracy was infiltrated and aborted in mid-August 1959 by three "dissident" majors, induced or forced by Castro to entrap the plotters: the U.S.-born soldier of fortune William Morgan and the leaders of the Second Front of the Escambray, Eloy Gutiérrez Menoyo and Jesús Carreras.[8] These officers, in concert with Castro, staged a revolt in the city of Trinidad. To discredit the operation, they encouraged a Trujillo connection and urged the Dominican dictator to dispatch arms and men to support the fake uprising. When Trujillo's plane landed, Castro and his aides, who were hiding near the airstrip, captured the invaders, ordered the arrest of the plotters in Havana and other cities, and heaped scorn on them.

When the news broke, I was having lunch with a group of friends at the Havana Yacht Club, one of five splendid private clubs in the outskirts of the capital. Unaware of what was happening, I had decided to unwind and socialize, if only for a few hours. Since the rise of Castro, I had not had much time to enjoy the attractions of club life. It was a bright, sunny day marking the celebration of a traditional sport event. But the ambiance was not quite the same as in the past. I saw traces of sadness in the flirtatious smiles of some of the young ladies. Family misfortunes under the revolution had left their mark on them. Drinking had increased—not really to heighten pleasure, but to escape from reality. Social conversations no longer centered on frivolous themes; they frequently turned to politics and sparked heated debates. Businessmen who had suffered government harassment and confiscation clashed with those who had not yet been "touched" by the revolution and thought they could buck the system. The Cuban phenomenon was still not well understood by the fading consortium of the rich and famous.

Conflicting opinions were often superficial and self-centered. The elite were conscious of the totalitarian drift, but many of them seemed paralyzed by fear or inhibited by a geographic, protectionist fixation. That attitude, known as the "ninety-mile syndrome," stemmed from the belief that the United States could not tolerate a Communist government ninety miles off its coasts and would eventually take appropriate action to save Cuba. This over-reliance on Washington was a legacy of the so-called Platt Amendment, which during the period 1902–1934 enabled the United States to intervene in the internal affairs of Cuba.[9]

Not all, however, was inertia and fatalism. Some of the younger members of the intelligentsia had the courage of their convictions and were prepared to play an assertive role in the events that were unfolding. I saw at the club several pale-faced friends who were actively conspiring. They were the ones who informed me that the cattlemen's plot had been quashed and that Eddy had been arrested.

I promptly left the club and drove to the Arango residence. There I found the family visibly shaken by the news. Eddy was being held incommunicado; no one knew where he was. We heard that as many as one thousand persons implicated in the plot had been detained in various parts of Cuba. After several hours of painful vigil, we got word that Eddy was well. Since no visits were allowed, we sent him some clothes and proceeded to find a litigator willing to take his case. The defense, however, proved to be an academic exercise, for the revolutionary tribunal was not bound by the niceties of due process of law. Eddy was sentenced to six years' imprisonment. He faced his accusers with dignity and received the verdict with composure. He made us proud.

A few days after the cattlemen's conspiracy was uncovered, my mother called me at the office. Her quivering voice projected anguish. She told me that six police officers were at home looking for me. She paused and then asked me: "What are you going to do?" I remained quiet for a while as I tried to marshal my thoughts under tension. I had not been actively involved in any anti-Castro conspiracy, nor had I formed or joined any opposition group. But I had been highly critical of government measures, and my inflammatory speech at the Cattlemen's Association had elicited harsh comments in official circles. I basically had two options: to seek diplomatic asylum and leave Cuba, or to appear before the authorities and risk arrest. Not wanting to leave the island, I decided to confront my inquisitors.

When the police agents fetched me at the office, they said they were going to take me to the nearest station to clarify an alleged traffic violation. They drove me instead to army headquarters at Camp Columbia—not precisely the place to conduct a routine investigation. The corridors were filled with people from all walks of life who had been detained and were waiting to be interrogated. In one of the adjacent rooms I saw a former classmate of mine proudly wearing the olive-green uniform of Castro's Rebel Army. I expected at least a comforting hello, but he turned his face and ignored me. Fearing for his security, he disavowed our friendship. Later I saw another young officer I knew quite well. This one did not avoid me, but looking nervously around whispered in my ear: "Nestor, I also have been detained." Given the pervading confusion, I decided to sit down and refrain from extending salutations.

After two hours of waiting, I was escorted to a large room where several officers were engaged in animated discussion. Seated in one of the corners of the office was a portly army auditor, sporting a well-groomed beard, who was going to interrogate me:

Captain Juan Nuiry. I felt more at ease when I realized who he was. Although I did not know him personally, I had heard through common friends that he was affable and fair, and not a Marxist militant. He greeted me with a smile and then called on two young assistants, saying: "Come and join me, because Dr. Carbonell, who is intelligent, might try to dupe me." I responded in kind: "Captain, since we are *all* on guard, no one is going to be tricked."

After some further jousting, Nuiry zeroed in on my purported involvement in the cattlemen's conspiracy. He listened to my answers but was not satisfied with my denials. He repeatedly referred to my blood ties with Eddy Arango and my friendly relationship with some of the other plotters. I, of course, acknowledged those links but asserted that they were not enough to establish conspiracy. I defied him to produce a single piece of document, a single witness, a single shred of evidence showing that I had participated in a plot to overthrow the government.

Nuiry's eager assistants counterattacked and tried to shift the thrust of the interrogation from conspiratorial activities they could not prove to counterrevolutionary statements I could not deny. They hurled rapid-fire questions and tried to confuse me with frequent interruptions. I could tell by their technique that they had been trained in dialectics. This shift spelled trouble for me, so I decided to ignore their pointed accusations and address my response to Nuiry. I told him that to the best of my ability, I had answered all the questions and dispelled all the doubts concerning my purported involvement in the conspiracy. Summarizing my position, I said: "I do not oppose the revolution; I only disagree with certain deviations from its proclaimed objectives. There are no fundamental differences between my views, as expressed in various publications, and the revolutionary goals proclaimed during the struggle against Batista."

I was fortunate that Nuiry was in charge of the interrogation and that his pressing priority was to round up active conspirators and not political suspects. He ended the discussion and told me that I could go home, but that I must remain available for further investigation. I had narrowly escaped imprisonment, but not surveillance. Having been branded a potential counterrevolutionary, I knew that I would be watched. The session at Camp Columbia was for me a sobering experience, a timely warning—not to abjure convictions, but to be more discreet.

CHAPTER 5

The Takeover

A few weeks later, I decided to visit Dr. Manuel Antonio (Tony) de Varona. A former Prime Minister of Cuba with impeccable revolutionary credentials, Tony had warned against the progressive radicalization of the Castro regime and had called for free elections. Since he was a close friend of my father's, we were able to converse in confidence. He shared my concerns about the Cuban situation, but insisted that before frontally opposing Castro and reopening the path of violence, we had to exhaust all possible means to resolve the crisis without bloodshed.

Following his advice, I drafted a paper listing ten reasons why the Cuban people should be allowed to vote as soon as possible. The document, in essence, was published as an editorial in *Diario de la Marina*. Castro, who had initially agreed to hold elections, now rejected them as a stratagem to thwart the revolution. He had cleverly conditioned the minds of the masses, linking politics to venal practices of the past. Those who spoke of elections were chastised as purveyors of corruption. Few dared.

By the third quarter of 1959, I was able to trace a totalitarian pattern, evidenced by increasing government pressures and controls in all spheres of life—political, social, economic, and cultural. This trend, however, was not clearly discerned by the general public. State interventionism continued to be wrapped in the silken shroud of "humanism" and was extended gradually, a step at a time, in order not to open too many fronts all at once. Only after most of the ranchers and farmers had been crushed or neutralized by the agrarian reform did the government initiate the purge of the labor unions. This was not easy. Violent quarrels erupted at the Tenth Labor Congress between the Communist militants shouting "Unity!" and the 26th of July activists chanting "Melons!" The latter suggested that the Communists were like watermelons—on the outside olive green, the color of Castro's Rebel Army uniform, but red inside. The Communists seemingly failed in their attempt to place their representatives in key positions. Yet failure was not defeat, for the unquestioned victor in the struggle, the 26th of July Movement, turned out to be a Communist front. Stripped of non-Marxist members, the movement eventually became the Trojan horse that opened the gates of Cuba to the Soviet Union.

Since not many people realized or understood the implications of the interventionist momentum, I wrote a sixty-page paper entitled "Where Are We Heading?" It analyzed the government actions taken by Castro and compared them with the Marxist-Leninist blueprint for the takeover of a country. This factual parallel was designed to open the eyes of influential sectors of the population. I decided to serialize fragments of the study and publish them under a pseudonym in *Diario de la Marina,* which was already waging a frontal anti-Communist campaign along with *Prensa Libre,* led by Sergio Carbó, and *El País,* headed by Guillermo Martínez Márquez, among others. The campaign was so effective in building awareness that the government intensified its attacks on the independent press, subjecting it to economic strangulation, labor unrest, systematic defamation, and statements of clarification dubbed *coletillas,* "little tails." The *coletillas* were stinging rebuttals inserted by government-controlled censors at the end of every news cable or article deemed contrary to the revolution.

Castro repeatedly denied any Marxist design. Close aides, however, started resigning or defecting, including the air force chief, Pedro Luis Díaz Lanz; the Provisional President of Cuba appointed by Castro himself, Manuel Urrutia; and a valorous and magnetic Sierra Maestra major who had strongly supported the revolution, Huber Matos. They all denounced the progressive Communist penetration. Castro did not waver or retreat. He accused them of treason for raising the specter of communism to justify foreign aggression. Díaz Lanz was able to escape to the United States. Urrutia was forced to resign after an unyielding tirade by Castro on television—the first known case of a TV coup d'état preceded by character assassination. Huber Matos was lambasted by Fidel during summary court proceedings and was sentenced to twenty years in prison. Thirteen other officers were acquitted, subsequently rearrested, and then imprisoned.

Shortly thereafter, a seemingly unrelated event rocked the nation. Camilo Cienfuegos, the commander-in-chief of the Rebel Army, the most popular man in Cuba after Castro, was reportedly lost over the sea in a flight to Havana. A major search was carried out, but not a single trace of the alleged accident was found. Suspicions of a government purge rapidly spread and created further unrest.

To stave off or contain ideological dissent, Castro declared that anticommunism was counterrevolutionary and intensified police terror. Still, a large number of Cubans kept their faith in Fidel. They continued to blame his brother, Raúl and Che Guevara for radical excesses and believed that *El Líder Máximo* would eventually "shake the tree," expel the Communists, and steer the revolution to shore. Fidel played on the perceived rift by saying: "If something happens to me, you'll get my brother, Raúl."

Later, the regime's trained propagandists took a different tack. To prepare the masses for the eventual disclosure of Castro's true colors, they launched a major campaign centered on the slogan "If Fidel is a Communist, then put me on the list. He's got to be right." The subtle reasoning went like this: Castro was presented as a messiah—a savior who had conquered an army, destroyed a dictatorship, and brought freedom and prosperity to a desperate nation. Castro could not be connected with anything evil. Whatever he was had to be good. Therefore, if he was a Communist, then "put me on the list"; I'm with him. It was vintage Pavlov permeating minds and conditioning reflexes.

In October 1959, I received a message at the office to go home at once. The cryptic note bore the unequivocal sign of another family crisis. When I got to the house I saw a cordon of police cars encircling the premises. It was a raid. My father, who had arrived ahead of me, reported that my grandfather Cortina had been detained and taken to a police station. Secret agents apparently had found some hunting rifles at my grandfather's farm, and were now going to search our residence. I rushed to my room with a colleague from the office who had accompanied me. I had to dispose of a .38 Magnum revolver I kept in the closet. Where to conceal it? After pondering for a few moments, I asked my friend to place it among the numerous antique arms my grandfather had on display on the third floor of the house. There, I thought, no one would notice it.

I stayed alone in my room grappling with another problem. I didn't know what to do with the highly sensitive paper I had written on the Marxist-Leninist trends of the Castro regime. As I desperately searched for a place to hide it, one of the maids, the robust and inscrutable Eulalia, entered the room. She had worked for my grandparents for many years, and I had no reason to question her allegiance to the family. Still, no one could tell how employees or even friends and relatives would react under the fear of arrest for conspiracy and the temptation of rewards for spying. She saw me trying to remove the carpet and spotted the incriminating document on the floor. I could sense by her look that she knew what was going on. Without uttering a word, she grabbed the paper and ran out of the room. My fate was literally in her hands. She quickly returned and told me not to worry. She had concealed the document under her uniform, pressing it tightly against her chest. To save me from prison, she had actually risked her own freedom. I was deeply touched by her loyalty and valor. I embraced her with emotion—she had tears in her eyes.

The police did not find any cache of arms at the house. One of the agents, however, spotted my revolver when he was inspecting my grandfather's collection of antique weapons. Without asking any question or making any fuss, he took the revolver and casually put it in his pocket. He liked my Magnum.

Before the police left, I inquired about my grandfather. A taciturn officer lackadaisically informed me that he might have to stay at La Cabaña fortress until the whole matter was clarified. I could not believe what I was hearing: Cortina, the eighty-year-old statesman, to be taken as a criminal to La Cabaña. Controlling my rage, I told the officer: "Lieutenant, if those rifles you found at the Arroyo Naranjo farm belong to us, I'm sure we have the necessary licenses. Give us a couple of days and we'll produce the documents. As to my grandfather, his arrest is unwarranted and his transfer to La Cabaña, given his age and delicate health, would be tantamount to a death penalty. I am sure the government does not have that in mind. If you need to retain someone pending satisfactory resolution of this inquiry, I volunteer to stay in his place. In any case, please let me know where he is being held so that I can see him and deliver some medication."

Since the lieutenant had no authority to decide, he telephoned his superior. I overheard him stressing the health condition of my grandfather and the risks associated with the transfer to La Cabaña. After he hung up, he curtly told me that my grandfather would be released but placed under house arrest. The rifle licenses had to be produced within forty-eight hours; otherwise formal criminal proceedings would be instituted. Despite the implications of the ultimatum, the family felt relieved. My grandfather returned home that afternoon—somewhat haggard, but in fine fettle. We feverishly looked for the licenses and found them at the bottom of one of the files we kept at home. My grandmother was so happy that she invited the family to celebrate. She was not too interested in unraveling the mysteries surrounding the arrest; all that mattered was that her husband was back and well.

By the last quarter of 1959, the confiscation of land and the takeover of sugar plantations and cattle ranches were proceeding at breakneck speed. As I had anticipated in my speech at the Cattlemen's Association, the so-called agrarian reform affected not only the *latifundistas* but any owner of rural property or agricultural enterprise, regardless of its size or type. Many of those who still thought that Castro was not behind this systematic assault on capitalism were jarred by the startling revelations of a young "second chief of zone" of INRA who in October attended a highly confidential meeting of government hierarchs. The young man, Manuel Artime, was so incensed and alarmed by what he heard that he denounced the betrayal of the revolution, left the country, and later became the civilian leader of the ill-fated Bay of Pigs invasion.

As described by Artime, with whom I conversed at length in exile, the crucial meeting—the Second National Assembly of INRA—was held at its central headquarters in Havana. Given the rank of the leaders present—Fidel and the new rulers of Cuba—and the sensitivity of the topics to be aired, extreme security measures were taken. The building was guarded day and night by heavily armed bearded soldiers. None of the participants was allowed to leave the premises except to sleep. The managing director of INRA, Núñez Jiménez, underscored the confidentiality of the discussions and told the group that they constituted the genuine government of Cuba; that INRA was the real Cuban state, and that all the other government institutions were just a screen.

Then Castro explained the true objectives of the Agrarian Reform Law and drew a parallel with his guerrilla experience. He said: "We must proceed as during the war: first we take the countryside, and when the countryside is ours we then attack the cities, which will fall without much resistance," Describing the phased destruction of private enterprise, Fidel commented with sarcasm: "Within a short time the investors will have to become geniuses in order to find places to invest their money, because the state is going to have everything. If they doubt it, let them ask where they can invest. In housing? There is a rent [reduction] law already written and in effect which is immovable. Besides, I have another law prepared for when . . . the tenants will become owners of the homes they rent. . . . In land? With INRA at work, they would be insane to invest in this. Besides, the sale and purchase of land is prohibited. . . . In industry? They will have to step over the dead body of Che Guevara. . . ."

Che advocated that the profits of the state cooperatives be limited. When someone indicated that this would be like fixing a daily minimum wage for their peasant members, Che retorted: "Never mention the word 'wage' (*jornal*), because it reveals one's intentions. Continue speaking of a limited profit. And continue repeating to the *guajiros* that the profits of each cooperative will be divided among its members." When in the course of the discussion Castro said that "to those whose lands we expropriate we shall pay in agrarian bonds, but at the price which suits us and not that which they seek," Che replied with a smile: "Fidel, we can pay them the price they want. . . . The bonds are worthless." They all burst into laughter.[1]

Just prior to the INRA meeting, the Castro regime had seized my family's hacienda pursuant to the Agrarian Reform Law. Located in the far-western province of Pinar del Rio, near the picturesque town of San Diego de los Baños, the hacienda was endowed with fertile valleys, medicinal springs, and scenic mountains tapestried with pine trees. More than two thousand *guajiros* lived there and worked its various enterprises: cattle, forestry, and growing of tobacco, coffee, vegetables, and fruits. They formed a proud and industrious community eager to excel. From them I heard ingenious answers to many of the riddles and paradoxes of the countryside. Blessed with a fecund imagination and a delightful drawl, the *guajiros* had an explanation for just about everything. What they didn't know they would invent, usually with a thread of logic and a dash of humor.

A few days after the occupation of the hacienda—euphemistically called "intervention"—my grandfather Cortina was summoned to appear before government officials in Pinar del Río. Given the enormous scope of the agrarian reform, he did not expect to retain any significant area of the hacienda. He did harbor the hope, however, of keeping the part closest to his heart—the family quarters he had beautified over forty years with exotic plants, fragrant roses, classic sculptures, and cascading fountains. Waiving his right to be represented by counsel, he decided to attend the meeting himself. I accompanied him on the fruitless journey.

As we drove to Pinar del Río, vivid recollections of the hacienda assailed me. It was there that I had learned to enjoy the golden splendor of Cuba's sunrises, the purple mystery of its sunsets, the graceful elegance of its palm trees, the luscious fruit of its orchards, the pungent flavor of its coffee, and the sensuous aroma of its cigars.

But what attracted me most was the family quarters (which we incorrectly called *batey*) with its pastoral colonial house with red-tile roof. It had been a focal point where our family converged during the holidays. There, around a large oak table, we chatted and debated. My grandfather Cortina would lead the lively discussions, which ranged from history to agriculture, from politics to art. If the tone became too ponderous or polemical, my grandmother, *Yeya*—a sprightly lady of Andalusian descent—would interject a humorous comment or point to a poster on the wall that carried Victor Hugo's dictum "Laugh even if you are Homer. Laugh even if you are Cato!" These were some of the cherished memories that ran through my mind during our two-hour drive.

Shortly after we arrived at the provincial headquarters of the Agrarian Reform Institute, several uniformed officers greeted us. In their stern gaze I could read animosity. After brief perfunctory remarks, they homed in on the takeover of the hacienda with inexorable coldness. Since some of their statements were ambiguous, Cortina specifically asked them whether the *batey* would be included in the final expropriation. Their terse answer shattered all hopes: "The *batey* is an integral part of the hacienda's economic unit. You cannot keep it. You may apply, however, for compensation based on authorized acreage."[2]

Cortina seemed unperturbed, but as I casually looked under the table I saw him stubbing out a cigarette with the palm of his hand. Controlling his emotions, he responded with a grave voice: "Sir, the *batey* is not part of an economic unit. It comprises our family residence and gardens, which cannot be treated simply as land. It contains many works of art and intangibles which cannot be measured or appraised by the yard. But all of that is irrelevant, because the *batey* is not for sale. You can take it if you will, but it is not for sale!"

The meeting ended rather abruptly. Further debate seemed useless. When we entered the car, the chauffeur asked Cortina whether he wished to stop at the hacienda on the way back to Havana. He vacillated for a moment, but answered in the negative. He could not face the poignancy of a last visit. He reminisced for a while and then fell asleep. Deep furrows indented his forehead. It was not the placid expression of a man who was resting. It was the somber look of a soul in pain.

As we approached the end of 1959, government pressures mounted. New laws and regulations encroached upon the rights of the private sector and established the bases for further regimentation. All previous efforts to stem the tide of totalitarianism had failed. The Catholic Church, however, still offered some hope of containment or stabilization. Its influence was not as widespread as in several other Latin American countries, but it was nonetheless a powerful and cohesive institution—indeed the only one that had survived the collapse of the republic. In the void that ensued, the church became a natural rallying point, a gravitational force, which amalgamated those who feared the progressive radicalization of Cuba.

Castro was very careful not to antagonize the church in the early stages of the revolution. This enabled Catholic laymen to organize a national congress in Havana, in November 1959. More than half a million people from all over the island participated in the evening procession, carrying candles and waving white handkerchiefs. It was a moving experience that I shall never forget. Choruses of "Caridad" (referring to Caridad del Cobre—Cuba's patron Virgin of Charity) were heard in the same rhythm as the revolutionary slogan "*Paredón!*" ("To the firing wall!") that was chanted in Castro's rallies. It was the Catholics' response to extremism and violence. Toward the end of the procession, the multitude burst into a cry that reverberated through the streets of Havana like a soaring echo of dignity, a stirring expression of defiance: "Cuba *Sí;* Rusia *NO!*"

Fearing the contagious spread of opposition, the government clamped down on demonstrations and curbed religious activities. Church ceremonies were broken up by militiamen singing communism's "International"; priests and ministers were ridiculed and harassed, and Marxist indoctrination was intensified. By May 1960, Msgr. Pérez Serantes, who had been an ardent supporter of Castro, crossed swords with the government in a historic pastoral letter: "It can no longer be said that the enemy is at the gates, for in truth he is within, as if in his own domain. . . . The true Chris-

tian cannot live without freedom. . . . it has always seemed better to us to lose all, even to shed blood, than to renounce liberty."[3]
No one was immune to persecution, not even the ailing primate
of Cuba, Cardinal Manuel Arteaga. Having learned that Castro
had ordered his arrest, the cardinal, disguised as a *guajiro,* sought
refuge in the Argentine embassy. When Argentina severed relations with Cuba in early 1962, the cardinal was transferred to the
Brazilian embassy, and there he died, tormented by the vicious
attacks on the church and the expulsion from Cuba of more than
130 priests.

The only other factor that could have perhaps checked or
delayed the course of events in Cuba was the United States.
Washington, however, chose to follow the policy of patience and
forbearance recommended by Ambassador Bonsal, and became
Castro's whipping boy. The ambassador's mild-mannered approach did not elicit much respect, nor did it abate the anti-Yankee
hate campaign. Bonsal was frequently ignored or kept waiting—
sometimes for several months—when he approached the Cuban
ruler. Admittedly, there were provocations that created antagonism and complicated the situation. Several U.S. senators, congressmen, and journalists of the far right saw in Cuba "a Red
under every bed" and relentlessly fulminated against Castro. But
their opinions did not carry much weight. Those who truly represented the American establishment showed more balance and perspective—some even a pro-Castro bent.

During the second half of 1959, President Eisenhower declared that the United States was not accusing the Cuban government of being Communist; Senator William Fulbright, chairman
of the Senate Foreign Relations Committee, advocated a policy of
understanding and restraint toward Cuba; and General C. P. Cabell, deputy director of the CIA, affirmed that "Fidel Castro is
not a Communist," and added, "It is questionable whether the
Communists desire to recruit Castro into the Communist Party,
that they could do so if they wished, or that he would be susceptible to Communist discipline if he joined."[4]

The Cuban leader paid no attention to these benign, if not
conciliatory, statements. Instead, he excoriated Admiral Burke for
disclosing that unidentified submarines had been lurking in Cuban
waters. And he accused the United States of perpetrating a "Cuban Pearl Harbor" by allowing the former air force chief, Díaz
Lanz, to fly from Florida and "bomb" Havana with anti-Castro
leaflets.

Theatrics aside, Castro took another step in late November 1959 to hasten the radicalization of Cuba. He removed Felipe Pazos, president of the National Bank and one of the last liberals in the government, and appointed in his stead none other than Che Guevara. Ambassador Bonsal later wrote that "the U.S. government was now forced to recognize that normal or quiet diplomacy had proved worthless in dealing with the Cuban government."[5]

These setbacks notwithstanding, Washington persisted in its efforts to negotiate with Castro. Unable to make any headway through normal U.S. diplomatic channels, in January 1960 the Eisenhower administration asked the Argentine ambassador to Cuba, Julio Amoedo, to explore a possible rapprochement with Castro. The proposal involved U.S. economic aid to finance the agrarian reform; the sum of $300 million was mentioned. Amoedo, who had developed a close relationship with my father, kept us abreast of the negotiations. He was quite encouraged by Castro's initial reaction. Fidel stopped his slanderous campaign against the United States and intimated that he was prepared to settle his differences with Washington. This proved to be a stalling device, as Amoedo confided later.[6] Castro was only gaining time to consolidate the Communist infrastructure and cement his relationship with Moscow. He also turned down a parallel offer involving U.S. military assistance, which was made to his Finance Minister by Dr. Mario Lazo, a top Cuban attorney and legal adviser to the U.S. embassy in Cuba.[7]

The visit to Havana in February 1960 of Soviet Deputy Premier Anastas Mikoyan added a conspicuous international dimension to the Cuban situation. The powerful member of the Politburo headed a trade mission to Havana and committed the Soviet Union to buying five million tons of Cuban sugar over five years—about a third of what was normally shipped to the United States—at a price well below that in effect under the American quota system. The Russians further agreed to sell to Cuba approximately a third of its oil requirements and to grant a $100 million credit to buy industrial equipment.

Before going to Cuba, Mikoyan had informed Washington of his plan to set up a trade mission on the island. Disregarding the authoritative opinion of State Department Kremlinologists that the mission would be a cover for "clandestine and subversive operations throughout the hemisphere,"[8] Washington sounded no warnings and continued to pursue indirect contacts with Castro.

Ambassador Bonsal raised the need to "persuade the Russians—perhaps on a reciprocal sphere-of-influence basis—to avoid actions that would encourage the Cubans in their aggressive designs on legitimate American interests." Bonsal was told, however, that "representations even of an informal nature were not feasible."[9] Relations between Moscow and Washington continued to be conducted in "the spirit of Camp David" (where President Eisenhower and Khrushchev held a cordial meeting in September 1959). In that context, bringing up the issue of Cuba seemed an unnecessary irritant.

Washington's reticence encouraged the Soviet Union to bolster its trade delegation in Cuba with more than one hundred Russian and former Spanish Civil War experts in disinformation, agitation, and espionage under the leadership of KGB Colonel Ulianov.[10] This was but the start of massive Soviet infusion of economic, technical, and military aid, which over the years has turned the island of Cuba into an awesome Communist base.

The lavish hospitality extended by Castro to Mikoyan and the portentous implications of the Soviet connection reawakened local opposition to the Cuban regime. A well-known journalist, José Luis Massó, cornered Mikoyan on television with a blistering question on the Soviet invasion of Hungary. University students rallied in front of the statue of Martí, destroyed the wreath that had been placed by Mikoyan, and confronted the police. And the independent media, outraged by the glaring Soviet tilt of the Cuban government, intensified their anti-Communist campaign.

To divert attention, Castro accused the United States of masterminding the explosion of the French cargo vessel *La Coubre,* which arrived in Havana on March 4 laden with arms and munitions for the Cuban government. More than seventy longshoremen were killed and two hundred injured. The preposterous accusation, vigorously rejected by Washington, served to inflame the masses and eclipse the negative effects of the Mikoyan embrace. Castro called the *Coubre* accident a new *Maine,* started to create a siege mentality, and hurled at Washington the gauntlet of challenge and bravado: "You will reduce us neither by war nor famine." Castro's melodramatic performance galvanized the crowds, but did not smother dissent. So within the next three months the government took over by force all of the remaining privately held newspapers, as well as all the radio and television stations.

The gifted writer Luis E. Aguilar dramatically described the situation in the last independent article that was published in Cuba.

He wrote: "The hour of compulsory unanimity has arrived. . . .
It is worse than censorship. Censorship obliges us to silence our
truth, [whereas] unanimity forces us to repeat the truth of others,
even if we do not believe in it. That is, it dissolves our personality
in a general and monotonous choir. And there is nothing worse
than that for those who do not have the vocation of cattle."

To resist the communization process, which had reached the
militias, labor unions, and some of the educational centers, the
then embryonic underground movement started to coalesce. It
gathered strength, particularly among students, Catholic activists,
and professionals. Internal resistance, however, was not enough
to cope with increasing Soviet intrusion and support; U.S. assistance was required. By the second quarter of 1960, there were
signs of a new Washington policy designed to stimulate opposition
to Castro. Moderate leaders who had fought against Batista, like
Tony Varona, left the island to form a democratic revolutionary
organization in exile. As an independent legal and intellectual adviser, I kept in touch with Varona and other heads of anti-Castro
groups who remained in Cuba. To help forge the vital alliance, I
drafted a statement of principles denouncing Castro's betrayal of
the revolution,[11] invoking our inalienable right to oppose totalitarianism, and proclaiming the goals of a new crusade for an independent Cuba with freedom and social justice under law. The
document, carried by special courier, reached Varona in time for
inclusion in the manifesto that marked the beginning of organized
national resistance against Castro communism.

The storm was gathering; the ring was closing; my days in
Cuba were numbered. We huddled at home and agonized over our
future and the future of our country. A decision was finally made.
The family would split: some of us would leave Cuba before the
Iron Curtain fell; others would remain on the island. I would be
the first one to go, given my highly exposed position and Varona's
request that I serve as one of his special assistants in exile. My
parents and Cortinas would follow. Most of the Carbonell relatives, however, decided to stay, and the Arangos, who had Eddy
in prison, would not leave him behind.

Departure from Cuba loomed as a harrowing experience, particularly for the elders who had to start afresh. Our family had no
offshore properties or deposits, only a small emergency fund that
had been created for my grandparents, the Cortinas. In the past,
we had attempted to minimize political and economic risks by diversifying our wealth within Cuba, but we had not protected our-

selves against the unthinkable contingency of the communization of our land. Now it was too late. Those of us departing had to leave everything behind—everything except our memories.

Under such traumatic conditions, we promptly realigned our priorities. Material possessions no longer counted; objects with sentimental value gained importance: a family photograph, a personal letter, an autographed book. I tried to savor every minute I had left in Cuba and to freeze in my mind resplendent images of the country, the family, and friends. The pain of separation was too intense to carry without the consolation of remembrances. I prolonged my stay until I could no more. On June 17, 1960, a brilliant sun bathed Cuba and enhanced the verdure of its luxuriant vegetation. That day I quietly left the island I loved—not to emigrate, but to prepare for liberation.

CHAPTER 6

On to Exile

W hen I arrived at the airport in Miami, my exiled uncle Manolo Cortina and my aunt Cusa were there to greet me. Manolo was a tall, elegant lawyer with a brisk temper and an insightful mind. During his career as a senior foreign service officer, he had invited me to attend memorable sessions at the United Nations and had counseled me on international affairs. Cusa was an attractive brunette with an exotic air reflecting her finishing-school days in Austria and her extended trips to other countries in Europe. She developed in Cuba a passion for plants and became the roving naturalist of the family, always eager to explore the beauties of the countryside.

My arrival brightened their lonely days in Miami and conjured up memories of our immediate relatives, endowed with contrasting personalities, but bound together by intellectual affinities, ancestral allegiance, and emotional ties. During most of my youth, we lived close to each other on a sprawling family compound in Havana, and we shared our joys and afflictions, our successes and misfortunes. Uprooted by communism, we now had to cope with the anguish of dispersion without the solace of home. But Manolo, Cusa, and I were determined not to let Castro confiscate the only thing we had left: sanity. Brushing off the shadows of depression, we reminisced about humorous episodes of our lives.

One of them had occurred during a traditional Sunday family gathering at the Cortinas'. When I arrived, I found my cousin Eddy Arango in the living room bending his knees to show my father how to start a race. Reluctant at first to account for his sudden interest in track, my father finally disclosed that during a professional baseball game at the Havana stadium, he was angered by the slowness of catcher Salvador Hernández and called him a "turtle even I could beat." Whereupon friends on the spot took my father's bluff and challenged him to a two-hundred-meter race against Hernández. Unable to back down, my father accepted.

The story triggered a heated debate at the Cortinas'. My mother thought it was ridiculous for a man of my father's age and standing to engage in such a competition. My grandfather opined that it could seriously endanger his health, given his heavy smoking and overweight. My uncle Enrique Arango, a former athlete, counseled him to postpone the date and shorten the distance.

Unperturbed, my father reaffirmed his commitment and briefly trained for the race. It took place at the Vedado Tennis Club with all the trappings and fanfare of a major event: pictures, banners, music, and reporters eager to cover the race of the season, pitting a congressman against a catcher. The bets were even. My father started ahead and easily kept the lead during the first hundred meters. It seemed that Hernández was a turtle after all. But during the final lap my father couldn't keep up the pace and yielded to the catcher. He lost the race but won the hearts of friends and spectators, who carried him off the field and applauded his spirit.

Trivial memories, if only for a few moments, helped to assuage the brusque realities of exile. Having arrived in Miami with only a few dollars hidden in my jacket, I had to cram into the small motel bedroom where Manolo and Cusa were living. I shared their lodging and meals until I was able to afford modest accommodations at a pension, pending the arrival of my parents. These frugal arrangements were not uncommon within the Cuban community, then comprising about 100,000 refugees. Most of them, including members of the former propertied classes, had to rebuild their lives from scratch, able to count only on the generous but limited aid provided by the Refugee Center.

Gone were the days when Cuban exiles and revolutionaries at large could transfer funds from the island. Now the well was dry and the channels were closed. I was particularly saddened by the plight of some of the old, non–English-speaking magistrates and professionals, reduced to working as janitors, busboys, and porters. They did not project bitterness or resentment, however. They carried their burden with dignity, rarely losing their zest and patriotic fervor.

Despite the hardships of expatriation, morale was generally high among Cuban refugees. We viewed our stay abroad as temporary and therefore did not worry about settlement or integration. The early return to a free Cuba was an obsession and seemed a certainty. Resistance inside the island was flaring up, and most exiles were sure that American support would be forthcoming. With unflagging confidence in the United States as the shield of freedom, the Cuban refugees tightened their belts and anxiously awaited their D-Day.

Once in Miami, I promptly joined the Cuban Democratic Revolutionary Front, a coalition of middle-of-the-road political and civic leaders who had opposed Batista, and of non-Marxist members of the Castro regime who had defected. Forming the initial nucleus were Manuel Antonio de Varona, the fiery and honest politician who had served as president of the Senate and Prime Minister during the last Auténtico government; Justo Carrillo, a seasoned liberal who had ably presided over the Agricultural and Industrial Development Bank under both Prío and Castro; Aureliano Sánchez Arango, an articulate and pugnacious revolutionary who had been Minister of Education and of Foreign Relations in Prío's cabinets; Manuel Artime, a young, impassioned physician and former captain of the Rebel Army who had denounced Castro's betrayal in late 1959 and founded the Revolutionary Recovery Movement; and José Ignacio Rasco, a talented and amiable professor who headed the newly formed Christian Democratic Movement.

None of the front directors was a *caudillo* who could rival Castro's charisma and riveting histrionics. They were, however, true democrats with sound principles and growing appeal. Mindful of the Cubans' woeful experience with messianism and deception, these leaders pitted integrity against the hollow rhetoric of demagoguery, institutions against the cult of personality, and freedom against regimented oppression.

The front had been constituted in May 1960, following a secret meeting held in New York between most of the above-mentioned Cuban hierarchs and Gerry Droller of the Central Intelligence Agency. Droller was a balding German-born agent who had worked for the OSS during the war and had subsequently served as a Swiss-desk officer for the CIA. Using the code name Frank Bender or Mr. B, he was now involved in the implementation of the "Program of Covert Action Against the Castro Regime" approved in March 1960 by President Eisenhower. The program consisted of political action, propaganda, and paramilitary operations, and

Bender was asked to steer the political thrust aimed at forming a "responsible and unified" Cuban organization in exile that would replace the Castro regime.

After lengthy and tense deliberations, those present at the New York meeting reached a "gentlemen's agreement" setting forth the bases for U.S. cooperation. Dr. Pedro Martínez Fraga, a former Cuban ambassador to Washington and to the Court of St. James's, acted as secretary and summarized the discussions in a confidential aide-memoire, a copy of which I have on file. The three salient points highlighted in the historic document were:

1. The U.S. government had empowered the CIA, represented by Mr. B, to provide assistance to anti-Castro revolutionaries in their struggle for freedom. Maximum discretion was urged. If asked, Washington would officially deny the entente.

2. The Cuban revolutionaries, through a central committee, would prepare, direct, and wage the war against Castro. All major anti-Communist groups would be invited to join the front, except those connected with Batista.

3. The CIA would make available and manage the funds required to organize and prosecute the struggle. The expense budget would be monitored and approved by the CIA, operating as Bender Associates (Group B).

This entente gave rise to contentious issues within and outside the front. A clandestine relationship with Washington was viewed by some as unnecessarily cumbersome and degrading, particularly since the Soviet Union, following Mikoyan's visit to Havana, was steadily moving in on Cuba and bolstering the Castro regime with trade, financing, KGB officers, arms, and technicians.

A further irritant was the fact that Mr. B was a low-level officer who had no knowledge of Latin America and could not speak a word of Spanish. To remedy this embarrassment, an engaging operative fluent in Spanish was charged with the task of maintaining day-to-day contacts with the Cuban exile leaders in Miami. This agent, who posed as "Eduardo," was Howard Hunt, who years later gained notoriety during the Watergate break-in. Assisted by the colorful Cuban-American Bernard L. Barker ("Macho"), also of Watergate fame, Eduardo spent much of his time dealing with Cuban intrigues, occasionally stirred by Eduardo himself.

It soon became evident that the front could not efficiently operate through a collegium of equally empowered members, so Varona was elevated to the position of coordinator. This led to the resignation of Sánchez Arango, who accused the front's executive committee of subservience to the CIA. To fill the vacancy and broaden representation, the front directors invited other personalities to join their ranks. They were able to advance the process of unification, but not to the extent required. Tactical disagreements and petty rivalries of factions jockeying for power irked a number of Cuban notables and kept them aloof. Moreover, Washington was not particularly keen about creating a single, mighty exile organization which could conceivably hold the United States hostage. War memories of the unyielding de Gaulle were still fresh and probably prompted the CIA to support and abet a number of splinter groups. The CIA clearly favored the front, but did not want to put all its eggs in that basket.

Another bone of contention was the system of unilateral subsidies or grants managed by the CIA. Some of the front leaders objected to the dependency inherent in the system and proposed that the United States formalize the Cuban-American alliance and make a war loan to be repaid by the government of a free Cuba. Given the secrecy of the operation and Washington's insistence on exercising control, the petition was turned down. The front representatives soon felt the "power of the purse" encroaching on their prerogatives and intruding upon the conduct of internal affairs. Frictions and clashes inevitably ensued, but the entente survived. Most of the front leaders believed that U.S. support was essential to topple a totalitarian regime increasingly backed by the Soviet bloc. So they gnashed their pride, mended their differences and forged ahead.

My first mission at the front was to work with its planning committee, which had been entrusted with the responsibility of drafting interim legislation for the post-Castro provisional government. The committee was like a mini-congress composed of a select but heterogeneous group of revolutionaries and politicians, former judges and functionaries, entrepreneurs and labor leaders, professors and young graduates. We were fortunate to have Dr. Pedro Martínez Fraga as our chairman. An experienced parliamentarian and diplomat, a man of broad culture, and a keen-edged wit, Don Pedro spiced the debates, compressed our longwinded discourses, and slashed the bombast. When he felt that we were losing time enmeshed in byzantine discussions, he would ceremoniously remove his glasses and admonish us with an ironic smile: "Stop splitting hairs and move on, lest our impatient friends on the banks of the Potomac present us with their own drafts . . . in English!"

The discussions centered on the Cuban Constitution of 1940, which had been the leitmotiv of the struggle against Batista. Castro reneged on the promise to restore the Constitution and carry out social and economic reforms within its purview. We could not do likewise, most of us argued. Regardless of intentions, we had no right to modify our fundamental system of law without the express consent of the people. To deal with de facto situations created by the Castro regime, the successor Cuban government would have to adopt extraconstitutional measures, we realized, but only as transitory provisions pending final determination by a duly elected congress or constitutional assembly. The committee upheld this principle and agreed on the exceptional legislation required to ensure a smooth and orderly transition from totalitarianism to representative democracy.

It was enlightening to study again the 1940 Constitution, which embodied many of Cuba's long-standing aspirations. During the constitutional convention, all of the then existing political parties embracing the entire spectrum of ideologies, including the Communists, were duly represented. My grandfather Cortina, who in the early 1930s had drawn up many of the essential bases for a constitutional reform, was elected president of the coordinating committee which produced the final draft. The debates were lively, particularly those with the Communist leaders Blas Roca, Salvador García Agüero, and Juan Marinello, who excelled as sharp polemicists and ardent orators. They tried to introduce seemingly innocuous clauses, wrapped in florid language, which could have undermined our free enterprise system. Cortina, the brilliant parliamentarian Orestes Ferrara, and other delegates uncovered their machinations by quoting from their well-concealed doctrinal source: the *Communist Manifesto* of Marx and Engels.

The debates at the constitutional convention, however, were not always tranquil exchanges of wit and wisdom. A stormy incident during the initial session triggered pandemonium. To avert the dissolution of the assembly, inflamed by unruly crowds, Cortina delivered an impromptu speech urging delegates and spectators to rein in their passions and place the republic above selfish interests and divisive ambitions. Then, extending his right arm and index finger, he shouted with the full resonance of his sten-

torian voice: "The political parties—OUT! The fatherland—IN!"
Emotions gradually subsided, order was restored, and the session
continued. After three months of spirited but constructive deliberations, the delegates, under the adroit chairmanship of Dr. Carlos Márquez Sterling, carried out their mandate, adopting a Magna
Charta which substantially addressed the needs and yearnings of
the Cuban people.

The Constitution was hailed as one of the most progressive
on the continent—in some respects ahead of its time. According
to the United Nations International Commission of Jurists, "it is
characterized by the rare balance it established between republican, liberal, and democratic postulates, on one hand, and the demands of social justice and economic advancement on the other."[1]

The charter recognized all individual freedoms and created a
special Tribunal of Constitutional Guarantees to shield the citizen
from the abuses of power. Labor rights included ample social security protection, a forty-four-hour week with salaries equivalent
to forty-eight hours, and a one-month vacation with pay. No worker
could be dismissed except for just cause. Labor tribunals with
independent judges were to be created to settle disputes. *Latifundios* were proscribed, and Congress was empowered to set maximum limits to landholdings as part of a comprehensive agrarian
reform without dislocations or confiscations. Private property was
guaranteed, but in the context of its social function. Foreign
investors were duly protected, but nationals enjoyed preferential
rights to employment and land tenure. To curb the power of Cuban presidents, the Constitution established a regulated parlia-
mentary system with some of the stabilizing features subsequently
adopted by de Gaulle in France.

Twenty years later, the 1940 Constitution remained Cuba's
symbol of legitimacy and most viable framework for national
progress with freedom. We didn't have to resort to the failed and
oppressive methods of Marxism-Leninism, or to any other form
of totalitarianism, to promote social justice in Cuba. The Constitution could have cured many of our historical ills and shortcomings, if only we had abided by it and not breached or circumvented
it. That is the message we decided to relay to the Cuban people,
beset by Castro's insidious allegations that the Democratic Revolutionary Front was intent on turning back the clock of history
to reinstate Batista, the "war criminals," and the "rapacious oli-
garchy."

Since there was no independent press left in Cuba, the front used a fifty-kilowatt radio station built by the CIA on Swan Island, 110 miles off the coast of Honduras. Under the direction of Dr. Andrés Vargas Gómez, a prestigious diplomat and grandson of one of Cuba's heroes of the war of independence, Máximo Gómez, we responded to Castro's diatribes, beamed uncensored news to Cuba, and conveyed to the people a message of hope. Thousands of families across the island started to tune in to the evening transmissions of Radio Swan. Castro went berserk and harassed the listeners as counterrevolutionaries. This was hardly a surprise, for tyrants who boast of armies and strength shudder when haunted by the voice of dissent.

As part of my responsibilities at the front, I provided guidance and support to Cuban exile delegations that had been formed in most of the Latin American capitals. These delegations played an important role in counteracting Fidel's slanderous campaigns and alerting the Latin American people to the peril posed by Castro communism. Since early 1959, the Cuban regime had taken part in four armed forays against other Caribbean countries and had frequently used its embassies to foment agitation and disseminate Marxist propaganda throughout the hemisphere. Thanks, in part, to the crusading activities of the Cuban exile delegations, which led to the discovery of subversive centers and spy networks, many of the Latin American countries started to respond to the threat and severed relations with Havana.

The Cuban regime did not rely solely on its mobile cadres of agitprop specialists to exploit prevailing unrest on the continent. Beginning in late 1959, the Castro-controlled *Prensa Latina* extended its radio arm to beam half-hour programs to sixteen Central and South American countries. These programs consisted of "revolutionary chats"—primarily tapes of Castro's speeches accusing the United States of imperialistic aggressions. These charges, subsequently echoed by influential American journalists and professors such as C. Wright Mills, author of *Listen, Yankee,* attributed Castro's hostility to the United States to Washington's narrow-mindedness in defending unfettered capitalism and fueling anti-Communist mania.

Castro stirred up these accusations by cleverly managing the chain of actions and reactions that eventually prompted the United States to break with Cuba. As noted by Prof. Theodore Draper, "By waiting for the opportune occasion, every aggressive action can be made to appear in a defensive light. . . ." And he added: "Fidel Castro and his inner circle have never been innocent victims of circumstances; they have always been the engine of this revolution in perpetual motion; they have leaped at one pretext or another to do what they wanted to do; they have incessantly increased their power by taking the initiative against their enemies and relentlessly pressing the advantage."[2]

Castro's strategy was simple, but very effective. He constantly provoked, vilified, and abused the United States, and when Washington finally decided to react, he played the role of David seemingly victimized by the implacable Goliath of the North. The clash was not accidental; it was foreseen and indeed fostered by Fidel himself. In a well-publicized letter he wrote to his secretary and confidante Celia Sánchez, on June 5, 1958, while he was still fighting against Batista in the Sierra Maestra, Castro predicted: "When this war is over I shall begin a longer and greater war: the war I'll wage against them [the Americans]. I realize that this is my true destiny."[3]

Contrary to the opinions emitted by numerous pundits in the early 1960s, the respected journalist Arthur Krock concluded that Washington was not guilty of alienating Castro and pushing him into the Soviet camp. Krock wrote:

From the time Castro assumed power until May 17, 1960, the United States made nine formal and sixteen informal offers to negotiate all differences with Cuba. . . . On February 22, 1960, Castro did propose—but for the first time—to negotiate with the United States on compensation to American citizens for their property in Cuba that he expropriated soon after his accession to power. However, his conditions were that during the negotiation the United States should bind both the Executive and Congress to refrain from any action which Cuba would consider to affect its interests, while he remained free to negotiate or procrastinate as he chose—conditions obviously unacceptable and, so far as Congress was concerned, constitutionally impossible.[4]

Although Castro did not receive the requested assurances from Washington, he did enjoy sufficient time to cement relations with the Sino-Soviet bloc before the United States decided to take economic reprisals. From December 1959 to June 1960, Cuba signed trade and payment agreements with Red China (December 31, 1959), the USSR (February 13, 1959), East Germany (February 20, 1960), Poland (March 31, 1960), and Czechoslovakia (June 10,

1960). By mid-1960 Castro was ready to provoke a clash with the United States. He demanded that three U.S.- and British-owned oil refineries in Cuba process two bargeloads of Soviet crude oil. The Castro regime had not paid these companies for a long time and had piled up a large debt of $16 million for oil imports and $60 million for previous refining. The three companies refused to take Russian oil, so the Castro regime intervened their refineries. A few weeks later, the Eisenhower administration suspended the 700,000 tons that remained of Cuba's total 1960 sugar quota of about three million tons. Castro retaliated with a decree expropriating American properties and enterprises in Cuba whose value exceeded $850 million.

Castro's wave of expropriations was not really driven by nationalistic fervor or sovereign pride. On October 13, 1960, with one sweep, Law No. 890 engulfed over 380 all-Cuban enterprises, including most of the banks, all remaining sugar mills, eighteen distilleries, five breweries, sixteen rice mills, and sixty-one textile factories. Clearly, the takeover of U.S. properties was only part of a much broader and radical transformation. Washington's suspension of 700,000 tons of Cuba's sugar quota was not the cause, but it served as a useful pretext.

Castro mounted a virulent international campaign accusing the United States of economic aggression. At the same time, he celebrated the liberation of Cuba from a sugar quota system which Che Guevara had called a "symbol of colonialism" and which Fidel himself had dubbed an "economic Platt Amendment designed . . . to kill us through hunger." Never mind the contradiction between aggression and liberation; verbal consistency is not one of Fidel's most prominent virtues.

The incident aroused memories of past controversies in Cuba over sugar which often left a bitter aftertaste. On one extreme were those who argued that "without sugar there was no country," and on the other were those who opined that sugar was the source of all our evils. Despite the glaring exaggeration of these statements, they were not totally flawed, for sugar in the case of Cuba has been both a blessing and a curse. Firmly rooted in history, it has conditioned the advancement of the Cuban people, colored their psychology, and marked their lives.

Brought by merchants and conquistadores from the East, passing through India, Persia, Arabia, Sicily, and Spain, the tall grass with the thick, tough stem we call sugar cane blanketed Cuba, an ideal habitat. There cane seldom needs water or artificial fertilizer and is not exposed to frost, which is a constant threat in

Louisiana and Florida. Given such favorable agricultural conditions and Cuba's unsuitability for heavy industry because of the lack of energy resources, it was not surprising to see the proliferation of sugar mills mushrooming like volcanic islands amid green oceans of cane.

Lured by Cuba's business prospects at the start of the century, U.S. investors contributed capital and technology to rebuild the sugar industry, devastated by the wars of independence, and turned the island into the largest and most efficient sugar producer in the world. The affluent and secure U.S. market spawned periods of prosperity, particularly during the "dance of the millions"[5] in 1920, as well as after World War II and during the Korean War. The close relationship with the United States hastened the socioeconomic development of Cuba, ahead of most of the Latin American republics, and maintained the strength of the Cuban peso at parity with the dollar.

But along with the manifold benefits of sugar came nefarious consequences. The need for cheap, unskilled labor to cut and haul the cane prolonged slavery in Cuba and retarded the island's independence. Foreign capital—mostly American—spurred the sugar mills' modernization during the first decades of the century, and gained control of the industry. Absentee owners amassed large tracts of land and created *latifundios,* and the eight-month dead season that followed the harvest increased unemployment. Focusing on sugar to the detriment of other industries slowed down diversification, and concentration on a single export market—the United States—led to overdependency on that country. Finally, the fluctuations of world sugar prices and quotas and their ripple effect on the Cuban economy accentuated political instability and gave rise to a speculative sugar mentality.

In contrast to sugar, tobacco, which is not capital-intensive, remained a truly national industry and was not subjected to the dictates of any single market. Optimum climatic and soil conditions, along with exacting techniques handed down from father to son, made Cuban cigars world-acclaimed ambassadors of pleasure and fame. Positioned as a sort of paradigm of indigenous virtues, tobacco was pitted against sugar's alien, corruptive sway. Cuba's renowned sociologist Dr. Fernando Ortiz, in his classic book *The Cuban Counterpoint of Tobacco and Sugar,* analyzed the profound influence exerted by both products. Weaving their contrasting characteristics with delightful artistry, Ortiz sided with tobacco in its symbolic feud with sugar.

Ortiz viewed tobacco as:

proud, distinguished, aristocratic, dignified. It always goes alone
and seeks individuality. Sugar, its counterpoint, is common, in-
distinct, undistinguished. A uniformed mass, from cane to cake,
it always needs a companion, a chaperon. Tobacco is the de-
light of primates and princes; sugar is the solace of commoners.
Tobacco is cultivated not plant by plant, but leaf by leaf. It
requires expert and individual handling. Sugar, conversely, demands many workers, cheap, untrained and easily disposable.
Tobacco, proud of its heritage, remains brown after the leaf is
cured; sugar, ashamed of its dark past, is processed and whi-
tened. Tobacco relies on individual skills, which are essentially
Cuban; sugar depends on automation, which is primarily alien.[6]

Although critical of sugar, Ortiz was not suggesting the scrap-
ping or replacement of an industry that represented 30 percent of
Cuba's GNP and accounted for over 80 percent of its exports. He
and other personages, like the noted historian Ramiro Guerra,
pressed, however, for much-needed structural changes involving
the Cubanization of the industry and complementary diversification. By 1957–1958 the required reforms had not yet been completed, but the trends were in the right direction. Cubans had gained
substantial control over the sugar industry—they owned 121 mills
(of a total of 161) generating 62 percent of national production,
and most of the twenty-two refineries. Moreover, the country already had 38,000 industrial centers, and non-sugar agricultural
production income was approaching the $385 million sugar agri-
cultural level.

The country also benefited from other positive developments
within the sugar industry. Mill owners had reduced their vast
landholdings by 20 percent over the period of 1949–1958, and sugar
cane farmers had grown from 30,000 in 1939 to almost 65,000 in
1958. Protected by the Sugar Coordination Law of 1937 and subsequent legislation, those farmers who did not own the land outright enjoyed the security of tenure for life, subject only to a 5
percent rent. This right, which could be inherited, sold, or mort-
gaged, was almost equivalent to full ownership of land but without the concomitant obligations. Moreover, small sugar growers
had guaranteed "grinding quotas," and the industrial and agricultural workers—among the best-paid in Latin America—were entitled to receive close to 50 percent of gross income from sugar
cane. The balance was split between the farmers (26 percent) and
the sugar mills (24 percent).

Cuba's vulnerability to the fluctuations of the world sugar

market was tempered by her special agreements with the United States, which established annual import quotas for Cuban sugar at prices usually higher than those prevailing on the world market. To protect this privileged relationship, which in return accorded the United States major trade and tariff concessions, Cuba was able to obtain an undertaking from Washington that it would at all times make every appropriate effort to safeguard the island's sugar position in the American market. This undertaking was embodied in the notes exchanged in 1941 between the U.S. ambassador to Cuba, George S. Messersmith, and Cuba's Foreign Minister, José Manuel Cortina.

It was this singular arrangement, which had enabled Cuba during the period of 1948–1959 to supply almost 45 percent of the United States' total sugar requirements, that Washington suspended in July 1960. Castro had provoked this action not to exact more favorable terms, not to achieve economic independence, but to raise the specter of "Yankee imperialism" and create an emergency climate for totalitarian rule at home and alignment with Moscow abroad.

As soon as Washington suspended the Cuban sugar quota, Moscow declared that it was prepared to take the 700,000 tons of sugar that the United States had spurned. Castro was not too concerned about the economic implications of the switch. Under the five-year commercial treaty signed with Mikoyan in February 1960, he had accepted terms that were disastrous for Cuba. Russia's price for Cuban sugar was set at 2.78 cents a pound; the world market price then was 2.90 cents a pound, and the U.S. quota price was 5.11 cents. And Moscow was to pay only part of the price in dollars; the balance would come in "industrial equipment," which turned out to be chiefly Soviet arms and military matériel. The terms of sale for the 700,000 tons were not as onerous, but the price agreed to, 3.25 cents a pound, was still significantly below the U.S. level.

At the Democratic Revolutionary Front's headquarters in Miami, we were alarmed by these developments. It seemed to us that the emerging Soviet-Cuban compact was not prompted simply by Castro's realignment of trading partners. There were other deeper and more sinister motives, we felt. The background of the USSR's first ambassador to Cuba under Castro, Sergei M. Kudryavtsev, increased our suspicions. As embassy first secretary in Ottawa in 1946, Kudryavtsev had to leave with haste following the disclosures of Igor Gouzenko which led to the uncovering of

Canada's atom spy ring. Gouzenko had been military intelligence code clerk and reportedly identified Kudryavtsev as chief of the GRU *rezidentura*. After serving in Vienna as deputy high commissioner and in Paris as minister-counselor, he was assigned to Cuba in mid-1960 as a senior representative of the international section of the Soviet Communist Party.[7]

Apart from Kudryavtsev's appointment, what opened the eyes of many to Moscow's growing political and strategic interest in Cuba was Nikita Khrushchev's speech before the All-Russian Teachers' Congress in Moscow, July 9, 1960. In that speech, Khrushchev accused the United States of mounting an economic blockade against Cuba, pledged to support the besieged "brothers" of the socialist countries, and pronounced this startling challenge:

> Figuratively speaking, in case of need, Soviet artillerymen can support the Cuban people with their rocket fire if the aggressive forces in the Pentagon dare to launch an intervention against Cuba. And let them not forget in the Pentagon that, as the latest tests have shown, we have rockets capable of landing directly in a precalculated square at a distance of 13,000 kilometers. This, if you will, is a warning to those who would like to settle international issues by force and not by reason.[8]

President Eisenhower, who had been rather detached and reticent on Cuba, was shaken by this blatant threat. In a statement issued under his name, he declared that Khrushchev's bluster "underscores the close ties that have developed between the Soviet and Cuban Governments. It also shows the clear intention to establish Cuba in a role serving Soviet purposes in this hemisphere. . . ." Invoking the Monroe Doctrine, the President responded to Khrushchev's admonition:

> I affirm in the most emphatic terms that the United States will not be deterred from its responsibilities by the threat Mr. Khrushchev is making. Nor will the United States, in conformity with its treaty obligations, permit the establishment of a regime dominated by international communism in the Western Hemisphere.[9]

Unimpressed by Eisenhower's caveat, Khrushchev retorted with scorn:

We consider that the Monroe Doctrine has outlived its time, has outlived itself, has died, so to say, a natural death. Now the remains of this doctrine should best be buried as every dead body is so that it should not poison the air by its decay. That would be the correct thing to do and this is what will happen apparently.[10]

The Eisenhower-Khrushchev exchange had ominous implications. It rekindled the Cold War and drew a battle line in the very heart of the Western Hemisphere. Cuba was to play a pivotal role in the impending crisis. Why? To a certain extent, the answer lies with the impulsive Cubans and their egocentric ruler—prone to audacious feats and to dramatic swings in the pendulum of emotions. Yes, ethnic heritage played a part, but so did an external factor as powerful as the blood: the compelling geography.

Chapter 7

The Compelling Geography

Germany's Iron Chancellor, Bismarck, called geography "the only stable factor in history." But for Cuba and the Cubans, geography is more—it is destiny. As a student in Havana I was intrigued by the latter statement, rotund and categorical like most Spanish postulates. My initial reaction was to reject its implicit fatalism. The idea of destiny seemed to ignore or downplay human volition and disregard fortuitous circumstances. Yet as I delved into history, I realized that in the case of Cuba the importance of geography could not be overemphasized. Few other countries have been so dependent on or influenced by location as has Cuba.

Cuba is more than an island. It is a subarchipelago (part of the greater Antilles) comprising no fewer than sixteen hundred islands, islets, and cays with a combined area of approximately 44,000 square miles. Cuba proper—by far the largest in the chain—spans about 41,000 square miles, or the area of the state of Virginia. Cuba's preeminence in history bears no relationship to area or to population. There are many other larger and more populous countries around the globe whose imprints pale compared to Cuba's. What, then, has enhanced the influence of this relatively small island, which over the centuries has repeatedly surged as a magnetic pole attracting international conflicts and power plays? Its privileged geographical position has certainly played a part, as in the case of ancient Athens, Rome, and Carthage.

The Soviet Union, which views geopolitics in Clausewitzean terms as the "continuation of war through other means," has had its eyes on Cuba since the foundation of the Cuban Communist Party in the mid-1920s. Moscow appeared to be keenly aware of the island's unique geostrategic value: it sits astride the world's largest "mediterranean" sea (the so-called American Mediterranean), dominates the main entrances to the Gulf of Mexico through the "choke points" formed by the Straits of Florida on the north and the Yucatán Channel on the west, and commands the Caribbean Sea and the Atlantic approaches to the Panama Canal. Given the extraordinary leverage afforded by this prime piece of geography, it is no wonder that the Soviets have borne inordinate costs and taken unprecedented risks to control, bolster, and retain the Gibraltar of the Americas, the island the Spaniards centuries ago aptly called "Bulwark of the Indies and Key to the New World."

After Columbus's landing, the conquistadores capitalized on Cuba's strategic potential. Disappointed to learn that the island had limited supplies of silver and gold, they used her as a springboard for the exploration and conquest of the continent.

As the renowned Cuban geographer and historian Leví Marrero has recounted, most of the expeditions to Mexico, Central America, the Caribbean, and Florida originated in Cuba, and many of the conquistadores rose to fame with the backing of forces assembled on the island. Hernán Cortés, the conqueror of Mexico, was mayor of Santiago de Cuba, and there he wed and from there he sailed off for Mexico in defiance of Governor Velázquez's order to stop. Hernando de Soto, a veteran of the conquests of Peru and Central America who succeeded Velázquez as Governor of Cuba, set out at the head of an expedition to conquer Florida, following in the footsteps of Ponce de León, Pánfilo de Narváez, and Alvaro Núñez Cabeza de Vaca. In his absence, his wife, Isabel de Bobadilla, became the first and only woman to govern an imperial colony of Spain. For three years she paced the ramparts of La Fuerza fortress awaiting the return of her beloved, until she finally learned that he had died and was buried in the Mississippi. Twenty-five years later, in 1564, the Governor of Havana, Menéndez de Avilés, founded the first permanent settlements in the sunbelt of North America. Spain thus gained control of the great waterway from the center of the continent to the Gulf of Mexico, and Cuba became the key to "the two Floridas."

The island also served as the meeting place for the imperial fleets as they returned to Spain laden with precious metals and other products of the colonies. The navigation system called for two fleets, each consisting of fifty or more ships sailing under armed convoy. One fleet sailed in the spring for Veracruz (Mexico) and supplied most of Central America and the West Indies. The other one sailed in August for Panama and convoyed ships for Cartagena and other ports on the northern coast of South America. After loading their returns of silver and colonial products, both fleets would rendezvous at Havana and sail for Spain in the spring. The fleets' itinerary was thus centered on three critical points: Mexico, Panama, and Cuba. They formed a strategic triangle of such geopolitical salience that the constellation of monarchs who reigned in Europe following the discovery of America—Charles V, Philip II, Elizabeth I, and Francis I—shifted their lust for wealth and power to this part of the world.

During Spain's wars with England, France, and Holland in the sixteenth and seventeenth centuries, the Caribbean Sea attained pivotal significance in the quest for supremacy. At the outset, England lacked skilled seamen tempered in battle. The Caribbean was to provide the training, the booty, and zeal to those who eventually became legendary admirals of the Royal Navy— Francis Drake and John Hawkins, among others. If Waterloo, centuries later, was won on the playing fields of Eton, the Spanish Armada was vanquished by England in 1588 with the experience gained on the agitated waters of the Caribbean.[1]

It was the lure of riches and of a profitable slave trade that brought the pirates and the buccaneers. The Frenchman Jacques de Sores, the Dutch Pitt Hein, the English Henry Morgan, and many others ravaged Cuba's coastal cities. In an attempt to stop the smuggling, Spain unwittingly provoked an incident in 1739 that led to war. Having intercepted an unchartered English ship near Cuba, a Spanish officer boarded the vessel with his men, and in the battle that ensued slashed the ear of the British captain Robert Jenkins. The latter appeared before a committee of the House of Commons investigating alleged Spanish atrocities and displayed the dissected ear inside a bottle. Inflamed public opinion prompted Prime Minister Walpole to unleash a war against Spain that was fittingly called the "war over Jenkins's ear."

Hostilities spread to Cuba in 1741 as the English landed five thousand soldiers in the far-eastern province of Oriente. Five months later they were forced to withdraw to Jamaica in the face of local resistance and tropical diseases. In 1747 the English made another attempt to land, this time near Havana, but they were blocked by the Spanish navy. Finally in 1762 England fulfilled her dream. Backed by the most formidable armada that had been assembled in the Americas, the English under the command of Lord Albemarle seized Havana and remained there until the signing of the Treaty of Paris the following year. Pursuant to that treaty, England returned Havana to Spain, Spain yielded Florida to England, and France ceded Louisiana to Spain.

During the occupation of Havana, the British were often rebuffed and isolated by influential segments of the population who viewed them as invaders. Still, the Cubans benefited from free trade with England and its colonies, and the Americans, who started to visit the island in large numbers, became aware of its economic potential and geostrategic value.

The American Revolution sparked considerable interest in Cuba. Despite Spain's concern that the fire of independence might spread to her own American possessions, she yielded to the pleasure of seeing her longtime enemy England battered by growing insurrection. The Cubans were thus permitted—indeed encouraged—to come to the aid of the thirteen rebelling colonies, and in the process enlightened sectors of the population developed a yen for self-determination.

Cuba's role in the revolution was significant on several counts. The wealthy Havana businessman Juan de Miralles was appointed special representative to the Philadelphia Congress and became a personal friend and supporter of George Washington. Spanish troops from Louisiana, led by Governor Bernardo de Gálvez and backed by a strong Cuban expeditionary force, attacked and occupied two major ports held by the English on the Gulf of Mexico: Mobile and Pensacola. More than two thousand "redcoats," along with their chief, General Campbell, were taken as prisoners to Havana, then a most powerful naval base providing refuge and supplies to the American patriots and their French allies.

When the Continental Army and deGrasse's Atlantic fleet faced the most acute financial crisis of the war, just before the decisive battle of Yorktown, wealthy Havana ladies sold their jewelry to raise most of the funds desperately needed by deGrasse (1,200,000 *livres tournois*) to pay the salaries of five thousand soldiers for a period of four months. According to the historian Stephen Bonsal, this contribution, along with the £50,000 procured at the time by Rochambeau, "may with truth be regarded as the bottom dollars upon which the edifice of American independence was erected."[2]

Since the birth of the United States as a free nation, Cuba has occupied a place of singular importance in American foreign affairs. Few other countries have so deeply and continuously engaged the attention of the State Department as has Cuba. Lying within the southern defensive perimeter of the United States, this island has often ignited or influenced major controversies: the extracontinental threats that prompted the Monroe Doctrine; the prolonged dispute between the North and the South over the proposed annexation of Cuba; the Spanish-American War; U.S. interventionism under the umbrella of "Manifest Destiny"; the Battle of the Atlantic; the Bay of Pigs and the Missile Crisis; Communist subversion in the Americas, Africa, and the Middle East; and the efforts to woo the nonaligned nations of the Third World.

Thomas Jefferson was perhaps the first U.S. statesman to covet Cuba "as the most interesting addition which could ever be made to our system of States." But it was Secretary of State John Quincy Adams who in 1823 expounded on the rationale. He told the American minister to Spain:

> These islands [Cuba and Puerto Rico] . . . are natural appendages to the North American continent; and one of them, Cuba, almost in sight of our shores, from a multitude of considerations has become an object of transcendent importance to the commercial and political interests of our Union. . . . there are laws of political as well as physical gravitation; and if an apple severed by the tempest from its native tree cannot choose but fall to the ground, Cuba, forcibly disjoined from its own unnatural connection with Spain, and incapable of self-support, can gravitate only towards the North American Union, which by the same law of nature cannot cast her off from its bosom. . . .[3]

Fearful that Spain might cede the island to Great Britain, then a potential ally of Spain in a new war with France, Adams added:

> The transfer of Cuba to Great Britain would be an event unpropitious to the interests of this Union. . . . The question both of our right and our power to prevent it, if necessary, by force, already obtrudes itself upon our councils, and the administration is called upon, in the performance of its duties to the nation, at least to use all the means within its competence to guard against and forefend it.[4]

The Russians at the time were also trying to extend their colonial establishments to the New World. They felt so prepotent that they sent a note to Washington containing remarks on "expiring republicanism" which, according to the historian Samuel

Eliot Morrison, were as offensive to the American government then as was Khrushchev's bravado about "burying" us over a century later.

In order to address these challenges, Adams drafted President Monroe's vigorous message to Congress of December 2, 1823, known as the Monroe Doctrine. It declared the American continent would henceforth not be considered open to further colonization by any European powers, and warned that the United States would deem any such attempt dangerous to its safety. With respect to existing colonies or dependencies, (such as Cuba,) there would be no interference. Washington preferred Cuba to remain in the hands of a weakened Spain rather than fall into the grip of a stronger England, France, or Russia.

The United States also viewed any actions to incite or support the liberation of Cuba as inimical to U.S. interests. When the first Pan-American Conference was held in Panama in 1826 to protect the newly formed republics from European aggression and to promote the liberation of Cuba and Puerto Rico, President John Quincy Adams stated that the United States would not act in any way inconsistent with its neutral attitude toward Spain and her rebellious colonies. In the words of the leader of the conference, the liberator Simón Bolívar, the United States was "determined to maintain Spanish authority in the islands of Cuba and Puerto Rico" in the hope that they might be incorporated into the Union at a later stage.

Bolívar was right. The United States soon made several attempts to annex Cuba, influenced in part by the South's desire to extend slave territory. In 1848, President James K. Polk offered as much as $100 million to purchase the island, but Spain declined the offer and stated that "sooner than see the island transferred to any power, [Spain] would prefer seeing it sunk in the ocean."

In 1854 the administration of President Pierce believed the time was ripe for another bid to purchase Cuba for up to $130 million. The American ministers to Spain, Great Britain, and France met at Ostend, Belgium, to map the strategy for making the proposal. In their dispatch to Washington (the Ostend Manifesto), they stated:

> After we shall have offered Spain a price for Cuba far beyond its present value, and this shall have been refused, it will then be time to consider the question, does Cuba in the possession of Spain seriously endanger our internal peace and the exis-

tence of our cherished Union. Should this question be answered in the affirmative, then, by every law human and divine,
we shall be justified in wresting it from Spain, if we possess
the power.[5]

The manifesto was leaked to the press, and American public
opinion opposed the idea of seizing the island "by robbery or theft."
Spain's response was pointed and curt: ". . . to part with Cuba
would be to part with the national honor." The U.S. government
promptly rejected the manifesto and assured Spain that it had no
intention of taking the island by conquest.

In 1859 another attempt was made to acquire Cuba. A bill
was introduced in Congress to place funds at the disposal of President Buchanan so that he might have the means to negotiate
with Spain. The bill, however, met with strong opposition and
was finally tabled.

Meanwhile, in Cuba several efforts were made to spark a rebellion, including three expeditions launched from the United States
by the Venezuelan-born General Narciso López and his Creole
supporters. These efforts, however, did not materialize, and most
of the revolutionaries were executed. Spain's forces on the island
had been bolstered by loyalists who fled the liberated South
American colonies, whereas Cuban militants were weakened by
divisiveness. Some of the natives remained outright Spanish roy-
alists; others, including some of the opulent plantation owners,
favored annexation to the United States; still others strived for
political reforms that would lead to an autonomous colonial government. The latter, known as "reformists," did not wish to separate from Spain; they fostered evolutionary change within the
system.

Spain, however, dashed all hopes for reforms in 1867 when it
ignored the recommendations of the Cuban delegation (the Junta
de Información) and further increased taxes. Indignation in Cuba
gave way to rage. Distinguished members of the national elite,
including moderate landowners who had resisted violent measures, joined the "separatist" movement and prepared to overthrow the colonial regime.

The bloody revolt that ensued, known as the Ten Years War,
broke out on October 10, 1868. On that day, a well-to-do planter,
lawyer, and poet, Carlos Manuel de Céspedes, gathered some five
hundred rebels at his sugar mill near the far-eastern town of Yara.
In a moving ceremony, he proclaimed independence, unfurled the

national flag, and freed the slaves. For the first time the bell of the sugar mill did not call men to work; it summoned them to fight for freedom. My great-grandfather Néstor Leonelo Carbonell was one of the first to respond to the call to arms. Through him and others who survived the ordeal we learned of many an epic poem written with blazing machetes by the Cuban legionnaires.

Céspedes emerged as the leader of the uprising and was elected President of the Republic in Arms. He displayed exemplary courage. When the Spaniards captured his son Oscar and threatened to kill him if Céspedes did not surrender, he responded: "Oscar is not my only son; I am the father of all the Cubans who fight for freedom." Oscar was executed, and despite his grief Céspedes renewed his vow and pursued the struggle.

After the loss of the Central and South American colonies, Spain was determined to defend and retain, at all costs, her "most precious jewel of the crown." She thus deployed her best officers and soldiers to Cuba. Not strong enough to engage the Spaniards in conventional battle, the Cubans had to turn to, and master, guerrilla warfare in their quest for independence. Ironically, the Spaniards had developed this technique during Napoleon's invasion of Spain. Little did they know that it would be used against them by their last colony in the Americas. The stern Dominican-born strategist Máximo Gómez, and the indomitable Cuban mulatto Antonio Maceo, known as the "Bronze Titan," achieved continental fame in the art of outflanking superior Spanish forces and of wearing them down with bold ambushes and lightning strikes.

Military prowess and courage, however, were not enough to prevail. Insufficient resources, internecine feuds, lack of support from the western provinces, and sheer exhaustion forced the Cubans to accept Spain's promises of a general amnesty, political autonomy, and the emancipation of the slaves who had joined the revolt. Still, the Pact of Zanjón that was signed in 1878 did not really mark the end of the struggle; it only served as a fragile and ephemeral truce.

During the Ten Years War, the United States, though sympathetic to the rebels, was not in a bellicose mood. The administration of President Grant refused to recognize the belligerence of the Cubans and tried to use its good offices to end the civil strife, but the mediation efforts came to naught. In 1873, however, an international incident fired American public opinion and almost forced Washington to declare war on Spain. The side-wheeler *Virginius,* flying the American flag and with mainly American crew, was captured by a Spanish warship on the high seas between Jamaica and Cuba and taken into Santiago. Aboard were more than a hundred Cuban rebels led by General Oscar Varona and a large quantity of arms, medicine, and provisions. The passengers and cargo were on their way to join the patriots in the mountains of eastern Cuba.

On the instruction of the Spanish governor of Santiago, a summary court-martial was held and the passengers and crew of the captured ship were sentenced to death. The executions started: four the first day, and thirty-six, including the American Captain Fry, the next afternoon. Ninety-three others were to follow, and yet Washington only asked Spain for an investigation and ample reparation. The British vice-consul at Santiago, outraged by the massacre, which also included British subjects, used a more effective procedure to stay the hands of the executioners. He cabled Jamaica and ordered the British warship *Niobe* to sail to Santiago. On arrival, her commander, Sir Lambton Lorraine, warned the Spanish governor that if one more English or American was shot, he would shell the city.

The executions stopped, but Spain played for time in meeting Washington's demands of apology, indemnity, and punishment of the Spanish governor. At the height of the crisis, the U.S. Secretary of the Navy tried to deploy a flotilla of warships "for possible punitive action," but, according to the historian G.J.A. O'Toole, "the best the Navy could assemble was an assortment of rusty old hulks, most of which had not been to sea since the close of the Civil War eight years earlier."[6] Spain finally relented, but the *Virginius* incident was not forgotten. For years it reminded the Americans of the danger of military unpreparedness and the need to strengthen their navy. Cuba, yet again, had left its mark on U.S. foreign policy.

During the 1880s, a large segment of the Cuban intelligentsia favored autonomy, but Spain's continued oppression and corruption thwarted all peaceful attempts to promote self-determination. Convinced that there was no alternative but to fight for independence, the separatists unleashed their final war in 1895. The rousing force of that revolution, the heart and brains that galvanized the Cubans into action and inflamed them with a mystique, was José Martí, born in Havana in 1853. He strived to end Spanish domination in Cuba, ward off the annexation of the island by the United States, and pave the way for a national government under a democratic and socially just system of law.

The romance of Latin American independence started with Bolívar in Venezuela in 1810 and ended with Martí in Cuba in 1895. Martí was not only a liberator, but also a gifted writer, poet, orator, propagandist, and visionary. Having lived some fifteen years as an exile in the United States, Martí wrote myriad descriptions of the country and its personages. The Cuban Communists, eager to exploit Martí's prestige and influence, often point to his caustic remarks on the unbridled materialism and lust for territory and power that he observed in certain American quarters. They conveniently ignore, however, Martí's genuine admiration for the United States' unsurpassed qualities as an entrepreneurial and democratic nation, and ignore the sound advice he gave to Latin Americans on how to deal with the "Colossus of the North": "There is the America that is not ours, whose enmity is neither wise nor practical to instigate. But with a firm sense of decorum and independence, it is not impossible, and it is useful, to be its friend."

Martí's cult of individual freedom was tempered by his deeply felt compassion for the poor and the needy. He rejected, however, Marxist class struggle as the engine for progress, stating: "He who under the pretext of guiding the young teaches them . . . absolute doctrines and preaches to them the barbarous gospel of hate, instead of the sweet gospel of love, is a treacherous assassin, ingrate to God and enemy of man."

After he arrived in New York in 1880, Martí started to emerge as a magnetic leader. His genial personality, talent, and integrity won him the respect of older and more experienced patriots who initially were skeptical, if not outright critical, of Martí. "The Apostle," as he was later known, needed, however, a revolutionary organization to coordinate the efforts of the fragmented exiles, conciliate their differences, tap their resources, and direct the war. To achieve this goal, he sought and gained the support of the largest and most prosperous Cuban communities located in Tampa and Key West, and founded the Cuban Revolutionary Party.

When the final liberation war erupted on February 24, 1895, Martí insisted on going to Cuba to join the insurgents. Not a military man, he was recognized, however, as the supreme chief of the revolution. The revered generals Máximo Gómez and Antonio Maceo were entrusted with the conduct of the war. Nearly one month after they had landed in far-eastern Cuba, Spanish troops encircled Gómez and Martí near the hamlet of Dos Ríos. Gómez, about to counterattack, urged Martí to stay behind, but the latter did not heed the plea and exposed himself to fire. Martí died as he had foreseen—"facing the sun" in his quest for freedom.

Shaken by this terrible blow, Gómez and Maceo regrouped their men and waged a scorched-earth, all-out war the length of the island, which involved the destruction of plantations and mills that were supplying the enemy. More than 200,000 of Spain's crack troops tried to stop them with a series of blockhouses, barbed-wire entanglements, and ditches, but they proved no more effective than the later Siegfried and Maginot lines. Maceo broke through them and carried out his heroic invasion from one extreme of Cuba to the other before fatally collapsing under Spanish fire near the town of Punta Brava.

While the insurrection gathered momentum, American journalists roused U.S. public opinion against Spain. Joseph Pulitzer's *World* and William Randolph Hearst's *Journal* ran horrifying stories of thousands of Cuban families uprooted by the Spaniards and herded into concentration camps, where they died under brutal conditions. One story in particular, overlooked by most historians, caught America's attention—the romantic tale of Evangelina Cossío, published by the *Journal*.

Evangelina, an eighteen-year-old, convent-educated Cuban beauty, lived with her parents, who for political reasons had been deported to the Isle of Pines. A lecherous Spanish colonel, Berriz, tried to rape her one day, but she firmly resisted and cried for help. Beaten by outraged neighbors who came to her rescue, the colonel accused Evangelina of rebellion and had her condemned and transferred to a prison in Havana filled with depraved women. Pleas for mercy from the *Journal* and prominent American ladies were ignored by the Spanish governor, so Hearst went into action. A *Journal* reporter, Karl Decker, traveled to Havana, scaled a roof adjoining the prison, lifted the maiden out, and smuggled her aboard ship dressed as a boy. The enchanting Evangelina became an instant heroine. She was acclaimed by the crème de la crème of New York society and cheered at a huge rally in Madison Square.[7]

Disregarding public clamor, which was echoed by a congressional concurrent resolution on Cuba, President McKinley refused to recognize the belligerence of the insurgents with the same doggedness as his predecessor, President Cleveland. McKinley attempted instead to negotiate an armistice as a prelude to liberal reforms in Cuba under Spanish rule. This plan, supported by U.S. investors, who feared the devastations of war and the uncertainties of independence, was rejected by the Cuban patriots. On February 15, 1898, when the struggle had reached a virtual stalemate, the U.S. battleship *Maine,* sent down to Havana to protect American interests, mysteriously exploded in the harbor. More than 280 officers and sailors were killed. A court of inquiry found that the vessel had been destroyed by an underwater mine, but was unable to ascribe responsibility to any person or group. U.S. public opinion, however, was too incensed to worry about legal technicalities, so Congress, through a joint resolution, declared war on Spain.

The lofty terms of the resolution allayed fears of annexation or imperialistic conquest. Congress declared that Cuba "is, and of right ought to be, free and independent," and disclaimed any intention to exercise control over Cuba, except for the pacification of the island. Throbbing with missionary zeal, the nation took up the cry "Remember the Maine, to hell with Spain." Teddy Roosevelt relished the prospect of a "splendid little war" and braced himself for action. Few realized how woefully unprepared for battle the United States was at the time. The country relied on volunteers; guns were lacking. Some of the Southern regiments appeared with old Civil War muskets, and the uniform was still of heavy blue wool with overcoat and a blanket roll—not precisely the most appropriate attire for action in the Tropics. The soldiers, however, were not deterred by these minor inconveniences; they yearned for adventure, chanting: "Rough, tough, we're the stuff. We wanna fight and we can't get enough."

President McKinley sent off his famous "Message to García"—the general in charge of the Cuban forces in Oriente—who recommended the site for landing (Daiquirí) and helped devise a plan of combat to forestall massive deployments of Spanish troops. With General García's strong support, American soldiers, led by Teddy Roosevelt's Rough Riders, charged up San Juan Hill and prepared to take Santiago. Meanwhile, U.S. battleships blocked the Spanish fleet at Santiago Bay. Spain refused to surrender without a fight. Soon the wooden decks of her ships were ablaze. The Spanish fleet went down to defeat, but not without a burst of defiance and valor. Captain Phillips of the *Texas* uttered his unforgettable "Don't cheer, boys, the poor devils are dying!"

Hostilities ended on July 16, 1898, with the American forces making their triumphant entrance into Santiago—minus their partners in the war. To the Cuban leaders' anger and dismay, they were barred from participating in the celebrations and from unfurling their flag to the air. This offense left deep wounds. The author Erna Fergusson wrote, "As though the French at Yorktown had accepted the surrender of Cornwallis without the presence of George Washington, the United States Army marched into Santiago."[8] Adding insult to injury, the war was called Spanish-American and the Cubans were excluded from the Treaty of Paris.

During the U.S. military occupation of Cuba that followed the war (1899–1902), the island was governed by the generals John R. Brook and Leonard Wood. They instituted self-government in all the municipalities, modernized the school system under the direction of the noted Cuban philosopher-statesman Enrique José Varona, implemented public works programs, sanitized the cities, and revamped the legal system. Delegates to a constitutional assembly were duly elected in November 1900, and a U.S.-type charter was adopted.

Before completing what otherwise would have been an exemplary process of reconstruction and democratization, Washington demanded that the delegates add a constitutional appendix incorporating an amendment to a bill introduced by U.S. Senator Orville H. Platt. Prompted primarily by the fear of European intrusion in a free but inexperienced Cuba, the Platt Amendment granted the United States the right to pass on any foreign loan or treaty Cuba might contract, and the right to intervene for the preservation of Cuban independence and the maintenance of government adequate for the protection of life, property, and individual liberty. The Platt Amendment also provided for the cession of Cuban naval bases to the United States.

The Cuban delegates strongly objected to this constitutional appendix, which they viewed as a blatant violation of the 1898 joint resolution and a denial of the independence for which they had fought for almost a century. Faced, however, with the risk of prolonging indefinitely the U.S. military occupation of Cuba, the more pragmatic delegates finally mustered the votes necessary to incorporate the amendment into the Constitution.

Washington was pleased with the outcome, since the Platt Amendment was designed not only to promote commercial and political interests but also to protect the internal security of the United States. American government officials and opinion leaders firmly believed in the dictum of the renowned U.S. naval strategist Admiral Thayer Mahan, who held that "the security, nay, the very life of the U.S. depended on the control of the Caribbean [of which Cuba was the gateway]. Without such positive control, the

Panama Canal, the Atlantic seaboard and the great Mississippi Valley—the heartland of North America—all would be easy prey for attack."[9]

To strengthen American power in the area, the United States built in the early 1900s a formidable naval base in the port of Guantánamo, located in the southeast of Cuba facing the towering Sierra Maestra cordillera. In this region, which ironically enclosed Castro's former guerrilla hideout, the cordillera abruptly falls almost thirty thousand feet from the crest of the Pico Turquino to the ocean bottom's Bartlett Trough. This escarpment, one of the deepest in the world, was caused millennia ago by a folding of the earth's crust. The Guantánamo base became one of the U.S. Navy's most important defense and training centers and a symbol of U.S. predominance in the Caribbean. Today it stands as the only American enclave in a Communist territory, defying Castro's hostility and Soviet military might.

From a Cuban perspective, the Platt Amendment was demeaning and harmful. It retarded political maturity, sowed the seeds of discord, and weakened the fabric of the nation. As early as 1906, the Cubans started to feel the consequences. The first President of the Republic, Tomás Estrada Palma, whose administration had been generally honest and constructive, resorted to electoral fraud to ensure his reelection. The opposition protested, and armed revolt broke out, whereupon Estrada Palma asked Washington to invoke the Platt Amendment. Unwilling to reach a national settlement with his adversaries, he forced the resignation of his government and triggered foreign intervention. This was one of the by-products of American tutelage, which engendered in Cuba an overreliance on external factors and chance, an inclination to look abroad for the solution of internal problems, a tendency not to worry about local conflagrations, given Washington's readiness to put out fires.

President Theodore Roosevelt promptly filled the political void in Cuba and appointed the plump and personable Charles E. Magoon as provisional governor of the island. Magoon's administration (1906–1909) carried out several institutional reforms, including the enactment of electoral laws designed to prevent fraud. To pacify the country, Magoon assumed the role of arbiter of national disputes and power broker. Hardly a Metternich in the art of insightful mediation, he kept local factions content by handing out sinecures, pardons, and public works contracts as political inducements or rewards. Despite these practices, most of which predated the U.S. intervention, Magoon revitalized the country and held free elections. He withdrew in 1909, leaving Cuba poised for economic and social development, but not yet mature enough to maintain political stability.

In 1912, a minor "Negroes' revolt" erupted, and President Taft swiftly dispatched U.S. troops to the island. Cuba's Foreign Minister, the eminent patriot and orator Manuel Sanguily, protested vigorously, demonstrated that the government was in control of the situation, and staved off a third humiliating occupation.

Fraudulent elections provoked another uprising in early 1917. President Woodrow Wilson, fearful of unrest in Cuba at a time when the United States was about to declare war on Germany, asserted that Washington would not recognize any Cuban government resulting from a revolution. Buoyed by this indirect intervention and by the "dance of the millions" generated by high sugar prices, President Mario G. Menocal quashed the rebellion and prolonged his term. Geopolitics, yet again, influenced the course of events in Cuba.

Continued threats of U.S. intervention prompted the highly esteemed Cuban journalist and diplomat Manuel Márquez Sterling to wage a gallant anti-Platt campaign under the slogan "Domestic virtue against alien interference." He contended that the most effective way to avoid further encroachments on Cuba's sovereignty was to render the Platt Amendment obsolete by not giving Washington any pretext to invoke it. Democratic stability, government morality, and social justice were, in his opinion, Cuba's most potent weapons to fend off intervention. Determined to widen this campaign, Márquez Sterling and my paternal grandfather, José Manuel Carbonell, convinced Manuel Sanguily to lead a nationalist movement inspired on the liberal precepts of Mazzini's "New Italy." Prominent Cubans joined this moral crusade, but their efforts foundered amid opposition from vested political interests and skepticism from the press.

During the administration of President Alfredo Zayas (1921–1925), U.S. interference in the conduct of Cuban affairs was intensified. The central figure responsible for a "preventive" and much broader interpretation of the Platt Amendment was President Harding's special envoy, General Enoch H. Crowder, who arrived in Havana aboard the battleship *Minnesota* and used it as his headquarters for a period of time. Crowder viewed Cuba as a U.S. protectorate and sent off fifteen memoranda to Zayas outlining reforms that had to be implemented forthwith. Most of the reforms were plausible, but the threatening tone of the messages was degrading. It created animosity and rocked the government, assailed by political turmoil and economic depression. Zayas weathered the storm without curtailing freedom, but was reluctant to curb nepotism and corruption. My maternal grandfather Cortina, then Secretary of the Presidency, persuaded Zayas to heed Crowder's demand that the cabinet be reorganized with ministers of impeccable moral credentials. The new cabinet was well received and earned the appellation "Cabinet of Honesty."

This move, however, did not resolve the crisis. When Zayas later decided to replace a few ministers, the U.S. Department of State, goaded by Crowder, warned the President not to change the cabinet lest grave consequences should befall the republic. Faced with this veiled threat of intervention, which was leaked to the press and stirred up rumors of Congressional impeachment, Zayas sought the advice of Cortina. The latter urged the President to assert his constitutional right to appoint and remove members of the cabinet and to reject Washington's ultimatum as a matter of principle. "Crowder's rampant interventionism has to be stopped," Cortina postulated. "It is better to clash and fall than to accept such a fatal precedent. Now or never!"[10] Zayas followed Cortina's advice and dispatched a strong cable to Washington. Secretary of State Hughes backed down, indicating that the U.S. note was not intended to be a demand but a recommendation. Crowder mellowed his imperious tone, and President Zayas was able to complete his mandate.

Several years later, Crowder had second thoughts about the stinging memorandum he had sent Zayas on the subject of government graft. He candidly told Harry F. Guggenheim (subsequent U.S. ambassador to Havana): "When I returned from Cuba to Chicago and witnessed the corruption of municipal politics in that city, I felt a sense of shame in recalling that memorandum which I found necessary to send to President Zayas."[11]

Winds of violence lashed Cuba in 1933, giving rise to further U.S. involvement in the internal affairs of the island. President Gerardo Machado, who had been extolled as a progressive and dynamic leader during his first term, hatched a "cooperativist" scheme to neutralize the opposition, amend the Constitution, and extend his mandate from four to ten years. Several sectors of the population, led by the Student Directorate and the ABC revolutionary group, rose in protest, and Machado unleashed repression to snuff out dissent. President Franklin D. Roosevelt dispatched Ambassador Sumner Welles to Havana to mediate between the government and the opposition, but the situation had become too polarized for a settlement. After prolonged and bloody clashes, the army decided to depose Machado in 1933.

The suave Sumner Welles did not emerge unscathed from this major crisis. The students and other opposition groups, who rejected the constitutional succession engineered by Welles, accused him of frustrating the surging social revolution by denying U.S. recognition to Dr. Grau's provisional government. The hard feelings that this interference generated waned when the United States abrogated the Platt Amendment in 1934, following the Seventh Inter-American Conference in Montevideo. During that conference, the stalwart Cuban professor and historian Dr. Herminio Portel-Vilá waged a crucial battle against unilateral interventions in the Americas.

The demise of the Platt Amendment did not totally end U.S. intrusion in Cuba, as evidenced by Washington's behind-the-scenes maneuvering with Batista in the second half of the 1930s. It eliminated, however, the boldfaced tutelage symbolized by the constitutional appendix, which had sharply restricted self-determination and stained national pride. The Cubans, who are strident and impulsive but not resentful, had an opportunity to reaffirm their loyalty to the United States several years later, on December 8, 1941, immediately after Pearl Harbor. Voicing the sentiments of the great majority of the Cuban people, my grandfather Cortina, then Foreign Minister, informed Washington that Cuba considered "the dastardly and unprovoked attack made by the Japanese . . . as an attack against Cuba . . . calling for an immediate declaration of war . . . against Japan." The next day, December 9, the Cuban Congress declared war against Japan, and on December 11 it declared war also against Germany and Italy. While several of the other Latin American republics adopted a neutralist position, if not a pro-Axis bent, Cuba voluntarily sided with the United States in the defense of freedom.

As an extraordinary contribution toward the war efforts, Cuba refrained from enjoying the windfall of skyrocketing world sugar prices and sold its 1942, 1943, and 1944 harvests to the United States at the extremely low price of 2.65 cents a pound. Cuba also served as a major supplier of mineral resources. With five large deposits of nickeliferous iron ores, Cuba became one of the world's largest sources of nickel. The urgent need for additional supply of that metal during World War II and the Korean conflict led the United States government to make substantial investments in the Nicaro plant. Moreover, Cuba was a major producer of chromite, second only to the Soviet Union as a world source during the war.[12]

To protect and defend the approaches to the Caribbean, Cuba authorized Washington to build and operate two bases for heavy bombers: one in San Antonio de los Baños near Havana, and another in San Julián in Pinar del Río. These bases, which served also as training centers for American and British RAF personnel, reverted to Cuba after the war, only to fall under Soviet control in the 1960s.

The Cubans soon felt the deadly hazards of hostilities. The Nazis' fifth column in Cuba carried out acts of sabotage against cement and brick factories and commercial airlines. But what really wreaked havoc was the German submarines. They hung around Cuba like dolphins on the high seas, ready to attack unarmed ships carrying strategic minerals and raw material to the United States. In August 1942, U-boats torpedoed the Cuban vessels *Santiago de Cuba* and *Manzanillo,* and killed thirty-one sailors. A few months later the Cuban ship *Libertad* was sunk with twenty-five of its crew aboard.

Determined to stop the massacre, capture the attacking submarines, and seize their secret codes, an intrepid American writer took to sea for more than two years and went after everything that moved along the northern coast of Cuba. His name was Ernest Hemingway. With the consent and backing of the U.S. embassy in Havana, Hemingway overhauled his boat, *Pilar,* renovated its old gas engines, took aboard antitank guns, hand grenades, and dynamite charges, and set forth to confront the enemy. He was not able to engage German submarines in combat, as he had hoped, so he wrote *Islands in the Stream,* ''accomplishing through the magic of fiction what he failed to achieve in real life.''[13]

The Cuban armed forces fared somewhat better than the famed author. In June 1943, Lieutenant Mario Ramírez Delgado, commanding a submarine chaser of the Cuban navy, sank a U-boat off the Straits of Florida. Several months before, Cuban intelligence agents and FBI operatives had uncovered a Nazi spy ring headed by Enrique Augusto Luni, who had traveled to Cuba with a false Honduran passport. Luni operated a radiotelegraph transmission system from his home in Havana. He used large cages filled with singing canaries to hide his radio set and drown out the noise. Luni was arrested, found guilty of espionage, and executed.

For Cuba, these were significant anti-Nazi breakthroughs, but they hardly made a dent in the pivotal Battle of the Atlantic that was ravaging the Caribbean Basin. Admiral Dönitz and the German submarine command continued their offensive with unrelent-ing intensity. At their new Paris office on the Avenue Maréchal, a wall map of the Caribbean and the Gulf of Mexico shone with pins indicating the number of ships Nazi U-boats had sent to the bottom.

The Caribbean was an ideal assignment for the German sub-mariners. It had none of the Arctic extremes of the Murmansk route nor any of the inclement weather conditions of the North Atlantic. Moreover, the waters in the area, especially those around the Leeward Islands of the West Indies, were considered by the experts to be "good submarine water—deep, warm and difficult for antisubmarine forces, because changing thermal currents make it hard to trace submarines." [14]

Under these favorable conditions, a few Nazi U-boats, oper-ating primarily in the Caribbean, were able to undermine for some time the entire war policy of the United States. General George C. Marshall, then U.S. Army Chief of Staff, underscored the gravity of the situation:

> The losses by submarines off our Atlantic seaboard and in the Caribbean now threaten our entire war effort. The following statistics bearing on the subject have been brought to my atten-tion:
>
> Of the 74 ships, allocated to the Army for July by the War Shipping Administration, 17 have already been sunk.
>
> Twenty-two percent of the bauxite fleet has already been destroyed. Twenty percent of the Puerto Rican fleet has been lost.
>
> Tanker sinkings have been 3.5 percent per month of ton-nage in use.
>
> We are all aware of the limited number of escort craft available, but has every conceivable improvised means been brought to bear on this situation? I am fearful that another month or two of this will so cripple our means of transport that we will be unable to bring sufficient men and planes to bear against the enemy in critical theaters to exercise a determining influ-ence on the War. [15]

Fortunately, the United States promptly moved its tremen-dous industrial and war capacity into high gear, and the danger waned. But we learned that in times of crisis, vital Allied trade and supply lines could be interdicted or threatened by enemy sub-marines operating in the Caribbean—particularly if they had a permanent base in the area.

Against this backdrop, one can understand America's concern in 1960 over the progressive communization of Cuba, accented by Khrushchev's missile-rattling speech in July of that year and by the effusive embrace he gave Castro in New York during the September meeting of the United Nations. The feared contingency had become a reality. What the United States had guarded against for over a century and a half was actually happening: the strategic island of Cuba had fallen under totalitarian rule and was rapidly tilting toward the Soviet camp and becoming a most strident and violent exporter of anti-Americanism and subversion throughout the hemisphere.

The ensuing alarm colored political debate in the United States and influenced the results of the 1960 presidential election. As had occurred many times in the past, Cuba became a central issue of the campaign. Both candidates, Vice-President Richard M. Nixon and Senator John F. Kennedy, agreed on the necessity of "saving the free people of Cuba from communism." But Kennedy, carrying no government baggage, was more aggressive and called for support of "democratic anti-Castro forces in exile and in Cuba itself, who offer eventual hope of overthrowing Castro. Thus far," he added, "these fighters for freedom have had virtually no support from our government.[16]

This, of course, was not true, but the Vice-President was unable to refute that allegation, given the secrecy of the CIA-backed plan to topple the Castro regime. He could only refer to the economic embargo decreed in October 1960 by the Eisenhower administration, which was viewed by many as "too little, too late." Placed by the more telegenic Kennedy on the defensive, Nixon failed to regain momentum and lost the election by a very small margin.

The Cuban exiles were not particularly concerned about the outcome of the U.S. election. The majority preferred Republican continuity, but not because we felt that the liberation plans were at risk: both parties had publicly pledged to support our cause. No matter who occupied the White House, the United States would not tolerate the existence of a Communist regime ninety miles off its shores. Castro's fall was inevitable, we believed. Pressures as inexorable as that of gravity were involved. Even if history absolved Fidel, as he himself had proclaimed, geography, for sure, would condemn him. Or so we thought.

Chapter 8

The Underground

Alarmed by the burgeoning alliance between the Cuban government and the Soviet bloc, the CIA proceeded to implement the "Program of Covert Action Against the Castro Regime" approved by President Eisenhower in March 1960. Pursuant to this program, Richard M. Bissell, Jr., the CIA's flamboyant deputy director of plans, authorized the resurfacing of an old airfield at Retalhuleu in Guatemala and the construction of military barracks at a coffee plantation nearby owned by Roberto Alejos, right-hand man to the President of Guatemala, General Miguel Idígoras-Fuentes. The original objective was twofold: to train paramilitary cadres of anti-Castro Cubans, who would be infiltrated into the island to organize and lead the resistance movement; and to create a small, covert air-supply capability to support the insurgency.

Washington's Special Group or 5412 committee overseeing this program was intent on replicating the "Guatemala model"—the 1954 military coup staged by the CIA against the Guatemalan pro-Communist President Jacobo Arbenz. A force of about 150 Guatemalan exiles and a handful of World War II P-47 fighters piloted by CIA operatives proved to be sufficient to induce the army to overthrow the Arbenz regime, without major opposition.

Castro's Cuba, however, was no Guatemala. First of all, there was no standing army that could be swayed, for Castro had destroyed the remnants of that institution and created his own Rebel Army and militias. Second, Castro had promptly established a most effective apparatus of espionage and repression to stave off or smother internal resistance. Toward the end of 1960 he formed the so-called Committees for the Defense of the Revolution—a network of paramilitary units covering practically every block of every city and town in Cuba. These units were, and still are, the eyes and ears of the Ministry of the Interior, empowered to invade the privacy of the homes to weed out active or potential counterrevolutionaries.

Another factor that complicated the CIA's mission was that Cuba, as an island, shared no boundaries with other countries as Guatemala did. This made the task of supply and infiltration from abroad all the more difficult. Finally, Castro was much more cunning, audacious, and resourceful than Arbenz and wielded greater power as the leader of a triumphant revolution that had captivated the world. Drawing valuable lessons from the Guatemalan experience, Fidel lost no time in laying the totalitarian foundations of his regime and preparing for a CIA-backed assault. From his perspective, the clash was inevitable and indeed desirable to consolidate communism in Cuba, provided, of course, he could muster Soviet support without provoking an all-out American intervention.

Castro performed this balancing act with supreme dexterity. Undeterred by Washington, he received the Soviet assistance he needed in 1960–1961 to crush a major insurgency that could have crippled or severely undermined his regime prior to the Bay of Pigs invasion. Most historians have so far ignored or downplayed the Russians' covert involvement in this crucial episode. Castro's former G-2 officer, Juan Vivés, and other defectors disclosed what actually happened.

According to Vivés's testimony, anti-Castro guerrillas had sprung in various mountainous regions of Cuba, especially in the Escambray cordillera, located in the central province of Las Villas. The most prominent leaders were Evelio Duque and Osvaldo Ramírez, who had fought against Batista in the late 1950s. They were unable, however, to forge a unified command, given pervading rivalries and their reluctance to mingle with former officers and soldiers associated with the Batista dictatorship who also had taken up arms. Despite the internecine squabbles, the anti-Communist guerrillas in the Escambray soared to about eight thousand supported by a large number of *guajiros* and members of the underground.

Determined to quell the rapidly spreading rebellion, Castro deployed twelve thousand soldiers and eighty thousand militiamen to the Escambray in late 1960, but these forces made no significant headway. Then, on January 13, 1961, four hundred Soviet anti-guerrilla specialists arrived in Havana under the command of Lieutenant Colonel of the Red Army Anastas Grigorich, Lieutenant Colonel of the KGB Valentin Trujanof, and Colonel–Political Commissar of the KGB Mijail Furmanov. This contingent, assisted by Spanish-speaking Soviet personnel who served as interpreters, was immediately dispatched to a military compound in El Condado, near the city of Trinidad. According to Vivés, who visited the gloomy penitentiary galleries of El Condado, the compound soon became a KGB redoubt. From there, the Soviets secretly directed a major offensive to quash the insurgency.[1]

The operation involved the deployment of 70,000 Cuban soldiers and 110,000 militiamen. To cut off the rebel supply lines, the government uprooted most of the peasant families living in the area and dragged them into concentration camps located in the far-western peninsula of Guanahacabibes. Over eighteen hundred guerrilla prisoners were executed. Since Castro's obsessive goal was total extermination, his forces destroyed crops, burned huts, and contaminated springs as they systematically combed the region for rebels or suspects. Faced with this onslaught, the insurgents avoided direct confrontations with government troops pending the arrival of promised arms and reinforcements from abroad.

To support the insurgency, over fifty Cuban exile pilots received CIA training at the Retalhuleu air base ("Rayo") located some thirty miles off the Pacific coast of Guatemala. From that base, the pilots flew to Cuba and dropped arms and supplies in designated territories. Despite their valiant efforts, only 10 percent of the drops reached the hounded guerrillas. Various authors have attributed this failure to the lack of pinpoint navigational experience of the anti-Castro pilots; yet the latter were the same ones who displayed considerable daring and precision only a few months later during the Bay of Pigs invasion. Others have accused the CIA of unwillingness to back an autonomous and disjointed rebel movement perceived to be leaning to the left; yet notwithstanding this apprehension the Agency organized more than sixty-eight air missions to Cuba between September 1960 and March 1961. Still others have contended that the Democratic Revolutionary Front hierarchs in Miami showed no interest in fomenting local guerrillas not directly controlled by them; but despite the front leaders' manifest bias for an expeditionary force of Cuban exiles, they frequently pleaded for more U.S. support for the besieged Escambray rebels.

The failure of the air supply operation can be traced, at least in part, to the almost insurmountable hurdles faced by the Cuban pilots. As described by one of them, Captain Edward B. Ferrer, they had to fly "over the mountains of Guatemala, the highest peaks in Central America at over 13,000 feet, in antique, World War II, unpressurized, propeller-driven aircraft, at night, fully loaded, with no VOR, Inertial, Omega, or any other sophisticated navigational system [or reliable radio beacons]."[2] The round trip of sixteen hundred to eighteen hundred nautical miles reportedly took from eleven to fourteen hours depending on the type of aircraft and weather conditions.

To complicate matters, there was no direct communication between the guerrillas and the air force at Rayo Base. As noted by Captain Ferrer, "when the guerrillas requested an air drop, they used an intelligence network operating between Cuba and the United States. The agents in the U.S. would then inform the advisers at Rayo of the date, time and place of the scheduled drop. If, for any reason, the guerrillas had to move, there was no way for us to know. Many times, hours after leaving Rayo, we could not make contact with the guerrillas and would return home, cargo intact. On some missions, under the same circumstances, the captains decided to drop the cargo, hoping that the guerrillas who were supposed to be in the area would find the parapacks."[3]

This awkward, inefficient method of operation was the outgrowth of an egregious mistake: the notion that primitive facilities and flawed execution would serve to mask Washington's involvement. Throughout this risky period, disclaimer became a fixation. It was deemed essential to disavow U.S. participation ("plausible denial") at all costs, no matter the consequences. That is why the Cuban pilots were told by their CIA advisers that if they had to make a forced landing at the U.S. naval base of Guantánamo, the authorities at the base would surrender the crew to the Cuban government! Ferrer and his colleagues were stunned by this warning and wondered for a while whether they had two enemies instead of one.[4]

While the guerrillas were conducting their hit-and-run operations in the mountains, the urban underground was rocking the cities and the towns. During the latter half of 1960 and the first few months of 1961, the resistance movement unleashed, with sporadic CIA support, a major sabotage campaign aimed at the properties seized by the Cuban regime. Three major department stores in downtown Havana—Fin de Siglo, La Epoca, and El Encanto—went up in flames. Anti-Castro militants also destroyed telephone and electric lines, derailed trains, and burned a huge tobacco warehouse in back of the capitol building.

In the countryside, workers sabotaged sugar mills, and chemists raised the acid content of the sugar to make it inedible. Some of the *guajiros* also wreaked havoc. As described by Paul D. Bethel, who remained as the press officer for the U.S. embassy in Havana until Washington broke relations with Castro in January 1961, "the *guajiros* soaked rags in kerosene, tied them to the tails of rats, set them afire and threw them into the cane fields where the rodents would run wildly about, extending the fires so that the militia could not extinguish them readily."[5]

Government terror grew in step with armed resistance. Castro declared in the auditorium of the Federation of Cuban Workers: "We will answer violence with violence. We may not have God on our side, but we do have an infantry—and it's the finest in the world." 1961 had been officially designated the year of Education. However, in the face of mounting opposition, Captain Núñez Jiménez presaged that it would become the Year of the Firing Squad. His sullen prediction came true.

Hundreds of Cubans, most of them in the bloom of youth, like Virgilio Campanería and Alberto Tapia Ruano, were arrested and executed. Imbued with a mystique, they stood before the firing squad and shouted: "Down with Communism! Long live Christ the King!" Their stirring cries echoed through the two-hundred-year-old moats of La Cabaña fortress and were overheard by the poet Armando Valladares and many other political prisoners from their own cells. Castro eventually put an end to this blatant and contagious expression of defiance. After 1963, the patriots taken down to the gallows were gagged.[6]

Castro's bloody repression, however, did not stamp out opposition and unrest. The ranks of the various underground organizations swelled with freedom-loving militants from all walks of life. One of the most active groups was the Student Revolutionary Directorate, which had taken a public stance against the communization of Cuba during and after Mikoyan's visit to Havana in February 1960. Its leaders, Alberto Muller, Juan Manuel Salvat, Luis Fernández Rocha, and Ernesto and Tomás Fernández Travieso, belonged to the Agrupación Católica, a Catholic laymen's association whose members in the main had sided with Castro during the struggle against Batista and in the early stages of the new regime. Realizing that the revolution was being cast from a totalitarian mold, many Agrupación activists broke with Castro and joined the underground; others left for the United States to receive special sabotage and guerrilla training and were later infiltrated into Cuba.

Within my family, most of the young took an active part in the resistance movement, both prior to and during the Bay of Pigs invasion. We did not follow any preordained path or patriarchal master plan; each one of us abided by the dictates of his or her own conscience. Despite our differing tactics, we all shared a common goal, free of political strings or ideological tones: the liberation of Cuba.

Among our family's war stories, the one we treasure most is the gripping tale of Manuel Puig and his wife, Ofelia Arango—a tale of valor, passion and tragedy. Manuel's patriotic fervor prompted him to accept a highly risky mission in the Cuban underground; Ofelia's romantic love drove her to his side. They were both caught by Castro's security police. He was executed; she survived—scarred for life.

Manuel (known as Ñongo) and Ofelia first met in Havana in 1945. Ñongo was a tall and handsome twenty-two-year-old athlete with a cheerful countenance and an imposing physique. A consummate oarsman, he won many crew regattas, including a memorable one which afforded him the privilege of representing Cuba in the 1948 Olympics, held in London. Ñongo, however, did not flaunt his muscles with brazen ruggedness. He was a gregarious and soft-spoken gentleman with a warm and honest heart. He enjoyed club life, but he was happier when he visited the countryside to rediscover nature. Ñongo left the structured environment of the university to pursue studies on his own. He read avidly and had a penchant for painting. A born salesman, articulate and convincing, Ñongo started to excel as a hard-working distributor of wines and spirits. He was intensely motivated and eager to succeed, but money was never his driving force. He always remained a romantic at heart.

When my cousin Ofelia first met Ñongo, she was sixteen years old, a striking blue-eyed, statuesque brunette with a beguiling smile and a disarming wit. Convent-educated in Cuba and the United States, she mischievously challenged the starchy rigidities of cloistered life. Both at school and at home she displayed unconventional frankness and will, with occasional flashes of rebelliousness. In society's fashionable salons, Ofelia's enchanting personality and beauty attracted quite a few admirers and potential suitors, but she remained unresponsive and aloof until she met

Ñongo–her first and only true love. Their encounter sparked an ardent romance, strained in part by Ofelia's very strict family upbringing.

Ñongo was enamored of Ofelia, but was somewhat reluctant to surrender his independence and end his bohemian life. After four years of intermittent but passionate courtship, Ñongo finally succumbed to Ofelia's charm. Radiating joy, they were married in 1949 with the blessings of both families. Following a one-year stint in New York, where Ñongo studied art, they settled in Havana— Ñongo as a keen salesman, and Ofelia as a devoted housewife eager to start a family.

Nine years later, with four children and a prosperous business, Ñongo and Ofelia were lured, along with many other young, nonpolitical couples, by the lofty ideals proclaimed by Castro during the struggle against Batista. They joined the 26th of July Movement and raised funds for the revolution, deployed arms, and harbored persecuted rebels. When Batista fell, they celebrated the advent of the new regime with unflagging confidence in the future.

For Ñongo it was hard to accept that Castro was intent on implanting Marxism-Leninism in Cuba. Credulous and trustful as he was, Ñongo rejected for several months the notion of deception. I well remember the frequent discussions I had with him in early 1959. Ñongo acknowledged the excesses of the revolution, but he was convinced that the dust would settle and that democracy would flourish. When he became aware of Castro's Communist design, Ñongo was incensed. He felt deeply hurt and personally betrayed. Saddened by the need to resort to violence, yet again he joined the underground.

Working initially with the group Acción Cubana Revolucionaria, Ñongo immersed himself in clandestine activities: anti-Castro propaganda, purchase of arms, and sabotage. His courage and dedication soon earned him stature within the underground community. Secluded in the family's vacant Veneciana beach house, Ñongo, with Ofelia's assistance, held countless meetings with experienced conspirators and young militants to build a solid infrastructure. Just as the organization started to expand, Ñongo received the staggering news of his brother Rino's arrest.

Rino had been actively conspiring against the Castro regime in concert with Ñongo. In October 1959, Rino visited the U.S. naval base of Guantánamo on the pretext of a sales call on behalf of Bacardi Corporation. Rino met privately with the second-high-

est-ranking officer at the base, provided information on the totalitarian plans of the Cuban government, and requested military
supplies to fuel resistance. The cordial but somewhat unresponsive officer did not share Rino's alarm and responded: "I don't
really think this is communism. To me, this revolution is like a
tropical storm: it lashes but it passes."

With undampened zest, the Puig brothers, along with hundreds
of other more seasoned activists throughout the island, helped build
an anti-Castro network which included various officers of the Rebel
Army. Buoyed by the tremendous response, Ñongo and Rino intensified their efforts, without realizing that Castro's secret police
had penetrated one of their cells. On October 22, 1960, when Rino
knocked at the door of a "safe house" near Havana, the welcome
he received was the cold muzzle of a machine gun pressed to his
temple. Rino was arrested and condemned to fifteen years of imprisonment, which he underwent with dignity under most brutal
conditions.

The news of Rino's detention distressed Ñongo no end. Rino
was his youngest brother and very much like him—athletic, out-
going, and dapper. To complete the parallel, Rino had also married
a glamorous Arango girl, Ileana, Ofelia's younger sister. Faced
with the imminent danger of capture (the two brothers belonged
to the same cell), Ñongo and Ofelia sought refuge in a cousin's
house a few hours after Rino was ensnared. It was a very long
and painful vigil. Pondering with Ofelia the few options open to
him, Ñongo resolved not to remain in Cuba, defenseless and exposed to persecution and arrest. He decided instead to join the
exiles undergoing paramilitary training abroad and return to the
island with sufficient arms and support to pursue the struggle. Alluding to Castro's secret police, he said to Ofelia that evening,
"They won't catch me like a sitting duck. Not without a gun; not
without a fight." He left for Miami the following morning.

As soon as he arrived, Ñongo came to see me at the Revolutionary Front headquarters. He apprised me of developments in
Cuba and asked me to expedite the processing of his application
for covert military training at the CIA-controlled infantry camp in
Guatemala ("Trax Base"). Under a cloak of secrecy and camouflage, Ñongo was escorted to Trax, where he commenced his
training in earnest. The forests and mountains exhilarated him,
but the exercises fell short of his expectations: he found them
"too easy." Determined to stretch his endurance, he took up trot-
ting along the winding ridges with a heavy log on his back.

After several months of military instruction, Ñongo elected to join the "infiltration teams," composed of a select group of young recruits who were going to receive additional training in guerrilla warfare and be spirited off to Cuba ahead of the invasion. All of the volunteers were transferred to the U.S. Army "jungle warfare training camp" at Fort Gulick in the Panama Canal Zone. There, military experts who had honed their skills fighting guerrillas during the Hukbalahap rebellion in the Philippines and the Malaysian insurgency subjected the Cubans to grueling drills under most rugged conditions.

Upon completion of their training in late February 1961, Ñongo and his colleagues were flown to Florida for a few days while arrangements were made to drop them in Cuba. They stayed at a tightly guarded tomato farm near Miami. Ñongo managed to slip away one evening, and called me. "I have to see you," he said. During our brief and furtive meeting, Ñongo described his "survival" training in the deep jungles of Panama—"wet, without food, and entertained by snakes." He had lost weight, but he looked as muscular and fit as when he had made the Cuban Olympic crew.

In the course of our conversation, he referred to his underground mission with the zeal and conviction of a crusader. He then spoke of Ofelia and their four young children, all of whom had remained in Cuba. Having been totally incommunicado, he had not seen or heard from them for several months. Conscious of the risks he was about to take (the odds for survival were reportedly one to ten), he told me that he was going to call Ofelia in Havana and ask her to fly to Miami, if at all possible. He wanted to see her if only for a few hours before being infiltrated into Cuba, because he had been told that he would be stationed far from Havana. Ofelia answered the phone with her usual calmness, not knowing who was calling. But when she heard the long-awaited voice of Ñongo, she barely could control her emotions. Suspecting that her phone was tapped, Ñongo spoke to her in cryptic terms: "Pepe has just left the hospital. He is well and eager to see you." Ofelia needed no further prodding. In less than forty-eight hours, overcoming the barriers faced by those trying to leave Cuba, she managed to get the required departure permit and flew to Miami.

My uncle Humberto Cortina and I greeted Ofelia at the airport. She inquired about Ñongo and asked us with growing impatience: "When and where can I see him?" Humberto informed her of the secret rendezvous he had painstakingly arranged, and told her they could get together for a few hours, after dark. Before the encounter, I had a private conversation with Ofelia. I cautioned her not to distress Ñongo with her fears and laments, since he was irrevocably committed to the impending underground task. I shall never forget her response. Looking straight at me with her enormous blue eyes, she said: "I did not come to Miami to dissuade Ñongo from landing in Cuba. I came to embrace him and to tell him about my total involvement in the resistance movement. When he lands in Cuba, I will be at his side, undertaking the same mission and facing the same risks."

Ofelia fulfilled her pledge. She spent a few hours alone with Ñongo conversing and reveling in blissful embrace, and then returned to Cuba to await his arrival. Ñongo followed her a few days later aboard the *Texana III,* a converted subchaser with concealed deck armaments. The ship was used by a former Cuban industrialist, Alberto Fernández, and his crew, headed by the fearless Tony Cuesta, to shuttle anti-Castro conspirators between Florida and Cuba. Sailing with Ñongo in the *Texana* was a mysterious and restless personage, Humberto Sorí Marín, a former *comandante* of the revolution and leader of a major anti-Castro plot involving top government and military officials.

As Minister of Agriculture in Castro's cabinet, Sorí had refused to sign the Agrarian Reform Law drafted behind his back by Captain Núñez Jiménez and other Marxists. Having lost the government's favor, Sorí was placed under house arrest in late 1959. He boldly escaped by removing an air conditioning unit from the wall and sliding through the hole. Pursued by Castro's secret police, Sorí hid in the house of Ramón Font and his wife, who had been close friends of Fidel. From there, Sorí continued to conspire against the regime. By the end of 1960 he had enlisted the support of Castro's secret police chief, Aldo Vera; Major Julio Rodríguez, deputy commander of the San Antonio de los Baños air base; several key navy flag officers; the military superintendent of Camagüey province, and other influential government figures.

Noting Sorí's strong personality and stature as military leader of the powerful Unidad Revolucionaria organization and his anti-Castro plot, the CIA brought him to Miami to hasten the coordination of efforts to topple the Cuban regime. Sorí chose not to remain in exile; his goal was to erode and overturn the regime working primarily from within. To achieve that objective, Sorí was named chief military liaison of the resistance movement and was entrusted with the responsibility of unifying the civilian leadership of the major underground groups in Cuba.

Ñongo met Sorí for the first time aboard the *Texana* on March 13, 1961. During the turbulent journey to Cuba that evening, Ñongo chatted at length with the *comandante*. Having struck an immediate rapport, Sorí asked that Ñongo be assigned to him in Havana instead of sending him off to the province of Camagüey, as originally planned. Ofelia was happy with that decision, since it enabled her to remain close to Ñongo from the very first day of his arrival.

Sorí worked in Havana at a feverish pace to finalize the plans for the crucial offensive. Sabotage campaigns in Havana and other major cities were building to a climax, and plotters within the armed forces, especially the navy, were anxious to revolt. Moreover, there were signs that the invasion would soon be launched, but Sorí and his colleagues were not apprised that it was imminent. They were indeed kept in the dark. Still, the coordination of the major underground groups under a single leadership had to be accomplished, so Sorí convened a top-secret meeting of chiefs involving Rafael Díaz ("Rafael"), Rogelio González Corzo ("Francisco"), Domingo Trueba Varona ("Mingo"), Ñongo, and Sorí himself. The first two, Rafael and Francisco, whose groups had attracted the largest following, headed the roster of legendary figures of the underground.

This was to be the most important and risky anti-Castro parley held within Cuba. It was scheduled for March 19 in the afternoon. Extreme precautions were taken. The venue was disclosed to the participants only one hour before the start of the meeting. Ofelia drove Sorí and Ñongo to their destination. Both were armed and visibly tense. Fearing recognition, Sorí held a handkerchief close to his face, and he told Ofelia: "Don't drive alongside other cars. Avoid red lights. If stopped, we'll shoot."

All of the conspirators safely reached the meeting place—the residence of a retired engineer and his wife, located on a tranquil street in Havana's Siboney suburb (formerly Reparto Flores). While Ofelia and two other girls played cards in the living room to allay suspicion, the underground chiefs gathered in the back of the house around a heavy table covered with street maps. They were pinpointing the massive incendiary assaults against the downtown district of Old Havana that were to touch off planned military uprisings.

In the course of their intense discussions, a purely accidental chain of events prompted the secret police to storm the house. Nemesio Rodríguez, a guerrilla who had been detained by security officers in a suburb close by, having to justify his presence in

Havana, gave the address of a relative. It happened to be the house adjoining the underground leaders' meeting place. When the officers proceeded to search Nemesio's reported residence, the young housewife who opened the door panicked and ran to her neighbor's house, unaware of the crucial summit that was being held there. This triggered the fateful raid.

In a matter of seconds, heavily armed agents who had followed the young lady barged into the house and caught everyone by surprise. One of the officers immediately recognized Sorí and exclaimed: "Look who is here, the big fish, and we never suspected it." As the security men rounded up the plotters and pushed them against the wall, the daring Sorí dashed like a hounded deer through a partly open door, crossed a vacant lot, and tried to flee. The guards, however, who carried snub-nosed Czech machine guns, wounded Sorí and foiled the desperate escape.

All the detainees, including the women, were taken to the G-2 secret police headquarters and subjected to torturous interrogation for extended periods of time. This wrenching experience notwithstanding, the prisoner's mood remained upbeat. Mingo Trueba, for one, intoned flamenco songs which resounded across the halls and lifted the spirits. Nena, Francisco's assistant, who had developed a close rapport with Ofelia, would draw laughter with her sparkling wit. Ñongo and Ofelia also kept their courage up. Confined in separate cells, they managed nevertheless to exchange a few words when under heavy guard they met in a corridor one afternoon. Ñongo, looking tired, had not lost his sense of humor. Kidding Ofelia, he said: "I hear you're giving them a hard time. Behave yourself." Ofelia smiled.

A few weeks later, all the conspirators were transferred to prisons pending summary trial—the women to Guanabacoa penitentiary, and the men to La Cabaña fortress. The presence of Sorí at La Cabaña was expected to provoke confrontations with former Batista followers, who were waiting to be judged, and possibly executed, under the revolutionary law that Sorí himself had drafted in the Sierra Maestra. The feared clashes did not occur; civility prevailed in the face of adversity.

Just before the start of the summary trial, Silvio de Cárdenas, a prominent businessman who had also been imprisoned in La Cabaña, witnessed a moving scene between Sorí and Comandant Mirabal, former deputy chief of Batista's military intelligence. Mirabal approached Sorí and said: "Good luck, *comandante*." Sorí, who was using a walker because of his bullet wounds, turned around and responded: "Good luck to *you, comandante*. My fate has already been sealed."

Sorí was very pessimistic, even though Fidel had personally promised Sorí's mother that nothing would happen to her son. The trial he and his colleagues went through on April 19, two days after the Bay of Pigs landing, could hardly be called a judicial process. It took place at a military courtroom in La Cabaña. The attorney representing Ñongo and Ofelia did not appear—he had been arrested. Ofelia's father, Enrique Arango, a corporate lawyer who had not been involved in the case, had to assume on the spot the representation of his daughter and son-in-law.

Enrique and the other attorneys made an extraordinary effort to bolster the defense. They demonstrated that the most damning accusation—an alleged plot to eliminate Castro—was not supported by any evidence. But the prosecutor, whose record of performance had earned him the appellation "Blood Bath," continued to demand the death penalty for Sorí, Ñongo, and the other underground leaders, including Nemesio Rodríguez and Eufemio Fernández (who had been added to the case), and thirty years' imprisonment for Ofelia and the remaining defendants.

The behavior of the five members of the military tribunal showed beyond any doubt that the defense was futile. When they were not delivering acrimonious tirades, which militiamen watching the trial applauded with gusto, they would chat among themselves with their feet perched atop the table. Occasionally they would play games with paper balls and laugh loudly.

Through most of the twelve-hour trial, Ofelia just gazed at the spectacle, which seemed so unreal to her. Numbed by the suffering and fatigue, she could not gauge the full intensity of the unfolding drama. It was only at the conclusion of the trial that she realized that Ñongo's end was near. When the president of the tribunal pronounced the death penalty for Ñongo and the other six defendants, Ofelia felt a staggering jolt. In anguish, she turned to her husband and cried out: "Ñongo, if they're going to do something to you, defend yourself. Don't let them hurt you!"

Ñongo's last words still ring in Ofelia's ears. Looking at her with unbelievable serenity, he gently whispered: "Ofelia, to die is nothing. We all have to die—a little sooner or a little later. At least I know what I'm dying for. My death has meaning. Don't worry, Ofelia, I'll be all right."

The seven prisoners, standing upright, with their hands tied in the back, were then taken to a secluded section of La Cabaña known as *la capilla* or "death row" to await the results of the appeal that followed the trial. The proceedings barely lasted fifteen minutes. Soon after the attorneys had made their opening statements, the president of the appellate court mumbled a few words, signed the death sentences, and collapsed on the table. He was drunk. The cruel farce was over.

Ñongo and the other brave underground leaders were immediately told that their appeal had been denied. Without any opportunity to bid farewell to their loved ones, they were led, one by one, to a wooden stake before a wall of sandbags. Facing their executioners with unflinching dignity, they voiced their allegiance to God, fatherland, and freedom. With spotlights trained on them amid a murmur of prayers coming from the cells above, they were shot at 2:00 A.M., April 20, 1961.

That evening, at the Guanabacoa penitentiary, Ofelia and the other inmates kept their vigil, waiting for the dreaded news. They paced the gallery in silence, lost in their agonized private thoughts. Only an occasional sob or a prayer broke the oppressive stillness of the night. They had to wait until 6:00 A.M., when the government generally announced on the radio who had been shot the night before. Ofelia was well aware of the desperate situation, but she still hoped that, somehow, a miracle would save her husband. Then came the chilling radio statement. "This morning, at 2:00 A.M., the following prisoners were executed . . . Manuel Puig Miyar . . ."

Stunned by the news, Ofelia remained for several days in a state of shock, tearless and immovable, sleepless in bed. All the inmates tried to console her, to no avail. When she was released some time later, she didn't want to leave the penitentiary. Ofelia explained her conflicting feelings: "To leave prison meant that I had to face the outside world, and I could not cope with that. I didn't want to see anyone, not even my children. I feared the sight of them because they would remind me that I had to go on living and that I had to inflict pain on them. I had to tell them that their father had been shot, and there was no way I could avoid that."

In August 1961, Ofelia left for Miami with her four children. Shortly thereafter, she came back to Havana to exhume and identify the remains of her husband. She decided to go through that ordeal because she didn't know, for sure, if Ñongo was dead. Like all political prisoners who were executed by the Castro regime, he was secretly buried without the presence of any relatives or friends. Overcoming innumerable government obstacles, she completed the traumatic process of verification and persuaded a cemetery guard to let her inter Ñongo's body in the family grave.

Ofelia then prepared herself to return to Miami to rejoin her children. She applied for the permit required to leave the country, but to her consternation, the officials delayed the paperwork, alleging that her passport had been lost. Ofelia knocked on many doors and pleaded her case, but the unnerving delay continued. Determined to force a resolution after three months of waiting, she decided to request a meeting with Blas Roca, the aging leader of the Cuban Communist Party who had debated against our grandfather Cortina during the 1940 constitutional convention.

Blas Roca's secretary greeted her with extreme cordiality. While they waited for Blas, the secretary tried to instill in Ofelia animosity toward the United States. Alluding to Washington's foreign policy of "exploitation and abandonment," the secretary said: "Yankee imperialism will squeeze you like an orange until there is nothing left but dried pulp. Then they'll dump you. When this happens, call us—we'll receive you with open arms."

Ofelia remained silent until Blas Roca arrived. She then explained to him why she had to leave Cuba—her children's presence in Miami being the primary reason—and asked for his assistance in obtaining the requisite permit. Blas Roca was polite but pessimistic. He indicated to Ofelia that, given her counterrevolutionary record, it would be very difficult to grant her request. Realizing she had nothing to lose, Ofelia gave vent to her despair. With hardly a quiver in her voice, she bluntly told Blas Roca: "I am a desperate woman. You are my declared enemies. You have killed my husband. If I stay here, it would be only to hurt your revolution. It's better that I go!"

Taken aback by Ofelia's emotional outburst, Blas Roca promptly ended the meeting, saying: "I'll see what I can do, but I can't promise anything." Forty-eight hours later, Ofelia received her passport and left for the United States.

Almost three decades have elapsed since those tragic events took place. Although the past still haunts Ofelia, she agreed, at my urging, to recount her harrowing tale. It was not easy for her to begin, but once she did, she felt compelled to tell me everything: the words, expressions, and feelings that faithfully described what she and Ñongo went through. And so, with painful determination, after long hours of thought and introspection, Ofelia drew the details of this story from the locket of her most hallowed memories.

CHAPTER 9
The Faltering Alliance

The arrest of Sorí, Ñongo, and the other underground chiefs on March 19, 1961, less than a month prior to the Bay of Pigs landing, was viewed by Cuban exiles as a serious setback, but not as a catastrophe. Although severely weakened by the capture of these leaders, the underground still had sufficient resources to spur the liberation offensive, which was expected to be supported by the unassailable power of a U.S.-backed expeditionary force.

By the fall of 1960, the CIA task force in charge of the Cuban Operation had concluded that guerrilla efforts alone (the original "Guatemala model") could not overthrow Castro and had started to prepare for an amphibious and airborne assault. There were several reasons for this new trend of thought. Air drops into Cuba to energize the insurgency had proved to be difficult to accomplish. Soviet-bloc arms shipments to Cuba had soared, and Castro's police state, shaped with the help of KGB specialists, had considerably tightened its control over the civilian population.

According to the report of the Board of Inquiry on the Bay of Pigs (the so-called Taylor Investigation), which was ordered by President Kennedy following the debacle, there is no evidence that the Special Group (the interagency committee overseeing the Cuban Operation) formally approved this revised plan at the time. The Director of Central Intelligence, however, briefed President Eisenhower on the new paramilitary concept on November 29, 1960, and received the nod to expedite the project.[1] Thereupon, the CIA directed its officers in Guatemala to reduce the guerrilla teams in training to sixty men, who would be infiltrated into Cuba prior to the invasion. The remaining cadres (then about four hundred strong) and all new recruits were to be trained as an amphibious and airborne assault brigade equipped with extremely heavy firepower.

The effects of the change from guerrilla operation to conventional force were felt immediately at Trax Base in Guatemala. The sixty recruits who volunteered to form the infiltration teams (Ñongo Puig being one of them) left the base to receive further guerrilla training in Panama. All of their instructors, headed by the Philippine guerrilla expert Colonel Vallejo, departed as well. They were replaced by a much more cohesive and professional group of officers led by a U.S. Army colonel known as Frank—a sandy-haired, energetic commander with a penetrating gaze and forceful manner.

Frank commenced immediately to create an assault brigade under the leadership of Pepe San Román, a wiry, reserved, twenty-nine-year-old Cuban regular army officer who had undergone training at Fort Belvoir, Virginia, and Fort Benning, Georgia. Second in command was Erneido Oliva, a black, magnetic, twenty-eight-year-old career officer who had graduated in Cuba from the Mariel Military Academy. The brigade consisted initially of four battalions: the 1st Battalion of Paratroopers, commanded by Alejandro del Valle; the 2nd Battalion of Infantry, led by Hugo Sueiro; the Armored Battalion, headed by Oliva; and the Heavy Gun Battalion, led by Pepe's brother, Roberto San Román. Battalions 5 and 6 were later added under the command of Ricardo Montero Duque and Francisco Montiel, respectively.

Determined to turn Trax into a true military camp, the CIA ordered the construction of more barracks, installed an electric plant, built a new kitchen, and shipped in large quantities of modern weapons and ammunition. To foster *esprit de corps,* Frank suggested that the men choose a name for the brigade. Moved by the fatal accident of Carlos Rodríguez Santana ("Carlay"), the first of the recruits to die in Guatemala, the brigade adopted his serial number, 2506. The emblem of Brigade 2506, also known as the Bay of Pigs or Cuban Brigade, carried those numerals along with the tricolor Cuban flag superimposed on a plain white cross.

Training was proceeding as planned when an incident occurred in late January 1961 which threatened to dismember the brigade. A letter from Manuel Villafaña, chief of the brigade's air force, accusing the Cuban military staff in Miami of conspiring against the brigade commander, touched off an internal feud that had been brewing since the removal of Captain Oscar Alfonso Carol as head of the Cuban cadres. To the astonishment of the CIA advisers, battle lines were drawn between two factions: on one side, the brigade headquarters loyalists (who vehemently rejected the scurrilous label *batistianos*), and on the other, the Democratic Revolutionary Front standard-bearers (who just as vehemently dismissed the pejorative term *políticos*). Latin temper flared, clouding judgment and polarizing the environment. A general strike broke out, and 230 out of the more than 500 men at the base resigned, including the members of the 2nd and 3rd Battalions. Plotters stealthily moved guns and grenades in the dead of night, and there was talk of a coup d'état.

The situation became so tense that "Bernie," the acting chief of Trax Base in the absence of Frank, assembled the brigade and bellowed: "A lot of you people have never seen me, but I am the boss here, and the commander of this brigade is still Pepe San Román."[2] At Bernie's behest, Pepe reasserted his authority, and all but one hundred men followed him. Assured that leaders of the Front would soon come to Guatemala to hear their complaints, the diehards finally resumed their training, except for a group of seventeen who were transported to the Petén jungle, in the northernmost part of Guatemala, and held there incommunicado until after the invasion had taken place.

Reports of disturbances at Trax Base shook Miami. Tony Varona, the Revolutionary Front chief, raged because the CIA had not let him visit the camp. After several weeks of emotional clashes, Varona and two other front directors, Dr. Antonio Maceo, grandson of the revered "Bronze Titan" of Cuba's war of independence, and Manuel Artime, were escorted to Guatemala. Following a stormy session with the brigade commanders, Varona became more conciliatory. When he addressed all of the members of the brigade, he praised their chiefs, urged discipline and sacrifice in the struggle for freedom, and ended his peroration by saying: "A page of history is waiting for the legend of your triumph."

Before he left the base, Varona had a private conversation with Colonel Frank. When Varona questioned whether the brigade could stand up against the thousands of men Castro had under arms, the colonel responded with a reassuring smile, "Don't worry, Dr. Varona. We will have complete control of the air, and Castro won't be able to move a single car or truck anyplace in Cuba."[3] The colonel also promised to discuss the invasion plan with Varona before D-Day.

After Varona returned to Miami, the front stepped up the recruitment drive. Word spread that the planned assault would soon be launched, and the Cuban exiles rejoiced. Not even the resignation of Martín Elena as the front's head of military affairs dampened their enthusiasm. Martín Elena was a former colonel of the Cuban army who had given up his regimental command in protest over Batista's 1952 coup. No one disputed his honorable background, but some criticized his rigid and humorless personality. The crisis, however, was not triggered by his demeanor, but by a direct question he had asked the CIA: "When will I be allowed to see the invasion plans?" Not satisfied with the answer he got, he discreetly resigned.[4]

The front's executive committee understood Martín Elena's difficult position, rebuffed by the brigade and blocked by the CIA. An effort was made to select a replacement with sufficient stature and experience to overcome these hurdles, but no consensus was reached. The CIA resisted such appointment on the grounds that the operation was "too complex to be left to Cuban generals." The exile leaders were disturbed but not overly alarmed. Most of them felt that the Americans knew what they were doing and had no alternative but to support the invasion and win.

This assumption, which accounted for many of the exiles' actions and failures to act, was not too farfetched. Indeed, it was validated by history. When President Eisenhower authorized in 1954 the CIA-backed operation against the pro-Communist government of Guatemala (which did not pose as serious a threat as Castro's Cuba), he reportedly told his chiefs of staff and senior advisers: "I'm prepared to take any steps that are necessary to see that it succeeds. If it succeeds, it's the people of Guatemala throwing off the yoke of communism. If it fails, the flag of the United States has failed."

I was not immune to the contagious belief in the inevitability of our triumph. This conviction was reinforced, in my case, during the private meeting Dr. Guillermo Alonso Pujol and I had at the Pierre Hotel in New York on January 19, 1961, with Gerry Droller ("Frank Bender"), the CIA's Headquarters Chief of Political Action, Cuba Project. Dr. Alonso Pujol had been Cuba's last constitutional Vice-President (pre-Batista). A sagacious yet highly controversial "Talleyrand of Cuban politics," he had not been invited to join any of the exile groups, but even his critics sought his counsel and tapped his mind. Since he was not fluent in English, he invited me to attend the New York meeting as his interpreter.

Dr. Alonso Pujol raised many issues during the three-hour parley with Bender, including the urgent need to revitalize the Escambray insurgency and to bolster the front leadership. Of all that was said at the meeting, what really caught my attention was Bender's comment when we expressed concern about the recurring leaks to the press of the brigade's planned assault. Bender told us: "There is nothing we can do about the leaks, but bear in mind that the brigade's strike is only part of a much larger amphibious and airborne operation involving resources beyond those assembled in Guatemala. Shortly after the brigade's landing with complete control of the air, the U.S. will respond to the call of the Cuban government-in-arms and provide full support." Bender did say, however, that this comprehensive plan was still subject to the final approval of the new administration.

Dr. Alonso Pujol, much more knowledgeable than I was about the vagaries of international affairs, was skeptical of Washington's commitment, but I was generally satisfied with Bender's explanation. President Kennedy's inaugural speech the following day kindled my optimism, particularly when he pledged: "Let every nation know, whether it wishes us well or ill, that we shall pay any price, bear any burden, meet any hardship, support any friend, oppose any foe to assure the survival and the success of liberty." If not in Cuba, I asked myself, where? If not now, when?

By mid-March 1961 I had completed my assignments at the front's planning committee, which included the drafting of communiqués to be issued by the government-in-arms requesting diplomatic recognition and military support. Realizing that the brigade would soon depart for Cuba, I decided to enlist as a private. My parents and friends, including Varona, tried to persuade me to remain at the front headquarters, arguing that my intellectual skills would be more useful to the cause than my insignificant military abilities. I felt, however, a sense of moral commitment. Having called for a war of liberation, how could I, at the moment of truth, fail to practice what I preached? I thought of my paternal grandfather, who at the tender age of fifteen fought for the independence of Cuba. What counted in his case (and perhaps in mine, I thought) was not the experience that he lacked, but the passion that he gave and the example that he set.

Just before I left for Guatemala, some of my colleagues persuaded me to join a newly formed unit—"Operation Forty"—which was to be integrated into the brigade and charged with the occupation and temporary administration of liberated territories. (I later heard bizarre stories, echoed by noted reporters and historians, about the purported sinister task of this unit: that of eliminating "leftist" leaders, including Miró, who might stand in the way of "reactionary" plans!) This unit was composed of about eighty men, most of them young professionals known to me, and was headed by an amiable former colonel of the Cuban army, Vicente León, who had honored his uniform throughout his career.

Phase one of our brief training was conducted in Miami, where we were subjected to polygraphic tests and apprised of our mission as guardians of public order and custodians of human rights. Then one evening we were asked to board army trucks with rear canvas flaps pulled down. We rode in total darkness to an abandoned airbase in Florida, Opa-locka. Soon we were airborne inside an old C-54 military transport with metal seats placed along the fuselage, and windows painted black and covered with masking tape. We felt claustrophobic—enclosed in what seemed a long, narrow vault piercing the night. We were naturally apprehensive about many unknowns. But we had faith. We believed in the righteousness of our cause and had confidence in our staunch ally.

My short stay at Trax Base in Guatemala—about three weeks—was an unforgettable experience. By the time I arrived there, all of the rustic training facilities had been completed in the heights of cloud-shrouded mountains. I was extremely happy to see my nineteen-year-old cousin Humberto Cortina displaying his usual zest and effervescence. He had become a deft radio operator, and was fit and keyed for action. I also met many old friends and made new acquaintances—Cubans of all ages and from all social classes. I saw proud fathers with their young sons preparing for battle. I saw political adversaries burying their differences for the good of the common cause. The feuds that had initially marred the brigade were gone; a spirit of kinship and a sense of mission pervaded the ranks. I saw the commingling of races without any sign of discrimination. Nepotism and corruption had not surfaced their ugly heads. Sons and relatives of exile leaders were not accorded any special privileges. Scions of families that used to be symbols of wealth and power marched side by side with men of humble origin.

Among the latter was the lanky and affable Francisco Guerra, my father's chauffeur in Havana. Despite his limited education, he saw through Castro's rhetoric with greater perspicacity than some of the sophisticated captains of Cuban industry. Unwilling to live under Communist rule, he left his family and fled Cuba on a small boat, but only to receive military training and return to the island bearing arms. When I saw him at Trax Base, he was pale and gaunt, yet ecstatic. He arrived from Miami with the last group of volunteers allowed to join the brigade. After hugging me in the Cuban tradition, he said with an air of triumph: "I made it! There was nothing that I wanted to do more than to participate in the liberation of our land."

Except for a few undesirable characters who had slipped through the cracks of the enlistment process, the fourteen-hundred strong brigade was a cross section of the new Cuba, tempered in adversity and committed, in the main, to a progressive and lasting democracy. I did not notice any alarming militaristic influence— only 10 percent of the men had had any prior army experience. But the training received by at least half of the recruits was impressive, and so was their concentrated firepower. This helped temper my disappointment over our numerical inferiority. I had expected a much larger Cuban force.

While the brigade in Guatemala was finalizing its training, the Revolutionary Front in Miami was under great pressure to broaden its base. The prestigious Latin American triumvirate of the "democratic left"—Rómulo Betancourt from Venezuela, José Figueres from Costa Rica, and Luis Muñoz Marín from Puerto Rico—along with some of the New Frontier officials insisted that the front restructure its executive committee and join forces with several liberal leaders. Their prime candidate was Manuel Ray, Castro's former Minister of Public Works, a skilled organizer credited with the formation of a vast anti-Castro network inside Cuba. Ray's detractors, however, discounted his underground strength and accused him of fostering a socialistic program dubbed "Fidelismo sin Fidel" (Castroism without Castro).

In the face of mounting antagonism which threatened to undermine the exile movement, the CIA promptly settled the dispute with the persuasive eloquence of power. On behalf of the Agency, the Spanish-speaking New York engineer William Carr assembled the Revolutionary Front chiefs at Miami's Skyway Motel on March 18 and told them point-blank that no further American aid would be forthcoming unless the Cubans constituted a new organization that embraced all anti-Castro elements.[6] This meant liberal groups not connected with Batista. After four days of heated discussions, the Cuban Revolutionary Council was formed to weld the alliance between the front and Ray's group, the People's Revolutionary Movement.

Elected president was Dr. José Miró Cardona, the talented and mild-mannered criminal lawyer and university professor who had presided over Cuba's Bar Association and had served as Castro's Prime Minister during the first six weeks of his regime. He was not a politician in the strict sense of the word, but he was a shrewd negotiator who could reconcile the differences among the council members and coordinate their efforts. Not all the groups in exile hailed the alliance, however. Dr. Aureliano Sánchez Arango again impugned his colleagues for their docile submission to Washington, and Dr. Juan Antonio Rubio Padilla, a well-known Catholic leader backed by conservative elements excluded from the alliance, took exception to the leftist tilt of the council.

Undeterred by these and other admonitions, the council rallied its forces and pressed ahead. Miró, accompanied by Tony Varona and three other members of the council, went to Guatemala in early April to review the troops. Following the military exercises, Miró addressed the brigade. A large number of the men were indifferent, if not hostile, when he started to speak, but by the time he finished he had aroused their enthusiasm and won their support. What really moved them was his pledge to join the brigade on the battlefront. "In support of my pledge and unswerving commitment to the cause," he said, "I leave with you what I treasure the most: my son and the memory of my father who fought for the independence of our homeland."

On our way to the chapel, I had a brief conversation with Miró. When I voiced apprehension about the scant resources of the brigade, he told me: "I'm also concerned, but Colonel Frank has assured me that we will be able to count on thirty thousand U.S. soldiers, including those stationed on the island of Vieques, plus the backing of three Latin American countries and complete control of the air." Not satisfied with the colonel's promise, Miró added: "In the next few days I will go to Washington to seek confirmation."

Colonel Frank's assurance, although perhaps inflated, was not essentially at variance with the full-fledged assault that was conceived during the latter part of the Eisenhower administration. Unbeknownst to Bay of Pigs historians, this plan was reportedly outlined to the President of Argentina, Arturo Frondizi, in late 1960.

According to the records of the Argentine chancellery,[7] Roy Rubottom, then U.S. ambassador to Buenos Aires, was asked to deliver to Frondizi a piece of paper bearing the name of a White House emissary and the hotel where he was staying. As in-

structed, Rubottom told Frondizi that whatever the emissary had
to say carried the same weight as if uttered by Eisenhower himself. After stating with obvious annoyance that he had no idea
what the confidential message was, Rubottom curtly added: "My
mission has ended; I have nothing further to tell you."

The mysterious presidential envoy informed Frondizi that the
Pentagon and the State Department had concluded that the Castro
regime was Communist-controlled and subservient to the Soviet
bloc—a situation which violated the principles of the inter-American system and threatened the security of the United States. The
emissary then indicated that among the options available to deal
with the threat, the American government had chosen "the invasion." As communicated to the Argentine President, the plan called
for the landing of some one hundred Cuban exiles, who would
plant the flag in an isolated spot on the island, trigger uprisings,
and request military support from the United States. When Frondizi raised pro forma objections to the unilateral intervention,
the envoy responded that he came to inform, not to seek con-
currence.

A further indication of the U.S. involvement contemplated by
the Eisenhower administration was the assignment entrusted to
Whiting Willauer, former U.S. ambassador to Costa Rica. On December 10, 1960, Secretary of State Christian Herter, at the request of the President, asked Willauer to evaluate the invasion
plans jointly with Tracy Barnes of the CIA. The ambassador was
not a military man, but he had lived at the right hand of General
Chennault and his China Flying Tigers from 1942 to 1953, and had
learned air strategy. With his Far Eastern experience, Willauer
felt that one of the great weaknesses of the Cuban operation was
the lack of provision for jet air cover for the low-level strafing
missions of B-26 bombers, which were designed to secure a
beachhead. He firmly believed that the invasion "should not be
done or undertaken unless there was practically no chance that it
would fail, and that we should have to commit ourselves in advance to see that it was backed up, so that it could not fail."[8]

This was the very same position taken by Eisenhower when
he personally briefed President-elect Kennedy on January 19, 1961.
As confirmed by historian Trumbull Higgins in his recently published book *The Perfect Failure,* ". . . Eisenhower told Kennedy
that it was Kennedy's responsibility to do whatever was necessary to overthrow Castro because the United States could not let
the present government there go on."

Shortly after the Kennedy administration was installed, Ambassador Willauer was abruptly cut out of the Cuban Operation without being debriefed. The CIA task force, however, pursued the development of a plan of action for the overthrow of Castro which contemplated U.S. involvement in ascending degrees. Following consultations with the Joint Chiefs of Staff, the CIA presented to President Kennedy on March 11, 1961, the so-called Operation Trinidad, named after the Cuban town which was to be the site of the main landing. The operation, which the Joint Chiefs of Staff supported as one having "a fair chance of success," called for:

1. An amphibious/airborne assault by the Cuban Brigade at Trinidad-Casilda, south of the central province of Las Villas and near the Escambray mountains where most of the anti-Castro guerrillas were operating. The assault was to be preceded by a diversionary landing.

2. Concurrent tactical air support with the intensity required to provide full protection to the expeditionary force. (The jet cover recommended by Ambassador Willauer was rejected because "the operation had to look to the world as one exclusively conducted by Cubans.")

3. Seizure of a beachhead with access to an airfield and to suitable terrain for guerrilla operations, if necessary.

4. Constitution of a Cuban government-in-arms on free territory, which would serve as a rallying point and legal basis for military support by the United States and other friendly countries.

President Kennedy vetoed Operation Trinidad as "too spectacular" and directed the CIA to come up with another plan for a "quiet" landing, preferably at night, without having the semblance of a World War II–type amphibious assault. The ensuing changes, which whittled down and emasculated the operation, reflected serious doubts and vacillations at the White House. Only a few weeks after taking office, President Kennedy faced the need to match his anti-Castro campaign rhetoric with decisive action. Yet he wasn't prepared to commit the resources necessary to ensure success, nor was he willing to cancel the invasion to avoid disaster.

The President's ambivalence stemmed from genuine philosophical and geopolitical issues. Specifically, was the Castro regime just "a thorn in the flesh" warranting only toleration and isolation, as the influential Senator William Fulbright insisted, or was it a real and growing threat requiring surgery? The Kennedy administration's April 1961 white paper on Cuba, penned by the historian and presidential assistant Arthur M. Schlesinger, Jr., underscored the seriousness of the menace. From the middle of 1960 to April of 1961, it was reported, the Soviet bloc had shipped to Cuba more than thirty thousand tons of arms with an estimated value of $50 million. The January 1961 Havana military parade displayed a large number of the new Soviet tanks and field and assault guns received by Castro. Thanks to the mounting military aid, the Cuban forces had become the largest in the hemisphere, except for the United States.

Moreover, the Castro regime was expecting the imminent return from Czechoslovakia of about one hundred Cuban pilots who had been receiving intensive training in MiG flying. Their arrival would significantly alter the military situation, particularly since U.S. intelligence operatives in Cuba had already spotted mysterious crates which reportedly contained unassembled MiG planes. During the April 1961 executive sessions of the Senate Foreign Relations Committee (the records of which were declassified only in 1984), CIA Deputy Director Richard M. Bissell stated: "We do expect, sir, that the offensive weapons will appear very soon in Cuba. We have estimated that within another two months we would expect to see some MiGs appearing there and some pilots coming back from training." Bissell also disclosed that there were already in Cuba at the time fifteen hundred to two thousand Soviet-bloc personnel of one kind or another.

The consensus of the U.S. military community was that the transformation of Cuba into a Soviet satellite was not an end but a beginning, and that it was "likely to grow stronger rather than weaker as time goes by." Accordingly, they recommended the implementation of the paramilitary operation without delay.

Another issue that troubled the President was the legitimacy of the operation, even with covert, scaled-down U.S. participation. Senator Fulbright had warned him that it would violate the OAS charter, hemispheric treaties, and our own federal legislation. And Arthur Schlesinger had alerted him to the probable consequences of having to send in the marines to support the rebels. Much of the world would interpret this, Schlesinger affirmed, "as calculated aggression against a small nation in defiance both of treaty obligations and of the international standards as we have repeatedly asserted against the Communist world."[9]

These arguments carried substantial weight. Except in the case of self-defense, the United States was obligated to invoke the Rio Treaty and seek the advice and consent of the other OAS members before taking any direct or indirect military action against the Cuban regime. However, Castro's repudiation of the inter-American system and repeated interventions in the domestic affairs of sister republics did not accord him sufficient credentials to lecture the United States on public morality or international law.

There were other extenuating circumstances as well. According to Secretary Dean Rusk's Senate closed-door testimony on the Bay of Pigs situation, "we were in touch with a great many of the governments in the hemisphere, and there were perhaps half of them who were prepared for some formal OAS action, with the exception of perhaps one or two. The others were prepared to encourage action against Castro, but did not feel that they could do so publicly because of the situation which they confronted in their own countries."

"Indeed," Secretary Rusk added, "the reluctance of some of these countries to do so publicly is in part a measure of the degree of penetration which the Communists and Castro-type movement had effected within this hemisphere."[10]

The nations supporting military action against Castro were not only the so-called banana republics of the Caribbean, close to the center of turmoil. Even the ambassador to Cuba of a proud and distant South American country was secretly backing the invasion. He met with the CIA in Miami in early 1961 and urged prompt action. "Each day that passes," he warned, "helps Castro consolidate his grip on the island."[11]

Despite these manifestations of support, President Kennedy insisted on sharply reducing the "noise level" of the operation to mask American involvement. He did not seem to realize that the U.S. invasion plan had already become an open secret. In its issue of November 19, 1960, *The Nation* published an editorial under the heading "Are We Training Cuban Guerrillas?" On January 9, 1961, the *New York Times* also published a story under the headline "The U.S. Helps to Train Anti-Castro Forces at Secret Guatemalan Air-Ground Base." The *Miami Herald* followed on January 11 with a write-up containing specific details of how Miami's anti-Castro airlift worked. So public were these "covert" efforts to topple Castro that Cuba's Foreign Minister, Raúl Roa, in speeches made at the United Nations in early January, accused Washington of planning aggression against Cuba through "mercenaries" being trained in Guatemala and Florida.

Pursuant to President Kennedy's instructions, the CIA scrapped the well-thought-out Operation Trinidad and hastily developed three pared-down landing alternatives, which were superficially evaluated by the Joint Chiefs of Staff. Instead of reexamining the operation *in toto,* from start to finish, the CIA tried to patch up the remnants of the original proposal—a grave mistake. Of the three alternatives presented, the Chiefs of Staff preferred the Bay of Pigs, on the Zapata Peninsula on the southern coast of Cuba. Although Trinidad remained their first choice, they supported the Zapata option because its airstrip could accommodate the brigade's B-26s, and its few access roads would make it difficult for Castro to deploy his troops. They also assumed that if the landing forces could not hold their positions, they would "melt" into the mountains and become guerrillas.

This assumption sounded plausible but was in fact infeasible. Most of the members of the brigade had not been trained for guerrilla warfare, and the landing area was surrounded by uninhabited, alligator-infested swamps with no mountain hideouts and not enough food supply to sustain resistance. General Máximo Gómez, the undisputed master of guerrilla warfare during Cuba's long quest for independence, expressly avoided the Zapata Peninsula as a "geographical and military trap." [12] Clearly, the U.S. strategists had not thoroughly studied Cuba's geography, much less its history. To paraphrase James Reston's dictum on Latin America, they were prepared to do anything for Cuba, except read about it.

The chances of success of Operation Zapata—the Bay of Pigs landing—were slight and hinged primarily on air supremacy. This essential condition was fatally compromised by international political sensitivities, which prevailed over military considerations. Pressed by the State Department to truncate further the proposed invasion, the President rejected an all-out air strike on the morning of D-Day, as recommended by the CIA and the Joint Chiefs of Staff, and accepted only limited air strikes on D-2, D-1, and D-Day. (The D-1 and D-Day sorties were eventually canceled, and those scheduled for D-2 were carried out by eight planes instead of sixteen, as planned.) [13]

The Joint Chiefs of Staff did not favor the D-2 air strikes because of their indecisive nature and the danger of prematurely alerting the Castro forces. They went along, however, on the assumption that subsequent strikes would knock out or neutralize the remainder of the Cuban air force and naval vessels before the brigade ships made their final run into the beach. "If this is not done," they forewarned, "we will be courting disaster." Ignoring the military's premonition, the political advisers tipped the balance and carried the day.

On March 16, the President authorized the CIA task force to proceed with the curtailed invasion plan, but reserved the right to call it off before D-Day. He was still unresolved and unconvinced. What finally prompted Kennedy to give the green light was what Allen Dulles called the "disposal problem" of the brigade—the political and psychological consequences of disbanding the aggressive and vocal anti-Castro forces trained in Guatemala. As recorded by the White House's historian-in-residence, Arthur Schlesinger, the President said: "If we have to get rid of these eight hundred men, it is much better to dump them in Cuba than in the United States, especially if that is where they want to go." [14]

The Cuban exile leaders were not privy to this appalling solution to the disposal problem, nor to the specifics of the Washington invasion plans and attempts to eliminate Castro with the help of Mafia chieftains (Operation Mongoose). Kennedy biographers and Bay of Pigs chroniclers have stated, however, that the president of the Cuban Revolutionary Council, Dr. Miró Cardona, was privately informed by the President's emissaries a few days before the invasion that the brigade would be on its own and that no United States forces would be involved.

Miró steadfastly refused to give his own account of the conversations he had with Kennedy officials. He did not want to stir up a controversy that would only favor Castro. But following the publication in 1965 of Schlesinger's book *A Thousand Days,* which purportedly contained the White House version of events, the usually calm and genial Miró was enraged. He wrote to Dr. Ernesto Aragón, a close friend and executive assistant who accompanied Miró to all of the post–Bay of Pigs government meetings: "If I had been told that Yankee support had been denied, I would have stopped the invasion with a megaphone in Central Park!" Miró also dismissed the allegation that he misunderstood the message because his "knowledge of English or the translation was sadly at fault." Most of the discussions were "conducted in Spanish," Miró retorted. (His principal U.S. interlocutor, Adolf A. Berle, spoke Spanish fluently.)

Realizing that he had to set the record straight, Miró started to write a book titled "The Itinerary of a Defeat." Although he died before completing the project, he left handwritten notes which shed fresh light on his meetings with U.S. government officials.

Having had access to Miró's private files, zealously guarded by his son José ("Pepito"), a Bay of Pigs veteran, and Miró's devoted secretary, Ascensión C. Pérez ("Nena"), I will now summarize Miró's unpublished version of the pre–Bay of Pigs meetings.

According to Miró's notes, the first meeting, arranged at his request by the Washington representative of the Cuban Revolutionary Council, Carlos Piad, took place at the State Department on April 5, 1961. In attendance were Adolf A. Berle, a former member of Franklin D. Roosevelt's brain trust, who chaired the meeting as head of the Latin American Task Force at State; Arthur Schlesinger, representing the White House; Philip Bonsal, the last U.S. ambassador to Havana; William Bowdler, a State Department official; and Miró and Piad. Following the customary salutations, Berle asked Miró whether he was an advocate of the left—that seemed to be a password for New Frontier support. Adept as a barrister at circumlocution, Miró did not answer directly, but he expounded his views on the Cuba of the future. When Berle complimented Miró on his "socially advanced vision," the latter told him that he was simply enunciating the principles embodied in Cuba's progressive 1940 Constitution. Miró later noted with surprise that Berle seemingly knew nothing about this document.

The U.S. delegation objected to the draft they had seen of the council's manifesto (written by the jurist Dr. Antonio Silió), because it was too legalistic and lacked broad social appeal and revolutionary flair. Miró concurred and decided to revise the draft. He also agreed to assemble the council members in New York, where they would be in a better position to present the exile case to the United Nations.

After reaching consensus on these and other political matters, Miró proceeded to raise military issues. Berle told him that they were not in a position to discuss them, but he stated: "We're not deaf. We will listen." Somewhat baffled by the answer, Miró touched on the points he had covered with Colonel Frank in Guatemala and insisted on being kept informed, since, he said, he was "assuming a tremendous responsibility toward my compatriots." The U.S. representatives paid heed to Miró's observations and promised to get back to him shortly.

The following day, April 6, William Carr informed Miró that Adolf Berle was ready to see him, preferably alone. Their meeting, apparently not known about by Bay of Pigs historians, took place that afternoon at Berle's Georgetown residence. Dr. Ernesto Rojas, a perceptive Cuban lawyer then representing one of the revolutionary groups in Washington, accompanied Miró to Berle's house and waited for him at a gas station nearby. According to Miró's notes, Berle told him that the military plan was proceeding very well, that the invasion forces would have "control of the air" (he didn't use the term "air cover"), and that they would be supported by fifteen thousand additional troops. When Miró pointed out that Colonel Frank had promised thirty thousand, Berle responded firmly that a reinforcement of fifteen thousand men would suffice.

Miró was encouraged by Berle's assurance, coming as it did from a high-level U.S. government official and not from mysterious spooks with aliases. Nevertheless, Miró underscored the responsibility he was assuming and asked for a more explicit guarantee. Berle understood his concern but pointed out that the United States could not enter into a formal alliance. He gave the Cuban exile leader, however, his word of honor (*parole d'honneur* was the expression he used). Berle urged Miró to stress publicly that only Cuban patriots would be involved in the operation, and then added: "The United States cannot admit that it is backing the invasion, but it will have our total support." Berle's categorical statement was not inconsistent with the position on Cuba he had taken at the meeting held with President Kennedy and his advisers on April 4. Berle reportedly declared then that "a power confrontation with communism in the Western Hemisphere was inevitable anyhow." As for the U.S.-backed invasion, "Let 'er rip" was his counsel.[15]

Before the meeting with Miró ended, Berle stated that several Latin American republics were willing to support the invasion. He also confirmed massive U.S. economic aid to a post-Castro Cuba and informed Miró that a Spanish-speaking Harvard professor, John Plank, expert on Latin American affairs, would act as special adviser to Miró and as liaison between him and Washington. According to Berle, that appointment added further substance to the tacit alliance.

Dr. Rojas, who escorted Miró back to the hotel, recently told me that the Cuban revolutionary leader was euphoric when he left the meeting with Berle, "and the euphoria was not self-delusion," Rojas noted. He clearly remembers Miró's recital of Berle's assurances: control of the air, capture of a beachhead, recognition of a Cuban government-in-arms, fifteen thousand additional troops with symbolic representation from several Latin American republics, and a multimillion-dollar aid program for the reconstruction of Cuba.

Six days later, on April 12, President Kennedy stated in a press conference: "There will not be, under any conditions, an intervention in Cuba by the United States Armed Forces. . . . The basic issue in Cuba is not one between the United States and Cuba. It is between the Cubans themselves. I intend to see that we adhere to that principle and as I understand it this administration's attitude is so understood and shared by the anti-Castro exiles from Cuba in this country." Miró and the other Council leaders were stunned by this pronouncement, but held some hope that the President might have been playing to the gallery or trying to confound the enemy. At the urging of Dr. Arturo Mañas, a renowned sugar expert and authority on U.S.-Cuban relations, Miró immediately requested through John Plank a meeting with Berle to seek clarification of the presidential statement.

The parley, a spirited lunch discussion, took place the next day, April 13, at the Century Club in New York, with Berle, Schlesinger, and Plank in attendance. The discussion was conducted in Spanish, since all the attendees save Schlesinger were proficient in that language. According to Miró's notes, Berle informed him at the outset that the Soviet embassy in Washington had privately expressed some interest in exploring with them a peaceful solution to the Cuban problem which would enable the exiles, including the council leaders, to return to the island. When Miró flatly rejected the proposal as a Castro-Soviet diversionist ploy, Berle told him: "We just wanted to hear your views on the subject, but please keep this in confidence."

The Soviet message had been transmitted by Georgi Kornienko, the counselor of the Russian embassy in Washington, to Arthur Schlesinger, who immediately informed the President and Secretary Rusk. Schlesinger referred in his book to this intriguing episode and indicated that neither Kennedy nor Rusk saw much in it. The famed historian, however, did not mention that the subject was taken up again on April 13, this time with Miró. The reason for resurrecting this seemingly dead issue, four days before the invasion, escapes me.

The discussion at the luncheon soon centered on the pivotal question of United States military support. According to Schlesinger, Berle tried to convince Miró that American assistance was conditional and limited: "If there is an internal uprising . . . we would provide . . . the things necessary to make it successful,"

he said, and ". . . once the provisional government was established on the beachhead, we would offer all aid short of United
States troops."[16] Miró's version differs sharply. He wrote: "When
I expressed concern about the President's statement, Berle explained that for the very same reason that I proclaim that the invasion will be Cuban, the President has to deny U.S. participation.
But—Berle emphasized—our agreements stand (*nuestros pactos
quedan en pie*)," which Miró interpreted to mean that the understanding reached at Berle's home on April 6 remained in effect.

Having received this assurance, Miró told Berle that he could
not continue in the dark as far as the invasion plans were concerned, and requested that a high-level U.S. military liaison be
designated to brief him. Berle agreed with Miró and promised to
fulfill his request. The following day U.S. General Barley met with
Miró and Varona at the Blackstone Hotel in New York. The general listened to Varona's recommendation that the brigade land in
Trinidad, but was rather circumspect, saying that "in times of war
the civilian leadership must yield to the military." However, he
gave advance notice to Miró of the pre-invasion raids on Castro's
airfields that took place the following morning (April 15).

Given the discrepancy between Miró's and Schlesinger's versions, I recently asked Dr. Aragón whether the two had ever aired
their differences. Aragón responded affirmatively, saying that the
brief exchange took place at the White House office of presidential assistant Richard Goodwin shortly after Stewart Alsop had
stated in his June 24, 1961, *Saturday Evening Post* article "The
Lesson of the Cuban Disaster" that Berle and Schlesinger had
warned the exile leaders in advance that under no circumstances
would American forces be involved.

When Miró took exception to Alsop's statement and started
to recount to Goodwin what transpired at the Century Club luncheon on April 13, the latter called Schlesinger and asked him to
come to his office. According to Aragón, who had accompanied
Miró to the White House, Goodwin said to Schlesinger when the
latter arrived: "Arthur, as you are a historian, I called you in case
you wish to comment on what Dr. [Miró] Cardona has started to
tell me about a meeting at the Century Club in which he says that
you, Berle, and Plank were present." Before Schlesinger could
utter a word, Miró reportedly sputtered in his broken English:
"You might not remember—perhaps because the conversation
between Berle and me was in Spanish—but he did confirm to me
our understanding on U.S. armed support and promised to ap-

point a military liaison to brief me on the invasion plan. Don't you agree?'' According to Aragón, Schlesinger, somewhat befuddled by the unexpected question, said something to the effect that he could not remember exactly what was said because he had been unable to understand everything, but what Miró had recounted might well be true, more or less. Thereupon Schlesinger excused himself, saying he had urgent things to do, and left the room.

Even after Miró's and Aragón's stark testimonies, doubts may still linger on the whole issue of promised U.S. support. But one thing is certain: the deployment of a large American naval task force to the Bay of Pigs theater of operations. As disclosed by Admiral Arleigh Burke to Captain Edward B. Ferrer, it comprised twenty-two warships, including a submarine, the aircraft carrier *Essex* with its jet fighters, the helicopter carrier *Boxer* with a complement of two thousand marines, and twelve destroyers.[17] It also involved additional troops in combat readiness on the island of Vieques and at Guantánamo base. Despite President Kennedy's assertion that the United States would not send troops to Cuba, the tangible elements of a military alliance were there to back the liberation thrust. Tools to do the job were not lacking; what failed was the determination to use them—the will to win.

CHAPTER 10

The Bay of Pigs

At the end of March, while President Kennedy and his advisers were whittling down the invasion plan, Colonel Frank was lifting the spirits of the brigade chiefs in Guatemala. He confided to Pepe San Román and Erneido Oliva that the expeditionary force would soon gather at an unidentified base he called Trampoline—the springboard. From there U.S. warships would escort the brigade flotilla to Cuba. The marines would not actually land with the brigade, Frank explained, but they would be ''close to you when you need them.'' He also assured the young Cuban commanders that their air force would include fighter planes as well as B-26 bombers. Once the brigade secured a beachhead and a Cuban government-in-arms was constituted, Frank added, the support of the United States and other friendly countries of the hemisphere would be overt and unrestrained.

Then, early in April, Frank shook the brigade chiefs with the news that forces in the Kennedy administration were trying to block the invasion, and that he might be ordered to abort it. Pepe San Román recalled Frank's next words: ''If this happens, you come here and make some kind of show, as if you were putting us, the advisers, in prison, and you go ahead with the program as we have talked about it, and we will give you the whole plan, even if we are your prisoners.''[1] After providing details on how to cut communications with the outside, Frank then laughed and said: ''In the end we will win.''

The brigade leaders, including Manuel Artime, who had re-

156

mained at Trax Base as the council's civilian representative, were flabbergasted by this turn of events and by Frank's bizarre conspiracy. They kept quiet, however, convinced that Frank's military superiors were backing him in a desperate effort to salvage the operation from the snare of appeasement. The suspense lasted only a few days. On April 9, Frank received the long-awaited order to begin the three-day move to Trampoline.

San Román assembled the brigade the next day and told us that the invasion was imminent. He used no oratorical flourishes, yet his voice carried the vibrance of a military leader about to embark on an epochal mission. He said: "Fight fiercely, but protect the civilians and respect the prisoners. . . ." "On to victory," was his rousing finale, "freedom is our goal; Cuba is our cause; God is on our side!" We clapped and cheered wildly.

Two unexpected developments dampened my growing enthusiasm. First, because of a serious staph infection, my index finger —the very one I used to discharge my M-3 submachine gun— puffed up like a red balloon and had to be operated on two days before we left. The attending physician performed the incision with limited surgical tools and virtually no anesthesia. Most of the medical supplies already had been shipped to Trampoline. Friends mockingly accused me of theatrics, of concocting a ruse to stay behind. I waved the finger at them—not precisely the index one.

The second development that disturbed me was that Operation Forty had been split, and I was no longer assigned to the affable Colonel León, with whom I had built a close relationship, but to the stout and boisterous Captain Zorrilla. This puzzled me, since León had just appointed me as one of his aides. When I inquired about the change, the colonel assured me that the separation—decreed for logistical reasons—would only be temporary and that all of the members of Operation Forty would gather as a group on the beachhead. I never saw León again. Some say he died in combat along with several of my friends; others affirm that he shot himself at the Bay of Pigs before running out of ammunition and falling into the hands of Castro. All I know is that he was not captured; he did not surrender.

We left Trax in a joyful mood, singing popular songs and shouting *vivas*. Were it not for the camouflage uniforms that we were wearing and the deadly weapons that we were carrying, we could have been mistaken for a throng of college students on their way to a football game. Our caravan of large trucks moved slowly down the mountains to Retalhuleu. Along the winding roads In-

dian peasants waved and wishéd us well. Our "covert" mission
was anything but secret. At the air base, transport planes with
taped windows awaited us. We left just before midnight for Trampoline. Location unknown.

When our plane landed, I saw a quaint coastal town with
primitive houses and a long pier with railroad tracks jutting out
into a harbor. Trampoline turned out to be Puerto Cabezas, a port
in northeastern Nicaragua. Preceding us, the equivalent of fifty
freight-car loads of aerial bombs, rockets, and firearms had been
airlifted into Trampoline by unmarked U.S. C-54s, C-46s, and
C-47s. In addition, some thirty U.S. C-124 Globemasters had roared
in to off-load cargoes of rations, blankets, ammunition, and medical equipment.

This impressive display of military power and logistical efficiency contrasted with the hulking and dilapidated merchant vessels which formed our flotilla. My colleagues and I had envisaged
large, well-equipped ships like the ones we had seen on war news-
reels. Instead we got five rusty old tubs of the García line: *Atlántico, Houston, Río Escondido, Caribe,* and *Lake Charles.*

Our misgivings abated, however, when we saw two World
War II LCIs on port: the *Blagar,* which was to serve as the command vessel and carry arms for a thousand men, and the *Barbara J,* which would supply five hundred. Also heartening was
the announced addition of an LSD (landing ship dock) containing
three LCUs (landing craft utility) and four LCVPs (landing craft
vehicles and personnel), full of tanks, trucks, and other military
equipment. Not bad, we thought, for the first wave of a perimeter
landing.

Before moving into our assigned ships, we were asked to rest
for a while at the pier. In the darkness I heard the muffled snore
of a tall, sturdy man with silvery hair who was lying on a log. It
was Dr. Laureano Falla, an eminent Cuban gastroenterologist, who,
along with other well-known exiled doctors from Miami, had volunteered to trail the brigade flotilla aboard the promised hospital
vessel. On arrival in Puerto Cabezas they learned, to their surprise, that the vessel had been cancelled. CIA officers argued that,
given the lightning thrust of the planned invasion, the doctors didn't
really need a hospital ship. They could use at the outset the brigade's field hospital, and then, as the liberation forces advanced,
they could avail themselves of the island's own medical facilities.
Although miffed by the unexpected change of plans, most of the
doctors agreed to join the brigade and boarded the *Lake Charles*
together with our Operation Forty unit.

Living conditions on the five transports and the two escort ships were less than adequate. Many of us lay on deck, wherever we could spread our sleeping bags, and ate C-rations, either cold or heated by Sterno lamps. Smoking was prohibited. We were carrying more than thirty thousand gallons of gasoline to supply the brigade's air force once the field near the landing area was seized. Our ships were floating powder kegs. A stray match or spark could touch off a huge explosion. I tried not to think of this cataclysmic contingency, and prayed.

Before we sailed, Frank and other U.S. intelligence officers briefed the brigade chiefs and their staff on the impending operation. The first day the briefing was very general and cryptic—the map of Cuba was partially covered with acetate to conceal landing sites. But the following day the American officials removed the acetate and disclosed the details of Operation Pluto, as the invasion was dubbed.

The brigade was to capture and defend a beachhead extending forty miles along Cuba's southern coastline, in the area of the Bay of Pigs. From that base, ground and air operations would be carried out, and a government-in-arms formed by the council's leaders would request diplomatic recognition and military support.

The invasion called for landings at three points: Playa Larga or "Red Beach," deep inside the bay; Girón or "Blue Beach," at the center; and "Green Beach," east of Girón, cutting the road to Cienfuegos. Oliva was to land at Playa Larga with the 2nd and 5th Battalions of Infantry, and Pepe San Román would disembark at Girón with the 6th Battalion of Infantry, the 4th or Armored Battalion, and the Heavy Gun Battalion. The latter was to give support to the 3rd Battalion of Infantry, which would land at Green Beach.

The 1st Battalion of Paratroopers would be dropped along each of the three access roads crossing the swamps that surround the Bay of Pigs. Alejandro del Valle, the paratroop commander, would establish his headquarters at San Blas, which was to become the brigade's front-line position fifteen miles inland.

Operation Pluto would be preceded by a diversionary landing in Oriente province and by a simulated attack, accomplished with special sound equipment, in the province of Pinar del Río. Specially trained underground agents were to bomb power plants and bridges, derail trains, and disrupt Castro's communications network. Brigade planes would drop leaflets calling on the Cuban people to join the rebellion. More than seventy-two tons of arms, ammunition, and equipment would be unloaded on D-Day to support four thousand men. Additional supplies of armaments exceeding fifteen hundred tons were allocated for the subsequent weeks.

Castro's fledgling air force was to be destroyed prior to the invasion. Enemy troops, trucks, and tanks would not be able to reach the brigade; they would be blasted from the air. To allay any fears of a Castro counteroffensive, the CIA briefer asserted that an "umbrella" above would at all times guard the entire operation against any Castro fighter planes that might remain operational.

The U.S. officers assured the brigade chiefs that the beaches selected for the landing were sandy. The shadows that appeared on aerial photographs were just seaweed, they affirmed. The intelligence experts also indicated that only a few civilians involved in the construction of tourist facilities lived in the vicinity of the Bay of Pigs, and that the nearest telecommunication post was forty miles away.

When Frank's turn to speak came, he emphasized that the brigade was to hold the beachhead for seventy-two hours. Then he added: "We will be there with you for the next step. But you will be so strong, you will be getting so many people to your side, that you won't want to wait for us. You will go straight ahead. You will put your hands out, turn left, and go straight into Havana."[2]

Buoyed by the assurances and the infectious optimism, the brigade commanders asked few questions and prepared to depart. It was about 5:00 P.M. on April 14 when the invasion vessels left Puerto Cabezas—all except the *Lake Charles,* which, for reasons still unknown to me, was ordered to sail two days later and not allowed to disembark. An air of exhilaration permeated the ranks. The men of the brigade lined the railings and sang the national anthem. Each battalion and special unit had been assigned a different-colored scarf. We all waved them—blue, red, yellow, black, white—as the ships moved slowly out to sea and the sun sank on the horizon.

We were no longer concerned about our old, rusty merchant flotilla bereft of adequate antiaircraft protection. Military experts of the country that had led the Allied forces to victory in Normandy were directing our operation. They knew—we thought—how much was at stake in the battle against the first Communist stronghold in the Americas. And since our interests were seemingly intertwined, we were convinced that Washington would provide the support required to succeed. Early signs were positive. At a distance, the imposing silhouette of several American destroyers could be seen. We were not alone; the United States was backing us with its might. Confidence was strong and hopes were high. We could not fail.

The following day, April 15, our morale received a further boost when we heard on the radio the news of the raids on Castro's military airports. As communicated to the brigade pilots at the air base in Puerto Cabezas (named "Happy Valley"), this was to be the first of three strikes scheduled for D-2, D-1, and D-Day. The objective was to destroy or neutralize Castro's military aircraft: five Lockheed T-33 jets carrying rockets under the wings and two .50 caliber machine guns with a lethal fire rate of seventeen hundred rounds per minute; five single-engine British-built Sea Furies, which carried four 20mm machine guns on the wings and had exceptional maneuverability; and six B-26 medium-range bombers.

The brigade's sixteen B-26 piston-type bombers were no match for Cuba's armed T-33 jets and Sea Furies. They were even at a disadvantage against Castro's own B-26s. So that the extra fuel necessary for the long flight to Cuba could be carried, the tail-gun turrets of the brigade's bombers had to be removed. The pilots at Happy Valley counted on a devastating first strike to offset this major drawback. They also relied on the promise of fighter protection.

Captain Edward B. Ferrer, one of the brigade's pilots, well remembers the answer he got when he voiced apprehension about the vulnerability of the B-26s without tail guns. Wade Gray, a CIA officer, put his hand on Ferrer's shoulder and said: "I know, I know. But don't worry. We're gonna have 'Cuban' pilots who don't speak Spanish and who have blond hair and blue eyes taking care of us, and an aircraft carrier which is loaded with the latest model fighters."[3]

When the brigade pilots gathered on April 13 for a pre-mission briefing, emotions were sky-high. "Gar," one of the chief CIA advisers at Happy Valley, announced: "Gentlemen, this is it! We will select the crews that will make the first strike on the fifteenth against Cuba. But first, we need a volunteer for a very important mission, one that must be flown alone . . ." Since they all raised their hands, Gar proceeded to choose one of them, Mario Zúñiga, to carry out the task—a ploy designed to cover up the raids from Happy Valley. Zúñiga was to land in Miami posing as a defector who had bombed a Cuban airbase just before fleeing the island.

As the briefing continued, Gar made a statement that staggered the group. Only eight crews were to carry out the first air strike instead of sixteen, as originally planned. The Cuban pilots protested vehemently. They contended that the first wave of attacks was crucial, given the element of surprise, and insisted that all of the brigade's B-26s be used. Gar let them argue for a while, and then responded categorically: "Orders from the top call for eight aircraft to take off and not one more than eight."[4] (The "top" in this case was President Kennedy himself. On April 12, when he learned that sixteen bombers were going to participate in the initial air raid, he told Bissel: "Well, I don't want to on that scale. I want it minimal.")[5]

Despite their anger and concern at having to ground half of their B-26s, the selected brigade pilots did not hesitate to embark on their daring missions, code-named Gorilla, Linda, and Puma. After a hairy takeoff (the aircraft were overloaded with fuel and heavy demolition and fragmentation bombs), the first two crews flew to Antonio Maceo Airport in the city of Santiago de Cuba on the eastern tip of the island. Skirting the fierce barrage of antiaircraft batteries, they each made five bombing passes and returned to Happy Valley with fuselages decorated with dozens of bullet holes.

A second group of three B-26s flew south of Havana and blasted the San Antonio de los Baños Airbase, braving a hail of enemy fire. One of the pilots, Alfredo Caballero, who had refused to abort his mission when he reported that his droppable fuel tanks were not feeding properly, could not make it back to Happy Valley and was forced to land at Grand Cayman.

The most perilous of the operations was the raid on Camp Libertad (formerly Columbia), located close to Castro's national military headquarters in suburban Havana. To fulfill their mission, the three chosen crews tried to neutralize the potent Czech-made four-barrel antiaircraft guns that protected the base. Captain Danny Fernández-Mon, an experienced pilot, fired several rockets at one of the batteries. As he roared through, a second battery opened fire, tearing holes in the fuselage and damaging the left engine. Undaunted, Danny made a turn and completed his pass, but this time an emplacement on the north side of the base struck like a bolt. The B-26 instantly burst into flames, killing Danny and his navigator, Gastón Pérez—the first two members of the brigade's air force to die in combat.

Although the pilots displayed skill and valor, their raids were less than devastating—half of Castro's military aircraft remained intact. The mood at Happy Valley was not one of despair, however. Additional air strikes had been planned for the next forty-eight hours, and the pilots were convinced that they could destroy the balance of Cuba's fighters and bombers on the ground. It didn't cross their minds that Washington would halt the raids and, yet again, change the plans.

Shortly after the air attacks had taken place, the U.S. ambassador to the United Nations, Adlai Stevenson, vigorously denied Castro's charges of American aggression. He unwittingly echoed the cover-up story of Cuban "defectors" bombing air bases before leaving the island, and even showed a picture of Zúñiga's aircraft after he had landed in Miami. When Stevenson subsequently learned the facts, he was incensed. Feeling "deliberately tricked," he expressed outrage and urged the White House to stop the madness and avoid further embarrassment. Strong pressure also came from Moscow, determined "not to allow the United States to attack Cuba." At a tense meeting of the United Nations, Soviet Ambassador Zorin warned: "Cuba is not alone today. Among her most sincere friends the Soviet Union is to be found."

Against this background of veiled threats and political turmoil, Secretary of State Rusk concluded that further strikes from abroad would raise the international noise level to an intolerable degree. At his urging, and without prior consultation with the Joint Chiefs of Staff, President Kennedy canceled all further raids until the brigade's aircraft could appear to be launched from the beachhead. CIA's deputy director, General Charles P. Cabell, appealed to the President through Rusk, but the decision was final.

Miró and the other leaders of the Cuban Revolutionary Council, who had gathered in New York to hold a press conference, were not aware of the President's fiat. They were pleased with the reports of the air strikes and were expecting to join the brigade before heading for Cuba, as promised. On April 16, when CIA officers whisked them away in Philadelphia to board a private aircraft, they thought they were going to rendezvous in Guatemala. Much to their surprise, they landed at the deserted, blacked-out airfield of Opa-locka in Florida. There they were held incommunicado pending the outcome of developments in Cuba.

The news of the canceled air strikes left everyone at Happy

Valley dumbfounded. Why would Washington call off the additional pre-invasion raids necessary to destroy the remainder of Castro's T-33s and Sea Furies? The pilots asked themselves this question with visible consternation. It was bad enough that the first strikes were carried out with only eight aircraft instead of sixteen as planned. Now Castro had forty-eight hours to mobilize troops without the pressure and disruption produced by continuous air attacks. One who fully understood the fatal consequences of the cancellation was General Reid Doster, the commanding officer at Happy Valley. Doster became so angry that he cursed the fainthearted presidential advisers, hurled his cap to the ground, and shouted: "There goes the whole fuckin' war!"[6]

Castro was taken aback by the April 15 raids. Although he knew that the invasion was coming, he wasn't sure how and where the brigade would strike. He had sounded the alarm from the national military headquarters in surburban Havana, where he spent sleepless nights, but his pilots failed to heed his instruction to disperse their aircraft and were taken unawares. What saved the remainder of Castro's air force was on the one hand the powerful four-barrel antiaircraft guns protecting the bases, and on the other the White House's order to ground half of the brigade's bombers.

Moreover, Washington's decision to cancel the additional pre-invasion raids, coupled with the tranquilizing public assurance that no U.S. troops would be involved, gave Castro breathing space to regroup and counterattack. During the April 16 funeral oration for those who had died in the bombing raids the day before, Castro boldly revealed his radical design. For the first time he publicly characterized the revolution as "Socialist." He declared to a crowd of ten thousand, mostly militia: "The United States sponsored the attack because it cannot forgive us for achieving a Socialist revolution under their very noses." Thereupon, disciplined agit-prop agents led the crowd to chant: *"Fidel, Khrushchev, estamos con los dos!"*—"we are with you both."

Realizing that the April 15 raids were a prelude to the invasion, Castro promptly mobilized his vast security and espionage network to ward off any attempt on the part of the underground to spread the insurgency. In an unprecedented wave of arrests, more than 150,000 suspects, including women and children, were packed indiscriminately into public halls, theaters, auditoriums, and ball parks. Among those detained were many prominent members of the resistance movement who were not apprised of the impending invasion. Although the CIA's plan did not assume a general uprising (very difficult under a highly militarized totalitarian regime), it did call for acts of sabotage and subversion to sow confusion and stimulate the accretion of forces in support of the brigade. Fearful, however, of the Cubans' penchant for indiscretion, the CIA did not alert the underground leaders and thus enabled Castro to catch many of them off guard.

Even the members of the brigade infiltration teams were kept in the dark, José Basulto, for one, received his coded instructions to rise, interrupt communications, and blow bridges only after the invasion had taken place and Castro had decimated the resistance movement. Deeply disturbed by the unforgivable tardiness, yet retaining his biting sense of humor, Basulto wired back: "Impossible to rise. Most patriots in jail. Thanks for your damned invitation. Closing transmission."[7]

Another setback for the liberation forces was the inability to effectuate a diversionary landing in Oriente province just prior to D-Day. The operation was to be carried out by a group of 168 Cuban combatants, trained by the CIA in New Orleans and led by Nino Díaz, who had once fought alongside Raúl Castro in the Sierra Maestra. They twice made an attempt to land in the indicated area, some thirty miles east of Guantánamo, but their reconnaissance platoons reportedly saw "militia waiting for them, cigarettes glowing in the dark and stationary lights set to shine on them." They thought it was a trap and refused to land. The Taylor investigation, however, attributed the fiasco to "weak leadership."

The men of the brigade were unaware of these setbacks as their flotilla quietly approached the Bay of Pigs on a moonless night, Sunday, April 16. At 11:45 P.M., five Cuban frogmen crouched in two rubber rafts with their rifles, ammunition, and battery-powered signal lights. Accompanied by Gray, the CIA agent who had trained them, they were going to place white and red lights on the beach to mark the landing zone at Girón. About eighty yards from the shore, the boats scraped against a hard bottom. They had hit razor-sharp coral reefs, which CIA photo interpreters had summarily dismissed as seaweed. This serious flaw in the invasion plan delayed the landing several hours and exposed the brigade flotilla to air attacks the following morning.

The frogmen soon found out that the beach area was not virtually deserted, as had been reported. Shortly after the first landing light was placed, a menacing jeep moved rapidly toward the coast. The frogmen, led by Gray, opened fire. This touched off the alert, and a truck full of Castro militiamen zoomed to the beach. The placid resort instantly turned into a battlefield, with heavy shells pounding the coastline and tracer bullets igniting the sky. Under covering fire from the *Blagar,* the first troops came ashore, wading through chest-high water after the bottoms of three of their fiberglass landing boats were ripped open by the reefs. Additional problems arose with defective outboard motors that sputtered and choked out in the sea.

Faced with these pathetic conditions, the brigade commander Pepe San Román, became impatient and decided to land, ahead of schedule, with the 4th Battalion at Girón. He promptly established his headquarters and quelled the resistance, taking 150 prisoners, of which fifty enthusiastically joined his forces as volunteers. He also dispatched some of his men to seize the Girón airstrip and prepare it for immediate use by the brigade squadron. Off Playa Larga, twenty miles northwest of Girón, Erneido Oliva, deputy brigade commander, disembarked with the 2nd Battalion. They, too, ran into hidden reefs and were hampered by defective landing craft. However, with the help of the escort boat *Barbara J,* they completed the first phase of their landing, stormed the beach, and silenced the militia's machine-gun emplacements.

Meanwhile, at Happy Valley in Nicaragua, the brigade pilots were warming up six transport planes to drop the 1st Battalion of Paratroopers over the island junctions that controlled the passages to the Bay of Pigs. Strong, blue-eyed Alejandro del Valle, twenty-six years old, commanded the battalion. He exuded confidence and was proud of his men. Just before boarding the plane, he teased Captain Edward B. Ferrer: "Remember, we are the paratroopers and we have the biggest *timbales* [balls] in the whole army . . . except, of course, you goddam pilots." As their aircraft approached the Bay of Pigs, they passed within eight hundred feet of the USS *Essex*. It was an exhilarating sight that heartened the paratroopers. Standing on the mammoth deck of the carrier were hundreds of American sailors and officers waving at them. Captain Ferrer rocked the wings of his airplane, while a former Cuban navy pilot whistled "Anchors Aweigh."

Del Valle and the contingent assigned to him landed at San Blas, a strategic road center about fifteen miles northeast of Girón. Backed by the 3rd Battalion and a heavy weapons detachment, they seized the town and incorporated groups of local volunteers. Their outposts to the north and east, however, soon came under attack. Determined to hold the line, they buttressed the roadblocks to San Blas with 57mm cannons, bazookas, and 4.2 mortars, and awaited the onslaught of enemy forces.

Castro learned of the brigade landings sooner than anticipated. Microwave stations at Girón and Playa Larga relayed details of the invasion to Castro's headquarters at about 1:15 A.M. on Monday, April 17, scarcely one hour after the liberation forces had started to disembark. He swiftly dispatched several battalions to the western front at Playa Larga and to the eastern front at San Blas, and he ordered his air force to take off at dawn and attack the ships facing Playa Larga and Girón. Time was of the essence for Castro. He was determined to prevent at all costs the consolidation of a beachhead and the landing of the provisional government-in-arms.

At 6:00 A.M., Monday, April 17, as the remainder of the Heavy Gun Battalion and all of the 3rd and 6th Battalions were landing at Girón, a B-26 flew over and dipped its wings in salute. Convinced it was one of the brigade bombers, they all waved back with joy. Shots from the plane abruptly ended their elation. It was one of Castro's military aircraft strafing the coast to blunt the invasion. This first strike posed daunting problems but did not impede the landing of these battalions. Although wet, scattered, and exhausted, most of the men were able to reach Girón and salvage their heavy weapons and armored vehicles, including five tanks.

Subsequent air attacks, however, were more intense and devastating. At 6:30 A.M., two of Castro's T-33 jets and a Sea Fury zeroed in on the *Houston* off Playa Larga, as the 180 men of the 5th Battalion started to disembark. One of the planes made a direct rocket hit, and the ship started to take on water. Miraculously, the *Houston,* which was laden with ammunition and gasoline, did not explode, and its courageous captain, Luis Morse, Sr., succeeded in grounding it three hundred yards from the coast. But the members of the 5th Battalion had to jump into the oily water and were strafed by Castro's aircraft. Some thirty men died in the sea, and the rest, dispirited and without weapons, landed in swampy areas and never got to the battlefront at Playa Larga.

At 9:30 A.M., Castro's air force dealt another staggering blow. Diving out of the sun like a blazing bird, a Sea Fury hit and sunk the freighter *Río Escondido* off Girón beach. It was an irreparable loss, for the ship carried ten days' supply of food, ammunition, and gasoline, as well as the brigade's communications trailer—the primary method of communications with the battalions, the flagship, and the rear base in Nicaragua.

In the face of relentless air attacks and no effective cover, the freighters *Atlántico* and *Caribe,* along with two LCIs and three LCUs, put to sea without unloading the ammunition they were carrying. The plan was for them to return at night to discharge their cargo. Considering, however, the mutinous attitude of the crews and the risks involved, the CIA flagship requested the escort of a U.S. Navy destroyer or low jet cover to execute the operation. Washington refused to grant authorization and directed the ships to rendezvous some sixty miles south of the Cuban coast, where they remained most of the time until the beachhead fell. The brigade was thus deprived of vital supplies (except for sporadic airdrops) and was unable to operate the airport that had been seized near Girón.

Despite the ease with which Castro's T-33 jets could destroy the brigade's obsolete B-26 bombers, the latter flew 720 miles from Happy Valley, rotated over the beachhead through D-Day, sank one gunboat, and made effective strikes against enemy troops. A total of thirteen combat sorties were flown on April 17, in the course of which four brigade B-26s were lost to enemy T-33 action and crashed. In the same period, Castro's air force lost one Sea Fury and one B-26 to antiaircraft fire.

In a belated attempt to destroy Castro's remaining aircraft on the ground, Washington authorized a bombing attack on the San Antonio de los Baños base the night of April 17–18. Six brigade aircraft flew over the target in two waves of three each, but the mission could not be carried out because of heavy haze and low clouds. Castro's lethal jets remained untouched.

These contretemps delayed but did not forestall the advance of the brigade on April 17. At Playa Larga, on the western front, Oliva and his men obliterated Castro's 339th Battalion of militia as they came down one of the access roads to the coast. With tanks, mortars, cannon, and bazookas, as well as the support of two B-26s, Oliva led the victorious charge that crowned his fame. He also showed his mettle during the "Battle of the Rotonda," a strategic intersection a mile north of Playa Larga. There he confronted and defeated over two thousand of Castro's soldiers and militia, plus twenty Sherman and Stalin tanks.

After fighting bravely in the environs of Playa Larga, some of Oliva's men momentarily lost their nerve. They were very low on ammunition and extremely tired. Surprised by a Stalin tank that suddenly emerged from the shadows, some of the soldiers started to retreat. To set the example, Oliva, backed by the commander of the 2nd Battalion, Hugo Sueiro, grabbed a 57mm cannon, ran to the middle of the road, knelt down, and faced the enemy tank. When the troops saw what their leader was doing, they regained their confidence and rallied to his side. Luckily for Oliva, the tank stopped and the driver got out and approached him.

"Are you the commander of these men?" he asked Oliva.

"Yes."

"I congratulate you because these men are heroes. I would like to fight with you."[8]

Oliva and his soldiers were emboldened by their initial success. The invasion plan seemed to be working after all. Displaying superior discipline, strategy, and firepower, the brigade ground forces at Playa Larga held on during the first day against overwhelming odds and with minimal casualties (ten to twenty dead, forty to fifty wounded). In contrast, Castro's forces were disorganized, untrained, and overexposed as they moved like Chinese hordes through isolated roads surrounded by swamps. Their April 17 casualties at Play Larga were estimated at fifteen hundred (five hundred dead and one thousand wounded), and the number of militia deserting or surrendering started to mount. Oliva knew that the brigade had to hang on to the beachhead for at least seventy-two hours to enable the Cuban government-in-arms to land and secure diplomatic recognition and military support. Counting on additional ammunition and air cover, he braced his men to resist and hold the line.

By dawn of April 18, hopes had dimmed on the western front. Short of bullets and beleaguered, after fighting incessantly for many hours, Oliva and his men could no longer fend off the Castro forces, now swelling and shouting "Fatherland or death." He therefore ordered the release of the two hundred prisoners he had taken and implemented a phased withdrawal to Girón. There Oliva found the brigade chief, Pepe San Román, desperately radioing the flagship and asking for weapons, ammunition, medicine, and food. As remembered by Pepe, the dialogue with the American task force commander went like this:

Task force commander: "Hello, Pepe, how are you? . . ."

Pepe: "Where have you been, you son of a bitch? Where the hell have you been? You have abandoned us."

Task force commander: "I know that you have your problems, but I've had mine."

Then Gray, the American frogman, came on the air and said:

"Hello, Pepe, I want you to know that we will never abandon you, and if things are very rough there, we will go in and evacuate you."

Pepe's exact words, as recorded on tape, were:

"I will not be evacuated. We will fight to the end here if we have to."[9]

Gray then promised to deliver supplies and uttered the magic words that Pepe will never forget: "Jets are coming." Gray announced that six unidentified jets and several B-26s would arrive within two hours to support the brigade. Pepe was euphoric. He spread the good news and exclaimed with confidence: "Now we will hit them."

The jets came and went without engaging in combat. The White House had only authorized photo and visual reconnaissance, using unmarked naval aircraft, to gauge the situation on the beach.

Brigade bombers, however, flew six sorties during the afternoon of April 18, attacking a column of tanks and vehicles approaching Girón. The raid was very successful with heavy casualties inflicted on Castro forces, including destruction of seven tanks. In addition, three C-54 transports carried needed supplies to the beaches at Girón, but half of the drops fell into the sea.

Meanwhile, at San Blas on the eastern front, intense artillery barrage and enemy pressure had compelled a gradual contraction of the brigade's position around the town. The dashing paratroop commander Alejandro de Valle, backed by the Heavy Gun Battalion commander, Roberto San Román, resolved not to withdraw and launched a counterattack. Standing on top of one of his two tanks, del Valle led his men forward under heavy fire. He was hit and knocked down, but he immediately climbed back and the tank forged ahead. After a short but fierce battle, Castro's numerically superior forces broke and ran. Some of his troops tore off their shirts and waved them as flags of surrender. This marked the apex of del Valle's quixotic San Blas assault. It suggested Castro's vulnerability and lifted the hopes for liberation. But not for long. As del Valle and his men started to run out of ammunition, their offensive faltered and they were forced to recoil under enemy air attack.

Given the critical situation faced by the brigade, CIA Deputy Director Bissell requested an urgent meeting with President Kennedy and his key advisers following a formal congressional reception at the White House. The momentous discussion began at midnight and continued until 2:45 A.M. on April 19. Bissell argued that the operation could still be saved and laid out a string of options, including the use of jets from the *Essex*. Admiral Burke supported Bissell's recommendations and pleaded: "Let me take two jets and shoot down the enemy aircraft." When the President reminded Burke that he could not commit U.S. forces to combat, the admiral suggested that unmarked jets be permitted to fly over the beaches as a show of strength. Still unable to convince the President, Burke then requested authorization to bring in a destroyer to knock out Castro's tanks. At this point the President got angry and responded sharply: "Burke, I don't want the United States involved in this." Deeply distressed, the admiral shot back: "Goddammit, Mr. President, we *are* involved, and there is no way we can hide it. We *are* involved!"[10]

As a compromise, President Kennedy authorized the U.S. Navy to fly combat air patrol over the beachhead, but only for one hour from 6:30 to 7:30 on the morning of April 19. The purpose of this mission was to allow the brigade's B-26s to provide close support to the troops in the beachhead and cover for air resupply.[11] The patrol mission was flown to no avail. It appears that the sixty minutes of air cover had been scheduled in Washington and Girón time—Eastern Standard Time—without allowing for the one-hour time difference between Cuba and Nicaragua. So when the U.S. jets flew into the airspace over Girón, none of the brigade planes were in the combat zone. Two B-26s piloted by American volunteers had already been shot down by Castro's T-33s, and the other aircraft involved in the morning raids and in the rescue of a wounded pilot off Girón had completed their tasks under enemy fire and returned to Nicaragua.

The surviving pilots at Happy Valley were battered and exhausted. In four days of combat, beginning with the April 15 raids, the brigade air squadron had flown thirty-six missions in old B-26 bombers without tail guns or cover. Fourteen pilots had been killed, four of them Americans from the Alabama Air National Guard, who, in the darkest hours of the invasion, volunteered to fly in combat as a gesture of solidarity with their helpless allies. They were hopeful of receiving air cover from the *Essex,* but their desperate call—"MAY DAY! MAY DAY! Mad Dog Four! A T-33's attacking us!"—was unheard or unheeded. One of their planes plunged into the sea, and the other crashed near a sugar mill off the Bay of Pigs.

Meanwhile, at the beachhead, the brigade battalions were pulling back into Girón. Castro's armor had pushed along the coastal road from Playa Larga, and his air force was strafing and bombing the area. San Blas continued under heavy enemy fire. Del Valle and his men launched an audacious, if short-lived, counteroffensive, and then began to retreat. Pepe San Román's radio messages to the flagship that morning (April 19) poignantly describe the plight of the brigade.

5:00 A.M. "Do you people realize how desperate the situation is? Do you back us or quit? All we want is low jet air cover. Enemy has this support. I need it badly or cannot survive. . . ."

6:13 A.M. "Blue Beach [Girón] under attack by B-26. Where is promised air cover? Pepe."

7:12 A.M. "Enemy on trucks coming from Red Beach [Playa Larga] are right now three kilometers from Blue Beach. Pepe."

7:50 A.M. "We are fighting in the west flank of Blue Beach with tanks. Pepe."

8:15 A.M. "Situation critical left flank west Blue Beach. Need urgently air support. Pepe."

9:14 A.M. "Blue Beach under attack by two T-33s and artillery. Where the hell is jet cover? Pepe."

9:25 A.M. "Two thousand militia attacking Blue Beach from east and west. Need close air support immediately. Pepe."

9:55 A.M. "Can you throw something into this vital point in the battle? Anything. Just let jet pilots loose. Pepe."

Toward the end the messages carried the signals of despair: "In water. Out of ammo. Enemy closing in. Help must arrive in next hour." "Fighting on beach. Send all available aircraft now." [12]

Gray on the flagship urged San Román to continue fighting. Still hoping to receive the green light from Washington, he told Pepe: "Hold on, we're coming, we're coming with everything." The situation at the beachhead, however, was untenable. By midafternoon, Pepe radioed his last message: "Am destroying all my equipment and communications. Tanks are in sight. I have nothing to fight with. Am taking to the woods. I cannot wait for you." [13] Powerless and distraught, Gray and his colleagues listened to Pepe's heartbreaking farewell and cried.

Pepe dispatched messengers to Oliva and del Valle ordering them to disperse and go into the woods in small company units until reinforcements came from abroad. With his staff officers and forty-six men, Pepe headed into the Zapata swamps and awaited the promised support.

It never came. The brigade's last redoubts collapsed; the Bay of Pigs operation was over. Close to 1,200 men were captured by Castro; 114 died in combat or perished in the subsequent ordeal, and 60 were seriously wounded. It was a tragic end to a courageous undertaking, which if properly executed according to the original Operation Trinidad plan and decisively backed and followed through, might have averted the consolidation of communism in Cuba and changed the course of history.[14]

CHAPTER 11
In the Wake of Defeat

Most of the men of the brigade, either in small groups or alone, followed Pepe's orders and tried to hide in the wooded marshland or otherwise escape. In their desperate effort to survive, they had to eat grass and lizards and lick the dew off leaves in the morning. The impenetrable swamps, which had served as a buffer in the early stages of the invasion, now turned into a trap. Few succeeded in eluding capture by Castro's militia. But there were those who never made it to the prison complex.

At Girón, 135 of the brigade prisoners were forced into an airtight meat trucktrailer and ordered to pile in, one man atop the other, until the truck was packed with bodies. Then the heavy doors to the sealed and insulated cargo space were locked shut. The trip to Havana took eight hours. When the doors of the truck were unbolted, nine of the men lay lifeless on the floor, asphyxiated. Others made it because, in their frantic quest for air, they were able to scratch holes through the truck's aluminum walls with their belt buckles.

Some of the members of the brigade decided their best chance to escape was to head for the open sea in any sailboat or floating device they could find. They were hopeful that the U.S. destroyers that were cruising back and forth on the horizon would come to their aid. An evacuation attempt was indeed made, but it was hardly a Dunkirk. The conditions initially imposed by Washington to ensure plausible deniability (use of unmarked amphibious craft at night with crews in dungarees, and strict rules of engagement) severely hampered the humanitarian task.

The U.S. destroyers withdrew from the coast and were unable to spot and rescue several of the brigade escapee boats, including the one that carried the paratroop commander, Alejandro del Valle, and twenty-one of his colleagues. They drifted for fifteen days in the sweltering Gulf heat until they were salvaged by an American freighter. Only seven survived the ordeal of thirst, hunger, and exposure. Alejandro, a tall, muscular young man, had been able to endure the initial hardships of the journey. Grieved, however, by the agony of his weaker friends on board, he drew on his energy reserves and made a supreme effort to boat a large shark they had hooked. Halfway out of the water, the shark broke the line and fell back. Haggard and depressed, Alejandro didn't utter a word. He sat down and just stared at the sea. Next day, he was dead.

The fall of the beachhead and the capture or death of my brigade comrades had a devastating impact on me. Aboard the *Lake Charles,* together with my Operation Forty companions and a medical team, we remained near the theater of operations, unable to land or even to support or rescue our friends in need. Cryptic orders from the flagship, devoid of any clear rationale or explanation, kept us on standby some fifteen miles off the Bay of Pigs. At or close to 2:00 P.M. on April 19, the order to land finally came. Our ship veered to the left and sailed at full speed toward the beach. My companions and I, in combat gear, were pensive and tense. We knew that the situation was desperate and that in the absence of American support, our chances of success were virtually nil. Then, suddenly, something happened that brightened our prospects and lifted our spirits. Over the horizon we saw two U.S. Navy fighters leading the way. We thought they were providing air cover, but in fact they were conducting a reconnaissance mission. A few minutes later, our ship came to a halt. The order to disembark was countermanded. The "Last Stand of Girón" was virtually over.

Our trip back was long and dreary. The brigade had been crushed; our dreams were shattered. After the initial shock, our group spent many hours on deck reflecting on the disaster. Puzzling questions assaulted us. Why had Washington launched the Bay of Pigs operation if there was no determination to succeed? Why had the invasion been scaled down, emasculated, to such a degree that failure ceased to be a contingency and became an inevitable reality? Why hadn't the operation been coordinated with the resistance movement, and why had the vital air cover been denied?

We didn't know the reasons, but we could surmise the consequences. Some of us pointed to the severe loss of U.S. prestige and credibility resulting from the abandonment of a close ally and the appeasement of a dangerous foe; the unwillingness to stand up to communism ninety miles from U.S. shores; the inability to execute a not-too-complicated amphibious and airborne operation; the perceived perpetration of aggression without the vindication of triumph. Other members of our unit anticipated a major boost to Castro's influence after having beaten an invasion force organized, trained, supplied, and directed by "Yankee imperialism." Still others foresaw a stimulus to the USSR to complete the Sovietization of Cuba and to confront the United States in other parts of the world as well. Finally, our group pondered the loss of a unique opportunity to liberate Cuba without major international complications or risks. We now faced the task of overcoming the terrible blow inflicted on the Cuban underground, decimated by executions and mass arrests; on the remaining anti-Castro guerrillas, strangled in the Escambray mountains; and on the refugee community, demoralized by the defeat.

As we grappled with these troubling issues, another concern arose: we didn't know where we were going. The commanding officers had told us that we would be taken back to Nicaragua. However, after a day or two, the ship turned around and sailed toward the island of Vieques, off Puerto Rico. Then we learned of another change of plans . . . back to Nicaragua. At that point, a group of us became very suspicious, and started to fear that something sinister was being hatched. Determined not to take any chances, we. considered commandeering the ship ourselves. This idea was discarded when we received unequivocal assurances that we would disembark in Puerto Cabezas, Nicaragua, and then fly to the United States.

On our way to Puerto Cabezas, we turned on the radio and began to listen to the interrogation of the brigade prisoners in Havana. This was a media show staged by Castro to portray the liberation forces as a bunch of mercenaries and to induce them to vent their bitterness toward the United States. Offering the unique spectacle of a government head conducting a TV debate with prisoners who had come to overthrow him, Castro lectured, exhorted, challenged, and argued with the captives. At times he seemed magnanimous, as when he told the prisoners that he would try to convince the irate militiamen shouting *"Paredón!"*—"To the firing wall!"—that mass executions would "sully the revolution." Some of the prisoners applauded; a few, under the strain of defeat and intimidation, felt remorse and asked for forgiveness.

Most of the captives, however, held their own. Tony Varona's son Carlos spoke up bravely. "If you have so many people on your side," he pointedly asked Castro, "why don't you hold elections?" Fabio Freyre, a prominent sugar industrialist with a patrician bearing, defended his heritage and asserted his democratic beliefs. Felipe Rivero, connected with the family that owned the leading newspaper of Cuba, sparred for more than two hours with the ten members of the panel interrogating him. Pressed over and over to admit publicly that the Cuban Brigade was composed of mercenaries and cowards, Rivero answered sharply: "If you think that I am going to attack my comrades here because I am a foot from being shot, you are wrong. . . . We went on fighting knowing we were going to lose. We had resisted for five days— and you should know the history of No. 2 Battalion . . . under grenades, under the constant attack of the air force, under mortars. You will understand that at this moment the most that I can feel about being executed is sadness for my family, but it is not a thing that . . . terrifies me."[1]

At one point during the endless sessions, Castro singled out a black paratrooper, Tomás Cruz. Trying to exploit racial prejudice, Fidel asked Tomás: "You, Negro, what are you doing here?" Castro underscored the purported gains blacks had made under his regime and said that they were even allowed to go swimming with white men. Cruz coolly responded: "I don't have any complex about my color or my race. I have always been among the white people, and I have always been a brother to them. And I did not come here to go swimming."[2]

Perhaps the most moving statement came from my good friend Carlos Onetti, a young, spirited professional who had distinguished himself as a paratrooper in the battle of San Blas. Now, facing his inquisitors, he showed not only courage but eloquence. As recorded on the transcripts I have on file, Onetti stated: "Dr. Castro, I would like to explain to you the motive that brought us here. The motive was an ideal—the purest and worthiest ideal. We came to combat a despotic regime—communism; to establish a democratic system in our country; to restore the 1940 Constitution, free enterprise, and human rights. For all those principles we came to fight. We have been defeated and we accept the consequences. The most that we can now lose is our life, but those principles will live on forever."

Cheers and applause drowned out his words. Castro tried to turn the situation around with his piercing dialectics, and indeed scored some points. But he was not able to take full advantage of the propaganda offensive. His effort to coerce the prisoners into praising their captors was stymied. His attempt to discredit the brigade had failed.

When we returned to Puerto Cabezas, Nicaragua, the civilian leaders of the Cuban Revolutionary Council—Miró, Varona, and Maceo—were there to greet us. Their bloodshot eyes and pallid complexions revealed intense suffering, humiliation, and wrath. The CIA had kept them incommunicado at heavily guarded, shabby barracks at Opa-locka, Florida. They learned of the landing by chance when they turned on a portable radio they found in one of the rooms. CIA officers promised to fly them to the Bay of Pigs as soon as the local airport seized by the brigade was operational. Faced with contradictory reports and mysterious delays, the council leaders became very emotional and threatened to break loose.

At President Kennedy's behest, Berle and Schlesinger flew to Opa-locka on April 19 in the morning to tranquilize the council chiefs. Miró, grim and dignified, argued that with more pilots the battle could still be won. If not, he said, the men of the Cuban Revolutionary Council should be permitted to die with their troops on the beaches. The feisty Varona was more direct and confrontational. After asserting that they had been bypassed and deceived, he emphatically demanded reinforcements, air strikes, and transportation to the beaches. Then, clenching his fists in rage, he warned the Washington emissaries that his group would no longer tolerate being kept incommunicado. "We don't know whether we are your allies or your prisoners," he told Berle and Schlesinger. Regardless of surveillance, Varona added, "I plan to leave the barracks at noon to hold a press conference in Miami. Let them shoot me down if they dare."[3]

Apprised by Schlesinger of the explosive situation, Kennedy invited the council leaders to meet with him in Washington that afternoon. Looking "exceptionally drawn and tired," the President preempted all recriminations by assuming full responsibility for the failure. He praised the valor of the men of the brigade (among whom were sons and relatives of most of the council representatives) and shared their grief as a man who also had seen combat and lost a brother and a brother-in-law in the war. He reaffirmed his decision not to use American troops in light of the many fronts he had to protect, but indicated that American commitment to Cuban freedom stood firm.

As an immediate priority, the President asked the council chiefs to assist the U.S. government in its effort to rescue the men of the brigade who were still unaccounted for. That is why Miró, Varona, and Maceo had come to Puerto Cabezas. Their pilgrimage was bleak and painful. Every meeting with a survivor reopened emotional wounds and brought forth memories of their sons and other members of the brigade who had died in combat or been captured by Castro.

From Puerto Cabezas I flew to Florida. I rushed home to see my parents, who didn't know my whereabouts and feared the worst. It was very early in the morning; the house was dark and they were asleep. When I walked into their room and gently woke them up, they thought it was a dream. They had to touch me with their trembling hands to confirm that it was real. Only then did they give free rein to their emotions and weep. Tears of joy rolled down their cheeks, but they soon turned into tears of grief.

The family had taken a heavy toll during the liberation struggle. I learned through my parents that my cousin Ofelia had been arrested, and that her husband, Ñongo Puig, had been executed. His brother Rino, married to my cousin Ileana, remained in prison on the Isle of Pines along with my cousin Eddy Arango. They both had resisted their captors' brutality, and had suffered violent reprisals. In the case of Eddy, the situation was more serious. He started to develop symptoms of muscular atrophy, which fortunately receded over time.

The news of the Bay of Pigs landing on April 17 gave Eddy, Rino, and the other six thousand political prisoners on the Isle of Pines a shot of life. They suspected that the invasion had started when they heard machine-gun rattle and the boom of cannon on the 17th at dawn. A few minutes later, they saw one of the brigade's B-26 bombers take a dive at Castro's frigate *Baire,* anchored at the mouth of a river nearby. The pilot missed the target the first time as he dodged a barrage of artillery shells. But the second time he scored. The explosion of his rocket made the ship's stern leap out of the water and enveloped it with a mantle of black smoke.

The scene produced incredible commotion among the prisoners. They took out a small makeshift radio hidden in one of the galleries and listened to the first offshore bulletins on the invasion issued by Radio Swan. Shouts of *"Viva Cuba libre"* ("Long live free Cuba") resounded throughout the penitentiary as the inmates embraced one another and jumped with joy. The hour of liberation had finally struck—they thought. Some of the prison guards, who in the past had displayed abusive fanaticism, began to waver, fearing the imminent fall of the regime. One of them approached Eddy and discreetly said: "Remember we are all Cubans, and we have treated you well."

When Castro's air force sank two of the brigade's ships and the balance of the war started to tilt against the invaders, the guards changed their attitude and became vindictive. Fresh troops arrived and fired at the windows of the cells. Then a tarpaulin-covered truck with armed soldiers aboard screeched to a halt in front of the main gate. The soldiers began to unload their dreadful cargo— boxes of Canadian-made dynamite. The dynamite was deposited underneath the prison, in the tunnel to the central tower, and along the foundations. Demolition experts also arrived and proceeded to unload boxes of detonators, rolls of fuse, and other equipment required to set off explosions. As the prisoners subsequently verified and leaked to the outside world, this was not merely a defensive mechanism to paralyze and intimidate, it was a macabre device to blow up the entire penitentiary if the invasion advanced or if another one was launched.[4]

To compound my family's distress, we had lost touch with my grandmother's nephew Antonio Ramírez (a gallant exiled activist who was later caught inside Cuba and executed), and we had no information about my cousin Humberto Cortina. He had landed with the 2nd Battalion and fought at Playa Larga, but he disappeared after the beachhead fell. We didn't know whether he was dead or alive, captured or at large. Only weeks later did we learn that he had tried to escape together with four of his brigade companions. Wearing civilian clothes they had received from friendly farmers, they managed to reach the Covadonga sugar mill some twenty miles east of the Bay of Pigs. There they aroused suspicion and were stopped by armed militiamen.

"Who are you?" they asked Humberto. "I'm the son of old man Molina," he quickly responded. Unconvinced, the militiamen ordered him and his friends to raise their hands. When one of them started to frisk Humberto, my cousin hit him with his elbow and fired at him with a pistol he had concealed under his shirt. Two of Humberto's companions, Luis Morse, Jr., and Eduardo Lambert, also resisted, and shooting broke out. In a matter of seconds, Humberto found himself lying on the floor gushing blood. A hail of bullets hit both of his legs and severely injured the central nerves. He was taken to a military hospital in Matanzas province, where his mother, María, found him a few days later, scathed but unbowed.

Immediately after my return to Miami, my parents and I met with other members of the family at the home of my grandparents, the Cortinas. They all were eager to see me and listen to my tales. The subject of the Bay of Pigs debacle inevitably led to frenzied discussions and harsh condemnations. The interjections were so frequent and so loud that no one could be heard. Against a backdrop of anxieties and tribulations, the Bay of Pigs was the last straw that overwhelmed my relatives' patience and aplomb. My grandfather Cortina had to intervene to cool their passions and provide perspective. He had aged considerably since the Castro takeover, but remained lucid and impressive. In a deep, faltering voice he told us: "The Bay of Pigs is a dark chapter in the history of our ally. Military support did not match the valor of our boys. But this is not the time for remonstrances or laments." Reminding us that the battle for freedom was not yet over, he uttered these inspiring words, which I retained by dint of repetition: "Let us bind up our hearts, soothe our hurt, and resume the struggle. Only then can we say that those who are in prison have not been abandoned, and those who have fallen have not died in vain."

Cortina's plea flowed painfully from the heart. He had suffered immensely, but he stood up to the challenge and stoutly bore the brunt of adversity. I heeded his advice and promptly resumed my work with the Cuban Revolutionary Council. Although shaken by the Bay of Pigs experience, I renewed my commitment to the liberation of Cuba and maintained a flicker of hope.

After Miró and other council leaders had visited Guatemala, Nicaragua, and Vieques to round up the brigade survivors, they were summoned to Washington for a high-level parley. The meeting was held on May 2 in a private conference room at the Park Sheraton Hotel. Representing President Kennedy were Paul Nitze, then Assistant Secretary of Defense, and Richard Goodwin, a young White House presidential assistant who was in charge of Latin American affairs. The Cubans thought that the primary purpose of the meeting was to discuss new plans for the liberation of their country. The President's envoys, however, had a different agenda.

When Goodwin stated that he and Nitze were there at Kennedy's request to discuss the fate of the brigade prisoners and survivors, assistance to the families of the deceased, and relocation of the exiles who were swarming into Miami, the Cuban leaders exploded in anger. Before the interpreter could translate, they fired a string of rebukes in Spanish at their flustered interlocutors: "We didn't come here for this"; "We've been duped again"; "This is another betrayal"; "We want military support, not relocation."[5] Miró restored order and asked Goodwin to convey to the President that the Cuban Revolutionary Council was prepared to discuss the items on his agenda, but only after the liberation plans had been mapped out. Thereupon, Miró ended the discussion and informed the President's emissaries that he and his colleagues would return to Miami the following day.

Two hours after the meeting had concluded, Goodwin called to inform Miró that the President wanted to see him alone, but that Miró could bring his own interpreter if he so desired. The confidential meeting took place at the Oval Office on May 4. In attendance were the President himself, without aides, and Miró and his executive assistant, Ernesto Aragón, who acted as interpreter for both Miró and the President. Aragón, a reserved Cuban lawyer who for fourteen years had been a member of the board of directors of the National Bar Association of Cuba, was totally bilingual. During the period 1963–1967 he served as interpreter and translator under contract for the State Department.

According to Aragón's unpublished notes (a copy of which I have on file), the President greeted Miró Cardona warmly: "It's nice to see you again, Dr. Cardona." The President, looking chipper and relaxed, sat in a rocking chair between the two small sofas occupied by his guests. He lit a Havana cigar and commented that he was running out of them. Aragón did not miss the cue. "Mr. President, with all due respect, I hope you will exhaust your supply of Cuban cigars soon so that we can help you get some more." The President laughed heartily.

At Kennedy's request, Miró touched on the salient points covered in a memorandum in Spanish he handed to the President: recognition of the council as a Cuban government-in-exile; economic, technical, and military support; reinvigoration of the underground; and recruitment and training of Cuban military units to serve as the vanguard of a future liberation force.

The President listened carefully and promised to study Miró's memorandum as soon as it was translated. He did advance, however, some pertinent observations. Kennedy did not favor the formation of a Cuban government-in-exile because, lacking territory and coercive power, it could not exercise authority or command respect, as had occurred with the ineffectual Spanish government-in-exile. Basing his opinion on world war precedents, he thought that an organization such as the Cuban Revolutionary Council could have a major impact if backed and presented in a better light by Washington.

To that end, the President told Miró: "You and I should each designate a representative to discuss specific issues, forge consensus, and implement decisions. If our delegates fail to reach an accord, we should meet again." The President designated Richard Goodwin as his representative.

Regarding the proposed recruitment and training of Cuban military units, he was in favor, but wanted the process to be within the armed forces of the United States. "Having to depend on other countries to train the brigade for the Bay of Pigs operation proved to be a grave mistake," he affirmed. Kennedy also favored revitalizing the Cuban underground, but "details of this program and of the financial and technical support that the council will receive should be discussed by our representatives," he added.

The President ended the fifty-minute discussion by reiterating his full support of the Cuban Revolutionary Council, short of formal diplomatic recognition. He had established the channels for direct communications to and from the White House and had laid the groundwork for closer cooperation on several fronts. He expressed the hope that the new *entente* would further the cause of a free Cuba. Miró thanked the President and, accompanied by Goodwin, left the White House with a much-needed boost.

Despite the President's backing, Miró did not have an easy task ahead of him. His prestige had been severely tarnished by the Bay of Pigs fiasco. Vocal compatriots in Miami, inclined to blame Miró first, demanded his resignation. To reassert his authority, Miró restructured the council, broadened its base, and formed working committees focused on war, propaganda, and foreign affairs. He followed up with another private meeting with President Kennedy on July 13 and agreed with Goodwin on the parameters for various support programs. Implementation was slow, however, and Washington continued to bypass the council and secretly finance splinter groups.

Remembering the Bay of Pigs, Miró decided not to continue

assuming responsibility for actions or initiatives on Cuba not co-ordinated with and through the council. He so apprised the President in writing on September 11, and tendered his resignation. Kennedy averted the crisis with a letter under his signature dated September 13, which Miró kept in his personal files and never published. The President's letter states:

> Dear Dr. Miró Cardona:
>   I write to express confidence in your leadership of the Cuban Revolutionary Council. The United States government deeply admires the distinguished services you have already rendered to the cause of a free Cuba; and I hope you will continue to lead this fight until your country is liberated from the tyranny which has been imposed on it. I am sure that any problems arising from your relationship with the United States can be worked out in a spirit of mutual cooperation and common aspirations which lie behind all our efforts.

The framework of the Kennedy-Miró understanding was embodied in a document[6] dated October 31, 1961, which reaffirmed the council's leadership role, fixed the level of U.S. financial assistance, outlined the procedure to support Cuban underground and exile groups (including those not linked to the council), and provided for the training of Cuban military units. To provide impetus and substance to the tacit alliance, Washington assigned to Miró a seasoned Spanish-speaking military liaison, Colonel Johnson. He counseled the Cuban leader on intelligence and operational matters and helped improve communications between Washington and Miami.

In the wake of the Bay of Pigs and of the investigation that followed, the President was concerned not only about the Cuban Revolutionary Council and the underground. Fixed in his mind was the brooding presence of the members of the brigade—the vision, in the words of Arthur Schlesinger, "of the men on the beaches, who had gone off with such splendid expectations, who had fought so bravely and who now would be shot down like dogs or carted off to Castro's prisons."[7] That vision was to haunt the President for twenty months as if the prisoners involved were American hostages.

Castro well understood Kennedy's predicament and took advantage of it. On May 17, 1961, he declared: "History recounts that on a certain occasion the Spanish people exchanged Napoleon's soldiers against pigs. We, on this occasion, are going to be a little more delicate: we will exchange with imperialism the soldiers against tractors.'' This statement led to a series of negotiations with Castro which continued through the Missile Crisis and culminated with the release of the Bay of Pigs prisoners on December 23–24, 1962. Not all were freed, however. Five were executed (allegedly because of crimes committed under Batista), two died in prison, and seven had to serve up to twenty-five years in jail.

Kennedy instantly reacted to Castro's May 1961 proposal to exchange the prisoners for five hundred bulldozers (which Fidel claimed as ''indemnification for the material damages caused by the imperialist invasion''). The President asked Dr. Milton Eisenhower to form a Tractors for Freedom Committee, along with Mrs. Franklin D. Roosevelt and the labor leader, Walter Reuther, and to commence discussions with a delegation of ten prisoners Castro was sending to the United States.

The committee was formed but soon foundered amid a barrage of accusations, primarily from Republican legislators, who contended that the proposed deal was humiliating if not illegal, that it was tantamount to blackmail, and that it was dangerous (given the bulldozers' potential military use). Milton Eisenhower was angry at the President for maintaining the fiction that the whole affair was private, when in fact it had been instigated and abetted by the government. Weary and disappointed, Eisenhower and his colleagues bowed out, but not without trading epithets with the Cuban ruler. Fidel called Eisenhower a liar, Mrs. Roosevelt a silly old lady, and Reuther a labor baron controlling the lives of the workers. The committee retorted thus: ''Dr. Castro's latest proposal to the effect that a delegation of prisoners whom he holds captive under threat of death or long terms of imprisonment can be able to negotiate the conditions of their own freedom is ludicrous. It is further evidence of his brutality in cynically toying with the lives of the prisoners and that of the relatives.''[8]

In July 1961, a new committee was formed, the Cuban Families Committee, composed of parents and relatives of the Bay of Pigs prisoners. Headed by a former Cuban cattleman, Alvaro Sánchez, and supported by three dedicated lieutenants, Ernesto Freyre, Berta Barreto, and Enrique Llaca, the committee worked tirelessly but did not make much progress during its first six months of operation. So Fidel Castro decided in March 1962 to try the men of the brigade as war criminals.

The word spread rapidly within the Cuban refugee community and created consternation. We all feared that Castro would hand down death penalties, and we believed that the brigade chiefs and the sons of the exile leaders were especially at risk. Miró and the other members of the council had not participated in any of the prisoner negotiations. They were in a very delicate position, having to prosecute the war against the Cuban regime without jeopardizing the possible release of the captives. They had opted, therefore, not to get involved in the proposed exchange. This infuriated the members of the Families Committee, who expected the council's endorsement, and displeased the anti-Castro die-hards, who demanded an outright rejection.

Faced now with kangaroo-court proceedings and possible executions, the council could not remain aloof. Miró, Varona, and I visited many ambassadors in Washington, including the Vatican envoy, and requested their good offices. We asked not for clemency, but for the strict application of the Geneva Convention on prisoners of war to forestall the mock trial. The Foreign Affairs Minister of the Dominican Republic, José Bonilla Atiles, pleaded our case before the Organization of American States and obtained a favorable resolution.

The Cuban leaders then requested a meeting with President Kennedy. They anticipated mass executions in Cuba and wanted the U.S. government to exert more international pressure on Castro to avert them. Unable to see the Cubans, the President referred them to his Special Assistant for National Security, McGeorge Bundy. The meeting was held at the White House on March 28, the day before the commencement of the trial. Nervous and distraught, the exile leaders expected from the White House diligence and compassion. Bundy was polite, but blunt, and underscored Washington's constraints in the absence of diplomatic relations with Cuba. Perceiving chilly indifference, Varona vented his wrath: "If you allow Castro to execute the Bay of Pigs prisoners, their blood will forever stain the White House!" The meeting with Bundy ended on this sour note.

Varona was still livid when he returned to the Manger Annapolis Hotel, where I was waiting. Miró was quiet and melancholy, as if resigned to the prisoners' lot. Asked by the press to comment on the impending trial, he slumped in his chair and penned this brief statement: "Unable to assume the defense of the men of the brigade, I send them my warmest salute. Among them is my son. I stand by him with pride. May he accept his fate with dignity. It's a privilege to suffer and die for our homeland. God bless you all!''

Meanwhile, at the Príncipe Castle in Havana, where the prisoners had been confined, the largest mass trial in Cuban history was about to start. As the men were being led to the courtyard, a fight broke out when a militia struck one of the prisoners. Two of his inmates who came to his defense were bayoneted, and others were hit with rifle butts. A bloody riot seemed inevitable. A captain of Castro's army rushed to the brigade chiefs, San Román and Oliva, and beseeched them to control their men. San Román bellowed: *"Brigada, atención!"* Every prisoner stood still, eyes to the front, arms to the sides, heels together. Then Oliva addressed them: "Soldiers, maintain order and keep quiet during the proceedings. We will have time to shout 'Long live free Cuba!' when we face the firing squad."

This incident galvanized the brigade and restored *esprit de corps*. It also served to thwart Castro's effort to divide the prisoners and force them to admit their guilt and denigrate the United States. The tribunal tried everything—threats, enticements, forged documents, incriminating testimonies—but it didn't work. All of the prisoners declined the services of the court-appointed defense counsel, and most abstained from declaring. Restless and angry, the president of the tribunal kept on asking, row by row, anyone who had a statement to make, to stand up. The prisoners remained seated. After a long period of suspense, a tall Negro in one of the back rows, Luis González Lanlonry, broke away from the group and raised his hand. Castro's presiding officer pointed to him with an air of triumph. "Yes, stand up. What do you have to say?" "I want to go to the bathroom," the prisoner responded as his inmates roared with laughter.

The tragicomedy ended when the prosecutor ratified his charges that the prisoners had committed crimes against the integrity and stability of the nation, and asked for the most severe punishment, from death to life imprisonment to twenty years in jail. Then the "defense" counsel rose to speak. He called his "clients" cowards, traitors, and mercenaries, parroted some of Fidel's venomous tirades, and acknowledged that it was difficult for him to perform his duties as a defense counsel because he was a revolutionary and the defendants' guilt had been amply proved. He concluded his ninety-minute "defense" by asking the tribunal to render a "just and generous sentence."

The tribunal adjourned to deliberate, but Castro didn't bother with formalities. Four days later, he himself announced the verdict to the brigade chiefs. He told them privately that all of the prisoners were guilty, but that the revolution had spared their lives and sentenced them to thirty years in jail. However, since they were so valuable to the Yankees, he had placed on the brigade a ransom of $62 million. For the chiefs he demanded a payment of $500,000 each, and for the rest of the brigade, divided into three groups, the ransom would range from $25,000 to $100,000. To "sell" the deal, Castro decided to send to the United States sixty of the most seriously wounded prisoners. He reasoned, with keen if diabolic logic, that by parading the injured veterans before the American people he could sway the United States to support the humanitarian rescue and forget the iniquitous blackmail.

One of the most moving scenes I have ever witnessed was the arrival in Miami on April 14, 1962, of the sixty scarred warriors of the Bay of Pigs. Waiting at the airport was a tremulous crowd of twenty thousand parents, relatives, and friends who for hours braved the scorching sun to embrace their loved ones. As the silvery plane slid down, the whistled "Colonel Bogey March," the theme song of *The Bridge on the River Kwai*, flowed rhythmically from the loudspeakers, and a color guard carrying the American and Cuban flags and the banner of the Cuban Brigade stood at attention waiting for the veterans to appear.

One by one they came . . . this man with a leg off, that one with an arm gone, the other with a patch over an injured eye. Each one saluted the flags, and with dignified bearing, walked slowly toward a sea of fluttering handkerchiefs held by the teary crowd, as "The Colonel Bogey March" whistled on.

Among the wounded prisoners who arrived was my cousin Humberto. Our entire family in exile was there to greet him. But there was one conspicuous absentee—Humberto's father. He had died when the news came out that the wounded prisoners were coming. He wanted to see his son so badly that his weakened heart failed.

Humberto was taken to the hospital immediately upon arrival. He could hardly walk with braces and was in pain. As a result of his bullet wounds, the central nerves of both legs were almost gone. He needed neurosurgery, but that had to wait. After a few days of rest at home, Humberto embarked with three of his wounded companions on a fund-raising mission to several cities of the United States. They and the rest of the group considered themselves prisoners of war until all of the members of the brigade were set free. And they pledged to return to the Príncipe Castle if their negotiations failed.

The leader of the wounded prisoners was Enrique "Harry" Ruíz-Williams, a sturdy, black-haired forty-one-year-old mining engineer who had fought bravely with the Heavy Gun Battalion. He had been blown into the air by an enemy shell in Girón and hit by more than seventy pieces of shrapnel. Both of his feet were smashed, and he had a hole near his heart and a large one in his neck. Shuttling between Miami, Washington, and New York, this quiet, unassuming hero worked feverishly with the Cuban Families Committee and with the newly organized National Sponsors Committee, represented by Richard Cardinal Cushing, General Lucius Clay, Ed Sullivan, and Princess Lee Radziwill, President Kennedy's sister-in-law.

These committees started to raise funds and made significant headway, but the decisive behind-the-scenes push came from the Attorney General, Robert Kennedy. He was in touch with Harry Ruíz-Williams almost on a daily basis and masterminded many of the critical moves, including the selection of James Donovan, a shrewd lawyer who negotiated the exchange in West Berlin of the Soviet spy Rudolph Abel and the U-2 pilot Francis Gary Powers. After several months of hard and vexing bargaining, Donovan and the Families Committee reached an agreement with Castro which called for the payment of $53 million worth of food and drugs. Since the total pledges received by the committees at the time fell far short of that amount, Bobby Kennedy personally enlisted the support of the Pharmaceutical Manufacturers Association and of several baby-food companies, obtained a favorable tax ruling for them, and secured the balance of the contributions to clinch the deal.

Donovan choked up when he saw the prisoners lining up to board the planes for Miami. "It was like the slave trade," he remarked to a reporter. "All they lacked was the chains." He was less lugubrious when he bid farewell to Castro and signed a required receipt for the prisoners. Fidel was jovial and relaxed, puffing on a long cigar surrounded by militiamen. Teasing the Cuban ruler, Donovan said in a loud voice, "You know, Premier, I have been thinking of all the good I have been doing for the people of Cuba these past weeks. I have relieved you of almost twelve hundred liabilities and I also have been helping the children, the sick, the poor and the elderly among the Cuban people. I think that when the next election is held I'm coming back and run against you. I think I can win." Castro took a long puff on his cigar and replied with a puckish smile, "You know, doctor, I think you may be right. So there will be no elections."[9] The two men shook hands, and Donovan flew back to the United States.

December 23, 1962, was a memorable and happy day for the Cuban community in Miami. On that day the freed brigade prisoners arrived en masse at the Dinner Key Auditorium which was filled to capacity with families and friends. When the veterans entered the hall, the crowd broke and rushed forward. Their tears and screams were seen and heard by millions of Americans watching on television. One of those who was particularly moved and relieved was the President of the United States.

Four days later, on December 27, he invited the brigade chiefs to his villa in Palm Beach. There, flanked by two resplendent ladies, Jacqueline Kennedy and her sister, Princess Lee Radziwill, he greeted Manuel Artime, Pepe San Román, Erneido Oliva, Roberto San Román, and Harry Ruíz-Williams. It was a friendly and informal meeting without presidential assistants, save the press secretary, Pierre Salinger, who was present part of the time. Harry served as translator. After a cordial exchange of pleasantries, the President, turning serious, raised the subject of the Bay of Pigs and told the brigade commanders that he was sorry for what had happened.

As revealed by Pepe San Román and confirmed by his companions, the President explained to them why he did not provide further support to the brigade. Never before had he been so explicit on this sensitive issue. After the April 15 (D-2) air raid, Kennedy disclosed, the Soviet government had threatened to attack West Berlin if the United States continued to launch raids on Cuba and backed the invasion. The President described his agonizing dilemma: support the Bay of Pigs operation and risk a Soviet confrontation in Berlin which could touch off a large-scale war, or maintain world peace and risk the defeat of fourteen hundred men in Cuba. It was a difficult and painful decision, the President emphasized, but the priority was clearly world peace.

The brigade chiefs manifested no anger or resentment. They did not question the President's assumptions. Indeed, they appreciated his candor and efforts to free them, and they posed for photographs with him. Later they informed the press that the President would come to Miami on Saturday, December 29, to inspect the brigade in the Orange Bowl. At that ceremony, he would be presented with the brigade's most treasured possession:

the banner which had flown over the command post at Playa Gi-rón for three days and had been preserved by a soldier who suc-ceeded in obtaining diplomatic asylum.

The ceremony at the Orange Bowl stirred the spirits of thou-sands in the stadium. The members of the brigade, clad in khaki uniforms, and their families and friends, waving flags, poured out their hearts when the white convertible carrying the President and the First Lady glided over the field. After the bands had played the national anthems of the United States and Cuba, Pepe San Román read his opening remarks and then turned toward the President and said: "Mr. President, the men of the 2506 Brigade give you their banner—we temporarily deposit it with you for your safekeeping."

The President unfurled the flag, stepped to the microphone, and replied: "I want to express my great appreciation to the bri-gade for making the United States the custodian of this flag." He paused, and then his voice soared with emotion. "I can assure you that this flag will be returned to this brigade in a free Ha-vana." [10]

Forty thousand men and women of all ages rose and clapped wildly. Shouts of *"Guerra! Guerra!"* ("War! War!") and *"Liber-tad! Libertad!"* rocked the stadium for several minutes. I looked around, and few eyes were dry. The members of the brigade and the Cuban exiles at large had put behind the Bay of Pigs debacle, and, roused by the President's assurance, had renewed their vows.

CHAPTER 12

The Battle of the OAS

After the Bay of Pigs, Washington attempted to neutralize or contain the destabilizing activities of the Castro regime by promoting economic development and social reforms elsewhere in the hemisphere. The vehicle used was President Kennedy's Alliance for Progress. The strategy pursued was to "avoid other Cubas by attacking the root causes of communism: poverty, hunger, and social injustice."

Even though these were not the causes that catapulted Castro into power, few could quarrel with the lofty goals of the Alliance for Progress, which was to be fueled by extraordinary levels of foreign aid ($20 billion over ten years). The Alliance, however, was a long-term development program requiring business confidence to stimulate investments and political stability to consolidate democracy. It could not succeed if the Castro regime remained free to spread subversion leading to Communist regimes or military dictatorships. Defensive actions had to be taken to forestall or curtail externally financed and orchestrated violence. Otherwise, the Alliance would fail to meet its grand expectations and degenerate into a futile race to see whether dollars poured in by the United States could outpace dollars taken out by frightened Latin Americans.

Isolating Castro was a first step, but not the end solution, we pointed out to Washington. The Soviets, in our opinion, would not let their prized possession wither on the vine. Moreover, if Castro was allowed to remain in power, we contended, he would be viewed by many as the real father of the Alliance for Progress. After all, he had urged the United States at the economic conference held in Buenos Aires in May 1959 to grant Latin America $30 billion in economic aid over a decade. What was then derided by Washington as ridiculous was now essentially being offered as a socially inspired hemispheric venture, as a moral equivalent of the Marshall Plan. Fear of Castro, however, was perceived by cynics to the south as the driving force behind the massive economic aid. If left to their own devices, why would they want to terminate the fear that generated the aid?

We warned, therefore, that if the Alliance for Progress was not linked to an Alliance for Freedom, if economic aid was not inextricably tied to a collective commitment to eradicate communism from this hemisphere, neutralists and demagogues in Latin America would most likely court the radicals, take the dollars, and thank Fidel.

In diplomatic affairs, Cuban exile leaders were more assertive and less naive than in military endeavors. We did not question the United States' ability to wage war—hence our tendency, prior to the Bay of Pigs, to accept action plans without probing and to follow marching orders without doubting. But in the subtle and deceptive field of realpolitik, we were less sanguine about Washington's deftness. So when diplomatic strategies on Cuba were discussed, we grilled, we challenged, and we frequently differed.

To address multilaterally the threat posed by Castro communism, we strongly believed that it was necessary to energize the Organization of American States (OAS), the oldest existing regional organization and military alliance in the world. Its origin goes back to the 1826 Congress of Panama, which tried to crystallize the continental union dreamed by the liberator Simón Bolívar. That union was bolstered in 1947 with the adoption of the Inter-American Treaty of Reciprocal Assistance (the Rio Treaty), which obligates member states to repel any act of aggression (effected by an armed attack or otherwise) against the territory or the political independence of any American state. It also calls for collective measures, ranging from the breaking of diplomatic and economic relations to the use of armed force, to meet any extracontinental or intracontinental conflict, or any other fact or situation that might endanger the peace of the Americas.

The Rio Treaty, in essence, ratified and expanded the Monroe Doctrine (1823), which warned that this continent was not to be considered open to future colonization by any European power.

That doctrine ceased to be only a unilateral policy of the United States and became a multilateral commitment of the OAS—indeed, the cornerstone of the regional alliance.

Faced in 1954 with a pro-Communist government in Guatemala, the OAS, led by John Foster Dulles, adopted the so-called Caracas Declaration, which states that the Communist domination or control of an American state constitutes a threat to the peace of the hemisphere requiring the adoption of the collective measures stipulated in the Rio Treaty. Recognizing the totalitarian and expansionist designs of international communism, the American states agreed jointly to take appropriate defensive action in the event that any country in this hemisphere fell under Marxist-Leninist rule, regardless of whether there had been any overt Soviet intervention.

Despite the explicitness of these regional commitments, the United States, prior to the Bay of Pigs, had been unable to rally the support necessary to enforce them in the case of Communist Cuba. This became evident during the seventh OAS meeting of foreign ministers held in Costa Rica in August 1960. Castro had already intervened in the internal affairs of several Latin American countries, and Khrushchev had astonished the world by threatening to use, in "figurative" terms, "Soviet artillerymen to support the Cuban people with rocket fire."

Castro and his Foreign Minister publicly accepted Russia's potential military support and stated that Cuba was not bound by the Rio Treaty, characterized by them as an instrument of U.S. domination. They described the OAS as Washington's "Ministry of Colonies" and made mockery of any possible sanction. The United States chose not to meet the challenge directly, because it did not want to bully Castro. With hindsight, this was a mistake, since leaders have to lead to command respect and attract a following. Peru was the country that eventually convoked the Costa Rica meeting of foreign ministers to address the Cuban situation and the Soviet threat.

Several Cuban exiles and I were asked by the Cuban Democratic Revolutionary Front to attend the Costa Rica meeting. Our mission was to denounce the communization of Cuba, spurred by Castro's betrayal, and to call for collective action pursuant to applicable OAS treaties and agreements. Armed with special reporters' credentials issued by three Cuban newspapers in exile, we obtained the necessary visas and left Miami on a direct LACSA flight to San José. As our plane took off, a hurricane lashed the area. Lightning sparked a darkened sky and rain fell in torrents. These inauspicious signs foreboded trouble for our delegation.

When we arrived in Costa Rica, an immigration official with a stolid gaze and a bushy mustache placed us under investigation. (We later learned that he was a Castro sympathizer.) After a perfunctory interrogation, he informed us that we would not be permitted to stay in the country because the authorities feared that we would create disturbances. Our appeal was denied on the spot, and we were ordered to return to Miami on the same flight that had brought us to San José. The police escorted us to the plane. The door was closed and the crew started to prepare for takeoff. We were unaware that on the way back the flight was scheduled to stop in Havana.

In the meantime, friends and supporters at the airport who had learned of our predicament were making every effort to rescue us. One of them, "Che" Rojo del Río, an Argentine who had fought with Castro in the Sierra Maestra and had subsequently defected, worked at the airport and had access to the control tower. He called the pilot and asked him to alert us and allow us to flee at the end of the runway. As the plane started to taxi, the chief of the National Guard and several aides appeared on the scene. They signaled the pilot to stop the plane and asked us to descend. On the personal guarantee of Don Ricardo Castro Beche, the director of the leading newspaper in Costa Rica, we were finally allowed to enter the country. The following day the *Miami Herald* headlined our saga "EXILES HAVE CLOSE CALL." The story began: "Three exiled Cuban journalists, all known foes of the Fidel Castro regime, almost got sent to Havana by Costa Rican officials. . . ."[1]

The San José meeting commenced with high hopes of a rapprochement with Castro. The Foreign Minister of Peru set the tone. He said that the conference would be conducted with "absolute neutrality and a spirit of conciliation." He attributed the Caribbean tensions to economic factors rather than to political ideologies. He was more concerned about frictions between Cuba and the United States than about Communist penetration or Soviet threat. He praised the economic and social reforms implemented by Castro and invoked the Gospel of Saint Luke as he prayed for harmony and prudence to prevail.

U.S. Secretary of State Christian Herter tried to put the Cuban situation in perspective. He accused Castro of falsifying the democratic ideals of the Cuban revolution, of laying the foundations of a Communist regime, and of fostering Soviet intervention in this hemisphere. The speech was a well-documented but emotionless lawyer's brief lacking rhetorical flourishes to rouse the Latins. It censured Castro but failed to take a firm stand against the Soviets and to outline a meaningful course of action to impede their direct involvement in Cuba.

Castro's Minister of Foreign Affairs, Raúl Roa, a sardonic intellectual showman, displayed sharp dialectics and wit when he delivered his acerb anti-American invective. He said that Cuba had come to the meeting not as the accused, but as the prosecutor. He charged the United States with more than fifty acts of aggression and intervention since the start of the century. He rhetorically asked how the United States could teach democracy to Cuba when it had failed to resolve its own atrocious racial inequities. He ridiculed Herter's allusion to his (Roa's) alleged Marxist slogans by reciting some of Martí's admonitions about American expansionism and lust for power. After each quote, Roa challenged Herter to name the author as he chanted with rhythmic staccato: "It was not Karl Marx; it was José Martí. It was not Nikita Khrushchev; it was José Martí." Roa concluded his tirade by stating that Cuba stood ready to resolve its differences with Washington on a bilateral basis, but reserved the right to receive Soviet military support in the event of aggression.

Roa's speech made a strong impact. His audience included not only the foreign ministers gathered in San José, but the masses in Latin America, who enjoyed the blistering sarcasm and defiance directed against the "Colossus of the North." Herter's rebuttal was weak. Some of the ministers aligned with the United States were concerned lest the weakness be perceived as paralyzing guilt or fear to confront the Soviets.

Our group of Cuban exiles huddled and decided to counterattack. Eric Agüero Montoro, who had been Castro's first Deputy Foreign Minister, and José Ignacio Rasco, Fidel's classmate and founder of the Cuban Christian Democratic Movement, met with several foreign ministers and provided unusual insights into Castro's personality and secret plans. The rest of us took a full page ad in the leading newspapers of Costa Rica and replied to Roa's diatribes. We stated that Castro's emissary did not represent Cuba, but a regime that relied on deceit and force because it feared open debate and free elections. We described in detail the totalitarian model that Castro was building and denounced his plans to incorporate Cuba into the Soviet bloc. On behalf of freedom-loving

Cubans, we asked the OAS to take collective action against the Castro Communist regime in accordance with existing treaties. Failure to act promptly and vigorously, we said, would only invite subversion or aggression and open the doors of this hemisphere to Soviet imperialism.

Our public statement, which incensed Roa and his followers, appeared to stiffen the spine of a few of the ministers who were wavering. Still, there were not enough votes to pass an anti-Castro resolution, and a Venezuelan proposal condemning *both* intra- and extracontinental intervention (i.e., the United States and the Soviet Union) was gathering strength. If that proposal was adopted, the United States would be placed in the same dock as the USSR and would leave the conference as a culprit. Roa was ecstatic at the possibility of accusing the United States of "economic aggression" for having suspended the Cuban sugar quota. There were rumors that Fidel, confident that he could sway the crucial votes, was going to make a grand appearance at the conference. A member of the Guatemalan delegation dropped us a note saying: "If 'Gillette' [Fidel] comes, the 'Napoleon of Central America' [Guatemalan President Idígoras] will be here to confront him." The situation seemed to be getting out of hand. We feared that, absent strong U.S. leadership, the meeting would turn into a Latin round robin of swagger and bluster.

Washington finally reacted and flexed its muscle. The presidents of Venezuela and Peru promptly replaced their pro-Castro foreign ministers as heads of their respective delegations. All of the American states represented at the conference, save Cuba, approved a broad resolution condemning Soviet intervention and totalitarianism of any kind in this hemisphere. Roa and his aides did not stay for the signing. As they abruptly left the conference chanting provocative slogans, a shout of "Cuba *SÍ,* Comunismo NO!" rocked the theater. It was our delegation responding to Roa and waving a large Cuban flag that the anti-Castro student leader Alberto Muller had hidden in one of the balconies.

The Declaration of San José preserved the integrity of the inter-American system, but did not really address the Communist threat. In order to achieve a general consensus (as if the OAS had to be ruled by near-unanimity), the declaration was watered down and did not explicitly condemn, or even mention, the Cuban regime. This emboldened Castro, who proceeded to tear up the declaration at a mass rally, confirm his acceptance of Soviet support, and heap ridicule and disdain on the OAS.

Bearing in mind the results of the San José meeting and Castro's reaction, Washington did not pursue formal consultations with the OAS prior to the Bay of Pigs. The United States, however, was in close touch with most of the governments in the hemisphere. As noted earlier, many of them privately favored, or were inclined to accept, prompt, decisive action against Castro backed by the United States. They preferred, however, not to involve the OAS at the outset—before the fact—so as not to give Castro the opportunity to stir up trouble in their respective countries.

The first important inter-American conference following the Bay of Pigs took place in Punta del Este, Uruguay, on August 5–17, 1961. The purpose of the meeting was to launch the Alliance for Progress, hailed as a great revolutionary venture. Che Guevara, who was representing Cuba, argued the case for the coexistence of competing revolutions. Some of the Latin American delegates favored the inclusion of Cuba in the Alliance and were instrumental in toning down references to representative democracy, elections, private property, and free enterprise. Heartened by a climate of compromise and rapprochement, Guevara asserted during the final session that the Alliance charter indeed recognized and included a nation with different characteristics from the rest. He was, of course, referring to Socialist Cuba.

If left unchallenged, Guevara's statement would have nullified Washington's official policy of isolating Castro. Douglas Dillon, head of the American delegation, left no room for misinterpretation. He firmly replied that the United States did not, and would not, recognize the permanence of the current regime in Cuba. To do so, he added, would be to betray the thousands of Cuban patriots who were still waiting and fighting for the freedom of their country.

Despite Dillon's categorical statement, endorsed by the majority of the delegates with prolonged applause, Richard Goodwin, the White House Special Assistant on Latin America, met privately with Guevara. Although described as a casual social encounter when it leaked to the press, the confidential meeting raised serious doubts about the United States' anti-Castro stance.

Shortly after the Goodwin parley, President Arturo Frondizi of Argentina also decided to hold a meeting with Guevara shrouded in secrecy. On August 18, 1961, Frondizi instructed his military aide to go to Don Torcuato airport and await the arrival of the plane *Bonanza,* Mat CX-AKP, which was expected to land at 10:30 A.M. "You will see someone descend from the plane whom you are going to recognize," he told his puzzled aide. "Escort him to your car and bring him to Olivos [the presidential residence]. That man must talk to no one."[2]

According to the records of Frondizi's mediation efforts, the President met with the guerrilla leader for more than one hour. He told Guevara that he saw the need for a comprehensive understanding between Latin America and the United States, without excluding or isolating Cuba. And he stressed that only through social, economic, and cultural development, and not through violence, could Latin America resolve its problems.

Guevara, who respected Frondizi's intellectual acumen, did not mince words. He drew an "explosive" picture of Latin America and indicated that it would soon become "another Vietnam." Only through "armed struggle," he postulated, could the countries in this hemisphere liberate themselves from "imperialistic" influence. Guevara conceded that Cuba wished to remain within the inter-American system, as he had told Richard Goodwin, but reiterated that small and poor countries could not eschew the "path of violence."

The meeting ended with no agreement, but on a cordial note. Guevara had a *bife* lunch with Mrs. Frondizi, visited an ailing aunt in Buenos Aires, and then left for Brazil, where he was solemnly decorated by President Jânio Quadros. When the guerrilla maverick arrived in Havana, he was beaming with joy. He referred to the growing support that Socialist Cuba was receiving from leading Latin American governments and declared on television that plans to isolate the Cuban regime would not materialize.

Despite Guevara's brutal frankness in Buenos Aires and the political upheaval that the secret meeting had set off when it leaked to the press, President Frondizi continued to oppose Washington's plan to hold an OAS meeting to condemn and isolate Castro. In concert with Brazil, he had proposed a regional conference with the presidents of the "big powers" (the United States, Argentina, Brazil, and Mexico) to establish a live-and-let-live understanding that would set the ground rules for peaceful coexistence with Castro. Frondizi reviewed the proposal with UN Ambassador Adlai Stevenson in Buenos Aires in July 1961, and followed this up with a series of discussions in the United States which culminated in a December 1961 summit with President Kennedy in Palm Beach.

The Argentine head of state was emphatic and direct. Alone with Kennedy, he told him: "The United States is a reality, but so is Cuba with Soviet help. A negotiation is necessary, but no American statesman can [effectively] undertake it. There are basically two avenues for the negotiation: Latin America through the big powers of the region, or the Soviet Union."[3] Kennedy, who was pressing for the isolation of Castro, did not reject Frondizi's proposal. After having dismissed his State Department interpreter, he asked the Argentine leader to send him a memorandum, but not through the embassy or the State Department. "I want to receive it directly," he said. Frondizi was equally secretive himself. When an inquisitive functionary asked him on the plane what he had discussed with Kennedy, Frondizi casually replied, "Trivialities."[4]

In the meantime, Colombia's Minister of Foreign Affairs, Julio César Turbay Ayala, also developed a plan to pave the way for the return of the Castro regime to the inter-American fold. In order to achieve broad consensus, he discussed the proposal with twelve Latin American governments and reviewed it in Brazil with Ambassador Adlai Stevenson. On his way back to Colombia, the commercial airline carrying Turbay Ayala was mysteriously hijacked to Havana, where Castro regaled him with a succulent dinner and a stimulating discussion. Just before leaving Cuba several hours later, Turbay Ayala reportedly stated to the press that "in a somewhat curious way, international relations with Cuba have improved. Dr. Castro is a very sincere, tranquil, and amiable man. He did not indulge in Soviet banalities; he spoke as one man to another, very frankly, very courteously." This statement unleashed a political storm in Colombia, which had been the target of repeated Castro Communist interventions. President Alberto Lleras Camargo was compelled to disavow his Minister of Foreign Affairs and to replace him.

While Frondizi and Turbay Ayala were carrying out their diplomatic missions, we of the Revolutionary Council in Miami were concerned because there was no indication that Castro was sincere in his peaceful overtures. In fact, our intelligence reports showed increasing Communist military and subversive activities and deeper Soviet involvement in Cuba. We needed a Latin American leader who would denounce Castro's dilatory tactics, reject appeasement, and champion our cause. That leader was Manuel Prado, President of Peru. He came from a distinguished family of statesmen who had supported Cuba in her wars of independence. Now was his turn to back her in a new liberation struggle that involved the Americas. He was prepared and eager to help.

Tony Varona and I, along with other Cuban exiles, met with Prado in Miami in September 1961. He was on his way to Washington on a state visit. We gave him a personal letter from my grandfather Cortina, who had honored him in Havana years back, and reviewed a brief outline of our position, calling for collective action against the Castro regime under the Rio Treaty and recognition of our belligerence.

President Prado didn't need much coaching or prodding. He feared, as we did, that efforts to placate Castro or to reach an accommodation with his regime would only serve to give him time to Sovietize the island and convert it into a launching pad from which to subvert the continent. Firm in his beliefs, Prado went to Capitol Hill and stated before a joint session of Congress: "The moment is of utmost gravity. Grave moments call for grave decisions—bold action, courage, and faith. . . . Communism is the negation of the Americas, of its traditions and of its mission in the future. It must be expelled from the Americas!"

President Prado was cordially received in Washington, but his sense of urgency and dogged determination to meet the Cuban threat head-on was not shared by the White House and the State Department. They cautioned him not to recognize a Cuban government-in-exile and not to press at that time for collective action against Castro, since such a proposal could split the OAS. Prado was not dissuaded by this wait-and-see attitude. He was not willing to grant a veto power to the weakest links of the regional chain just because they ostensibly represented a large majority of the Latin American population. When he privately met in Washington with a few of my colleagues, he told them that Peru would support our cause and call for sanctions against the Castro regime under the Rio Treaty. He fulfilled his promise, and on October 16, 1961, his OAS ambassador filed a formal petition to start the process.

I was then promptly dispatched to Washington as Special Representative of the Cuban Revolutionary Council to the OAS. My mission was to support the Peruvian initiative and assist in mustering the votes necessary for collective action against Castro. Despite the fact that I did not represent an established government, I met with all of the ambassadors to the OAS, save Castro's emissary. My surnames helped to open doors, since many of the ambassadors had met or heard of my forebears. These contacts provided valuable information and enabled me to gain a better understanding of the diversity and complexity of the issues involved. With these insights, I tried to temper my impatience—not always successfully—and to remind some of my single-minded compatriots that Cuba, though important, was not the navel of the universe, and that Castro Communism, though alarming, was not the only problem facing Latin America.

After a quick survey of the situation, I realized that the Peruvian proposal had been blocked by several powerful countries (Argentina, Brazil, Chile, Ecuador, and Mexico), which were fostering coexistence with Communist Cuba. The hard-line anti-Castro governments, on the other hand, seemed divided and confused in the absence of clear signals from Washington, which was intent on reconciling differences and striving for near-unanimity.

Working jointly with friendly diplomats and several compatriots experienced in foreign affairs, including the former Cuban ambassador to Washington, Dr. Guillermo Belt, and the former Cuban ambassador to the UN, Dr. Emilio Núñez Portuondo, we were instrumental in forming a monolithic anti-Castro group composed of Peru and countries directly threatened by Communist subversion: Central America and Panama (known as CAP). To broaden the support base, we convinced the Peruvian ambassador to merge his initiative into a revised Colombian proposal, which was backed by Venezuela and other Caribbean countries. Colombia added considerable weight because its President, Alberto Lleras Camargo, was an illustrious statesman and intellectual, and its Foreign Minister, Dr. José Joaquín Caicedo Castilla, was a renowned jurist and foremost authority on OAS affairs.

In an unprecedented move, the Inter-American Peace Committee of the OAS invited us to appear before its members and present evidence of Castro's violations of human rights, interventions in the internal affairs of other countries, and subservience to the Soviet bloc. Our comprehensive and factual reports, as well as those submitted by Luis V. Manrara representing the "Truth About Cuba Committee," Fernando García Chacón on behalf of the Student Revolutionary Directorate, and Tulio Díaz Rivera for the economic sectors in exile, served to substantiate some of the findings that ultimately led to Castro's indictment.

We progressed in securing most of the votes required to convoke a meeting of foreign ministers pursuant to the Rio Treaty. But what finally gave impetus to our plan was Castro's stunning speech of December 1, 1961, in which he claimed that he had been a Marxist-Leninist since his student days and that he had concealed his ideology to enlist the support of the Cuban people and take power. He climaxed his speech with the cry "I am a

Marxist-Leninist, and I will be one until the last days of my life."

There is still much speculation about the whys and where-fores of Castro's cynical confession. Was he simply vaunting his deception and defying the inter-American system, or was he pub-licly pressuring the Soviets to solidify their commitment to a Communist Cuba? Whatever the purpose, the governments of Ar-gentina, Brazil, Chile, Ecuador, and Mexico continued to woo Fi-del without feeling in the least offended or rebuffed. But the representative of another neutralist South American government hardened his position and gave us his vote.

After Castro's speech, Ambassador Carlos A. Clulow of Uru-guay—a country that still maintained diplomatic relations with the Castro regime—greeted me at the embassy with open arms. He said: "I receive you as the legitimate representative of the Cuban people, betrayed by Castro and oppressed by communism. You and your freedom-loving countrymen deserve our support. His-tory, geography, and treaties bind us together. Our own security and honor are at stake in Cuba. I have not yet received instruc-tions from my government on how to vote on the Cuban issue. But I will follow the dictates of my conscience." True to his word, Ambassador Clulow cast his vote in favor of the meeting of for-eign ministers that was to judge and condemn the Castro regime. Unwilling to follow his government's order to abstain, he quietly resigned after the vote, his dignity unscathed.

The eighth OAS meeting of foreign ministers was held in Punta del Este, Uruguay, on January 22–31, 1962. I arrived in Monte-video a few days before, carrying letters of introduction signed by Ambassador Clulow. Among the Cuban exile leaders already there was Dr. Luis Conte Agüero, who delivered a rousing speech at the *Ateneo*. Knowing that the Uruguayan vote would again be essential to pass an anti-Castro resolution, I requested a private meeting with the Foreign Minister, Homero Martínez, a short but upright former naval officer with a resolute character and a mar-tial pace. Our dialogue was brief. The minister informed me that he was facing a crisis of confidence that might force him to resign. He asked me to call him in two days. "If I continue in my current post," he said, "I would be pleased to meet Dr. Miró Cardona, President of the Cuban Revolutionary Council, and you to discuss your petition to the OAS." His parting words reflected the vul-nerability of many Latin American governments in the face of widespread Marxist agitation. He said: "We would have to meet in a distant, secluded place, possibly near the lighthouse of Puerto

Carreta. When you call me at home, do not address me as 'Minister.' Just say, 'Homero, this is Néstor.' Unfriendly eyes and ears surround us these days. We have to be very careful.''

The meeting eventually took place, but in a small bedroom at the Lancaster Hotel in Montevideo, where I was staying. The minister arrived unannounced, without escorts or assistants. He carried a copy of the document we had submitted to the foreign ministers. I noticed that he had underlined several paragraphs, which seemed to indicate that he had read it. After a short preamble, the minister homed in on the critical issue of collective sanctions against Castro. He told us that he would support them only if they were followed by a more definitive action. He did not want to expose his country to a "diplomatic Bay of Pigs"— to halfhearted, ineffective cures that would only exacerbate the malady.

Miró addressed the minister's concern, stating that the Cuban Revolutionary Council viewed the sanctions not as an end in themselves, but as a means of weakening the Castro regime and facilitating the task of liberation. Miró assured the minister that the Cubans would ultimately prevail in their struggle for freedom, with the promised help of the United States and other countries willing to follow. After considerable discussion, the minister agreed to support collective action against Castro if we could convince, or at least neutralize, Uruguay's President of the Council of Government, Eduardo V. Haedo.

The meeting with Mr. Haedo was held at his summer residence, La Azotea, located in Punta del Este. He greeted us near the pool with a Basque beret shadowing his forehead and a slanted half-smile projecting sarcasm. Miró thanked him for receiving us and asked him to endorse OAS sanctions against Castro. Haedo reminded us that his country had a collegiate government and that he represented only one vote. With a twinkle in his eyes, he added: "I am a very controversial politician—half of the Uruguayans curse my father, and the other half my mother." In a more serious vein, he stated that he was against OAS action against Castro because he viewed it as a subterfuge to legalize U.S. intervention in Cuba.

I respectfully took exception to Haedo's final remark and affirmed that we were asking for collective action as prescribed by the inter-American system precisely because we did not want Cuba to become a "Cold War pawn in the hands of superpowers." "The members of the OAS," I said, "have an obligation to take appropriate measures under the Rio Treaty to oppose a Soviet-backed totalitarian regime that is fueling subversion throughout the hemisphere." I continued, "If Uruguay and other Latin American republics do not honor their contractual commitments, they will condone and indeed foster what they are trying to avoid: unilateral intervention by the United States to protect their own interests, or worse still, blatant intrusion by the Soviet Union to expand their empire."

Haedo listened without interrupting me. As a skilled dialectician, he seemed to enjoy the rejoinder and remarked: "It's an argument." It was his oblique way of saying *touché*. As the debate continued, Haedo softened his stance and became more receptive to our views. Toward the end of the meeting, he agreed to reconsider his position but suggested that we caucus in Montevideo with a key member of the Council of Government, Dr. Echegoyen, who, in Haedo's opinion, had the swing vote on the Cuban issue. We followed his advice. Miró drove back to Montevideo to meet with Echegoyen, elicited a positive response, and thereby secured the critical vote of Uruguay.

Meanwhile, at the San Rafael Casino in Punta del Este, where the OAS meeting was being held, the Inter-American Peace Committee rendered its report pointing to Cuba's systematic violations of human rights, its espousal of Marxist-Leninist totalitarianism under increasing Soviet control, and its frequent acts of intervention in the internal affairs of other republics. Based on these charges, Colombia's Foreign Minister, Dr. Caicedo Castilla, the chief architect and promoter of the conference, called for the breaking of diplomatic and economic relations with the Castro regime and for its exclusion from the inter-American system, among other measures. The foreign ministers of Peru, Venezuela, Central America, Panama, and the Dominican Republic supported the Colombian proposal.

The delegations of Argentina, Brazil, Chile, Bolivia, Mexico, and Ecuador acknowledged that the Cuban Marxist-Leninist regime was incompatible with the inter-American system, but opposed the sanctions and the exclusion. Chancellor Dantas of Brazil even recommended the adoption of a "special statute" that would govern the relations between Socialist Cuba and the rest of the hemisphere. This proposal assumed that Cuba could be neutralized or "Finlandized."

U.S. Secretary of State Dean Rusk tried to avoid a schism within the OAS by bridging the gap between the hawks and the doves. He supported the incompatibility resolution and called for the exclusion of the Castro regime. But he proposed to defer execution pending further consideration by the OAS Council, and he did not endorse collective sanctions, such as the severance of diplomatic and economic relations.

The head of the Castro delegation, President Osvaldo Dorticós, delivered a blistering speech against the United States, but was careful not to antagonize the neutralist countries. He felt that efforts to penalize, and possibly expel, the Castro regime could be stymied, and he wasn't particularly bothered by a broad declaration of incompatibility. The delegations of Central America and Panama, however, were incensed. They viewed the U.S. compromise proposal as a sellout to the "doves," and threatened to leave the meeting if the OAS did not condemn and impose sanctions on the Castro regime.

In the private discussions that ensued, Caicedo Castilla again emerged as the decisive figure. To break the existing deadlock, he convinced the hawks to withdraw the motion calling for diplomatic and economic sanctions against the Castro regime, but insisted on excluding it from the inter-American system without the need for any further action other than a pro forma resolution by the OAS Council. He rejected the thesis propounded by Brazil, Chile, and Argentina that the exclusion required an amendment to the OAS Charter (a three-to-five-year process) and argued that the foreign ministers were empowered under the Rio Treaty to expel a transgressor member state.[5] Caicedo Castilla's firmness interfered somewhat with Secretary Rusk's effort to achieve a broader consensus. President Kennedy in Washington had reportedly called President Lleras Camargo in Bogotá and asked him to instruct his representative to moderate his stance, but Caicedo Castilla would not budge on the issue of the immediate enforceability of the Castro exclusion.

I saw him as he left one of his meetings with the U.S. delegation. He looked tired, but composed. When I asked him how things were going, he discreetly pointed toward the American diplomats and said with a placid smile: "They leave me alone; they leave me alone. But I am made of iron." And it was this "Iron Chancellor," as he was called in Punta del Este, who successfully originated and steered six key resolutions of the conference, and who finally persuaded Secretary Rusk to support unequivocally the unconditional expulsion of the Cuban regime, after the United States had secured the missing vote of Haiti.[6]

The ministers unanimously resolved that the Marxist-Leninist ideology of the Castro regime and its acceptance of Soviet intervention in this hemisphere were incompatible with the regional system and constituted a threat to the peace and security of the hemisphere. By a two-thirds majority, the ministers excluded the existing government of Cuba from participation in the OAS. They also urged "the member states to take those steps that they may consider appropriate for their individual or collective self-defense, and . . . to counteract threats or acts of aggression, subversion or other dangers to peace and security resulting from the continued intervention in this Hemisphere of the Sino-Soviet powers. . . ."

Toward the end of the conference, when verbal clashes with the Cuban delegation had heightened tensions, three of Castro's armed henchmen cornered my colleague Eduardo Leal and me in one of the halls. They provoked us with abusive language and challenged us to settle the dispute outside. Fortunately, a Uruguayan intelligence officer saw what was happening. As we were being forced out of the building, he ran to the door, separated the two groups, and averted what turned out to be an attempt to kidnap us. When Leal and I had calmed down, I asked the officer why the Castro agents were allowed to carry guns at the conference. Without hesitating, the officer replied: "Because the other delegations refused to surrender their weapons." To prove his point, he took me to a large room bristling with modern arms which he said belonged to the U.S. security service. Later, he called a friendly bodyguard who came with the Guatemalan delegation and asked him to show me his *piñas* ("pineapples"). With a toothy grin, the young man opened his briefcase and displayed four hand grenades. Trying to appear nonchalant, I turned to the Uruguayan officer and said, "I guess Leal and I are the only ones here not prepared for intramural fireworks."

When the expulsion resolution was being passed, Dorticós blasted the OAS and the foreign ministers and subsequently left the conference with his delegation. Miró and I, along with other members of the Cuban Revolutionary Council, were then authorized to enter the general assembly room. Most of the foreign ministers and their assistants greeted us with applause. It was a spontaneous expression of solidarity, a clear indication that the actions taken by the OAS were not aimed at the democratic people of Cuba, but at their totalitarian oppressors.

The exclusion of the Castro regime from the inter-American system was tantamount to a withdrawal of recognition by the OAS. The ousted government was stripped of all its prerogatives, including legal protection under existing regional treaties. As declared by the ministers of foreign affairs, "no member state of the inter-American system can claim the rights and privileges pertain-

ing thereto if it denies or fails to recognize the corresponding obligations."

The OAS had handed down an unprecedented sentence, ex-
pelling and outlawing the Cuban Communist regime. While it did
not explicitly provide for effective ways to execute the sentence
(that is, to remove the outlawed government), it did open an opportunity for countries in this hemisphere to recognize and support an anti-Castro belligerent government pledged to democracy,
or to exercise their right of individual or collective self-defense
against Castro Communism. But along with the opportunity came
a major risk. In the absence of a strong preemptive action in Cuba,
the USSR could extend its military support to include a client
state that had been expelled from the OAS and left in limbo—
with no ties or obligations to the inter-American system.

We departed from Punta del Este with mixed feelings. The
anti-Castro resolutions adopted by the OAS were unequivocal and
far-reaching. That was encouraging. But we were concerned that
time was running out for action. Voids in geopolitics seldom endure. If the United States and its hemispheric allies did not promptly
follow through on Cuba, we noted, the Soviets would move in and
shield the island with their might.

On the way back to Miami, I stopped over in Lima, Peru, to
thank President Manuel Prado for the unswerving support of his
government, both in Washington and in Punta del Este. Before
my meeting with the President, I saw Victor Raúl Haya de la Torre,
the legendary *caudillo* of the APRA party, at a house on the outskirts of the city. Already in his mid-sixties, this oldest of Latin
American leftist democrats retained his magnetic appeal and revolutionary flair. He was not deceived, however, by Castro's rhetoric. He viewed the Cuban regime as an instrument of Soviet
penetration in the Americas and promised to combat it.

My meeting at the presidential palace with Manuel Prado was
brief but enlightening. The President, who knew that I had worked
closely with his ambassador to the OAS, Juan Bautista de La-
valle, greeted me very warmly. I thanked him for his assistance
and stressed the need for collective military action against the
Castro regime pursuant to the Rio Treaty. He pledged the backing
of Peru and started to name the countries that might join us. He
suddenly stopped and said with disarming frankness: "You are
really missing one vote . . . the vote that counts: the United
States."

Right, author's grandfather, Dr. José Manuel Cortina, former Foreign Minister of Cuba (1941)

Author's wife's grandfather, Dr. Raúl de Cárdenas, former Vice-President of Cuba (1944–1948)

Author's grandfather, Dr. José Manuel Carbonell, diplomat and former president of the Cuban Academy of Arts and Letters (1930)

Right, author's father, Dr. Néstor Carbonell Andricaín, former senator of Cuba (1948–1952)

Opposite page, author (center) and members of his family attending a cultural event in Havana (1950s)

Below, author's father (center) and Dr. Carlos Márquez Sterling (right) forming the Free People's Party in 1958 as a force against Batista and Castro

The Puig brothers, Manuel "Ñongo" and Rino, who married two of the author's cousins, played a prominent role in the anti-Castro resistance. They are shown here (standing right) with author's father-in-law, Gastón Arellano (center) and other members of Cuba's 1948 Olympic crew team.

Ñongo Puig and his wife, Ofelia Arango, author's cousin, at Varadero Beach. Active in the underground, they were both arrested by Castro's security police in 1961. Ñongo was executed; Ofelia survived, scarred for life.

Left, Rino Puig was arrested by the Castro regime in 1960 and condemned to fifteen years' imprisonment; Right, cousin Humberto Cortina before joining the Bay of Pigs brigade. He fought during the invasion and was wounded. Below, cousin Eddy Arango, hailed at a public rally in Havana, was arrested by Castro's police in 1959 and imprisoned for six years.

Above, Raúl Castro and Che Guevara in the Sierra Maestra (1958) (*AP/Wide World*)

Left, Soviet leader Khrushchev warmly embraces Fidel Castro at the United Nations in 1960. (*AP/Wide World*)

Dr. José Miró Cardona (center), Dr. Manuel Antonio de Varona (left) and
Manuel Ray (right), leaders of the Cuban Revolutionary Council, declaring
war on Castro (1961) (*UPI/Bettmann*)

Below, Dr. Varona addressing the Bay of Pigs brigade at the training camp in
Guatemala (1961) (*UPI/Bettmann*)

Left, carrier USS *Essex,* part of the naval task force that led the invasion flotilla into the Bay of Pigs, was base for jets that could have turned the battle's tide. (*AP/ Wide World*)

Below, members of the Bay of Pigs brigade captured by Castro forces after they ran out of ammunition (*UPI/Bettmann*)

Right, Joche Smith, one of the battle-scarred Bay of Pigs freedom fighters, embraced by his mother in Miami when Castro dispatched a delegation of wounded prisoners to collect ransom for the rest of the brigade (*Miami Herald*)

Below, President Kennedy addressing brigade survivors at the Miami Orange Bowl shortly after they were ransomed (December 1962). When presented with the brigade flag, JFK promised to return it in a free Havana. (*Diario Las Américas*)

THE WHITE HOUSE
WASHINGTON

September 14, 1961

Dear Dr. Miro Cardona:

I write to express my confidence in your leadership of the Cuban Revolutionary Council. The
United States government deeply admires the
distinguished service you have already rendered
to the cause of a free Cuba; and I hope you will
continue to lead this fight until your country is
liberated from the tyranny which has been
imposed on it. I am sure that any problems arising from your relationship with the United States
can be worked out in the spirit of mutual cooperation and common aspirations which lie behind
all our efforts.

Sincerely,

Dr. Miro Cardona
Cuban Revolutionary Council

Left, letter from President Kennedy to Dr. Miró Cardona, urging him not to resign as President of the Cuban Revolutionary Council after the Bay of Pigs debacle

VERY URGENT

July 20, 1965

My dear Bebo:

You will understand my state of mind at this moment
after reading what I have underscored - excerpts, it seems,
from several Life articles. I NEED YOUR ADVICE QUICKLY.

The meeting alluded to was requested by me, at the
urging of Arturo Manas, who was concerned over President
Kennedy's statement that the U.S. forces would not
intervene.

The meeting took place at the Century Club. In
attendance were Adolf Berle, Arthur Schlesinger, Professor
Plank and I. Responding to my prodding and concerns, Mr.
Berle affirmed that our agreements stand; that for the very
reason that I was obligated to declare that the revolution
was entirely Cuban, the President had to deny any plan to
intervene.

I then asked him to assign to me a ranking liaison
[officer], and he appointed a general whose name I have
recorded in my papers. I was apprised that day of the
air raid (Hotel Blackstone). If I had been informed then
that Yankee support had been denied, I would have stopped
the operation with a seraphone in Central Park.

You witnessed the confrontation provoked by Goodwin
with Schlesinger at the White House when I took exception to
Alsop's report.

I am so incensed now that I cannot continue.   I need
your advice QUICKLY.

Yours,

Pepe

Would Plank be willing to confirm these points?

Right, English version of a letter from Dr. Miró Cardona to his executive assistant, Ernesto Aragón, taking exception to the White House's allegations that Miró was informed that the United States would not provide military support for the Bay of Pigs invasion

Right, Secretary of State Dean Rusk and Dr. Miró Cardona during OAS meeting of Foreign Ministers held in Punta del Este, Uruguay (1962) to condemn and expel the Castro regime from the OAS

Below, the author, Dr. Miró Cardona, and Cuban exile activist Eddy Leal, during OAS meeting, thanking Colombia's "Iron Chancellor," Dr. Caicedo Castilla, for his strong stance against Castro communism

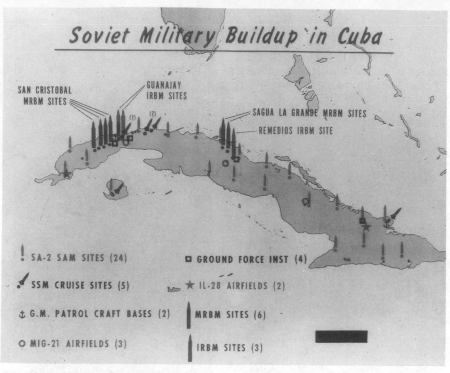

Soviet Military Buildup in Cuba

SAN CRISTOBAL MRBM SITES

GUANAJAY IRBM SITES

SAGUA LA GRANDE MRBM SITES

REMEDIOS IRBM SITE

! SA-2 SAM SITES (24)

◢ SSM CRUISE SITES (5)

⚓ G.M. PATROL CRAFT BASES (2)

⊘ MIG-21 AIRFIELDS (3)

□ GROUND FORCE INST (4)

★ IL-28 AIRFIELDS (2)

▌ MRBM SITES (6)

▌ IRBM SITES (3)

Above, while America slept in 1961–1962, the Soviet Union installed in Cuba a major strategic military capability. (*U.S. Department of Defense*)

Below, aerial photograph of Soviet intermediate-range ballistic-missile base in Cuba, October, 1962 (*U.S. Department of Defense*)

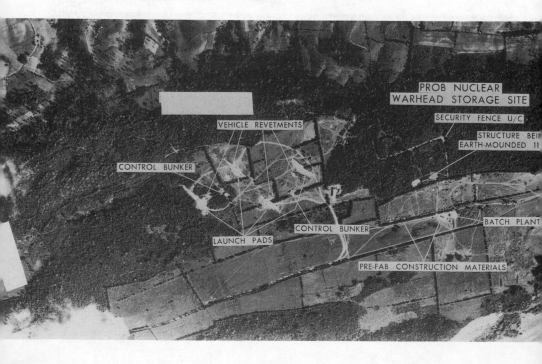

PROB NUCLEAR WARHEAD STORAGE SITE

SECURITY FENCE U/C

STRUCTURE BEI EARTH-MOUNDED 11

VEHICLE REVETMENTS

CONTROL BUNKER

CONTROL BUNKER

BATCH PLANT

LAUNCH PADS

PRE-FAB CONSTRUCTION MATERIALS

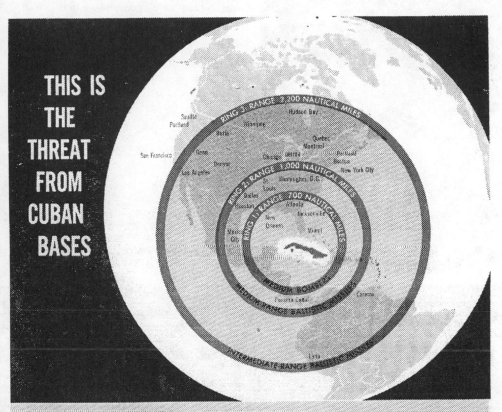

The threat posed by the installation of missile bases in Cuba (*U.S. News & World Report, Inc.*)

Left, Castro and speleologist Núñez Jiménez exploring one of the large Cuban caves, which were reportedly conditioned to conceal strategic arms (*Bohemia*)

Below, Soviet Premier Nikita Khrushchev honoring Castro in Moscow's Red Square on May 1, 1963 (*AP/Wide World*)

Above, one of more than twenty-four naval task forces deployed by the Soviet Union to Cuba since 1969 (*U.S. Department of Defense*)

Below, Fidel Castro and Daniel Ortega, intent on consolidating Marxism-Leninism in Nicaragua and beyond (*UPI/Bettmann*)

Portrait of Marx and Lenin held high at a Sandinista National Liberation Front (FSLN) rally marking the first anniversary of the revolution against Somoza, July 19, 1980 (*Owen Franklin/Sygma*)

CHAPTER 13

The Missiles and the Caves

On February 3, 1962, Washington formally instituted an embargo on trade between the United States and Cuba, but took no action and sounded no warning to stop the ongoing Soviet military buildup on the island. On March 27, the United States simply declared that the Sino-Soviet bloc had furnished about $100 million worth of military equipment and technical services to Cuba and that several hundred Cuban military personnel had received training in the bloc.

At the headquarters of the Cuban Revolutionary Council in Miami, we viewed the progressive Soviet involvement in Cuba with considerable alarm. The Castro regime was losing popularity with the dislocation of the economy and the stifling of freedom, but it was enhancing its power with totalitarian regimentation and Russian military support. Time, we felt, would only increase the cost of liberation and augment the risk of a major international clash.

Washington's inaction vis-à-vis the Soviets in Cuba led us to believe that President Kennedy had not fully recovered from Khrushchev's onslaught during the Vienna meetings in June of 1961. It had been reported that when the Soviet leader kept needling him on the Bay of Pigs, Kennedy rather testily countered: "Don't you ever make mistakes in your country, Mr. Chairman?" James Reston later confirmed what we suspected and feared. He wrote: "The President came into a dim room in the American Embassy [in Vienna] shaken and angry. He had tried, as always, to be calm and rational with Khrushchev, to get him to define what the Soviet Union would and would not do, and Khrushchev had bullied him and threatened him with war over Berlin."

Based on what Kennedy said in the embassy room, Reston concluded, "Khrushchev had studied the events of the Bay of Pigs; he would have understood if Kennedy had either left Castro alone, or destroyed him; but when Kennedy was rash enough to strike at Cuba, but not bold enough to finish the job, Khrushchev decided he was dealing with an inexperienced young leader who could be intimidated and blackmailed. . . ."[1]

In April of 1962 the Cuban Revolutionary Council had not yet received conclusive reports on the creation of a strategic military capability in Cuba, but it had gathered enough indications to realize that danger was looming on the horizon. Accordingly, Miró requested an urgent meeting with President Kennedy. It was to be their fourth in less than twelve months. Just prior to their discussion, I drafted an aide-mémoire for the Cuban exile leader. It stressed the need to prepare for military action against the Castro regime. Diplomatic and economic isolation, I contended, was not enough to topple a police state that was sustained and armed by the Soviets to serve as their arsenal for revolution. The memorandum emphasized the importance of accelerating the military training of Cuban exile units designed to form the front line of a liberation force backed by the United States and Latin American countries. Finally, the paper called for the formalization of the de facto alliance between Washington and the Revolutionary Council to facilitate the coordination of war efforts and the unification of exile groups.

The meeting between Miró and President Kennedy took place at the White House on April 10, 1962. Also present were Attorney General Robert Kennedy, presidential aide Richard Goodwin, and Miró's executive assistant and interpreter, Ernesto Aragón. During the one-hour discussion, Miró touched on the points covered in the aide-mémoire. The President was cordial and forthright in his response. He stated that "the Cuban problem was essentially military—of six divisions" and added that the Cuban Revolutionary Council should contribute as many combatants as possible. He instructed Goodwin to step up the recruitment and training of Cuban exiles, which had been bogged down in a mass of bureaucratic details.

There was nothing clandestine about the training. As confirmed by Roswell L. Gilpatric, Deputy Secretary of Defense, in his letter to Miró of August 28, 1962, the program called for the "recruitment of Spanish speaking individuals [Cuban exiles] who will receive their basic training in the Spanish language and in units made up primarily, if not exclusively, of their fellow countrymen. We will be able to accept applications for this program in New York, Chicago, Los Angeles, and New Orleans, as well as in Miami, and we are looking into the possibility of accepting applications in Puerto Rico. Under the new program, the fact that a man has several dependents will not be a bar to enlistment, and applicants will be informed that their training will prepare them specifically for combat-type assignments." The tag "but not necessarily in Cuba" was added, we thought, for security reasons. The program also included sixteen-week training courses at U.S. Army and Air Force schools for former Cuban officers.

Kennedy reiterated at the meeting that the program would be fully implemented as soon as possible, and assured Miró that any military action against Castro would be a joint effort, "not unilateral." Kennedy, however, did not deem it necessary to formalize the embryonic alliance with the council at that time. Alluding to the pressures and difficulties that Miró was facing with the restless refugee community, he told him at the end of the meeting: "Your fate is to suffer. Do not flag or waver. You have my support."

That evening, I joined Miró and Aragón at Washington's Manger Annapolis Hotel, where they were staying. They seemed reasonably satisfied with the outcome of the discussion, despite what I called the "persistent ambiguity." Both Miró and Aragón felt that the military solution alluded to by the President was not just a possible option or a contingency plan, but a committed course of action, and that Kennedy had been as explicit as he could be under the circumstances.

By late July 1962, we detected a significant change in the Soviet military buildup in Cuba. There was a sudden rise in the level of military aid. The average of Soviet dry-cargo ships per month increased from fifteen for the first half of 1962 to thirty-seven. In addition, we received many reports of ships unloading at night under strict security with all non-Soviet personnel being excluded from the dock areas. It was also reported that some of the arriving personnel were young, trim, physically fit, and disciplined, and that they formed in ranks of fours on the docks and moved out in truck convoys.

The U.S. intelligence community, working closely with anti-

Castro Cuban and European agents on the island, was doing a creditable job of gathering and processing large quantities of data on the deployment of the military equipment and personnel. According to the findings of the Preparedness Subcommittee of the Senate Committee on Armed Services (May 1963), the so-called intelligence gap on Cuba did not result from inadequate information, but rather from the flawed evaluation and assessment of the massive data—frequently colored by philosophical misconceptions, political biases, and plain wishful thinking.

Analysts were strongly influenced by the official notion that it would be contrary to Soviet policy to introduce strategic missiles into Cuba. Many in Washington believed that the USSR could be kept at bay, since it purportedly had no desire or need to bear the high cost and risk of establishing a client state in Cuba with offensive military capability. In the current nuclear era of intercontinental ballistic missiles and long-range bombers, it was argued, why would the Soviets want to have a strategic base in Cuba? Geography—i.e., proximity to the United States—seemed irrelevant to "the best and the brightest." Even at the height of the nuclear crisis, Washington Kremlinologists held that the missiles in Cuba were only a diversion and that the real Soviet goal was the seizure or neutralization of West Berlin.

The intelligence evaluators and political strategists had a tendency to dismiss Cuban refugee reports, which were occasionally inflated but basically correct. Overall, there was a disinclination to accept and believe the ominous signs arising from the raw data that had been collected. For example, the discovery of the surface-to-air-missile complex in the San Cristóbal area on August 29, 1961, did not lead to the logical assumption that they were being constructed to protect a strategic missile base, inasmuch as there was no existing military installation to safeguard in the area.

Without attaching any special significance to the increasing Soviet military involvement in Cuba, Washington simply took note in late July and August that large quantities of Soviet arms and technical personnel began arriving in Cuba. According to the official reports, the arms included surface-to-air missiles with a range of twenty-five miles, coastal defense missile installations with a range of thirty to thirty-five miles, a limited number of modern jet interceptors (MiG-21) possibly equipped with air-to-air missiles, and several Komar class guided-missile patrol boats. Washington also reported that about 4,200 Soviet technicians had arrived along with the shipments.

Despite the Soviet military escalation in Cuba and the confidential warnings given by Director of Central Intelligence John McCone before embarking on his honeymoon trip, the President seemed unflustered during his press conference of August 30. He said: "In response to your specific question, we do not have information that troops have come into Cuba, number one. Number two, the main [Soviet] thrust, of course, is assistance because of the mismanagement of the Cuban economy which has brought widespread dissatisfaction, economic slowdown, agricultural failures, which have been so typical of the Communist regimes in so many parts of the world. So that I think the situation was critical enough that they needed to be bolstered up."

The position taken by the White House and the State Department throughout this period was that the military buildup was justifiable, that the weapons being shipped by the USSR to Cuba were defensive, and that the Soviet-bloc personnel arriving with them were not soldiers, but technicians (many of them agrarian specialists). Despite the President's subsequent warnings that serious consequences would arise if these assumptions were incorrect, the general perception was that Washington really believed that the buildup was harmless.

As late as October 14, McGeorge Bundy, Special Assistant to the President for National Security, made the following remarks in a televised interview on the program *Issues and Answers*:

> Well, I don't myself think that there is any present—I know there is no present evidence and I think there is no present likelihood that the Cubans and the Cuban government and the Soviet government would in combination attempt to install a major offensive capability. . . . So far, everything that has been delivered in Cuba falls within the categories of aid which the Soviet Union has provided, for example, to neutral states like Egypt or Indonesia, and I should not be surprised to see additional military assistance of that sort. That is not going to turn an island of six million people with five thousand or six thousand Soviet technicians and specialists into a major threat to the United States, and I believe most of the American people do not share the views of the few who have acted as if suddenly this kind of military support created a mortal threat to us. It does not.

George W. Ball, Under Secretary of State, elaborated on the same theme in an article that appeared in the October 19, 1962, issue of *Washington World*. He wrote:

Our policy toward Cuba is based upon the assessment that Cuba does not today constitute a military threat to the United States. Without doubt it is an economic burden for the Sino-Soviet bloc. . . . The crash efforts of the Soviet Union to provide the Castro regime with economic technicians and to build up its military defenses is a demonstration of Cuban weaknesses. . . . We may take the events of the past month—regrettable as they may be in many ways—as evidence of the essential soundness of the strategy of isolation that we have pursued toward Cuba over the past two years.

Washington's toleration of the Soviet military buildup in Cuba was sending the wrong signals to friends and foes alike. Western allies were unwittingly providing logistical support to the Soviets during part of the buildup. As charged by Senator Kenneth B. Keating in the Senate on September 17, 1962, West Germany chartered ships to the USSR for the transport of strategic equipment to Cuba, Canada supplied pilot observers or guides for the flight of light bombers added to the Cuban air force, and Greece provided both shipping and refueling facilities for Russian cargo vessels on their way to Cuba.

From Senator Winston L. Prouty's perspective, the greatest threat to peace was the belief of Soviet leaders that the United States and perhaps the free world would not fight or resist in the event of a real showdown. According to a September 1962 article written by Joseph Alsop, Khrushchev had told UN Secretary U Thant that the United States would never fight. The Soviet Prime Minister reportedly made a similar statement to Robert Frost, adding afterward that we would simply sit "on one hand and then on the other." Based on this perception, it was not surprising that on September 11, 1962, the USSR warned Washington that any U.S. attack on Cuba "would be the beginning of the unleashing of war."

Unable to elicit from Washington any meaningful reaction to the Soviet-Cuban threat, Tony Varona (who was then in charge of the Cuban Revolutionary Council's external relations) and I met with Miró in early August to assess the situation and agree on next steps. By then we had enough raw data to support the charge that the Soviet Union had virtually occupied the island with troops and strategic arms. Varona and I argued that in light of the emergency, we could not rely solely on the White House and the State Department. We also had to present the facts to U.S. senators and congressmen on a bipartisan basis. Miró was concerned that our plan of action might jeopardize the relationship he had built with President Kennedy, but he did not stand in the way. "Just be careful and discreet," he counseled.

Varona and I, as well as representatives of the Student Revolutionary Directorate and other exile groups, met in Washington with a large number of senators and congressmen. Some of them echoed our findings and called for immediate action. Others relied on leaks from U.S. government sources and voiced alarm. The senator who had gathered more detailed and reliable information on Cuba was Strom Thurmond (then a Democrat from South Carolina). As a prominent member of the Armed Services Committee, he had access to the U.S. intelligence community and to the Pentagon. Relying on his own findings, Thurmond announced on September 3, 1962, that the Soviets were building IRBM bases in Cuba.

But the Cicero of the Senate who repeatedly warned of a nuclear-poised Carthage facing U.S. shores was New York's Republican Senator Kenneth B. Keating. From August 31 to October 12, 1962, he made ten Senate speeches and fourteen other public statements revealing alarming aspects of the Soviet military buildup in Cuba. Undeterred by White House accusations of irresponsibility and loose talk, he continued to play a major role in alerting the nation. Like Thurmond, Keating relied primarily on U.S. intelligence data and not on refugee reports.

Believing that sooner or later some type of military action had to be taken to address the threat, Varona and I pressed for the recognition of a Cuban belligerent government, not to vegetate in exile with meaningless titles, but to rally our forces for liberation. We enlisted the support of Senator George Smathers of Florida—a staunch anti-Castro leader and a personal friend of President Kennedy. Working diligently with the senator's staff, we found several precedents of U.S. recognition, from the Czechoslovak National Council headed by Masaryk in 1918 to the Polish government-in-exile based in France in 1939 and subsequently in England.

In all of the precedents, however, a formal state of war existed. This condition was missing in Cuba, but there were other factors that strengthened our case. The Castro regime had been outlawed by the OAS and, as a Soviet surrogate, was now posing a threat to the peace and security of the hemisphere. Moreover, Washington had already given tacit recognition to the Cuban Revolutionary Council, as evidenced by the ongoing relationship maintained with its chiefs. The time had come, we argued, to formalize that relationship and enable the council to enter into military alliances with the United States and other countries, unify anti-Castro refugees, and lead a struggle that should be viewed as a quest for Cuban freedom and not as a U.S.-Soviet conflict over hegemony.

Senator Smathers agreed with our approach and tried to obtain official endorsement as he pursued the initiative in the Senate. The State Department took a negative stance on the grounds that the various refugee groups lacked cohesion and sufficient constituency inside Cuba, and that the United States had never recognized a government-in-exile that was not driven from its home country by war. Efforts to rebut these allegations proved to be unsuccessful. Senator Smathers's proposal was shelved.

On August 20, the Revolutionary Council publicly denounced the Soviet invasion of Cuba with several thousand troops and strategic arms, and called for hemispheric action to repel the intervention. A U.S. State Department spokesman ridiculed the report and said that the troops "were more likely four hundred or five hundred agricultural and industrial advisers."

Incensed by Washington's procrastination, the Student Revolutionary Directorate decided not to engage in a fruitless debate with the U.S. government but to take direct action to highlight the Russian occupation and dramatize Cuban resistance. On August 24, at 11:30 P.M., a group of exiled students, nineteen to twenty-three years old, penetrated Castro's coastal defenses with two small vessels and shelled a Havana hotel that housed Soviet-bloc military officers. The audacious raid produced heavy damage, triggered a violent Castro protest, and earned headline coverage.

Washington admonished the attacking students but not the Russian invaders. Worried and perplexed, I sought the advice of my grandfather Cortina. He reminded me of President McKinley's reluctance to support the Cuban liberation war in 1898. "Now," Cortina affirmed, "the situation is much more serious because the internal security of the United States is at stake, and yet the White House refuses to act. As in 1898," Cortina added, "we have no alternative but to obtain a congressional joint resolution on Cuba." But he warned: "Don't rely solely on the Monroe Doctrine. We also should call for collective action pursuant to the Rio Treaty." And remembering the struggle he and others had waged to end American tutelage in Cuba under the Platt

Amendment, he emphasized: "Be sure to assert the right of the Cuban people to self-determination."

Convinced, as Cortina was, that congressional pressure was essential to move the White House from dangerous inertia to responsive action, Varona and I returned to Washington to resume our lobbying campaign. We carried the text of a proposed joint resolution on Cuba which I had drafted along the lines suggested by Cortina. Invoking the Monroe Doctrine and the inter-American treaties, the resolution called for the adoption of individual and collective measures deemed necessary to protect the security of the United States and other American republics, repel Soviet intervention in this hemisphere, and restore the right of the Cuban people to self-determination.

At Capitol Hill, Varona and I met separately with Senators George Smathers, Bourke B. Hickenlooper, and Strom Thurmond and Congressman William Miller (then chairman of the Republican Party). They reviewed our draft joint resolution and promised to support it in principle and seek the backing of their colleagues.

Spurred by the lobbying efforts and the continual reports of the Soviet military buildup headlined in the press, the notion of a congressional resolution soon gained momentum. On September 17, the Armed Services Committee and Foreign Relations Committee of the Senate met jointly to discuss the Cuban situation and provide a framework to address the threat. The meeting was not held at the request of the Executive to seek a mandate for action. It was convened at the behest of concerned senators to adopt a resolution on Cuba that would involve both chambers of Congress and possibly the White House. In sharp contrast to the situation in 1988, most of the legislators were more alarmed than the President and demanded a firm stand.

Secretary of State Dean Rusk, who appeared before the Senate committees, recommended a concurrent resolution, which would have reaffirmed certain underlying U.S. policies applicable to Cuba at the discretion of the Executive. The formidable chairman of the Armed Services Committee, Richard B. Russell, insisted, however, on a joint resolution, which requires the signature of the President and has the force of law. In his opinion, expressing the sense of Congress was not enough. It was essential to have the commitment of "the only man in the American government who can really speak for the United States in international relations," the President.[2]

Senator Russell prevailed after his colleagues had expounded on the seriousness of the Cuban situation and the need to reassert the Monroe Doctrine, the inter-American treaties, and the inherent right of individual and collective self-defense. The joint resolution, signed by the President on October 3, 1962, stated in part:

The United States is determined . . .

(A) To prevent by whatever means may be necessary, including the use of arms, the Marxist-Leninist regime in Cuba from extending by force or threat of force its aggressive or subversive activities to any part of this Hemisphere;

(B) To prevent in Cuba the creation or use of any externally supported military capability endangering the security of the United States; and

(C) To work with the Organization of the American States and with freedom-loving Cubans to support the aspirations of the Cuban people for self-determination.

Throughout the arms buildup in Cuba, the Soviets engaged in deception. On September 11, 1962, Moscow publicly stated: "The armament and military equipment sent to Cuba are designed exclusively for defensive purposes. . . . There is no need for the Soviet Government to shift its weapons for a retaliatory blow to any other country, for instance Cuba." And as late as mid-October 1962, Soviet Foreign Minister Gromyko told President Kennedy that he had been instructed to make it clear once again that Soviet assistance to Cuba "pursued solely the purpose of contributing to the defense capabilities of Cuba."

On October 16, 1962, the President was finally shown aerial photographic evidence of what Cuban refugees and concerned U.S. Senators had been reporting for some time: the existence in Cuba of medium- and intermediate-range ballistic missiles with launching pads and control bunkers manned by Russian troops, as well as Soviet jet bombers—all capable of carrying nuclear weapons and of striking most of the major cities in the Western Hemisphere.

In the words of Theodore C. Sorensen, Special Counsel to President Kennedy, "providing Cuban bases for their existing MRBMs and IRBMs [medium- and intermediate-range ballistic missiles] gave them [the Soviets] a swift and comparatively inexpensive means of adding sharply to the total number of missiles targeted on the United States, positioned to bypass most of our missile-warning system and permitting virtually no tactical warn-

ing between their launch and arrival on target. The fifteen-minute
ground alert on which our nuclear bombers stood by on runways
would no longer be sufficient."[3]

As recently disclosed by the retired career State Department
officer Raymond L. Garthoff in his *Reflections on the Cuban Missile Crisis,* the completion of twenty-four MRBM launchers and
sixteen IRBM launchers in Cuba would have increased Russia's
first-strike land-based salvo by 80 percent, from its then very low
operational level.

Faced with incontrovertible evidence that the Soviets had
stationed offensive weapons in Cuba (the first known case of Russian strategic missile emplacements outside Soviet soil), President
Kennedy immediately convened a meeting with his national security advisers and intelligence experts to interpret the photographs and then begin discussion on a course of action. According
to the sanitized transcripts of the recordings of the October 16
meeting, released in 1987 by the John F. Kennedy Library, the
President was puzzled by the missile emplacements and wondered
whether they made any strategic difference. "You may say it
doesn't make any difference if you get blown up by an ICBM
flying from the Soviet Union or one that was ninety miles away,"
the President mused. "Geography doesn't mean that much."

General Maxwell Taylor explained that these "pointed-at-the-
head" missiles "can become a . . . rather important adjunct and
reinforcement to the . . . strike capability of the Soviet Union."
Other advisers, especially Assistant Secretary of State Edwin
Martin, underscored the psychological implications of "sitting
back" and letting the Russians "do it to us." "It makes them
look like they're coequal with us . . ." conceded the President.
And that "we're scared of the Cubans," added the Secretary of
the Treasury, Douglas Dillon.

The discussions on October 16 reveal that the Executive
Branch was taken aback by the crisis, even though, according to
McGeorge Bundy, the Soviets "did make this decision [strategic
missile deployment into Cuba], as far as our estimates now go, in
early summer, and this has been happening since August." The
President candidly acknowledged: "We certainly have been wrong
about what he's [Khrushchev's] trying to do in Cuba. There isn't
any doubt about that. . . ." "Yeah. Except [CIA Director] John
McCone," interposed McGeorge Bundy. "Yeah," concurred the
President.

Despite the element of surprise and the lack of preparation, some of the presidential advisers, like Secretary of Defense McNamara, made a lucid and realistic assessment of the available courses of action. Others, like Secretary of State Dean Rusk, seemed to miss the mark. His idea of getting some word to Castro, possibly through the Canadian ambassador in Havana, "that Cuba is being victimized here, and that, uh, the Soviets are preparing Cuba for destruction or betrayal" (i.e., trading Cuba for Berlin), did not receive much support at the meeting.

After several hours of intense deliberation, the President ended the October 16 session convinced that the Soviet strategic missiles in Cuba had to be neutralized or withdrawn. Not yet knowing how best to accomplish that objective, he rose to the challenge and prepared to cope with the emergency. He summoned what later came to be known as the Executive Committee of the National Security Council, or Ex-Com, to evaluate all possible alternatives in absolute secrecy. After exhaustive discussions, the Ex-Com, steered by Robert Kennedy, rejected the option of a surprise air strike, favored by the top military advisers, because of the attendant risks and the perception of an "American Pearl Harbor in reverse." "My brother is not going to be the Tojo of the 1960s," the Attorney General passionately asserted.

A naval blockade, dressed up as a quarantine, was the course of action that was finally charted, but not without blunt disagreement. Former Secretary of State Dean Acheson, who had been invited to attend some of the meetings, challenged Robert Kennedy's Pearl Harbor analogy and called for the destruction of the missiles to ensure that they were definitely eradicated from the island, for a blockade "was a method of keeping things out, not getting things out." The most vehement opposition came, however, from Senator Richard B. Russell. During the private briefing the President gave the Congressional leaders on October 22, Russell, backed by Senator William Fulbright, objected to the blockade as a "half-measure" and forcefully argued for an invasion to resolve the Cuban situation once and for all. Fearing that the United States might surrender the initiative, he predicted: "If we get involved in negotiations in the United Nations and the Organization of American States and every other international body under the sun, we'll have a hollow victory and Khrushchev will still have Cuba."[4]

The President explained that the quarantine was an "initial" step, which did not preclude a surgical air strike or an invasion. He favored gradual escalation to avert a head-on confrontation which could bring Khrushchev to a "choice of either a humiliating retreat or a nuclear war." The general consensus was that the blockade provided a most effective display of measured power, enabled the United States to exercise other options, and laid the onus of initiating hostilities squarely on the Soviet Union.

Before addressing the nation and the world on the nuclear crisis, Kennedy ordered the U.S. Army, Navy, Marines, and Air Force to gear up for any eventualities. Moving swiftly and with amazing precision, the forces of the United States forged a ring of steel around Cuba. Over 350,000 men were mobilized, including the paratroopers of the 82nd and 101st Airborne Divisions and the Atlantic Amphibious Force. One hundred eighty-three ships of the U.S. Navy, encompassing fast destroyers, guided-missile cruisers, eight aircraft carriers, and detachments of submarines, were dispatched to the Caribbean to control the vital sea lanes surrounding Cuba. At more than eighty airbases in the United States and overseas, 2,500 aircraft were fueled, loaded with weapons, and readied to fly. And the ICBM launching crews, spread in complexes throughout the United States, were brought to full alert.

No leader has ever spoken from a position of such overwhelming strength as did President Kennedy on October 22, 1962. The quarantine announced that night was not just a desired objective, it was an accomplished and defiant reality. The warnings to Khrushchev were not the empty threats of a nation "too liberal to fight." They were the firm but restrained response of America, resolved to meet the unprecedented threat posed by the secret deployment of strategic weapons into Cuba.

The President's electrifying message evoked and made history. "The 1930s taught us a clear lesson: aggressive conduct, if allowed to grow unchecked and unchallenged, ultimately leads to war. . . . The path we have chosen for the present is full of hazards, as all paths are; but it is the one most consistent with our character and courage as a nation and our commitments around the world. The cost of freedom is always high—but Americans have always paid it. And one path we shall never choose, and that is the path of surrender or submission."

Following Kennedy's address and Stevenson's bravura performance at the United Nations, the free world stood behind the United States and called for the prompt dismantling and removal of all offensive weapons in Cuba, under the supervision of UN observers. Despite this unparalleled show of Western power and solidarity, Moscow did not initially cave in. Soviet ships continued heading toward Cuba; the Russians accelerated their work at the missile sites, with no signs of dismantling; Khrushchev started to send contradictory messages to Kennedy; and U.S. Major Rudolf Anderson, on a return U-2 flight over Cuba, was downed by a Soviet-manned SA-II antiaircraft battery.

At the headquarters of the Cuban Revolutionary Council in Miami the tempo increased as the crisis unfolded. But the normal buoyancy of the Cubans was now restrained. There was a clear consciousness of the gravity of the situation and of its far-reaching international repercussions. Miró had been in constant touch with high-level government officials since the October 14 meeting held at the Carrillon Hotel in Miami with Adam Yarmolinsky, special assistant to the Secretary of Defense, Robert Hurwitch, deputy chief of the State Department Cuban Desk, and several Pentagon officials. At that meeting, attended also by Tony Varona and Captain Ernesto Despaigne, the council leaders were urged to step up the recruitment of Cuban volunteers and trained officers. "Don't worry about age," they were told, "just focus on physical condition." During more than four hours they reviewed lists of existing and potential recruits and discussed procedures to augment the Cuban units being trained at Fort Knox. They also agreed to identify all available Cuban doctors in southern Florida, should their services be needed in Cuba.

The pressure mounted after the announcement of the quarantine. Then on Saturday, October 27—the blackest day of the crisis—Miró received an urgent call asking him to meet in Miami with several of his U.S. government contacts. He was informed at the secret parley that all enlisted refugees and officers were being kept in maximum readiness, pending possible orders to land in Cuba with a U.S. expeditionary force. Since an invasion seemed inevitable, Miró discussed final details concerning the establishment of a Cuban belligerent government on liberated territory.

Unbeknownst to the Revolutionary Council, the Attorney General, who was in frequent contact with Harry Ruíz-Williams on the fate of the Bay of Pigs prisoners, asked him to remain on standby and told him, "If we invade, I would like you and Roberto San Román to join our 82nd Airborne Division to rescue the prisoners." In the course of the discussion, it was agreed that Harry would land at the Príncipe Castle in Havana and Roberto on the Isle of Pines.

When Miró returned home on the 27th, he was visibly tense and reserved. Without disclosing the specifics of the plans, he told me that a massive landing of U.S. forces and Cuban contingents appeared to be imminent. He asked me to draft a proclamation addressed to the people of Cuba. It was to have the vibrance to lift the spirits and rally for victory, as well as the magnanimity to stimulate defections and unite for peace. I was asked to compose it immediately in a secluded room of the house.

I tried to picture the landing and the new dawn of freedom we had yearned for, but I was shaken by emotions. My mind wandered aimlessly through a kaleidoscope of blurry visions. It took me a while to concentrate, and then the thoughts started to flow. I wrote in Spanish. Here is an English version:

We have returned to our homeland after several years of painful expatriation. Marching with us, in close alliance, are the invincible forces of democracy.

We do not come with impulses of vengeance, but with a spirit of justice. We do not defend the interests of any sector, nor do we intend to impose the will of any ruler. We come to restore the right of the Cuban people to establish their own laws and to elect their own government. We are not invaders, inasmuch as Cubans cannot invade their own land. We aspire to the glory of liberating our country, which fell under the Soviet yoke through the perfidy and betrayal of some of its sons.

We come to oust forever from our soil the hatred that divides the Cubans, the firing wall that bloodies the families, the misery that ravages cities and towns, and the foreign domination that subjugates and disgraces the country.

The hour of rebellion—so eagerly sought—has finally struck. Members of the heroic underground: rise and help us rescue the unyielding political prisoners so that all of you can occupy a place of honor among the forces of liberation.

Members of the Rebel Army and the militias: break your ties with the Communist tyranny and join the legions of freedom. All those who abandon the enemy ranks to embrace the cause of democracy shall be our allies in war and our brothers in peace.

Our fatherland demands of us supreme sacrifices. Let every man be a muscle of rebellion. Let every woman be a torch of patriotism. Let every home be a trench line of dignity.

Cubans: Throw off the hammer and sickle of Communist oppression. Join the new battle for independence. Take up arms to redeem the nation, and march resolutely on to victory. Our sovereign flag proudly waves its splendid colors, and the island rises with the stirring cry of liberty!

As soon as I had finished drafting the proclamation, I handed it to Miró. He read it very slowly and didn't make any changes. Deeply moved, he gave me a warm Cuban *abrazo*. He then asked me to stay at home that evening and await the expected call that would summon us to action. That call never came.

The following day Washington informed us that at the very climax of the showdown, Moscow had retreated. Without having to fire a single shot, the President had secured a Soviet pledge to dismantle and withdraw the offensive weapons, under appropriate United Nations supervision, in exchange for a noninvasion guarantee. (We were not aware at the time of the Attorney General's secret offer to Soviet Ambassador Dobrynin to pull the Jupiter missiles out of Turkey.) Kennedy's measured response appeared to have worked. It gave the Russians a "decorous out" and averted a nuclear clash. The President was so euphoric that he welcomed "Chairman Khrushchev's statesmanlike decision" even before John J. McCloy had successfully negotiated the removal of the Ilyushin-28 bombers from Cuba.[5] No reference was made to the Soviet troops occupying the island. The world was not too concerned about these details. It hailed the settlement and reveled in peace.

Cubans on both sides, however, were unhappy with the outcome. Castro and his followers seemed angry for having been excluded from the negotiations and let down. A few hours after the Kennedy–Khrushchev compromise had been announced, Castro arrived at the Havana television studio with his entire cabinet and delivered an impassioned speech.

"We refuse to be the satellite of any nation," he declared. "We agreed to Khrushchev's offer to place missiles on our soil because he convinced us that it was indispensable for our revolutionary cause. We were not consulted about their removal.

"There is nothing we can do about it, but we want everyone to know that our principal weapon is not a missile, but our revolutionary honor and ideology. And these cannot be removed."

Castro sympathizers reacted emotionally. In the streets of Havana groups started chanting: *"Nikita, Nikita, lo que se da no se quita!*—"what you give, don't take away!" This became a slogan to vent anger in a very Cuban way: with conga rhythm.

To make the necessary arrangements for verification of the removal of the missiles, the Acting Secretary General of the United Nations, U Thant, flew to Havana and met with Castro on October 29. Curiously, U Thant chose not to represent the UN during this mission; he spoke on behalf of forty-five "neutralist" countries interested in world peace. He stated defensively, "This blockade has been an extremely unusual thing. Very unusual, except in times of war. . . ." And when Castro raged over the proposed inspection by UN observers, saying that the United States had no legal right to ask for it, U Thant replied: "This is my point of view. . . ." The Acting Secretary General ended his brief journey to Cuba assuring Castro: "I understand perfectly the sentiments of Your Excellency. . . ."[6]

In light of U Thant's fiasco, Kennedy agreed that Soviet Vice Prime Minister Mikoyan should try to talk reason to Castro in early November. After several days of seclusion, Castro met with Mikoyan but adamantly refused to accept the essential condition of on-site verification, even by the Red Cross. Informed of Fidel's obstinacy, Kennedy waived that condition (which has figured as the cornerstone of all disarmament negotiations) and acquiesced to inspection on the sea. Russian crewmen cooperated by pulling back canvas tarpaulins over what appeared to be missiles. This "striptease," as billed by humorists, enabled hovering U.S. helicopters to peek and photograph, but the metal casings that presumably protected the missiles were not removed, the holds were not inspected, and no boarding parties searched for nuclear arms. Nevertheless, Washington seemed satisfied with the procedure and announced in mid-November that forty-two MRBMs (SS-4)—the same number Khrushchev had admitted to—had left Cuba on Soviet ships. The IRBMs (SS-5) reportedly were stopped by the quarantine and never reached Cuba.

Cubans in Miami dismissed the notion that Mikoyan had genuinely tried to convince Castro to accept on-site inspection, but had failed. They called it a Russian stratagem that had been staged to conceal strategic weapons on the island. Castro, they claimed, appeared as an intransigent master of his destiny to provide an alibi for the Soviets, who did not really wish to show their secret military installations in Cuba. The exiles' denouncement was not taken seriously at the time. It was viewed as triggered by frustration, or as a scare tactic to provoke confrontation.

Soon, however, dispassionate voices were heard warning of a possible sham. Some of the Western European governments (whose intelligence agents in Cuba worked closely with the United States) were openly skeptical about the withdrawal of Soviet offensive weapons. West German Chancellor Konrad Adenauer, for one, told reporters on November 13, 1962—just before flying to Washington—that he doubted that Moscow had removed all of the strategic missiles and nuclear warheads it had installed in Cuba. He further declared that he did not trust the USSR, and that the only evidence that existed of the withdrawal of the missiles was "photographs of covered objects, which is not enough."[7] Adenauer's statement was supported and expanded in Washington in late January 1963 by the West German ambassador to Cuba, Karl von Spreti. He reportedly informed the Department of State that German intelligence agents based in Cuba had knowledge of eighty-four strategic missiles on the island—significantly more than were alleged to have been withdrawn.

Faced with conflicting reports carried by the press, Deputy Secretary of Defense Roswell L. Gilpatric candidly acknowledged in a television interview: "We never knew how many missiles were brought into Cuba. The Soviets said there were forty-two. We have counted forty-two going out. We saw fewer than forty-two. Until we have so-called on-site inspection of the island of Cuba we could never be sure that forty-two was the maximum number that the Soviets brought into Cuba." And Gilpatric added: "They [the Russians] have simply removed what they say were the missiles that were brought in. Beyond that, their performance has not yet gone."[8]

Another sensitive and embarrassing situation arose in connection with nuclear warheads. The Soviet government, in Telegram No. 1223, State to USUN, November 7, 1962, affirmed that "all nuclear weapons had been removed and that they were not going to reintroduce them." In truth, American intelligence agents had not detected any nuclear warheads in Cuba and did not verify any withdrawals. No issues were raised, however, because Washington did not wish to tempt the Russians to conceal and keep on the island any warheads that might have been brought there.

Informed senators and journalists wondered how the Soviets, with only seven ships, in just one week, had been able to remove all of their strategic missiles from the island. This was hard to believe, inasmuch as they reportedly had required about 165 ships to effect the missile buildup over a period of several months. They also raised questions about the IRBM launch rings that were necessary for the actual firing of the missiles. According to intelligence sources, six rings were photographed in Cuba but none on ships leaving the island. Moreover, only a few of the some two dozen launch stands and erectors spotted in Cuba were aboard the departing ships.

Not even Defense Secretary McNamara's dazzling perfor-

mance on February 6, 1963, quelled the debate. His detailed photographic review showed that the missile bases had been
dismantled, but without on-site inspection, no one could unequivocally assure that all of the strategic missiles had been removed
from the island. Even some of the so-called defensive weapons
systems that remained in Cuba created concern. Senator Strom
Thurmond pointed out that the one hundred Soviet cruise missiles
kept in four coastal defense sites had a range of approximately
twenty-five miles if controlled from a ground launching site, but if
controlled from an aircraft the range could be extended to approximately three hundred miles. He also indicated that the nuclear-
tipped FROG missiles in Cuba, mounted atop Soviet amphibious
tank chassis, had a range of up to three hundred miles.[9] Moreover, defense analysts warned that the forty-two MiG-21s that Cuba
already had in early 1963 could be easily converted from pure
interceptors into offensive aircraft capable of carrying nuclear
payloads from three hundred to five hundred miles on a round-
trip mission.

But what startled everyone was the presence in Cuba, not
disclosed or broached by Washington during the missile crisis, of
Soviet forces under the command of General C. O. Slazenko estimated to exceed 30,000. (Washington belatedly acknowledged
22,000.) As divulged in our January 1963 report titled "The Striking Military Power of Communist Cuba," that force included a
Soviet motorized division, an armored division and an elite guards
division, and was led by four Russian generals under Slazenko:
Colonel General N. I. Gusev, Chief of Staff of Air Force Units;
Major General Fedor Mikhaylovich Bendonesko, Chief of Staff of
Army Mechanized Groups and Support Units; Lieutenant General Sergey F. Ushakov, Chief of Staff of Antiaircraft Missiles,
and Lieutenant General Pavil B. Dankevich, Chief of Staff of
Strategic Rocket Forces.

Most of these elite officers and troops stayed in Cuba for more
than six months following the missile crisis. And they were not
basking in the sun or learning cha-cha-cha. They remained active
in secluded areas, close to the dismantled missile bases, where
underground installations were being rushed to completion under
a shroud of secrecy. Why?

Anti-Castro intelligence agents, farmers, and refugees leaving
the island gave a consistent explanation. They disclosed with considerable detail that Soviet strategic arms had been concealed near
the missile sites, in cave complexes that had been cordoned off,

reinforced, and conditioned prior to the October 1962 confrontation. Burrowing and tunneling continued at a feverish pace under the exclusive supervision and control of Soviet technical personnel.

For about fifteen years prior to Castro's rise to power, the noted Communist geographer Antonio Núñez Jiménez presided over the Cuban Speleological Society and explored and mapped some nine hundred caves and caverns, out of thousands that honeycomb the island. According to some of his colleagues who fled to the United States after Castro's ascent, Núñez Jiménez dispatched to Moscow in the early 1950s a copy of his comprehensive study "Subterranean Cuba." To the Soviet Union, the caves may have figured almost as prominently as Cuba's strategic geographical position. In a nuclear era, they are nature's own bomb shelters and silos for storing missiles. Cuba is ideally suited for that. Owing to intense orogenic activities and the erosion of underground rivers, clearly described in Gerardo Canet's *Atlas of Cuba,* the island is largely hollow. It rests on a vast labyrinth made up of complex chambers and corridors that stretch over the six provinces.

I am very familiar with one of those caverns, Los Portales, and with the adjacent Oscura and El Espejo caves, which are located within what used to be my grandfather's *hacienda* in Pinar del Río province, not too far from the San Cristóbal missile site. My family frequently organized horseback rides to visit the enthralling complex. We had to climb rugged mountains and cross one of the most gorgeous valleys in Cuba, Caiguanabo, a compact replica of the famous Viñales. Like most valleys in the province, Caiguanabo is dotted with distinctive monticules or *mogotes,* which rise from the cultivated fields like gigantic fortresses of rock. They were formed when subterranean rivers dissolved the limestone and left a vast network of corridors curtained by stalactites and stalagmites of beautiful colors. One of those hollow complexes of interconnecting caves is Los Portales.

In my early youth, my sister, my cousins, and I used to jump into the river that flows through Los Portales. While we swam, the rest of the family would prepare the typical country feast centered on *lechón asado,* or roast pig. After lunch, we explored the fascinating caves. Their entrance led to a huge gallery that had the configuration of a Roman amphitheater. From a protruding balcony that hung on one side, our shouts reverberated across the hall like echoes from the past. Armed with lanterns and flashlights, we would traverse an intricate web of passages and chambers flanked by eerie rock formations that resembled prehistoric animals gleaming in the night. We thought of many things, but we never suspected that caves like Los Portales would play such an important role during and after the first nuclear confrontation that shook the world.

Following Castro's rise to power in 1959, Núñez Jiménez was appointed director of the National Institute of Agrarian Reform. One of his first projects was to update and expand the existing data base on Cuban caves, purportedly to develop a national program to attract tourism. He employed boy scouts, along with trained personnel, to conduct a census which included the following details: name of the cave; town where it is located; persons who live nearby; sketch of the cave indicating dimensions, temperature, humidity, potable water, if any, entrances to the cave, and closest highways and access roads. This information was subsequently processed and used to select the caves that were to be conditioned for military purposes. Professor Osvaldo Aguirre, a long-standing member of the Cuban Speleological Society, and farmers who lived near the caves apprised us of the census and related activities.

During most of 1959, Castro and Núñez Jiménez were often seen visiting caves, including the Great Cavern of Santo Tomás in the province of Pinar del Río. In describing the cavern, Núñez Jiménez stated that it "presents the peculiarity of being the largest and most beautiful of all the caves in Latin America. . . . Its galleries and subterranean rivers, explored for many years by the author and his colleagues from the Cuban Society of Speleologists, span longitudinally more than fifteen kilometers [about nine miles], forming a complicated underground web of over twenty interconnecting caverns. Some of these galleries lead to secret valleys. . . ."[10]

In February 1960, Vice Prime Minister Mikoyan and Soviet military experts who accompanied him to Cuba visited some of the large caves as they strolled the countryside, ostensibly enjoying the natural beauties of the island. After they left, the Castro regime closed several of the caves to the public and started to clear the terrain as part of a feigned beautification program. In the fall of 1960 the American embassy in Havana received reports that Soviet engineers were secretly involved in the works. Paul D. Bethel, the U.S. press officer, tried to reach one of the caves (Soroa, in Pinar del Río), but large signs indicated that no visitors were allowed pending completion of a project initiated by the National Institute of Tourism. It did not escape notice, however, that the access roads were blocked by army troops.

In 1961, a group of speleologists from Poland, headed by Maciej Kuczynski, arrived in Cuba. The members of the expedition wore military attire and were escorted by Cuban Army Major Eladio Elso Alonso (who later became a staff member of the Cuban Nuclear Group). Bell Huertas, stationed in the Cuban Foreign Ministry in Havana at the time, reportedly informed Paul Bethel when the former defected in early 1963 that the Poles "were used as a screen, since the Poles are more 'respectable' Communists than the Russians." Behind this facade, Bell Huertas said, the Russians were pulling the strings and arranging for military construction to follow the explorations of the Poles.

Huertas also made this arresting comment: "A fundamental tenet in our teaching is always to show one thing openly to distract attention from what we are doing covertly. In other words, show something above ground to preoccupy the enemy while we proceed with the important work underground. Those caves could easily provide natural bomb-proof shelters for scores of missiles." [11]

Several months prior to the October 1962 Missile Crisis, Soviet-bloc personnel removed Cuban workers from some of the cave sites and took charge of the underground installations. To ensure adequate supplies of building material, the Russian Vasiliev Mendeviev ran the Titan Cement Factory at Santiago de Cuba and the El Morro Cement Factory at Mariel, and controlled national production of reinforced concrete. To condition the caves for military use, Soviet-bloc experts imported steel bars from Ostrava, Czechoslovakia, and prefabricated arches, refrigeration equipment to store liquid oxygen and sophisticated electronic devices, and lead lining to house radioactive materials. Within the vast cave complexes, the Russians built connecting tunnels, some of them with railway tracks to deploy heavy arms and troops below the surface.

When U.S. reconnaissance planes photographed the Cuban missile bases, Soviet-bloc technicians had virtually completed the reinforcement and expansion of the principal caves and caverns, particularly those lying on the perimeter of the four Soviet strategic complexes: the Great Cavern of Santo Tomás, near the San Cristóbal base; the Gobernadora Hill complex close to the Guanajay base; the Purio caves, adjacent to the Sagua La Grande base; and the Caguanes cavern, within the area of the Remedios base. It was thus quite easy for the Soviets to give the impression that they were withdrawing all of the strategic missiles, when they were possibly storing some of them underground.

Alarmed by these reports, Senate investigators summoned the head of U.S. Army Intelligence, Major General Alva R. Fitch, on March 6, 1963. Under heavy questioning, Fitch testified as follows:

"From the large volume and frequency of reports concerning the underground storage of ammunition, supplies, vehicles, and even aircraft, it is certain that there is considerable activity in connection with underground installations throughout the island. . . .

"There are several thousand caves in Cuba and many have been used for storage over the years. With the reported addition of dehumidification and air conditioning equipment, many would be suited to storage of both large and delicate electronic items."

General Fitch described the various kinds of tanks, artillery mortars, rocket launchers, and ground-to-ground missiles in Cuba today and then declared:

"With the introduction of this equipment into Cuba the potential firepower and mobility of ground forces has been increased considerably. . . . No nuclear warheads are believed to be in Cuba although it is possible that they could be used by some of the weapons systems present there." [12]

General Fitch and other senior members of the U.S. intelligence community were of the opinion that all strategic missiles and bombers had been removed from Cuba, but they readily acknowledged that, in terms of absolute, it was quite possible that offensive weapons remained on the island, concealed in caves or otherwise.

Given the prevailing uncertainty, the Senate Preparedness Investigating Subcommittee stated: "It is fair to say . . . that this [reports of concealed strategic weapons in Cuba] is a matter of great concern to the intelligence community. Based on skepticism, if nothing else, there is grave apprehension on this score. It is agreed that ironclad assurance of the complete absence of Soviet strategic missiles in Cuba can come only as a result of thorough, penetrating on-site inspection by reliable observers. The current intelligence estimate that they are not present is based largely on the negative evidence that there is no affirmative proof to the contrary. This, of course, was precisely the status of the matter prior to last October 14." [13]

Urging President Kennedy to insist upon on-site inspection,

the Senate Preparedness Subcommittee underscored the critical-
ity of the issue: ". . . Assuming maximum readiness at prese-
lected sites, with all equipment prelocated, the Soviet mobile
medium range (1,100 miles) missiles could be made operational in
a matter of hours."[14]

While informed senators voiced their warnings, Cuban refugees arriving in Miami in late 1962 and through most of the decade
provided alarming data on the continued Soviet military buildup
on the island. Among the hundreds of reports we received following the lifting of the U.S. naval blockade was the testimony of
thirteen *guajiros,* led by Manuel García Ramírez, who lived close
to the dismantled missile base in Remedios.

On arrival in Miami, on December 18, 1962, they declared
that some four thousand Russian soldiers were stationed at the
nearby farm of La Cantera. They were working constantly on underground installations, availing themselves of the large caves that
honeycomb La Puntilla hill. During the day militiamen hauled tons
of cement and other construction material up to the entrance to
the camp; from that point the Russians took over the trucks and
returned them empty for reload. At night Russian soldiers drove
enormous truck-trailers bearing long cylindrical objects covered
with tarpaulins. The *guajiros* ended their testimony by saying to
tell the Americans that "from the Remedios missile base the Russians have not even removed a firecracker."[15]

On January 20, 1962, the seventy-three-year-old White Russian Andrew Golochenko, who had designed the bronze lions that
flank the Paceo del Prado Boulevard in Havana, managed to leave
the island. Given his Russian background and language proficiency, he had been able to gain access to groups of Soviet-bloc
officers in Cuba. Immediately after he landed in Miami he divulged that he had heard—that "the missiles the Russians took
out are dummies; the real ones are in subterranean bases."

According to an underground report from the Student Revolutionary Directorate, evidence of the presence of strategic missiles came to light in a spectacular manner on March 20, 1964.
"At exactly 9:10 P.M. . . . . a fire broke out at La Guatana Soviet
base in Pinar del Río province. It was followed an hour later by a
series of twelve giant explosions which sent debris flying to a height
of 3,000 feet, covering an area of several miles. . . . The rest of
the night, and the following day, large Russian truck-trailers moved
a score of missiles from La Guatana to a Russian base located
at the Granja Escuela Ludovico S. Noda, a short distance from

the provincial capital of Pinar del Río. Only partially covered with tarpaulins, the missiles, ranging in length from 40 to 120 feet, were visible to onlookers who were quickly dispersed by Cuban militia." As revealed by the former owner of a neighboring farm, the explosions were caused by leakage of liquid oxygen, the propellant reportedly used for the Soviet missiles in Cuba.[16]

One of the most chilling eyewitness reports came a few years later from a Cuban escapee, Manuel Vidal. Driving his station wagon around 2:00 A.M. from the town of Punta Brava to Caimito, thirty miles west of Havana, Vidal noticed as he rounded a curve that some forty feet of guard rails and cement posts at the edge of the highway had been torn out. Vidal looked down and saw a truck-trailer that had overturned and a huge missile lying on the side. He parked his car and from a hillock watched the salvage operation. Russian military and civilian personnel promptly arrived and took charge of the removal of the missile. Two fire engines, cranes, and a Russian tank truck came to the site, and the work began. In recalling the scene, Vidal said: "Several cranes on caterpillar trucks pulled the truck-trailer out of the way, then stood the huge missile on end with its nose pointed toward the sky. There was a moment of panic," added Vidal, "when the missile began to give off a yellowish-orange vapor [a characteristic reportedly associated with ballistic missiles]. Then the Russian tank truck was brought into position, and streams of a milky colored liquid were poured over it."

Vidal pointed out that "water and milky colored liquid were also sprayed all over the ground in an area about 200 yards around where the missile had fallen. By this time, steam shovels had arrived, and they scooped out a carpet of earth one foot in depth over the entire area, and loaded it with great care into dump trucks which took it away."[17]

Despite the veil of secrecy covering the post–October 1962 Russian military constructions in Cuba, the incessant burrowing and tunneling by Soviet-bloc personnel, and the deployment of huge cylindrical objects reported by Cuban underground agents and escapees, Washington continued to affirm that there was no hard evidence that the Russians had kept strategic weapons on the island. The Cuban informants could show no photographs, and they allegedly lacked the necessary training to distinguish between offensive and defensive missiles.

Washington's denials notwithstanding, the Revolutionary Council lent credence to the persistent refugee reports of strategic missiles in Cuba, particularly after several disgruntled U.S. intelligence agents privately confirmed and elaborated on the council's data. As for me, I was intrigued and alarmed, even in the absence of conclusive evidence, by the confidential revelations of an exceptional witness—an embassy official of a NATO country who had been stationed in Havana for several years, before and after the Missile Crisis. He carried diplomatic credentials but only as a cover for intelligence missions, which he had fulfilled with distinction in several countries since the end of World War II.

His task in Cuba was, far and away, the most important and risky of the lot. Working closely with the U.S. intelligence community, he was involved in the early detection of the missiles and in monitoring the dismantling of the Soviet bases. He barely escaped arrest in Havana as the alleged head of a "CIA spy ring" in the mid-1960s, and fled with his family to the United States, where he died years later, isolated and forlorn. A daring operative in the twilight fronts of the East-West intelligence war, he will remain in anonymity at the request of his widow, who asked me not to publicize his name.

During the months that preceded the October 1962 confrontation, Mr. X (as I will refer to him) often flew to Mexico and Miami to meet with U.S. intelligence officers. Burly and balding, with a ruddy complexion and a zestful personality, he posed as an affable diplomat who came to relax and enjoy the epicurean attractions of southern Florida. Since my parents had developed a personal relationship with him before they left Havana, Mr. X frequently had dinner with us when he visited the Cuban "exile capital." He was rather circumspect about his covert assignment, but we knew that he availed himself of his embassy's diplomatic pouch to deliver top-secret data he and his team had gathered on Soviet military activities in Cuba.

During his sojourns in Miami, my brother-in-law, Ramón Acosta, used to drive Mr. X to a rendezvous in the Westchester residential area. Clutching a large briefcase filled with confidential material, he would wait for his contacts at a bar. He occasionally disappeared for several days to receive special CIA training on the use of ultramodern electronic gadgets, including underwater equipment.

About two years after the Missile Crisis, I had the opportunity to converse at length with Mr. X. No longer active in intelligence operations, he was more outspoken during our tête-à-tête at home. To start, I posed a question that had been bugging me all along:

"Why was the United States so late in detecting Soviet strategic missiles in Cuba?" Without any hesitation, he responded: "The lateness was not in detecting, but in reacting." He told me that in late 1961 the Soviets had commenced shipping strategic weapons systems to Cuba from the ports of Odessa and Riga, which were under close U.S and NATO surveillance.[18] Then he added: "Despite extreme security measures taken by the Soviets in Cuba, trained agents and I managed to photograph strategic missiles from afar." He wouldn't reveal the details, but he did say that they used very potent cameras with infrared rays to operate at night.

Was he sure they were strategic missiles? "Of course," he said with a condescending smile. "We had the expertise and ground capability to differentiate between strategic and defensive weapons." When I asked him if Washington had received the evidence prior to October 1962, he replied: "I presume the evidence reached intelligence quarters in Washington several months before the crisis. I personally delivered the photographs to my contacts in Miami, and believe me, the pictures were not just of SA-II surface-to-air missiles." He explained that Washington had to be cautious in order not to expose human intelligence assets inside Cuba, but, he pointed out, "there was no need to wait for the U-2 photographs of strategic missile bases to react. The October 1962 missile shock was not caused by the lack of military intelligence," he stressed, "but by the unwillingness of policymakers to heed it."

I then asked Mr. X whether the Soviets had miscalculated American resolve and had to back down. He answered thus: "I really don't know whether the Russians anticipated such a swift and awesome deployment of American might. But they certainly were prepared to use the specter of a nuclear clash to negotiate to their advantage." I urged him to be more specific. "The deal they struck," he said, "without on-site inspection, has enabled them to conceal some of their strategic weapons in huge underground installations and caves, on which they have been working since 1961."

When I asked him to give me an example, he opened a large map of Cuba I had in my room and pointed to La Gobernadora Hills, located between the towns of Quiebra Hacha and Cabañas, north of Pinar del Río province. "There," he said, "in those hills the Soviets have carved out their command post for the Western Zone of Cuba. We were able to monitor the deployment of medium-range missiles into a large subterranean complex with tunnels that stretch some eight miles from the hills to the vicinity of the port of Mariel. Two of the tunnels are large enough to accommodate two-way truck traffic, and another one is lined with lead plates or laminae . . . to store nuclear warheads, we suspect.''

"Did you apprise U.S. intelligence officers of the continued Soviet strategic buildup in Cuba?'' I asked Mr. X.

"Yes, to no avail,'' he replied. "Washington seems reluctant to reopen the Missile Crisis and confront the Russians again. This has enabled them to transform the island of Cuba into a virtually impregnable base for Communist agitation and subversion.'' Then, with a sudden flush that belied his coolness, he remarked: "Despite our overwhelming power at the time of the showdown on Cuba,[19] despite the total backing of the West, Washington flinched and the Russians stayed. . . . And they stayed with something they did not have before the crisis: a U.S. noninvasion pledge.''[20]

CHAPTER 14
The Unsettling Aftermath

Several Central American ambassadors to the OAS privately expressed to me displeasure and concern when they learned that President Kennedy had given Khrushchev assurances against an invasion of Cuba from the United States or any other country of the Western Hemisphere.[1] These ambassadors feared that the noninvasion pledge—binding Latin American republics without their consent or knowledge—would force Washington to accept and even safeguard the permanence of a Soviet-backed Communist regime in Cuba. In this connection, I heard allusions to Chamberlain's Munich, prompted by Kennedy's statement upon lifting the naval blockade that under certain conditions there would be "peace in the Caribbean."

A few months later, President Villeda Morales of Honduras, stating his views and those of his neighbors, publicly reminded the White House that "it is absolutely essential to win the battle of Cuba. . . . that battle cannot be considered ended with the mere withdrawal of Russian missiles. . . . it must end by returning millions of Cubans to liberty."[2]

In an effort to stem growing restlessness, Kennedy agreed to meet with the presidents of Central America in San José, Costa Rica, on March 18–20, 1963. The trip was a tremendous public relations success. The crowds acclaimed him as a hero, and the students cheered and applauded his eloquent peroration at the university: "Too much blood has been shed over too many years to preserve our independence from foreign rule. And we will never

237

be secure in our hemisphere until the Soviet Union goes the way of George III, the Spanish conquerors, Maximilian, and William Walker. And indeed it must and will.''

But the Central American leaders expected more than rhetoric. Just prior to the summit, Kennedy had vetoed a specific proposal for further OAS action to cut Cuba off from the rest of the hemisphere. Instead, the President recommended a higher dose of Alliance for Progress aid to immunize Central America from communism. Contending that economic assistance was not enough to counter Castro-driven subversion, the Central Americans outlined several options to stimulate internal resistance in Cuba. Kennedy was unresponsive and evasive. As reported by the *Miami Herald,* one of the Central American leaders later commented: "The U.S. Government seemed to be paralyzed by Russian atomic blackmail or by secret agreements entered into during the October Cuban crisis."[3]

The Cuban Revolutionary Council and the refugee community in Miami were also baffled and alarmed by the Kennedy-Khrushchev settlement. We believed, however, that the noninvasion pledge would not be binding, since the USSR had failed to comply with an essential condition: on-site inspection. We certainly did not feel bound by the semisecret superpower pact and were determined to pursue our efforts to destabilize the Castro regime and force the stalling Soviets out of Cuba.

The situation on the island was simmering with discontent. A large number of disgruntled *guajiros* had refused to work in the sugar harvest. Armed Forces Minister Raúl Castro acknowledged massive desertions from its labor ranks in his May 1, 1963, speech. He said: "Today we face an economic problem of the gravest nature. The revolution mobilized 50,000 people from their jobs in urban areas—factories, offices, and stores—and made them permanent volunteer cane cutters." Despite these draconian measures, the 1963 harvest plummeted to 3,800,000 tons from a high of 5,610,000 tons in 1958—the last pre-Castro harvest. Fidel accused the "enemies of the revolution" for the disaster and, on June 4, issued this warning: "Workers will do well to remember that the revolution is powerful enough to wipe them all out, to confiscate all that they own, in one day."

Sugar-production decline was not the only problem besetting the nation. The president of the National Institute of Agrarian Reform reported in July: "We find that we harvested only 40 percent as much corn this year as last; only 65 percent of the beans; 55

percent of the peanuts; 37 percent of the soybeans." To assuage severe food shortage in a fertile country that had never before experienced the rationing of essentials, in 1963 the Soviet Union allocated to Cuba $33 million of its total purchases of wheat and flour from Canada.

The mounting turmoil in the countryside soon spread to the urban areas. On September 11, 1963, the National Federation of Construction Workers staged a violent protest during a labor conference in Havana because Russian military personnel had been allowed to control all heavy construction in Cuba—cement plants, lumber mills, transport, and auxiliary industries—to satisfy their requirements for the subterranean bases. When old-guard Communist labor boss Lázaro Peña tried to address the demands of the irate workers to demilitarize the construction industry, meet urgent housing needs, and compensate them for the extended lay-off period, he was drowned out by cries of "We want freedom! We are hungry! We want to be Cubans!" Lázaro Peña was forced to break off the meeting and leave the Labor Palace, whereupon the rebellious delegates smashed chairs, tore out light fixtures, and wrecked the hall.

The underground movement capitalized on the pervading unrest to foment sabotage and uprisings. Anti-Castro agents were involved in five major train derailments from the end of December 1962 to March 1963. *Guajiros* burned cane fields on a scale far larger than that of the previous year. And guerrillas surged not only in the mountainous areas of Cuba, but also in the generally flat province of Matanzas, where armed counterrevolutionaries, by Fidel's own admission, pinned down 26,000 militiamen and troops and forced the government to clamp on a curfew.

The Russians did not remain idle. They trained Castro's crack forces in counterinsurgency techniques and participated in several military operations. Miguel Velásquez, a guerrilla who managed to escape to the United States, affirmed that Soviet troops were involved in crushing anti-Castro resistance. He said: "We operated in the hills of Oriente Province. The morning of March 26, a band of us attacked the garrison guarding the Nicaro mines. Our assault surprised the garrison, and we succeeded in wounding six and killing two others. As we withdrew we were attacked by a group of Russian soldiers dressed in Cuban army uniforms. They overpowered our smaller group, capturing twelve and shooting our commander Armando Govea."[4]

Confirmation that the Russians were indeed wearing Cuban

army uniforms came from the head seamstress of the San Ambrosio uniform factory, Mrs. Pérez Cabrera. Upon arriving in Miami in 1963, she said: "Just two months before I escaped, the supply officer of the Cuban General Staff issued an urgent order for us to manufacture 1,000 Cuban army uniforms daily. Great speed was demanded, and we worked overtime. The average size of the uniforms struck me as very peculiar. Cubans are relatively small people, but the order was largely in the 44 and 46 sizes. I thought it was a mistake, and examined the order again. The order stated clearly that the uniforms were for Soviet troops who are awaiting delivery."[5]

Meanwhile, in Miami, anti-Castro commando groups were preparing to strike. They wanted to boost internal resistance, put pressure on the Russians to leave, and demonstrate that the Kennedy–Khrushchev pact would not deflate or block the Cubans' effort to liberate themselves. On March 18, representatives of the exile organization Alpha 66 attacked the Soviet ship *Lgov* at the Cuban port of Isabela de Sagua. The Russians charged that a pirate vessel had fired several bursts from a heavy machine gun and blamed the United States for encouraging such actions, which, according to Moscow, violated "the agreement reached . . . on the settlement of the crisis in the area of the Caribbean Sea."

Actually, the White House was dead set against these attacks, which, in Kennedy's words, "could cause more harm than good." That is why Tony Cuesta, the leader of "Comandos L," had to prepare with cunning and secrecy the spectacular raid on the Russian freighter *Baku,* which marked a turning point in the Cuban exiles' relationship with Washington and in their struggle for freedom.

Tony had the daring and experience to launch that operation. A tall, determined onetime Havana businessman, he had become a seasoned seafaring captain infiltrating anti-Castro cadres into Cuba and carrying out coastal forays. This was to be one of the most dangerous undertakings, because the Cubans and the Soviets had tightened security measures and the American authorities were no longer winking at the raiders. After eluding U.S. surveillance, Tony and his crew left Florida aboard a mother ship and sailed to an inlet along the Anguilla Isles, bathed by the azure waters of the Bahamas. There they cast off the *Phoenix*—a converted twenty-two-foot speedboat—from the mother vessel and prepared for the adventurous journey.

Mario Alvarez, the agile electrician, worked on the faulty engines for three days. Ramón Font, the resourceful armorer, installed their heavy artillery—a lone 20mm cannon. Then he prepared their "torpedo"—an incendiary device strapped onto a homemade forty-pound magnet-equipped explosive mine. It was a nerve-racking job which only Ramón, who had the steady pulse of a neurosurgeon, could calmly do while humming "Twinkle, Twinkle, Little Star." Tony and the rest of the crew took care of the food supplies and the plastic-wrapped hardware—infantry rifles, carbines, pistols, ammunition, and cans of gasoline mixed with baby-soap flakes (the easiest sort of do-it-yourself napalm bomb). Not to be forgotten were the infrared lights and cameras of Andrew St. George, the *Life* photographer and chronicler of the venture.

At 3:30 on the afternoon of March 28, the *Phoenix* finally set off, cutting through heavy swells at ten to twelve knots. Just before midnight, Tony and his men could see the glow of the port of Caibarién. Anchored downwind was their imposing target: the bulky, round-bottomed Soviet freighter *Baku*. Tranquilino, the navigator, circled her very slowly and quietly. Tension was gnawing at all of the crew. Tony stared at the freighter and mused, "Wonder if they have lots of vodka aboard. Be a pity to waste it." The quip eased the stress, but not for long.

A low-silhouetted motor launch suddenly appeared on the scene, its spotlight sweeping across the *Phoenix*'s windshield. It was one of the new Soviet patrol vessels making her rounds. The raiders watched breathlessly as they held fast to their guns. The launch apparently saw nothing suspicious and disappeared into the darkness. A few minutes later, ten loud explosions shattered the silence. It was Ramón firing his cannon at the command bridge of the freighter. At less than ten yards, every rifle aboard the *Phoenix* shot at the deck of the *Baku*. Under the covering arch of fire, Tony impassively said, "*Ahora la bomba*"—"now the bomb."

As described by Andrew St. George, "Ramón leans out ready to drop the bomb, its fuse lit, overboard. But the bomb won't budge. The line attached to its float is tangled on the deck rail. Ramón tugs and yanks. The burning fuse has three or four minutes to go. . . . Ramón crashes his body against the railing. The railing gives, the line swings free. Someone leaps to help and the bomb is overboard. . . . Tranquilino swings the *Phoenix* away from the freighter. . . . There is a thud. . . . A geyser shoots up, way above the freighter's tall funnels. . . . Our boat shudders for a moment. From behind us I hear the crash of glass. The rifles on the *Phoenix* keep firing. Then all is silence as we speed away into the night."[6]

The blasting of a thirteen-foot hole in the *Baku* touched off the wildest international dustup since the October Missile Crisis. Moscow accused the United States of "dangerous provocation," hinted it might arm its merchant ships bound for Cuba, and pledged "aid and support" to Castro. Meantime, the Cuban ruler ordered two of his MiGs to fire on the U.S. transport *Floridian* in the high seas, and threatened to procure long-range bombers and naval equipment to convoy his ships. The Cuban commandos had underestimated the international repercussions of the incident. They certainly expected howling and pounding from their enemies, but they did not anticipate condemnation and persecution from their friends.

The U.S. authorities and most of the press held that such forays were counterproductive and dangerous, that they would strengthen the Soviet position in Cuba rather than weaken it and tighten Communist controls rather than loosen them. Sympathy with the cause of a free Cuba did not mean, the exiles were told, "that we are prepared to see our own laws violated with impunity or to tolerate activities which might provoke armed reprisals, the brunt of which would be borne by the armed forces of the United States."[7]

The Cuban exiles were not without vocal advocates—a testimony to the fairness and vitality of the American democratic system, which permits and indeed encourages healthy debates. Apart from supportive Republican leaders (who carried their own political agendas), well-known journalists came to the raiders' defense. David Lawrence reminded Washington that neutrality laws were plainly designed to apply to expeditions started on United States territory against countries with which the United States maintains friendly and normal relations, which was not the case with Cuba.[8] Roscoe Drummond challenged the assertion that the anti-Castro forays would make it harder to persuade Khrushchev to withdraw the Soviet troops. "If we insure the Soviets against any hazards for their troops in Cuba," he argued, "there is absolutely no incentive for Khrushchev to withdraw them."[9] Drummond also pointed out: "You may believe that the hit-and-run raids are only insignificant, hectoring pinpricks. So were Castro's first hit-and-run attacks on Batista. The only way to begin is to begin."[10]

Henry J. Taylor expressed deeper concerns. He wrote: "Who

would have dreamed that mighty America could have come full circle?—Here we said, as the minimum demand of the American people, that 'a Communist state will not be tolerated in the Western Hemisphere', that 'communism is not negotiable in the Western Hemisphere' . . . And what happens? We end up protecting, guaranteeing and solidifying Red Castro and the Soviet lodgment there with all the power of our great Air Force and the U.S. Navy!" [11]

Taylor's foreboding conclusion seemed exaggerated. But drastic measures taken by Washington soon gave credence to what he was saying. Pursuant to instructions from the Attorney General, the State and Justice Departments ordered a crackdown against all future raids on Cuba. Exile leaders and action groups were restricted to the land limits of Dade County, a 2,500-square-mile area which includes Miami. Speedboats owned by Cuban refugees were impounded. The Coast Guard set up an auxiliary station at Opa-locka airport, acquired six additional amphibian patrol planes and twelve surface craft, and increased its force by 20 percent to 3,600. To complete the quarantine of the Cuban exiles, Washington enlisted the support of the British authorities in the Bahamas to patrol adjoining seas.

Watching this impressive display of U.S.-British might, Henry J. Taylor remarked: "In tragic truth, Castro's Russian masters have outthought us, outmaneuvered us and cast us out of control of the situation. . . . How else—how else—could we now find ourselves forced to order a wrongway blockade against fighters for freedom instead of against Castro?" [12]

At the Revolutionary Council headquarters, pressure on Miró to act or resign reached an all-time high. Sensing that U.S. policy on Cuba was "drifting toward accommodation," as Arthur Schlesinger would later aver, Miró had sent off two memoranda to John H. Crimmins, who had been charged by the State Department to assume in Miami interagency coordination of Cuban affairs. Miró had asked for confirmation that the United States would support the liberation of Cuba and had outlined possible ways and means to further that goal through internal resistance backed from abroad. The Soviets had found a way to achieve just the reverse, Miró noted. "They give [Castro] all of the arms required to sustain the Cuban regime and penetrate Latin America, without risking a single Russian."

Having received no response to his urgent missives, Miró asked his executive assistant and interpreter, Ernesto Aragón, to follow

up in Washington. On April 1, 1963, Aragón met with Robert Hurwitch, deputy chief of the State Department's Cuban desk, at the
office of Joseph A. Califano, coordinator of Cuban affairs at the
Pentagon. Califano also attended the meeting, along with Colonel
Alexander Haig. Hurwitch asked Aragón to forward a copy of
Miró's memoranda, which apparently had not reached his office,
and then proceeded to inform Aragón that the training of Cuban
units at Fort Jackson, Fort Benning, and Maxwell Air Force Base
(involving some 2,700 recruits) would end forthwith. Aragón was
taken aback by the decision to discharge the Cuban forces (enlisted and trained pursuant to an agreement reached with President Kennedy) and asked Hurwitch whether that signaled a change
in U.S. policy toward Castro. "No," Hurwitch replied, "we're
discontinuing that program because of shortage of funds." He added
that as soon as the trainees returned to Miami they should "register at the Cuban welfare offices and seek employment."

Upon learning of these developments, Miró flew to Washington and had a long meeting with Hurwitch on April 3 at Aragón's
small office and *pied-à-terre* located at La Salle Apartments, 1028
Connecticut Avenue. During the discussions (conducted in Spanish, since Hurwitch was fluent in that language), Miró asked for
the continuation of the military training program, the release of
the Cuban commandos and their boats, and a well-coordinated
plan of sabotage and guerrilla warfare aimed at weakening the
Castro regime and facilitating the final Cuban-American thrust.
"A denial of these requests," Miró stressed, "would lead me to
believe that Washington has changed its Cuban policy, possibly
as a result of the Kennedy-Khrushchev Missile Crisis accord, and
would force me to so inform the council and tender my resignation."

Hurwitch strongly objected to the notion of a change of policy and told Miró that there were "secret plans" to resolve the
Cuban Communist problem, but that Hurwitch could not disclose
them. "You can't disclose them," Miró retorted, "because they
don't exist." Hurwitch countered, saying that the Cuban leader
was obfuscated, intractable, and emotional. Miró, irritated and tired,
said, "Bob, I don't want to know the secrets of the United States,
but I do expect and demand to know, and be involved in, any
plans that might affect the future of my country."

To summarize his position, Miró added: "We basically have
three options to liberate Cuba: joint Cuban-American military action; failing that, Cuban military action with the same type of [U.S.]

military and financial assistance for the Cuban exiles that the Soviet Union provides for the Castro regime; and failing that, Cuban
military action with no U.S. involvement other than a loan to the
Cuban Revolutionary Council to prosecute the war. I expect a
clear answer from the United States; otherwise I'll draw my own
conclusions.''

At Hurwitch's request, Miró remained in Washington three
more days to see the Attorney General, Robert Kennedy. The
meeting was held on Saturday morning, April 6, at the Attorney
General's office. While Miró and Aragón were waiting in the ante-
room, two of Robert Kennedy's young sons passed by with their
huge Labrador dog, Brumus. A few minutes later, the Cubans
were escorted to the Attorney General's office. He had removed
his jacket, loosened his tie, rolled up his sleeves, and left his shoes
under the desk. Despite his seeming informality, he was sullen
and tense. There was not even a hint of a smile in his steely gaze.
Since he was alone, Ernesto Aragón acted as interpreter and took
notes, which he recently disclosed to me.

Not wasting any time on perfunctory remarks, the Attorney
General bluntly told Miró: "You seem to be misinformed. We
have not changed our policy toward Cuba. The U.S. government
never represented to you that it had committed itself to taking
military action against Castro." Miró responded: "Since the be
ginning I was told, I think in your presence, that the Cuban problem was essentially military, requiring at least six divisions, with
as many Cubans involved as possible. I cannot imagine that the
six divisions meant Brazilians, Argentines, or anyone else except
North Americans." Visibly irked, the Attorney General shot back:
"I was not present when you allegedly were told that Cuba was a
military problem. That is not true, and besides, there are no military plans against Cuba."

Miró was flustered by Robert Kennedy's cutting remarks,
knowing full well that the Attorney General had been present when
the President affirmed that Cuba was a military problem and asked
Richard Goodwin to step up the training of Cuban units at several
U.S. camps. His integrity called into question, Miró responded
with anger. Stabbing the air with his index finger, he told the Attorney General: "You are a kid"—*chiquillo* was the term he used—
"speaking to a university professor . . . one of three generations
[of Mirós] who have fought for freedom . . . and I will not allow
you to cast a shadow of doubt on my word of honor!"

The acrimonious exchange did not abate. Robert Kennedy

lambasted the Cuban commando groups for their irresponsible and
ineffectual operations. "I will not tolerate any actions from U.S.
territory that are contrary to the laws of this country," the Attorney General emphatically asserted. Miró responded: "How can
you say that you support freedom-loving Cubans when you per-
secute them and bar them from fighting for the liberation of their
homeland?"

As further evidence that the United States had changed its
Cuban policy, Miró told Robert Kennedy that the council had not
been consulted prior to the crackdown on the raiders, that he (Miró)
had not been allowed to travel to Costa Rica during the presidential summit at San José, and that the U.S. government had forbidden him to visit Cuban exile trainees at Fort Benning, Georgia,
and Fort Jackson, North Carolina.

When Miró reiterated his intention to resign, the Attorney
General clenched his jaw and muttered: "Tell me, Dr. Cardona,
what is it, specifically, that you want?" Miró outlined the three
options to liberate Cuba he had discussed with Hurwitch, including a U.S. loan to the council to prosecute the war if Washington
preferred not to involve American troops or resources. "What is
the order of magnitude?" Robert Kennedy asked. "I am not prepared to give you an estimate without consulting with military
specialists," Miró replied. Robert Kennedy pressed him to give
him a rough number. "I really don't know," Miró said, "but if
you insist, fifty . . . one hundred million?"

The Attorney General promptly changed the subject and told
Miró that he did not understand why Miró wanted to resign and
urged him to think it over for thirty days and then meet with him
again. "But if you decide to resign and to issue a public statement," Robert Kennedy warned, "you must clear the text with
us first. Sensitive disclosures might be harmful to the security of
the United States and could be used against us by enemies of this
administration."

According to Aragón's notes, Miró stood up and somberly
replied: "I came here to seek clarifications regarding the Cuban
situation. After a careful assessment of the facts and of the re-
sponses received, I have concluded that you have changed your
policy toward Cuba and that you have no plans or intentions to
put an end to the Castro regime. I outlined possible courses of
action and they have been tacitly rejected. I am, therefore, impelled to resign. I cannot wait thirty days, and I do not intend to
consult with anyone on the text of my resignation. I assume full

responsibility for my actions. Good afternoon and goodbye." To the Attorney General's dismay, Miró, followed by Aragón, left the room. The long and fruitless discussion had finished.

Soon after Miró and Aragón had returned to the latter's apartment, Hurwitch appeared on the scene. Probably briefed by Robert Kennedy on the results of the meeting, Hurwitch tried to convince Miró not to resign. "The positions are irreconcilable," Miró said. "Nothing that you or Robert Kennedy has told me indicates that there is any intention of liberating Cuba." When Hurwitch tried to rehash his arguments, Miró interrupted him: "Listen, Bob, for two years I have been taking a lot of tranquilizers to keep me going and to believe what the government of the United States was telling me. I can assure you that I will no longer take tranquilizers."

Miró proceeded to type his long letter of resignation, which included a litany of broken promises and unfulfilled plans. He then flew to Miami with Aragón. An urgent message awaited him at home: "Please contact the White House immediately." Aragón returned the call on behalf of Miró and heard a familiar voice. It was Robert Kennedy urging Miró not to resign. "If he insists," the Attorney General added, "we expect him to give us a copy of his statement a few hours before he goes public, as the President had done prior to announcing the blockade on Cuba." The Attorney General paused, and then punctuated these words: "We still consider him an ally, and not an enemy of the United States." Aragón agreed to convey the message to Miró and to give an answer that afternoon to Robert Hurwitch at the White House.

Two hours later, Aragón informed Hurwitch that Miró was determined to resign and would give Hurwitch a copy of the statement when he deemed it opportune. According to Aragón's notes, Hurwitch stated that Miró's attitude would lead to a severance of U.S. relations with the Cuban exiles. "No single Cuban will ever be received in any government office in the future," the State Department official reportedly asserted. He also reminded Aragón that there were a number of legal reasons for canceling a U.S. residence permit—a "green card." When Aragón asked whether that was a personal or an official government threat, Hurwitch reportedly answered: "No, not at all, just a point of view prompted by Miró's incomprehensible attitude." He noted, however, that having spoken with the Attorney General and a presidential adviser on this issue, he assumed that their stance reflected the thinking of the President.

Miró remained firm in his decision to resign but, given the implications of Hurwitch's message, asked Aragón to walk over to a public telephone, call the Costa Rican ambassador in Washington, Gonzalo Facio, and inquire about the possibility of obtaining Costa Rican visas for Miró, his family, and Aragón. Aware of Miró's predicament, the ambassador immediately gave pertinent instructions to his consul in Miami, who issued the requested visas the following day.

On April 9, a few hours before Miró tendered his resignation to the council, he handed a copy of his public statement to Hurwitch, who had flown to Miami. When the latter read it, he was furious. "You can't do that, Pepe," he shouted. "You've gone crazy. You would be helping Castro and betraying the United States!" After an equally vehement riposte, Miró asked Hurwitch to leave his house. As he waited outside for a taxi, Hurwitch asked Aragón to help Miró regain his equanimity, and said: "I assure you that if he waits and does not release his letter of resignation, we can reach an accord that will enable us to continue working together until we achieve the liberation of Cuba." "Are you giving this assurance on behalf of the State Department?" Aragón asked. "Yes, I am," replied Hurwitch. "Please convey this to Miró and let me know if he is willing to wait."

The council did not accept Miró's resignation and asked him to withhold his public statement pending a resolution of the crisis, as requested by Hurwitch. The State Department, however, made no effort to reconcile the differences. Instead, availing itself of the copy of Miró's statement delivered to Hurwitch (the only one that had been released), State started leaking to the press fragments out of context, conveying the impression that Miró was about to resign because Washington had refused to bow to his ultimatum of a $50 million loan and a pledge to invade Cuba.

Incensed by this attempt to discredit him with misrepresentations and innuendos, Miró tendered his resignation on April 18 and released for publication the twenty-four page appendix explaining the motives. Although it was addressed primarily to the exile community, the document received wide coverage in the United States and abroad. It had the effect of a political and diplomatic bomb. Washington vigorously counterattacked, denying the allegations made by the exile leader and accusing him of fabricating commitments and distorting facts. Miró decided not to fuel the acrid polemic with counterallegations. That is why he did not publish the additional confidential information, pre– and post–

Bay of Pigs, which I have included in this book.

I saw Miró a few days after he resigned and flew to Puerto Rico. He was under tremendous and conflicting pressures, but he was steadfast in his resolution and at ease with his conscience. In a brief aside, he told me: "You know, throughout the process, I have been able to withstand the impatience, even the diatribes, of my compatriots because I had confidence in our friends in Washington, who promised me to support the liberation of Cuba. Now, however, with the Kennedy-Khrushchev pact and the resulting change of policy, my faith has been dashed." Frowning more than ever, he added: "Washington is seeking, I am convinced, an accommodation with Castro . . . but I will not be a party to that disgrace. The son of General Miró Argenter will never play the shameful role of Marshal Pétain!"

Ten days after Miró had been snubbed by Washington and compelled to resign, the international wire services reported that the "Cuban Premier Fidel Castro, wearing a fur hat and a trenchcoat with sleeves far too long, flew into Moscow . . . and received the warmest, most tumultuous welcome ever accorded a foreign dignitary in the Soviet Union." [13] During his forty days in Russia—probably a record in the annals of state visits—Fidel journeyed to fourteen cities; inspected the Northern Fleet and strategic forces rocket base; delivered innumerable speeches at stadiums, factories, monuments, and town squares; reviewed the May Day Parade from the top of the Kremlin Wall; received the title of Hero of the Soviet Union, the Order of Lenin, and the Gold Star; and spent scores of hours conversing and chuckling with Nikita Khrushchev and his successor-to-be, Leonid Brezhnev.

Meanwhile, in Miami, the political environment was heating up. Miró's resignation had set off a virulent controversy among Cuban exiles. Some of those who had accused him in the past of being too readily yielding to the Americans now reproached him for breaking with Washington. Others who had charged him with weaving dreams now censured him for prophesying disaster. Within the council, Tony Varona, who assumed the presidency, disagreed with Miró's posture. "Even if his perception were correct on the implications of the Kennedy-Khrushchev accord," Varona contended, "we cannot give up. We've got to open the eyes of the Americans and continue the struggle." Varona rallied the troops and persuaded me to stay with him until 1964, when the council finally was disbanded and I decided to rebuild my life, marry, and pursue professional activities in New York and abroad.

Most of the other action groups kept their militancy alive through 1964–1965. They were heartened, and often supported, by the Miami CIA operation, then the largest in the world outside Langley, with about four hundred case officers, each running between four and ten Cuban "principal agents." They had a large flotilla of small boats, used primarily for intelligence operations in Cuba. Forays were generally forbidden. Only those who abided by the rules, like Manuel Artime and his MRR group, were able to operate training camps in Central America and launch a few raids, like the May 12, 1964, attack from the sea on a sugar mill on the south coast of Oriente.

The Student Revolutionary Directorate, which had played a leading part in the Cuban underground movement and in the exile fronts, was angered and distressed by Washington's clamp-down following the Missile Crisis. Despite their links with the CIA, the students had always maintained a certain degree of autonomy, of youthful irreverence and defiance, which enabled them to circulate to the Senate intelligence reports on the Soviet buildup edited by José Antonio González Lanuza and to carry out unauthorized operations such as the August 1962 raid on Havana.

Now, however, the CIA had issued stern warnings not to cause trouble. José María de Lasa, a twenty-two-year-old Cuban student who through family connections had met Deputy CIA Director Richard Helms, was summoned in early 1964 to CIA headquarters in Washington. After a cordial greeting, Helms reportedly told him in no uncertain terms to refrain from launching any forays; otherwise the students involved would be expelled from the United States.

Back in Miami, José María caucused with the student leaders Juan Manuel Salvat, Luis Fernández Rocha, Isidro Borja, and Miguel Lasa (José María's older brother, who had managed to escape from Cuba after being wounded by Castro's security police). The students decided to heed the CIA directives and not to launch any attacks from the United States. They opted instead to operate from an offshore base, which they assumed would be acceptable to Washington. After raising funds at a concert held in Miami, they obtained authorization from the government of the Dominican Republic to use a small military camp on the island of Catalina, off La Romana. José María and other young members of the Student Directorate moved to the island with a converted speedboat and commenced their training.

After four months of drills and preparation, just as the students were about to launch their first assault, the Dominican authorities informed them that because of "pressure from the Americans," they had to abort the operation and dismantle the base. For José María and his colleagues, this was a stunning blow. It proved to them, beyond any doubt, that the Kennedy noninvasion pledge protected Castro from any attacks, even if planned and executed outside the United States. In the words of José María, "Washington had sadly become the custodian of the Soviet satellite in Cuba." A few months later, the Student Directorate was dissolved and many of its members decided to pursue university studies. José María was admitted to Yale University, where he earned a law degree. Working now as an associate general counsel for a major U.S. pharmaceutical company, he recounted to me this telling episode of the post–Missile Crisis era.

The Kennedy-Khrushchev accord not only bound Latin America, it leaped the Atlantic and impinged on Europe. As part of the deal, Kennedy had privately agreed to withdraw the outmoded Jupiter missiles from Turkey, but the withdrawal was to be according to its own schedule and not tied to any explicit agreement with the Soviets. Secretary Rusk recently disclosed, however, that to settle the Cuban crisis the President was prepared to "trade" the American and Soviet missiles without the consent or knowledge of the NATO partners. To control the political damage that would ensue, the swap was to be positioned as a proposal made by the acting Secretary General of the United Nations, U Thant. Since the bargain was never publicly spelled out, Washington thought that the dismantling of the Jupiter bases in Turkey (and Italy) would be perceived by the NATO allies as part of a logical process of removing vulnerable missiles and upgrading defenses.

This was not the case with General de Gaulle, who had steadfastly backed the United States during the Cuban Missile Crisis. In April 1963, the *Revue Militaire d'Information,* regarded as the most authoritative publication issued under the aegis of the French Defense Ministry, denounced that "there was . . . indeed an agreement between the great powers on the 'demissilization' of Western Europe, an operation evidently demanded by the Soviets in return for their own nuclear disengagement in Cuba." "Western public opinion was tricked," the publication declared. "Under the pretext of modernizing the armaments of Turkey and Italy [with seagoing Polaris missiles], the United States has cleverly disengaged itself [from mainland Europe]."[14]

Kennedy's pledge to remove the Jupiter missiles and not to invade Cuba had a profound effect on General de Gaulle. According to C. L. Sulzberger, the French leader early on had told Richard Nixon: "As the Soviet Union develops the capability to strike the cities of North America, one of your successors will be unwilling to go to nuclear war for anything short of a nuclear strike against North America."

"For the General," noted Sulzberger, "this analysis was confirmed by the 1962 Cuba confrontation. Once the Russians had nuclear-tipped rockets emplaced in the Caribbean, they agreed to remove them only when U.S. missiles were withdrawn from Turkey and if Washington promised to leave Castro alone. De Gaulle reasoned: 'If the Americans will not fight for Cuba, 90 miles from the United States, they will not fight for Europe 3,500 miles away. I must draw conclusions from this.' " And as Sulzberger pointed out, "These conclusions included a weakened NATO—of which France is now a 'yes, but' partner."[15]

For all of de Gaulle's prescience, anticipating Moscow's nuclear strategy to decouple the United States from Europe, he didn't quite fathom the ambivalence of Washington's policy toward Cuba following the Missile Crisis. Unbeknownst to him (and to most of the Cuban exile leaders), while the State Department was honoring the noninvasion commitment and making overtures to Cuba, the CIA was trying to carry out Operation AM/LASH, which called for the elimination of Castro by one of his *comandantes,* Rolando Cubela.

According to the findings of the Senate Intelligence Committee investigating assassination plots involving foreign leaders, Cubela accepted the assignment under two conditions: delivery of an effective assassination device and a meeting with Attorney General Robert Kennedy. The meeting was set for October 29, 1963, in Paris. The Attorney General did not attend, but Desmond Fitzgerald, a social friend of the Kennedys and the CIA man in charge of the Cuban task force, did meet with Cubela. Fitzgerald's professed credentials as a personal representative of the Kennedys apparently satisfied the Cuban *comandante,* and they agreed to proceed with the plot. At the next meeting, Fitzgerald reportedly gave Cubela a ballpoint pen rigged with a hypodermic needle the point of which was so fine that its victim would not feel the injection. This critical encounter took place on November 22, 1963— the very same day President Kennedy was shot in Dallas.

Thereafter, the CIA stopped dealing with Cubela except through Manuel Artime, who had been the civilian leader of the Bay of Pigs invasion. Artime acceded to Cubela's additional demands—a silencer and some small, highly concentrated explosives—but the plan never crystallized. Cubela was arrested in 1966, sentenced to twenty-five years in prison, and released by Castro in the mid-'70s.

The Senate Intelligence Committee tried to determine whether there was any connection between the plot to kill Castro and the assassination of President Kennedy, and whether Cubela was a double agent or a security risk. No conclusive evidence of a connection was uncovered during the investigation, but some of the members of the committee, particularly Senator Robert Morgan (D-N.C.), saw a link between the Dallas tragedy and the Castro threat conveyed through the Associated Press reporter Daniel Harker on September 7, 1963: "United States leaders should think that if they are aiding terrorist plans to eliminate Cuban leaders, they themselves will not be safe."[16]

During the balance of the decade of the 1960s, the Soviets reduced their troops in Cuba but improved the quality of their military installations and dug in. They expanded their central headquarters in the outskirts of Havana (Managua) and connected them, through tunnels, to outer perimeter bases in El Sitio, El Chico, Wajay, Calvario, and El Cano. As in other parts of Cuba, they availed themselves of a huge cave complex ("Cura") on the hills between Jaruco and Tapaste to store what underground agents have described as strategic weapons.

The Soviets also enlarged and fortified the major air bases, including San Julián, seventy miles from Havana on the western neck of the island. According to intelligence sources, that base was equipped with a system of subterranean hangars and missile vaults several stories deep in the ground. In this secluded place alone, the Russians are capable of lifting one aircraft to ground level every three minutes.

While very active in the 1960s, the Soviets did not overtly increase their military presence in Cuba. Refugee reports notwithstanding, it seemed that they were honoring the Kennedy-Khrushchev accord and that Washington's decision to restrain the exiles was paying off. Then, starting in 1969, the Russians resumed their military escalation in Cuba. This time, however, it was tentative and gradual. As noted by Christopher Whalen, who thoroughly researched this buildup and published his findings in the book *Cu-*

ban Communism, edited by Irving Louis Horowitz, each incremental move was a test, each minor achievement was a precedent to build on.

The arrival of a seven-ship Soviet naval squadron in July 1969 marked the start of this new chapter of Russian expansionism, which to date has brought more than twenty-five Soviet naval task forces to Cuba. For the first time since the destruction of the Spanish fleet off Santiago de Cuba in 1898, the naval force of a rival extracontinental power entered *mare nostrum*—the Caribbean Sea. This squadron included a guided missile carrier, two guided missile destroyers, and a November class nuclear attack submarine. The submarine did not put into any Cuban ports, but several surface vessels visited the port of Cienfuegos. There was no Washington reaction.

The Soviets then decided to include Cuba in their global naval exercises, Okean '70. They began occasional flights from Murmansk to Havana of Tu-95 Bear turboprop reconnaissance aircraft (capable of carrying nuclear payloads if reconfigured as a bomber). Unchallenged, the Russians soon started to conduct from Cuba reconnaissance missions along the East Coast of the United States. Another precedent was set, and still there was no vigorous Washington response.[17]

A second naval squadron visited Cuba in May 1970, including an Echo II class nuclear-powered cruise-missile submarine equipped to carry nuclear warheads. According to a special report issued by the Center for Strategic and International Studies of Georgetown University, "The visit of the nuclear Echo II to Havana is believed to be the first time that a Soviet nuclear attack submarine has entered a non-Russian port."[18] On this visit, the Russian ships openly used Cuban ports for resupply, thus moving up another notch in their escalation. Still, no Washington reaction.

Then in September 1970, a third Soviet squadron was sighted en route to Cuba. This force, including submarine tenders and a barge to handle nuclear waste, rendezvoused outside Cienfuegos harbor, where the Soviets were rapidly building a submarine base to extend the range of their nuclear-powered fleet. This strategic base was viewed in Washington with utmost seriousness. Congressional leaders called for action. The specter of another U.S.-Soviet confrontation loomed anew. President Nixon vigorously warned Moscow that "the servicing of nuclear submarines . . . either in or from Cuba," or the servicing "anywhere at sea" by submarine tenders operating from Cuba, would be considered a violation of the Kennedy-Khrushchev accord of 1962.

Once again, the Soviet Union was seemingly forced to "back down" by the United States. Yet less than three months after the 1970 "understanding," another nuclear-powered November class submarine, accompanied by a Kresta-I guided-missile cruiser and a submarine tender, put into Cienfuegos and was serviced. There was no American reaction to this Soviet defiance. Since then, nuclear submarines from the USSR have called in Cuban ports and patrolled the southern and eastern coast of the United States.

Despite the Soviet fleets' maintenance capability for extended periods of time, a base in Cuba affords the Russians major advantages, such as dry docks, repair and specialty shops, provisioning and victualing, and immediate access to spare parts and resupply. Associated with these services are special training, housing, and recreation facilities in ideal climatic conditions. Strategically, the gains include more "on-station" time for Soviet submarines, a considerable prolongation of the core life of nuclear reactors, shorter warning time in the event of war, and an approach from the south where U.S. defenses are weakest.

Since the late 1970s, there have been other Soviet violations of the Kennedy-Khrushchev accord, or attempts to circumvent it. In addition to the more than 150 MiG-21s held by Castro, a newer ground-attack variant of the MiG-23, the MiG-23F, was spotted in Cuba in 1978. With potential capability of carrying nuclear payloads up to twelve hundred miles, this aircraft is far superior to the IL-28s that the Soviet Union was asked to remove from Cuba during the 1962 Missile Crisis.

Based on satellite and Blackbird photo reconnaissance, as well as HUMINT (human eyes and ears) reports, Washington concluded in 1978 that the MiG-23Fs seen in Cuba were not equipped to handle nuclear payloads. Nevertheless, the intelligence community recognized that the aircraft could be rapidly reconfigured for a nuclear role.

In the absence of any meaningful U.S. resistance or protest, the Soviets have shipped to Cuba about forty MiG-23Fs, and they also reportedly have delivered an equal amount of the more advanced MiG-27. Nine Cuban airfields can handle these planes. But of even greater significance is the existence of at least three that can service the Soviet Backfire strategic bomber, which, from Cuban bases, could hit any target in North America and easily make it back to the USSR.

In July 1979, Senator Richard Stone of Florida, apparently

tipped off by Defense Intelligence Agency officers, inquired about
an alleged three-thousand-strong Soviet combat brigade in Cuba
at a Foreign Relations Committee hearing on SALT II. Subsequent official confirmation of these troops unleashed a stormy
debate and forced President Carter to declare in September:
"We consider the presence of a Soviet combat brigade in Cuba to
be a very serious matter . . . and that this status quo is not acceptable."

To address this new crisis, Washington had virtually no
leverage, inasmuch as the Kennedy-Khrushchev accord covered
only offensive weapons. Moreover, since the Kennedy years the
permanence of Soviet forces in Cuba had been known in Washington and had gone unchallenged. Attorney General Robert Kennedy even attached significant benefits to these forces. In his
recently published memoirs he asserted: "I don't know why there
was a political matter to be concerned about—the Russians in
Cuba—because they weren't posing any threat, really. I didn't see
what the problem was—the Russians in Cuba. I mean, I'd rather
have the Russians running the SAM [surface-to-air missile] sites
than the Cubans running them."[19]

Moscow chose to ignore the brigade flare-up—partly fueled
by electoral pressure on the chairman of the Senate Foreign Relations Committee, Senator Frank Church—and the Russian troops
stayed on the island, along with ten or twelve thousand Soviet-
bloc military and civilian personnel. As a direct consequence of
this new superpower clash over Cuba, *détente* was dealt a mortal
blow and SALT II was shelved.

The brigade incident was short-lived, but it gave rise to some
critical questions. What are these soldiers and military specialists
doing in Cuba? Are they there only to protect or control Castro?
Soon, fresh intelligence information uncovered other motives as
well. The brigade, we were told, is providing security for a major
electronic intelligence station in Cuba whose large antennas
eavesdrop on U.S. and international civilian, military, and space
satellite messages and picture relays. This advanced monitoring
complex, atop a limestone hill at Lourdes, east of Havana, has
been officially described in Washington as "the most sophisticated Soviet [intelligence] collection facility in the world outside
the Soviet Union itself."

But that is not the only role that the Soviet military personnel
play in Cuba. Russian units continue to operate and control some
of the strategic military installations pinpointed by the Cuban un-

derground in the wake of the Missile Crisis. Other contingents are stationed around the Punta Movida military complex, recently built by the Soviets and linked by rail to the Cienfuegos naval base. This facility is off limits to the Cubans and, according to underground reports, is being used to service nuclear weapons from Soviet submarines.

Not far from this area is the nuclear power plant that the Russians are building for the stated purpose of diversifying Cuba's limited sources of energy and reducing its dependence on petroleum. Apart from the risk of disaster, as in Chernobyl, the construction of a nuclear power facility capable of producing plutonium poses potential nuclear proliferation and security issues. In the case of Cuba, these concerns are very real, given Castro's refusal to sign key international agreements controlling the spread of nuclear weapons, as well as his interventionist foreign policy. Even if the Soviets do not relinquish control over this facility, we could still be faced with a dreadful surprise. The operation of the plant reactors provides the opportunity to produce nuclear weapons in Cuba.

More than twenty-five years have elapsed since the Cuban Missile Crisis stunned the world. In hindsight, it can be said that the settlement that was reached in October 1962 did not resolve the fundamental issues inherent in the crisis; indeed, it may have aggravated them. Having waived the essential condition of on-site inspection, we don't know for sure what the Soviet troops so zealously guard in huge underground military installations in Cuba. Having focused solely on the removal of the missiles of October, Washington implicitly recognized the permanence of a Soviet-backed Communist regime in the Western Hemisphere, which was considered to be "nonnegotiable." And having accepted and honored a noninvasion pledge (despite occasional U.S. representations to the contrary), Moscow has been able to build in Cuba a formidable bastion with much greater electronic, bomber, and submarine capabilities than in 1962.

Prior to this tremendous Soviet buildup, NATO naval exercises in the Gulf of Mexico and the Straits of Florida were carried out infrequently by five or six ships that make up NATO's so-called standing naval force in the Atlantic. More recently, however, recognizing the potential threat to allied shipping in any wartime emergency from Cuban or Soviet ships, planes, and submarines operating in Caribbean or Gulf waters, NATO's naval exercise in the area involved twenty-eight ships and eighty aircraft from six NATO nations.

This is not to say that the Soviet-backed military complex in Cuba poses today a threat that could not be neutralized by the United States on a war footing. But it shows that it is sufficiently powerful to secure what perhaps was the main objective pursued through the missile scare: a strategic sanctuary facing the United States from which to wage conventional and unconventional wars in three continents without the fear of reprisals.

CHAPTER 15

From the Horn of Africa to the Caribbean Basin

By chance, I witnessed the formation in Cuba of what was to become a mobile and invisible army of international guerrillas. In February 1959, just a few weeks after the advent of the Castro regime, I visited my grandfather's hacienda. Searching for solace and quiet, I went horseback riding, meandering along steep mountains covered with pine, mahogany, and Spanish cedar trees. Not far from the trail, I spotted groups of armed men engaged in military exercises. They spoke in Spanish, but I could tell by their accents that they were not Cubans.

Alarmed by what I saw, I asked the administrator of the hacienda to find out who these people were and what they were doing. After a cursory investigation, he informed me that most of them were Nicaraguan, Panamanian, and Haitian rebels who were preparing to invade their respective countries from Cuba. "There is nothing we can do about it," the administrator said, shrugging his shoulders. "The foreigners have the blessing and support of the Castro regime." He also heard that there were other guerrilla training camps on the island, but he didn't know where.

This was not the first time that Cuba had instigated or sponsored military actions abroad. During the late 1940s, two Cuban presidents and several Latin American leaders of the "democratic left" had organized the Caribbean Legion to topple the authoritarian governments of Nicaragua and the Dominican Republic, among others. Castro himself had joined one of the expeditions that was aborted. Now that he had ascended to power—with the

259

glow of revolutionary triumph—it was not surprising to hear him boast that he would "turn the Andes into the Sierra Maestra of Latin America." Hyperbole, after all, was expected of *caudillos*.

Fidel's high-flown pronouncement, however, was not just empty talk. Between April and August 1959, he aided and abetted four armed expeditions with the objective of overthrowing or destabilizing the governments of Panama, Nicaragua, the Dominican Republic, and Haiti. Except for Panama, all of the targets were unpopular dictatorships, so not many voices rose in righteous indignation to condemn the ill-fated assaults.

The Castro regime was unquestionably involved in these incursions. OAS investigations confirmed that Panama was invaded by a group of eighty-six Cubans and Panamanians headed by the Cuban César Vega, who declared when deported to Colombia that the expedition had been backed by Fidel Castro and Che Guevara. Those who invaded Nicaragua (including the Cubans Onelio and Marcelo Fernández, killed in combat) had been trained in La Cabaña fortress by Che Guevara. And the guerrillas who landed in Haiti were led by members of Cuba's Rebel Army.

But the most flagrant of the 1959 Castro-supported invasions was the one launched against Trujillo's satrapy. On June 14, fifty-six men boarded a plane near Manzanillo in Oriente province and headed for the Dominican Republic. The expeditionary force landed at the airport of Constanza, but was not able to make it to the mountains. Clad in distinctive uniforms fairly easy to identify, many of the guerrillas were cut down by machete-wielding peasants. The military chiefs, Enrique Jiménez Moya and Delio Gómez Ochoa, were both *comandantes* of Castro's Rebel Army. Cuban frigates escorted two vessels carrying arms and provisions for the invaders. Just before the vessels reached the Dominican coast, they were sunk in a combined action by Trujillo's air force and navy.

During the first half of 1960, more than fifteen members of Castro's foreign service were accused of intervening in the internal affairs of various Latin American republics and were declared *personae non gratae*.[1] In most cases, they used the Cuban embassies as centers for Marxist propaganda, espionage, and agitation. Independent analysts were baffled by these interventions, which, by the end of 1961, had compelled thirteen governments in the hemisphere to sever diplomatic relations with the Castro regime. Were the widespread subversive activities prompted by romantic excesses of revolutionary zealots, as most Castro sympathizers opined, or were they part of an orchestrated plan, amateurishly executed, to foment "wars of liberation or popular insurrections against [Yankee] imperialism," as the Cuban exiles claimed?

By early 1963, the CIA had gathered a mass of concrete evidence of Castro's systematic campaign to propagate communism through all of Latin America. On March 1, Director of Central Intelligence John A. McCone disclosed before the House Foreign Affairs subcommittee that between 1,000 and 1,500 Latin Americans had received guerrilla and sabotage training in Cuba in 1962. Pointing out that we were no longer facing the haphazard challenge of revolutionary dilettantes, McCone warned: "Today, the Cuban effort is far more sophisticated, more covert and more deadly. In its professional tradecraft, it shows guidance and training by experienced Communist advisers from the Soviet bloc, including veteran Spanish Communists."[2]

According to McCone, trainees from practically all of the countries in Latin America were asked "to mark bridges and other similar demolition targets on detailed maps of their country. . . . These trainees were also required to fill out a lengthy questionnaire on sabotage targets, possibilities for subversion of police, methods of illegal entry and travel, suitable drop zones for air supply, possible points of attack against police and military posts, and similar information necessary for direction of subversion and insurrection."[3]

Despite McCone's alarming report, distinguished pundits and scholars continued to dismiss the notion of a Soviet-backed subversive campaign from Cuba. They believed that Castro was alone in his misguided adventurism, and that we should not polarize the situation with exaggerated visions of the Cuban threat, stemming from alleged distortion of facts and rigid anti-Communist dogmatism. The inference was that the CIA and right-wing demonologists were stirring up fear to justify a confrontational policy toward Castro.

This theory, however, was negated by the February 8, 1963, report of the Special Consultative Committee on Security of the OAS, which could hardly be accused of fabrication or bias. The committee concluded that the Castro offensive was linked to Moscow's design to further Communist expansion by exploiting the desire of the West to avoid war and by using hidden aggression or subversion—the most effective and "least costly way of acquiring peoples and territories without exaggerated risks."

According to the OAS report, the Castro regime was employing all of the prescribed techniques to spur subversion in this hemisphere: recruitment and training to form cadres of men and women "who will dedicate not only their free afternoons to the revolution, but their entire lives"; infiltration to penetrate and control non-Communist organizations and institutions in the Americas; psychological impregnation to condition the minds of the masses through the repetition of slogans and the dissemination of misleading information; dislocation to exploit existing grievances and weaken the social structure; and militarization to perfect all methods of violence, from sabotage and terrorism to guerrilla warfare.

The enunciation of these techniques was no major revelation, but the confirmation that they were being applied by Cuba on a large scale as part of a Soviet-inspired continental campaign to train, arm, and finance Latin American subversives was indeed astonishing and disturbing. To support its findings and underscore the magnitude of the challenge, the OAS listed some of the many specialized Marxist-Leninist training centers then functioning in Cuba:

Blas Roca School, in Los Pinos, Havana province
Marcelo Salado School, in Luyanó section of Havana
El Cortijo School, in Pinar del Río province, especially for military personnel
La Cabaña Fort, in Havana, especially for young people
Minas Río Frío School [in Oriente Province], for training guerrillas.
San Lorenzo School, in the Sierra Maestra, Oriente province, for training guerrillas
Ciudad Libertad School, in Marianao, Havana province, under Russian instructors
Boca Chica School, in Tarará, Havana province, director General Alberto Bayo
Julio Antonio Mella School, in Marbella, Havana province, for training and instructing [labor] leaders

Most of the member states of the OAS recognized the gravity of the situation, but took no collective action to address the threat. Only in November 1963, when a fisherman discovered three tons of war equipment hidden in a place called Macama on the seacoast of Falcón state in Venezuela, was the Rio Treaty invoked. The arms came from Cuba and included automatic rifles, bayonets, submachine guns, mortars, rocket launchers, and demolition charges. The arsenal was to be used for raids on Caracas by Venezuela's "Armed Forces of National Liberation," whose leaders had been trained in Cuba.

The rifles found in the arms cache on the Venezuelan beach had been purchased by Comandante Ricardo Lorié back in February 1959 under Castro's personal instructions. Lorié signed a contract with the Belgian National Arms Factory which included the sale of 22,500 automatic FAL rifles. Castro was furious with Lorié because the rifles had been numbered and engraved with Cuba's coat of arms (a standard international practice). Lorié later testified: "Castro's reaction to the numbering on the arms indicated to me that he most certainly had something sinister in mind."[4] Just how sinister was revealed by the OAS mission to Venezuela, which verified that the arms found were those purchased by Lorié. The serial numbers and the Cuban coat of arms had been filed from the rifles, but through the application of acid they were raised and identified.

As a principal source of petroleum and iron ore, Venezuela had become a prime target of international communism. But strategic considerations and ideology were not the only factors driving the onslaught. Another important element was the personal clash, the battle of wills, between Castro and the Venezuelan President, Rómulo Betancourt—a prestigious left-of-center statesman determined to achieve progressive reforms under a democratic system. Betancourt had denied Castro in 1959 a $300 million loan to carry out what Fidel called the "master plan against the *gringos*."[5] The Cuban leader neither forgave nor forgot.

After confirming the acts of subversion and aggression denounced by Venezuela, the OAS condemned the Castro regime in July 1964. All member states, except Mexico, severed diplomatic and economic relations with Cuba. The near-isolation of the island had finally been achieved. Many thought that the ostracized Castro regime would refrain from further interventions and mellow with time.

Civil war in the Dominican Republic in April 1965 dashed our hope. The breakdown of law and order created a void that was promptly exploited by some forty Cuban-trained Marxist operatives, intent on seizing control of that country, then ruled by a powerless triumvirate. Military and political instructions were being imparted by telephone from Cuba; rebel arms were pouring in, and Communist radio broadcasts were fanning the flames.

Under those circumstances, President Lyndon Johnson or-

dered the landing of U.S. Marines near Santo Domingo. He moved
swiftly and resolutely to avert another Cuba. However, he initially bypassed the OAS and disregarded consultative procedures.
Alarmed by the implications, the Costa Rican ambassador to the
OAS, Gonzalo Facio, and four other Latin American leaders
pleaded with Washington to turn the unilateral intervention into
collective action under the Rio Treaty, and to place the U.S. Marines under the symbolic command of an Inter-American Peace
Force. This move was accomplished with the requisite vote of
two-thirds of the OAS members. The Peace Force stabilized the
Dominican Republic, reorganized the army, and paved the way
for free elections supervised by several hundred international observers.

    Despite this peaceful resolution, the subject of the 1965 U.S.
intervention in the Dominican Republic continues to spark heated
debates. A number of respected analysts hold that Washington's
fear of a possible Communist takeover in Santo Domingo was totally unfounded. And yet, an unimpeachable witness, the Brazilian ambassador Ilmar Penna Marinho, had this to say about the
chaotic situation then prevailing in that country: "It was a no-
man's-land. There had been a complete collapse of public authority. The Dominican Republic had disappeared as legal and
political entity—arms had been given to a disorganized nation of
fanatics and adolescents who were in a frenzied state egged on by
subversive broadcasts—anarchy reigned—and any organized group
that made a landing in the Dominican Republic could have dominated the situation."[6]

    After their foiled attempt to exploit and control the insur-
gency in Santo Domingo, Fidel Castro and Che Guevara remained
adamant in their commitment to armed struggle. They clashed with
Latin American Communist leaders who advocated opportunistic
political alliances with other parties under a united-front strategy.
By late 1966, tactical divergences had widened to the point of
straining Cuba's relations with the USSR. Critical of Moscow's
overcautious expansionism, Che Guevara landed in Bolivia with
the aim of creating "two, three, many Vietnams" in this hemisphere. He had vanished from Cuba in the early part of 1965 for
reasons never fully explained. Nevertheless, Castro assigned Rebel
Army officers to Che's guerrilla detachment, supplied and financed the expedition, and maintained frequent radio contact with
him until the very end.

    The Moscow-oriented Bolivian Communist Party, however,

refused to provide arms and men to Guevara, and the peasants withheld their essential support. Beset by a recurrent asthmatic condition, Che's health sharply declined in the jungles. Brooding over lost opportunities, he unsuccessfully tried to revitalize and augment his forces. In October 1967, Che's group, pared down to seventeen men, was encircled by Bolivian counterinsurgency units trained by U.S. Green Berets. Most of the guerrillas, including Guevara, were captured and killed.

This was a major blow to Castro's subversive goals, but not the only one. Also unavailing were his efforts to engineer Marxist takeovers through the Tupamaros in Uruguay, the Montoneros in Argentina, and the M-19 guerrillas in Colombia. These setbacks, though, were not total failures in the context of communism's multipronged strategy to undermine and supplant democracy in Latin America. Castro-backed agitation unleashed the pendulum of violence. Terrorism gave rise to repression. Demagoguery and turmoil led to military dictatorships. The net result was that Communist rule was averted, but often at the price of freedom and human rights.

In September 1970, Salvador Allende's electoral victory in Chile, with a 36 percent plurality, ushered in a Marxist government that had to contend with existing democratic institutions and a standing army. Fully cognizant of Allende's vulnerability, Castro lent him his total support in an effort to establish a totalitarian infrastructure before the opposition struck back. Like a Roman proconsul, Fidel traveled to Chile in November 1971 and stayed there three weeks. He visited nine provinces, rallied the workers, roused the students, and reinforced Allende. Castro's backing, which included an array of Cuban political and military advisers based in Santiago, failed, however, to provide a safety net. Mounting unrest, stimulated by the CIA, led to the 1973 army coup which ousted Allende and introduced military rule into the country.

By the mid-1970s, the Castro regime had significantly diminished its subversive activities in the hemisphere and moderated its tone. Encouraged by these developments, several Latin American republics reestablished relations with Cuba. Washington thought the time was ripe for an accommodation and conducted secret negotiations with Havana envoys for almost a year. In the spirit of détente, the United States no longer insisted that Cuba break its ties with the Soviets. Just when differences seemed to be narrowing in 1975, Castro started to send combat troops into Angola.

Washington warned that it would cancel its plans to normalize relations with Cuba if Fidel did not stop the invasion. Castro sneered at the threat. "What is there left to cancel that they haven't already canceled in vain?" he asked. "What can they take away which has not already been taken away? Nothing! The situation is one of absolute impotence on their part."

Castro's involvement in the African continent actually started in 1960 with the dispatch of arms to the Algerian National Liberation Front led by Ben Bella. This was followed by small shipments of military equipment, troops, and guerrilla instructors to Guinea, Gabon, Cameroon, Congo, Mozambique, and Malawi. Despite the breadth of Cuba's military commitments announced during the 1966 Tricontinental Conference held in Havana, Washington did not seem overly concerned. Policymakers considered that Castro was acting on his own and lacked the Soviet logistical muscle to carry out his interventionist plans. They seemed to have underestimated Moscow's geostrategic interest in the second-largest continent in the world, which has mineral and oil resources estimated at several trillion dollars in value and commands "choke points" and sea lanes of vital interest to the West.

In 1975, the USSR decided to increase military aid to the Marxist-dominated Popular Movement for the Liberation of Angola (MPLA), which was to seize control of most of the country following independence from Portugal. At the same time, Moscow assisted the Castro regime in airlifting Cuban combat troops into Angola. This task was facilitated in January 1976 through the enactment of Senator Dick Clark's amendment banning U.S. covert aid to the non-Marxist Angolan rebels (represented primarily by Savimbi's UNITA movement). Although by early 1976 there were already fifteen hundred Cuban soldiers in and around Luanda, the capital of Angola, the majority of U.S. senators viewed this invasion as an isolated case provoked by South African incursions, and not as a dangerous precedent. Andrew Young, U.S. ambassador to the UN under President Carter, would later describe the Cubans as a "stabilizing force" in Angola.

In 1977, U.S.-Cuban relations seemed to improve with the opening of reciprocal Interests Sections in Washington and Havana, and their signing of fishing, health, and maritime agreements. Cuban officials even began to discuss the possibility of withdrawing troops from Luanda. A few months later, to the dismay of Washington's optimistic "Cubanologists," Castro sent seventeen thousand troops into Ethiopia to crush the Somali invasion of Ogaden. Some of these soldiers subsequently joined Soviet forces in a major buildup of strength in the Red Sea–Persian Gulf strategic area.

Today, there are more than eighty thousand Cuban troops and military and civilian advisers spread over thirty African, Middle Eastern, and Latin American countries. Given their ubiquity, resilience, and toughness in battle, they have been called "the globetrotting Gurkhas of the Russian empire." If it weren't for the Cubans' subservience to Moscow's neocolonialist interests, the term would not be demeaning. The Gurkhas, after all, are the quintessential warriors from the mountains of Nepal who earned their fearsome reputation fighting alongside the British in many a battle around the world—from Gallipoli and Neuve Chapelle in World War I, to North Africa, Borneo, and Malaya in World War II, to the Falkland Islands in 1982.

The Gurkhas are short in size, but long on legends. The most terrifying ones center on decapitations with one swift stroke of the traditional *kukri*, a heavy-curved dagger all Gurkhas carry. A joke tells of a Gurkha swinging his *kukri* at an enemy with a deft sideways cutting movement. "You missed," cries the opponent. "Try shaking your head," retorts the Gurkha.[7]

Although the Cubans have traditionally distinguished themselves for their intrepidness and grit, those in Angola could hardly be compared to the indomitable Gurkhas. Castro's soldiers were able to shield and bolster the MPLA government, but UNITA forces started to make headway, particularly since the U.S. Congress authorized the shipment of arms to them in 1986. As in Afghanistan, ground-to-air Stinger missiles supplied by Washington proved to be a wondrous weapon against the Cuban-and Angolan-flown MiG-21 and Mig-23 jets and the Mi-8 and Mi-24 helicopters. In 1986 alone, the Stingers' "intelligent" heat-seeking heads hit more than thirty government aircraft.

Low morale and inadequate training also impaired the effectiveness of Cuban troops in Angola. Rafael del Pino, the Cuban air force general who recently defected, told of large numbers of casualties and desertions. Referring to the treatment of young military recruits, he disclosed that they were often dispatched to Angola with very limited training, and then sent into battle immediately. The general further stated that when Cuban soldiers died in combat, they were buried in Angola and relatives were not allowed to take their bodies back home.[8]

Castro's unfettered internationalism in Africa has been taking a heavy toll on the Cubans at large. This seems to be the price they have had to pay for Moscow's continued subsidy of their impoverished economy and massive military aid. Angola, moreover, has provided Castro an ideal platform for Third World leadership, as well as a source of much-needed hard-currency funds. Payments by the MPLA government to Cuba are estimated to have exceeded $300 million annually. Paradoxically, the United States largely contributed to these payments. Ninety-five percent of Angola's exports are in oil, produced by a complex in Cabinda which is partly owned by the American company Chevron. The United States, by far the largest customer, paid out about $1 billion for Angolan oil in 1985 alone.

In an effort to end the Angola conflict, Washington is currently negotiating a step-by-step withdrawal of Cuban troops from Launda in exchange for South Africa's agreement to refrain from further forays and her consent to Namibia's independence. Optimists believe that Angola's president, José Eduardo dos Santos, is desperate enough for Western credits and technology to be willing to forgo his Marxist credo, Soviet military assistance, which in 1984 reached $2 billion,[9] and Cuban armed support. Skeptics, however, warn of a possible ploy to have Washington pour dollars into Angola, neutralize UNITA's anti-Marxist guerrillas, and drive the South Africans out of Namibia in exchange for nothing more than promises of a nonaligned Angola without Cubans. Through skillful negotiations, skeptics contend, Angola and its allies plan to attain what they have not been able to achieve through a decade of fighting.

Despite Angola's heavy drain on resources, the Soviets and their Cuban surrogates were active in another region of significant strategic and psychological importance to the United States: the Caribbean Basin. Within that region, the initial targets of opportunity in 1975–1976, the year of the Cuban invasion of Angola, were the islands of Jamaica and Grenada.

In Jamaica, Castro worked closely with the Marxist government of Michael Manley to train and arm local militias and Communist brigades. Manley's electoral defeat in 1980 impeded the consummation of the progressive takeover. And in Grenada, Cuban forces had penetrated the ruling New Jewel Movement and were rapidly turning the island into a captive military base. As in the case of the Dominican Republic in 1965, the perceived emergence of another Cuba with Soviet help led to the 1983 invasion of Grenada by the United States and several Caribbean islands.

Central America, though, is the area that affords the most suitable conditions for Communist infiltration and control. There the Soviet-Cuban axis has been exploiting deeply rooted discontent caused by many years of social injustice and political oppression. Castro's role, particularly since the XI Festival of Youth held in Havana in July 1978, consisted in galvanizing and unifying feuding factions under local Marxist leadership aligned with Cuba. In the case of El Salvador, the centralization of command was effected in Havana in December 1979, with the formation of the Farabundo Martí Front. Since then, Castro has leveraged his power by providing arms and supplies only to those Salvadoran rebel groups that abide by the dictates of the front.

The real Marxist breakthrough in Central America, however, was achieved in 1979, with the ascent to power in Nicaragua of the Sandinista movement following the collapse of the Somoza dynasty. The revolution against Somoza had garnered widespread support, both inside Nicaragua and abroad. Venezuela, Panama, Costa Rica, Mexico, and Cuba, along with the international socialist movement, openly backed the rebel forces. The United States eventually cut off all aid to the dictatorship, and the OAS tipped the balance in favor of the insurgents by demanding the resignation of Somoza and the holding of free elections.

These external factors precipitated the fall of the Nicaraguan regime. However, no action was taken, by or through the OAS, to ensure a peaceful and democratic transition. When Somoza resigned, the Sandinistas emerged as the only cohesive force ready and able to grab the reins of power. They promptly started weeding out dissident non-Marxist elements from government and converting the country into a police state, propped up with Soviet-Cuban economic and military aid.

Today, after more than twelve years of strife and civil war, the majority of the Nicaraguans and their neighbors yearn for a settlement that could bring peace with freedom to the turbulent region. Given the internationalization of the struggle, with the Soviet Union and Cuba backing the Sandinista government and the United States endorsing the Nicaraguan rebels (the contras), many people wonder whether a lasting democratic solution is possible under the terms of the Arias peace accord subscribed to by all of the Central American heads of state.

To determine the chances of success, I delved into the background of the current crisis and reviewed the circumstances that propelled the Sandinistas into power. No one is better qualified to shed new light and provide perspective than the U.S. ambassador to Nicaragua during the last two years of the Somoza dictatorship, Dr. Mauricio Solaún. Although he has been rather reserved and circumspect, pending the completion of his memoirs, he readily agreed to share his insights with me when I recently visited him at the University of Illinois. Our friendship goes back to our school days in Havana, and Solaún spoke to me with unusual frankness and candor.

A short, dark-haired, unassuming scholar who peppers his intellectual acuity with dashes of wit and banter, Solaún was born and raised in Cuba, where he studied law. Following Castro's ascendancy in 1959, he left the island and earned an M.A. degree in economics at Yale University and a Ph.D in sociology at the University of Chicago. When President Carter appointed him U.S. ambassador to Nicaragua in July 1977, Solaún had completed his tenth year as Professor of Sociology at the University of Illinois and had undertaken a number of consultancies and field assignments in Latin America.

Ambassador Solaún's primary goal in Nicaragua, as outlined by the State Department, was to "promote democratization and improvement in the human rights situation while maintaining neutrality." When I asked Solaún whether he was in accord with this intrusive role, he replied: "Yes, Nicaragua needed a change, and the United States could no longer remain aloof." What bothered him, however, was that his task had a narrow human rights focus and no global political plan or vision. It did not take into account the repercussions of Washington's pressures on Somoza to liberalize the regime, nor the dynamics of the struggle which usually accompany destabilizing changes.

Solaún explained to me his predicament. "I was to be a catalyst for change amid increasing turmoil," he said, "but I was forbidden to mediate the crisis, steer the process, and help to avert a political vacuum that could be filled by the radicals. My limited involvement was, in diplomatic parlance, interference without intervention—a way of inducing internal reforms without assuming responsibility for the outcome."

"Given your constraints," I teased Solaún, "it seems to me that you were a rebel without a cause, a missionary without mission."

"Not really," the ambassador snapped back. "I was just a crusader without power. Challenger of Somoza's dictatorial excesses, I was not allowed to leverage the full weight of my government to ensure a democratic succession."

These misgivings notwithstanding, the initial impact of President Carter's human rights policy was encouraging. It forced Somoza to lift the state of siege he had imposed at the end of 1974 and stimulated the moderate opposition to be more vocal in criticizing the dictator and demanding reforms. Fearful that a change in government might freeze them out, the Sandinistas (the *tercerista* faction) sought political respectability through a group of establishment backers known as *Los Doce* (the Twelve). Much as Castro did in Cuba via the 26th of July Movement, this faction concealed the Sandinistas' Marxist-Leninist goals and developed a "General Political-Military Platform of Struggle" which promised political pluralism, a mixed economy, and international nonalignment.

The Sandinistas managed to broaden their popular base by the end of 1977, but were not yet a threatening force. There was still an opportunity to vitalize the moderate opposition and press Somoza for liberal reforms and free elections (without the dictator running) in 1981. That is what Ambassador Solaún initially fostered within the purview of his mandate. Shortly after arriving in Managua, he met with representatives of the unarmed opposition, the church, captains of industry and commerce, civic spokesmen, and professional leaders and urged them to unite in what was called the Committee of National Dialogue, which sought to commence negotiations with the government. At the behest of the American ambassador, Somoza met with the committee in December 1977, and he agreed to proceed with the dialogue two months later, after the scheduled municipal elections.

In the interim, an unexpected and tragic event occurred which derailed the plans and inflamed the nation. On January 10, 1978, Pedro Joaquín Chamorro, the director of the newspaper *La Prensa* and one of the most distinguished and stalwart anti-Somoza leaders, was shot dead as he drove to his office. Although a Cuban-American physician was the one who reportedly organized the killing as a personal vendetta, most of the enraged population held Somoza responsible for the death. Mass demonstrations, strikes, and clashes rocked the major cities. The Committee of National Dialogue, led by Archbishop Obando y Bravo, canceled the meeting with Somoza. Seasoned business and political leaders realized that continued violence would only benefit the radical guerrillas. They were unable to control the situation, and many of them hoped the United States would help to arbitrate the power struggle and prevent chaos.

In Washington there was sharp disagreement on this issue,

but the view that prevailed was that the U.S. ambassador should not meddle in the internal political affairs of Nicaragua. "We don't want to be accused of imposing a 'Made in USA' formula,'' the saying went. The Nicaraguan situation was to be dealt with only as a human rights problem, through economic and psychological pressures aimed at specific goals, such as freeing prisoners and establishing due process of law.

Since any U.S. official attempt to address the root problem of Somoza was forbidden, Ambassador Solaún was compelled to use circuitous routes and elliptical language. In February 1978 he subtly persuaded the dictator to declare publicly that he would retire from the government and the National Guard in 1981, when his six-year term would expire. Owing to the highly polarized environment, however, the opposition rebuffed the offer.

Solaún became convinced that the dictator had to leave sooner to avoid a prolonged civil war and a radical takeover. Barred by Washington from taking a firm stance or even playing a mediation role, the ambassador met in April with Somoza's uncle, Dr. Luis Manuel Debayle, a colorful and outspoken patriarch who was not particularly overawed by his nephew. ("Uncle Light,'' as he was called after presiding over the Energy Department, used to say sarcastically that Somoza considered himself the "mother of Tarzan.") Knowing full well that his off-the-record comments would probably reach the dictator, Solaún measured his words. Speaking as a concerned citizen, not as an ambassador, he told Dr. Debayle that Somoza had isolated himself and seemed to be unaware that it behooved him to find a political, democratic solution to the existing turmoil. "There is growing opposition to the dictatorship from all quarters,'' the ambassador affirmed. "All indications are that the dynasty of the Somozas, including young Tachito [who was emerging as the head of the National Guard], won't last through 1981.''

Dr. Debayle generally concurred, but stressed the need to develop what he called a "slide-type formula" to ensure a gentle descent. By that he meant a negotiated settlement that would enable him and his family to remain in Nicaragua. Although Debayle urged Solaún to express his views directly to Somoza, he promptly visited his nephew and gave him his own version of the ambassador's remarks.

Somoza was fuming when he called the ambassador to his office. "What is this message you have sent me through my uncle,'' he sputtered, "that the Nicaraguans accuse me of being a dictator and have turned against me, that Tachito has to leave the National Guard, and that the Somoza dynasty has to end before 1981?'' Solaún let Somoza blow off steam and then calmly replied: ''We have maintained good relations, Mr. President, so we don't need to exchange messages of substance through intermediaries. I certainly don't intend to establish that precedent.''

The ambassador then stated his views on the need to find a political solution to the acute crisis that was convulsing the nation. Finally, when Somoza seemed calmer, Solaún touched on the delicate subject of the dictatorship. With unconventional frankness (which Somoza occasionally enjoyed), the ambassador quipped with a roguish smile: ''I know you don't like to hear about the dictatorship. But after all, Mr. President, with all due respect, you are a dictator.'' More surprised than annoyed by the blunt remark, Somoza for once dropped his pretense and chuckled.

Following this meeting, the dictator tempered somewhat his proverbial haughtiness and became more responsive to the ambassador's prodding. In June 1978, he announced a series of liberalization measures which included the amnesty of some political prisoners, an invitation to the OAS Human Rights Commission to conduct a survey in Nicaragua, guarantees for the safe return of exiled members of the Twelve, and a promised reform of the electoral system.

Instead of keeping the pressure on Somoza to make sure he honored his promises and shortened his term, the White House made an incredible about-face and decided to approve new AID loans to the government and to send a letter of appreciation to the dictator over President Carter's signature. Ambassador Solaún strongly objected to the loans and the letter on the grounds that they would send the wrong signals to Somoza and convince him that he could ride the waves of U.S. policy through 1981 and beyond. In view of the White House's obduracy on these issues, the ambassador then requested authorization to transmit the message orally without handing over the letter. Washington again overruled Solaún, forced him to deliver the missive to Somoza, and approved the loan.

As foreseen by the ambassador, the dictator became more intransigent, and the anti-Somoza groups, which coalesced under the aegis of the Broad Opposition Front, became more aggressive. They demanded the dictator's immediate resignation and prepared for a national strike. Convinced that time was running out for a negotiated settlement, Solaún met in August with Dr. Julio Quintana, Nicaragua's Foreign Minister, and extraofficially urged him to work out a political solution with the nonviolent opposition before a wave of radicalism swept the country. "The oppositionists," the ambassador said, "want Somoza out yesterday, and the government diehards give the impression that they want Somoza in not only through 1981, but forever. I don't know whether the compromise is 1979 or 1980, but both sides will have to yield if a peaceful and democratic solution is to be found."

Not surprisingly, Dr. Quintana informed Somoza, who instantly summoned Ambassador Solaún to the Bunker, as his office was called. This time there was no opportunity for a dialogue, much less a quip. The dictator, clad in athletic attire, his eyes bulging, let loose a tirade: "Didn't I warn you not to tell anyone that I had to leave before 1981? If you persist, the one who will have to leave is you! I am not about to quit just to please the liberals in Washington. I would rather continue fighting and be condemned by the OAS as the pirate of the Americas than deliver an easy victory to my enemies. I want you to communicate this to the State Department and the Department of Defense. And if they don't like it, let Carter come and get me!"

Shortly after this tempestuous meeting, a Sandinista guerrilla unit under "Comandante Cero" (Eden Pastora) attacked the national palace and held fifteen hundred people, including the president of the Chamber of Deputies, as hostages. To end the siege, Somoza agreed to release about fifty political prisoners, pay $500,000 to the Sandinistas, and publish vitriolic communiqués signed by the Ortega brothers and Víctor Tirado. About half of the raiders and the former prisoners went to Cuba to be trained, and subsequently returned to Central America to join the insurgency.

The spectacular palace assault, which was followed by guerrilla attacks and popular uprisings in four major cities, finally convinced the Carter administration that the Nicaraguan situation could no longer be handled within the general framework of the human rights policy. Accordingly, Washington agreed in September 1978 to sponsor an OAS-backed mediation commission led by William P. Bowdler, a U.S. career diplomat who was then director of the Bureau of Intelligence and Research. Ambassador Solaún was not requested to participate in the mediation, but, pursuant to instructions from the State Department, he convinced Somoza to accept the good offices of the commission, and in less than one week brought together representatives of a broad spectrum of society to commence negotiations.

The objective was to ensure a smooth transition to a democratic regime through the creation of a government of national unity in which the Sandinistas would have only minor participation. Many felt that Washington was uniquely capable of achieving that goal by offering guarantees to Somoza if he cooperated and threatening to isolate his regime and deny him asylum in the United States if he balked. The mediators believed that direct, unequivocal pressure was essential to force Somoza to step aside before the precarious opposition coalition disintegrated and the Sandinistas picked up the pieces. The White House, however, refused to issue any ultimatums, and Somoza resisted making any meaningful concessions.

When the mediation degenerated into a fruitless debate over minimum conditions for a plebiscite, Castro started to play a more active role in the insurgency. On December 26, 1978, the Cuban radio announced that the three factions of the Sandinista Front had agreed to end their tactical disputes and merge their forces politically and militarily. Making armed assistance conditional on this unification, Castro induced the factions to accept a Marxist-Leninist hard-liner, Tomás Borge, as the coordinator of the amalgamated Sandinista forces.

Meanwhile, Ambassador Solaún officially warned Washington on December 13 that if the mediation broke down, the anticipated violence and deterioration of public order would require an immediate U.S. response. "The hope of a majority of Nicaraguans in such a situation," he asserted, "would be direct intervention either by the OAS or even by the U.S. unilaterally. If such direct actions were not forthcoming, the credibility of the U.S. would be undermined not only in Nicaragua, but also within and possibly beyond the hemisphere."

Washington ignored this advice, and when the mediation collapsed in early 1979, there was no effective U.S. policy or contingency plan to break the crippling stalemate. As a feeble reaction, the Carter administration decided in February to end military aid to Nicaragua (which had been virtually suspended since September) and to withdraw about half of the embassy personnel. Ambassador Solaún was allowed to return home, too, when the CIA uncovered a Sandinista plot to kill him. None of these measures had any impact on Somoza, who continued to stonewall the proposed settlement and defy the United States.

The failure of the mediation and Washington's display of impotence had dire consequences. The moderate opposition sectors in Nicaragua were left hanging on the horns of a dilemma: join the Sandinista-controlled insurgency or make peace with the dictator. U.S. allies in the area, particularly the leaders of Venezuela, Costa Rica, and Panama, were disappointed by Washington's ambivalence and decided to proceed on their own. Hoping naively to influence the course of the rebellion, they cast their lot with the Sandinistas and gave them military and logistical support. And Havana, eager to exploit the upheaval and exercise control, became the rebels' principal headquarters, training center, and source of supplies.

According to subsequent investigations conducted by the Costa Rican National Assembly, from December 1978 to July 1979 some sixty flights, mainly from Cuba, carried war matériel into Panama for transshipment to Costa Rica. On arrival in San José, most of the crates laden with arms were delivered to the Sandinistas, who trucked them to their operations area in Guanacaste.[10] With this massive influx of arms, followed by a sharp increase in the number of guerrillas, the insurgency gathered momentum and the moderate opposition lost credibility and power.

In June 1979, at the peak of the Sandinista offensive, Washington finally decided to abandon the "noninterventionist policy." Through its new ambassador to Nicaragua, Lawrence Pezzullo, the United States gave Somoza an ultimatum and sponsored an OAS resolution calling for the immediate replacement of the dictatorship with a democratic government that would hold free elections.

Dr. Zbigniew Brzezinski, then head of the National Security Council, was not optimistic about the prospects for democracy and peace. He reportedly clashed with State Department officials who were hoping that "some middle-of-the-road regime would somehow or other miraculously emerge in the wake of Somoza."[11] Wary of the probable collapse of the National Guard and of the powerlessness of the splintered non-Sandinista opposition, Dr. Brzezinski pressed for a U.S.-led multinational peacekeeping force that would move into Managua to help the transitional government establish its authority and avoid a Castroite takeover. A halfhearted attempt was made to obtain OAS approval, but the Latin American governments were unwilling to compromise their professed noninterventionism (as they did in Santo Domingo in 1965) and risk leftist agitation to follow the faint and belated trumpet of a giant with cold feet. Dr. Brzezinski then argued for a U.S. unilateral intervention, but President Carter and Secretary Vance rejected that option.[12]

Absent a strong, cohesive force to contain the triumphant Sandinistas, they grabbed the reins of power when the Somoza dynasty fell in July 1979, and they gradually started to build a Marxist-Leninist infrastructure with Nicaraguan characteristics. As they implemented their plans and became more outspoken, the Sandinistas' true colors started to show. At present, their Communist bent or ideology is no longer in question, at least among informed Americans. What continues, however, to spark passionate debates is the role the United States should play in Nicaragua given the involvement of Moscow and Havana. American public opinion, colored by political sectarianism, is fundamentally split into two extreme but not mutually exclusive camps: those who believe we should resume or increase U.S. support to the contras to prevent a second Cuba, and those who favor a negotiated disengagement to avert another Vietnam.

The National Bipartisan Commission on Central America (Kissinger Commission), formed by President Reagan in 1983, tried to forge a national consensus on a comprehensive U.S. policy for the region, encompassing economic assistance, proactive diplomacy, and military aid. But the bipartisanship achieved was short-lived. Congressional opposition soon resumed its relentless attacks, and the embattled White House, trying to circumvent legislative constraints, entangled itself in the Iran-contra spider web.

The U.S. approach to the simmering problem of Nicaragua hardly testifies to inspiring statesmanship in our time. We have lacked a credible and sustained strategy with clear goals. How can we expect to persuade public opinion that our security is at stake in Nicaragua when the military aid requested for the contras (less than 15 percent of that provided by the Soviets to the Sandinistas) bears no proportion to the stated threat? Given our ambivalent stance, we have not even been able to persuade Nicaragua's beleaguered neighbors to exercise jointly with us their inherent right of self-defense. And to magnify the prevailing confusion, instead of recognizing under international law the belligerence of the touted freedom fighters, we have maintained diplomatic relations with the very government we have been trying to destabilize or overthrow.

Today, as peace talks on Nicaragua are spasmodically pursued, we don't have a solid U.S. front to influence the negotiations. Nor do we have a broadly accepted contingency plan to bring more pressure to bear on the Sandinistas through a Nicaraguan government-in-arms, through an inter-American police force, or otherwise, should the negotiations turn out to be a calculated Marxist ploy to break the spine of resistance. Failure to react promptly and decisively (as occurred in early 1979 when the mediation efforts under Somoza foundered) would aggravate the current crisis. Our emboldened foes would exploit our weakness, and our disheartened friends would spurn our unreliability.

Without prejudice to our moral commitment to democratization and social reforms, Nicaragua should be viewed in the context of the United States' strategic interests in the Caribbean–Central American Zone. As noted in the Kissinger Commission's report, through the sea lanes intersecting this area pass almost half of our foreign trade, more than half of our imports of crude oil, and a large portion of the military supplies our NATO partners would require in the event of war.

The Soviet Union and its Cuban surrogates appear to be keenly aware of the geopolitical significance of gaining another foothold in this crucial part of the Western Hemisphere—this time on the mainland itself. While we flagellate ourselves for past and present sins and impair our ability to protect U.S. interests in the region, they continue to deliver large quantities of modern arms to Nicaragua. Since 1979, the Soviet Union had shipped more than $2.5 billion in military aid to Managua, over half since 1985—a walloping investment from a country under economic pressure which professes not to be interested in Central America.

In addition to these huge military shipments, which are sometimes rerouted to the Marxist guerrillas in El Salvador, Warsaw Pact engineers are constructing the El Bluff deepwater port on Nicaragua's Caribbean coast, similar to the Cienfuegos naval base in Cuba for Soviet submarines. They are also building a ten-thousand-foot airfield at Punta Huete, north of Managua. This runway could accommodate Soviet bombers or long-range reconnaissance and antisubmarine missions along the U.S., Canadian, and Latin American coasts and out to Hawaii.

Moreover, Soviet-bloc and Cuban engineers are reportedly studying the feasibility of digging a canal through the narrowest strip of land in Nicaragua to link the Pacific Ocean with the Caribbean. If they carry out this project (originally conceived by U.S. experts back in the nineteenth century), the Soviet Union would significantly enhance its naval deployment capability. Russian warships do not have access to the Panama Canal, and currently have no better alternative than to sail the lengthy route around Cape Horn.[13]

The Soviet-Cuban inroads into the Caribbean Basin, while unsettling, do not necessarily mark an irrevocable trend for the rest of the hemisphere. If there is a tide today in South America, it is the tide of democracy. Ten years ago most of the continent was ruled by generals. At present they run only two South American countries. Although plagued with macroeconomic problems, the large nations below the Rio Grande have made strides toward industrialization and higher levels of education, and are potentially poised for the great leap into the developed world in the next few decades, if a solution can be found to the debt crisis.

Despite these encouraging signs, however, democracy remains vulnerable in South America. The political institutions are fragile, the trade unions, the students, and the military are restless, and social ferment is widespread. Furthermore, Castro and his Soviet backers, who are currently exploiting a new leftist wave in Latin America, have not really renounced violence. They have softened their tone and mended relations, dispatching diplomatic and commercial missions that ooze goodwill and vie for trade. But behind this facade of civility and peaceful interchange lies the deadly network of subversion directed by the Americas Department of the Cuban Communist Party. This apparatus was established in 1974 to centralize Havana's operational control over covert revolutionary activities throughout the hemisphere.

No Latin American country escapes its reach. In the case of Colombia, beset by a twenty-four-year guerrilla war, Castro has been supporting and funding the M-19 revolutionary group in concert with drug traders. In 1982, a Florida grand jury indicted the former Cuban ambassador to Colombia, Fernando Ravelo, and other Cuban officials on charges that they conspired to use Cuba as a staging point for smuggling Colombian drugs into the United States in exchange for arms shipments to the M-19 guerrillas. Subsequently, Havana and Managua were implicated in the M-19 assault on Colombia's Palace of Justice. In a twenty-eight-hour siege abruptly ended by the army, close to one hundred people were killed, including eleven Supreme Court justices.

Chile has also been a prime target of Castro Communist subversion. In August 1986, Chilean security forces discovered the largest clandestine arsenal ever found in the Western Hemisphere. Buried in ten sites north of Santiago, the arsenal included more than 3,300 American-made M-16 rifles captured after the fall of Saigon, 117 Soviet-made rocket launchers, and 2,000 rocket-propelled grenades made in Bulgaria. These weapons were brought to Chile's shores on Cuban trawlers as part of a major international offensive to bolster the local Marxist guerrilla group, the Manuel Rodríguez Patriotic Front. A month later this group claimed responsibility for the assassination attempt against General Augusto Pinochet that left five presidential bodyguards dead.

Not even the present leftist government of Peru can guarantee immunity from Castro Communist subversion. The Cubans have been financing and supplying arms to one of Peru's two guerrilla groups, the Tupac Amaru Revolutionary Movement, since it started to operate in 1982. Named after an Inca leader who fought the Spaniards in the seventeenth century, Tupac Amaru is largely an urban terrorist group involved in recent bombings, kidnappings, and assassinations. Violence in Peru today is so pervasive that it has overshadowed its economic woes. In the words of a foreign banker, "The only activity there gaining momentum is terrorism, and the only industry showing vitality is security."

Closer to our shores, Castroite subversives known as Los Macheteros have been intent on undermining Puerto Rico's U.S. Commonwealth status. In 1981, these terrorists destroyed nine A4-D Corsair jet fighters at the Muñiz Air National Guard base, and in 1983 they carried out a $7.2 million robbery of a Wells Fargo armored truck. They also have been responsible for a number of terrorist activities on the island in past years, many of them directed against U.S. military personnel and federal and local law enforcement agencies.

More recently, the Castro regime came to the rescue of Panama's besieged General Manuel Antonio Noriega. The Panamanian strongman had helped Castro bypass the U.S. trade embargo and had shared with him U.S. intelligence data. The Cuban ruler returned the favor by supporting Noriega's drug-trafficking activities. (On February 26, 1988, two U.S. federal indictments involving Noriega charged seventeen people with smuggling Colombian cocaine into Florida through a Cuban military base.)

When Washington recently tightened the economic screws on Noriega in an effort to remove him from power, Castro shipped to Panama forty-eight tons of weapons along with a Praetorian Guard composed of Cuban security officers and henchmen. Emboldened and protected, the Panamanian dictator overcame the crisis, at least for the time being, and sneered at Washington's proposed deal.

Commenting on the United States' bumbling diplomacy, the *Economist* of London quoted Machiavelli: "Among other evils

which being unarmed brings you, it causes you to be despised.''
Then the usually balanced and restrained magazine issued this
pungent admonition: "In the violent and ill-governed region just
to its south, the United States has disarmed itself by its chronic
inability to define what it wants there, and by shrinking from the
only means—the credible and consistent threat or use of military
force—which would let it accomplish its goals. Central Americans already smirk about the United States for its inconsistency
of purpose and lack of will. Unless it pulls itself together, it
may face much more than derision: it could jeopardize its own security.'' [14]

Soviet-Cuban expansionism in this hemisphere and beyond is
not limited to the military realm. One of its key long-term goals is
to condition the minds and shape the political attitudes of selected
foreign students who have the potential to lead or sway the intelligentsia in their own countries. This intensive program takes place
principally in Cuba's Isle of Youth (formerly the Isle of Pines).
Located some sixty miles from the southern coast of Cuba, it used
to be considered a sportsman's paradise, with almost 1,200 square
miles of game preserve for hunters and fishermen. Its mangrove
swamps and hidden coves, sown thick with caches left
behind by the buccaneers, inspired Robert Louis Stevenson's im-
mortal novel *Treasure Island*.

Under Castro, more than thirty thousand foreign students—
grammar school through university—have visited this island, but
not to cruise along the shores to locate the fascinating spots described by young Jim. They have come with scholarships provided by Cuba to undergo indoctrination in Marxism-Leninism and
to learn a variety of skills, from engineering and paramedicine to
espionage and terrorism. Students from such dissimilar countries
as Namibia and Nicaragua arrive at the age of twelve to fourteen
and remain on the island for about six years. When they return to
their home countries they will be prepared to assume important
roles—some as educators and technicians, but most, alas, as
apostles of hatred and architects of violence.

Castro's example will influence their feverish minds. The aging Cuban ruler is no longer the ravishing folk hero of the early
days of the revolution, nor the harbinger of economic progress
and political freedom. But in the eyes of many of the Third World
nations he remains an imposing transcontinental power, an arresting revolutionary figure. Secure in his Soviet-backed sanctuary,
he fans the flames of subversion from the Horn of Africa to the

Caribbean Basin. His conquests so far are limited, yet his energy and capacity to spawn unrest are boundless. He draws on the financial and military resources of the Soviet Union. But he also counts on a potent intangible force: psychological contagion generated by his ability to defy the United States and the West with virtual impunity.

CHAPTER 16

Inside Cuba

During the thirty years that Castro has remained in power, I have received many and varied reports on the situation inside Cuba. Coded messages from the underground, statements from newly arrived refugees, impressions from Cuban exiles and foreign observers who have visited the island, unsigned letters from relatives and friends who have stayed behind—all of these sources of information have enabled me and others to keep abreast of developments in Cuba.

One of the most touching and revealing nonpolitical accounts I have received came from my wife's younger sister, Elodia Arellano Fanjul, a petite and vivacious brunette who lives in Florida with her husband and three teenage children. Having left Cuba when she was twelve, Elodia seized the opportunity to visit her homeland in 1979, if only for two days.

It was a sad journey prompted by the death of her maternal grandfather, Dr. Raúl de Cárdenas, a former constitutional Vice-President of Cuba and a renowned jurisconsult of sterling integrity. Although on several occasions he was able to obtain temporary exit permits from the Cuban government to visit his progeny in the United States, he decided to reside in Havana with his wife, even at the price of destitution and silence. In the twilight of his honorable life, he fervently clung to the island he loved.

When his daughters and relatives learned of his passing, they resolved to send a small family delegation from Miami to attend his funeral. Not knowing how to proceed on such short notice,

Dr. de Cárdenas's grandson, the enterprising Eduardo Arellano, picked up the phone and called Celia Sánchez, then Castro's secretary. After introducing himself, Eduardo explained the reason for his call and requested authorization to fly to Cuba on a twin-engine charter plane along with five members of his family. Since the Castro regime was planning to capitalize on the death in Cuba of such a conspicuous representative of the capitalist era, permission was given for the aircraft to land in Havana.

On arrival, the group—Elodia; Eduardo; his father, Mario Arellano, Cuba's premier interior designer; his wife, Fina; and her cousins, the Pérez Estables—were courteously greeted at the airport. They passed quickly through immigration and customs, but Elodia received a chilling reminder. When she presented her U.S. passport, a testy officer asked her: "Where is your Cuban passport?" "I lost it," replied Elodia. He did not make a fuss over the issue, but tartly warned her: "Your American passport has no validity in Cuba. *Here*, you are a Cuban."

A relative of hers who lives in Havana drove the group to Dr. de Cárdenas's residence, where the wake was going to be held. The family had been able to fend off government overtures to have the body lie in state at the national capitol. Elodia was dismayed by what she saw at the house, or perhaps by what she did not see. There was practically no food there; water, ice, coffee, and sugar were all she found. No soap was available. Layers of dust blanketed the floors; the drapes were torn and the windows were broken. Few pieces of furniture were left in the room. The Vice-President had been impelled to sell most of them for subsistence.

Yet, despite his deprivations, he was not abandoned. When his wife had passed away, two of his nieces had looked after him, and two former maids, grateful for the roof he had continued to share with them, had provided assistance in their spare time without pay. Dr. de Cárdenas, who died at the age of ninety-five, remained lucid until the very end. Acting as a private mentor or counselor, he drafted documents, rendered opinions, and interpreted regulations, for which he occasionally received compensation in kind. Many of those who had sought his advice, from intellectuals to workers and technicians, came to the house that evening to pay their last respects.

Several young members of the government, including the Party official in charge of coordinating the funeral arrangements, attended the wake. They were disciplined and well dressed, and seemed to thrive in the Castro milieu. The others at the house, mostly elders, looked ashen and dejected. Wearing mended clothes of bygone times, they huddled in the hallways and conversed in low voices. Some of the ladies approached Elodia and discreetly dropped in her purse scraps of paper bearing the names and telephones of relatives in the United States. No particular messages were to be relayed, just regards. One of the ladies, with a black dress and a dignified presence, whispered to Elodia: "The only way to leave this inferno is as your grandfather did: horizontally." For her and others in her station, death was the sole means of escape.

The night was emotionally exhausting, and not bereft of surprises. When the guests had departed, the house looked even more barren than before. Upon taking inventory of Dr. de Cárdenas's personal possessions, Elodia and her family noticed that most of the small *objets d'art* he had left—porcelains, frames, and bibelots—had vanished. They later learned that some of those who attended the wake, driven by their grueling struggle for survival, had filched the Vice-President's belongings for resale in the black market.

The interment took place the following morning. About one hundred friends accompanied the family to the cemetery. The Party official delivered a graveside eulogy, praising Dr. de Cárdenas as an exemplary statesman and subtly linking him to the Communist revolution. There was a moment of tension. Eduardo Arellano, the eldest of the grandchildren, felt he had to respond. Without notes, his knees shaking, he said that, having left Cuba as a young boy, he was not qualified to evaluate his grandfather's political achievements, and would defer to history. But as a grandson he was able to affirm that Dr. Raúl de Cárdenas was a man of unswerving democratic and Christian principles, devoted to his family, loyal to his country, and true to his friends. He then respectfully thanked the official for his eulogy and all those present for their condolences.

Carefully choosing his words, Eduardo had made his point without triggering an embarrassing and potentially dangerous incident. The Party representative did not seem to mind the indirect rejoinder. After the brief ceremony, he left, but told Eduardo that he would see them again at the airport that evening just prior to their departure. He left them a car with a chauffeur and a guide (euphemism for secret service agent), in case they wished to drive around Havana.

After a quick but rather traumatic vist to the Arellanos' former family compound in the Biltmore suburb, now turned into a run-down complex for Cuba's Olympic athletes, the group went to see Mercedes, the black nanny who had nursed Elodia and her six brothers and sisters. She lived in a small room provided by the government, and was very frail and practically blind. When Elodia arrived, Mercedes did not recognize her at first. "Who have they brought to me?" she anxiously queried, sensing it was someone she loved. Elodia could not control herself. She threw her arms around Mercedes and sobbed. "It's me," Elodia sputtered, "*tu gorda*"—"your chubby one." "Yes, I know," Mercedes replied, tears trickling down her cheeks. "I could tell by the way you cried." She hugged Elodia with her trembling arms and said: "I knew you would come. But tell your brothers and sisters that this Negro is not about to die. I will be waiting here for all of you." The young Communist guide, who witnessed the scene, muttered to the driver: "They couldn't have been that bad, after all."

In the course of the visit, it became clear that the underprivileged, like Mercedes, were not better off under the current regime. With nonmilitary construction significantly lagging behind demographic needs, the housing shortage in Havana had sharply worsened. Mercedes told Elodia: "We've all had to cram into this small room—my daughter Prieta and her husband using one bed, and their teenage children sharing mine." "What about your daughter Pinta?" Elodia inquired. "Oh, she married a sergeant," Mercedes answered, twisting her face in a wry grin. "They gave them a nice house at the Biltmore, but I'm not allowed to visit them. They belong to a different class."

With time running out, Elodia and her relatives said goodbye to Mercedes and drove off to Old Havana. They stopped at the Floridita Bar, which Mario Arellano had decorated and Ernest Hemingway had made famous, and sipped the still-delicious frozen daiquiris. Then they toured the old city. Elodia well remembered the entrance to the harbor, flanked by the imposing Morro Castle and La Cabaña fortress; the elegant Paseo del Prado boulevard, lined with laurels; the spacious Plaza de la Catedral, paved with cobblestones; and the elaborate colonial buildings, laced with balconies.

Despite the general state of disrepair,[1] Elodia was deeply moved and impressed. "Even in its present shabby condition," she told me, "Havana is beautiful. I'm glad I went. My visit brought back treasured memories of my childhood. But when I left the island this time, I was not homesick. Having felt the frightening tensions of the system, I knew I did not belong there.''

A more recent and equally insightful account of life in Cuba came from Pedro Alvarez,[2] an articulate fifty-year-old professional residing in Venezuela who visited the island early in 1988 with a group of prominent businessmen. Born into a middle-class family from the central province of Las Villas, Pedro left Cuba several years after Castro's ascent. He was eager to return to his country of birth and see for himself the changes that had taken place.

Shortly after he arrived in Havana, government officials greeted his delegation with cordial hospitality at one of the villas near the old Country Club of Havana, which used to belong to affluent members of Cuban society. These villas, Pedro reported, were now luxurious enclaves for government hierarchs and official guests. Describing what he saw, Pedro said that the life-style there was not much different from what it was in pre-Castro days. Exquisite antique pieces adorned the villa, and smartly attired waiters served canapés with caviar, well-seasoned Cuban food, and a fine selection of imported wines.

Despite the government's courtliness and desire to attract foreign investors, the business discussions did not reach fruition. As Pedro noted, Cuba's foreign investment decree lacks adequate legal safeguards, bars the enterprise from contracting workers directly (only through a state entity can this be done), and raises serious concerns about management control and profit remittance. ''All that puts a damper on joint ventures under the current regime,'' Pedro said.

A possible exception, according to Pedro, is tourism. In this area, the Cuban government seems to have made some progress, joining forces with Western European investors in a $400 million program to improve hotel facilities. Still, in 1987, Cuban tourism generated less than $200 million. In comparison, Puerto Rico, which is one-twelfth the size of Cuba, raked in that year more than $1 billion in tourism revenues.

Pedro pointed out that not all the systems in Cuba were antiquated. ''When I asked a Party leader to help me locate a friend in the interior of the island,'' Pedro told me, ''I received all of the particulars in less than three hours, including my friend's whereabouts, his employment and revolutionary record, and the activities of his family." Pedro quipped, "If the economy were as efficient as the police system, Cuba would be one of the most prosperous countries in the world."

Pedro gave me his own description of Havana today. "The city is not as boisterous as in the past, with fewer and older cars. There are no blaring radios and no shouting street vendors or beggars. Life now is more subdued and predictable; its Latin impulse is controlled by ration books, bureaucratic forms, and government fiats. I saw shopping bags of all types carried by throngs of Cubans lining up along the sidewalks. They have become a symbol of the daily quest for sustenance."

Pedro welcomed the elimination of gambling casinos and public centers of licentiousness. But he was alarmed by the high consumption of alcoholic beverages, notably beer. What depressed Pedro the most, however, was his uncle. Expansive and affectionate before Castro, he had become taciturn and cold. His sons had been indoctrinated in Marxism and were active members of the Communist Party. He worked as a doctor in one of the government hospitals and seemed content with his life and supportive of the revolution. Just before Pedro left Cuba, the uncle managed to see him alone—away from the scrutiny of his militant sons. Only then did he open up and ask the question that was tormenting him: "How can I get out of here?"

Another perceptive report, this one with a rural flavor, came from Lucio González, a modest but alert Cuban *guajiro* who for many years worked at my maternal grandfather's hacienda in the province of Pinar del Río. Lucio and his family recently left the island and now reside in Miami.

Lucio did not mince words in describing conditions in rural Cuba. "The government," he said, "claims to satisfy the basic needs of the people for food. And yet, there have been years when even sugar was rationed, when we had to relieve our hunger with surplus corn, and when mango became an essential element of our diet. The situation is not any better today—there is still much shortage of food. This is unforgivable in a country as fertile as Cuba."

Lucio attributed the failure of the system to lack of incentives. "Few farmers own the land they till," he said, "and those who do have to sell most of their crops to the government at very low prices." I inquired about the social benefits afforded by the revolution. "Free medical services are generally available," he acknowledged, "but pharmaceutical products are expensive and scarce. Education at lower levels is widespread, but so is Marxist indoctrination.''

I asked him whether, in his opinion, the majority of the *guajiros* supported the Castro regime. "Look," he replied in his high-pitched voice, "we've got to give the government their due. They are very effective in mobilizing and controlling the population. But that doesn't mean that the majority of the *guajiros* like the regime.''

Lucio talked about the heroic guerrillas who had fought in the mountains before and after the Bay of Pigs and the Missile Crisis, hoping that support would come from abroad. He also referred to the local recalcitrants like Fela, who worked as a cook at my grandfather's hacienda. When asked to prepare a banquet for Castro and his entourage, who were visiting the ranch, she adamantly refused, saying: "I only cook for the owner, Dr. Cortina.''

Lucio explained that there are many *guajiros* and workers who are unhappy, but dare not band together for fear of reprisals. There are plenty of opportunists who feign allegiance to the government in order to advance. Most dissidents remain quiet and await "the day." "Of course," Lucio conceded, "there is a segment of fanatics and beneficiaries of revolutionary privileges who firmly support the regime. But even they waver in times of danger." To support his assertion, Lucio disclosed that during the U.S. invasion of Grenada, he and others who had applied for authorization to leave Cuba started to receive friendly messages from hard-liners. "I guess they wanted to hedge their bets," Lucio remarked with a big grin, "to be on good terms with both God and the devil.''

Adjusting to life in the United States has not been easy for Lucio and his family. "One of my sons," he said, "had a nervous breakdown shortly after arriving in Miami. For several months, I had to rely on the generosity of friends for food, a roof, and two sofas to share with my family. But I have no complaints or regrets. This is heaven compared to the straitjacket of Communist Cuba.''

These and many other accounts of life in Cuba today can only be understood in the context of the Marxist-Leninist system implanted in the island. In spite of, or perhaps because of, the individualistic traits of the Cubans, the totalitarian features of the Castro regime tend to be more radical than in most Soviet-bloc countries. Stalinization in Cuba is evidenced by the concentration of power in a single individual, the deification of Castro and un-bridled sloganeering, the extreme collectivization of the economy and the militarization of labor, and, above all, the rigorous suppression of all forms of dissent.

The Committees for the Defense of the Revolution—the remarkably effective network of informers and spies that exists on every block in Cuban municipalities—enable the Ministry of the Interior to watch all movements, check all visitors, monitor all sensitive communications (particularly opinions expressed on political issues), track reception of foreign radio broadcasts, and even record conspicuous home consumption. This system relies not only on continuous and penetrating surveillance, but also on computerized data culled from "verification forms" or individual report cards for job applications like the following:

a) Participation in assignments (e.g., voluntary work in agricultural areas, block vigilance, mass rallies, blood donations):

b) Social conduct and morality:

c) Does he/she maintain relations with any counterrevolutionary elements? Explain.

d) Does he/she have any religious beliefs? Explain.

e) Does he/she maintain communications with anyone abroad? In which country?

f) Does he/she have any relatives arrested or convicted? Specify type of crime and family connection.

g) How does he/she get along with the neighbors? Explain.

h) Does he/she maintain relations with any antisocial elements? Explain.

The stringent control exercised by the Cuban regime over every facet of life has inexorably led during the last thirty years to mass arrests, executions, and deportations. To improve his image, Castro occasionally releases groups of political prisoners at the behest of international personages and with a theatrical sense of timing. Among his grandstand gestures was the agreement he reached with the Rev. Jesse Jackson in 1984 to free twenty-seven Cuban prisoners, including Dr. Andrés Vargas Gómez, a sixty-nine-year-old poet and former career diplomat who had served twenty-one years in a series of eight or nine prisons and cells.

Dr. Vargas Gómez was grateful for Jackson's intervention, but declared when he arrived in the United States that it would be a "moral offense" to let Castro "use political prisoners as a form of merchandise to buy respectability." Dr. Vargas Gómez added, "This was no humanitarian feature. All of those released had finished their sentences several years before." He also described his ordeal in captivity—the psychological torture he had to undergo, for long periods incommunicado, eating watery boiled rice, without clothing except for a diaper made out of a sheet. "My only companion," he said, "was the stench of my body odor. I was not allowed to bathe . . . visits to the bathroom were merely a dream."

This was no isolated case. The poet Armando Valladares, who after twenty-two years in Castro's jails was released thanks to the efforts of French President François Mitterrand, described his harrowing experiences in two books of poems smuggled out of Cuba: *From My Wheelchair* (deprived of food, he suffered in prison from "deficiency polyneuropathy"), and *The Heart in Which I Live*. Now in exile, he has published *Against All Hope,* an extremely well-documented and terrifying account of systematic brutalities inside the Cuban *gulag,* which in the case of the valorous student leader Pedro Luis Boitel led to a fifty-three-day hunger strike and death.

The United Nations Human Rights Commission has recently reported that more than 120 long-term political prisoners are still confined in Cuban cells. Most of them are known as *plantados*—recalcitrants who refuse to accept political reeducation or be classified as common criminals. Their sentences of from fifteen to twenty years or more are deemed the most severe in the Communist bloc. If we add all the political offenders serving lesser terms, plus the several thousand Cubans in prison for attempting to leave the country, and the conscientious objectors who have been jailed for refusing to serve with Cuba's overseas forces, then the number of prisoners could well reach ten to twelve thousand. (The Castro regime acknowledges holding fewer than five hundred political prisoners, and has started to release some of them.)

Summary execution of opponents has been a constant practice of the regime since it came to power in 1959. Although the show trials of the earlier period have stopped, secret executions have continued, albeit on a smaller scale. As communicated to the U.S. Congress by the Department of State, "in August [1986], Antonio Frías Sosa, a seventeen-year-old high school student and photographer reportedly working with the Cuban Committee on Human Rights, died mysteriously while in police custody within a few hours of his arrest. Police allege that he committed suicide.

In late 1986, nine persons jailed for religious activities reportedly were awaiting execution in Combinado del Este prison."[3]

 The Cuban dissident leader Ricardo Bofill, who has been imprisoned several times and forced to leave the refuge of the French embassy in Havana, denounced in January 1988 the death of five political prisoners as a consequence of cruel treatment. He also declared that between July 1986 and June 1987, seventeen prisoners had been executed by firing squad for alleged crimes against state security. Bofill's detailed report was smuggled out of Cuba in early 1988 and delivered to the Human Rights Commission of the United Nations in Geneva.

 Cuba today is hardly the "workers' paradise." Solidarity-type unions are not allowed to surface on the island; they are nipped in the bud. Just when labor protests were gaining momentum in Poland, five Cuban workers were sentenced to death for "industrial sabotage." All they did was to talk to some fifty employees of the need to form a labor union separate from the government-controlled Cuban Federation of Workers. The defendants were originally sentenced to imprisonment. However, during a retrial ordered by Castro, the five were given the death penalty. Because of the international outcry that ensued, their lives were spared and the sentences were changed to thirty years' imprisonment. The trial's chief magistrate, who had protested against the severity of the death penalty, landed in jail. And the defendants' four attorneys were imprisoned as well.

 Reprisals are also prevalent in rural areas. In April 1983, two hundred farmers in the area of Sancti Spiritus were arrested. They had refused to sell their crops to the government, which was offering them a price below cost and had denied them permission to retain part of the harvest for personal consumption. Enraged, the farmers burned their crops in front of a state warehouse. Eleven of them were sentenced to death and shot.

 Despite these sanguinary excesses, Castro did tolerate for some time, beginning in the early 1980s, a modicum of financial freewheeling and private enterprise. Farmers were allowed to sell about 20 percent of their output on the open market at prices not regulated by the government. Moonlighting for extra income started to spread among Cubans with special skills—plumbers, shoe cobblers, tailors, carpenters, key makers, auto mechanics, and other artisans and craftsmen, who worked mainly from their homes after doing state jobs.

 Then, in early 1987, at a time when other Communist countries were easing restraints on entrepreneurship, Castro launched a crackdown in Cuba. Alleging that too many Cubans were behaving like "capitalists in disguise . . . trying to get rich individually," he ordered the farmers' stands replaced by state-run enterprises and curtailed the budding home businesses. As a result, farm productivity has continued to ebb, and the quality of services in urban areas remains dismal.

Politically, the country has not fared any better. Cuba is totally controlled by the Communist Party, which in turn is dominated by Castro. Members of the Central Committee and the Politburo are chosen by a small group of Party hierarchs. Elections simply confirm selections previously made. The National Assembly of People's Power meets twice a year, but solely to rubber-stamp decisions already made by the Party. No political opposition is allowed, and any attempt to organize or explore the possibility of forming an independent political organization is ruthlessly punished. As recently reported by Amnesty International, the forty-year-old Cuban engineer Andrés Solares was sentenced to eight years' imprisonment for having drafted letters (not actually sent) to French President François Mitterrand and U.S. Senator Edward Kennedy, asking them for information and advice on how to form a political party. Charged with "enemy propaganda," Solares was held at Combinado del Este prison. He was recently released thanks to the intervention of Kennedy and other U.S. legislators.

Religion also has borne the brunt of the revolutionary onslaught. After the nationalization of all private and parish schools, the prohibition of processions, and the mass expulsion from the country of priests, ministers, and rabbis in the early 1960s, overt government persecution did wane. But religion has been reduced to liturgical rites conducted inside the 120 Catholic churches left in Cuba, out of over 1,000 before Castro. Although three synagogues remain on the island, there are no permanent rabbis to minister to the eight hundred Jews living in Cuba. Traditional religious ceremonies, including Christmas, have been suppressed, and even small Christmas trees are looked upon as counterrevolutionary.

The Cuban Communist Party has repeatedly called for systematic dissemination of scientific materialism and the use of administrative measures to hamper religion and isolate believers. In this environment, only a few parishioners, mostly the aged, run the risk of going to church. Young people who attend service are stigmatized as counterrevolutionary and usually barred from admission to universities and denied job promotions.

Certain religious denominations continue to be harassed by the government, such as Jehovah's Witnesses, Evangelical Gideon's Band, and Seventh-Day Adventists. Three members of the Jehovah's Witnesses order were sentenced to death in the mid-1980s. The alleged crime was that of spreading "propaganda to promote armed revolts against the revolution." The mimeograph that was presented as incriminating evidence against the three detainees was used only to reproduce the scriptures. That did not matter. They were shot, accused of promoting the very same thing they had condemned and abhorred: violence.

At present, church-state relations seem to have improved. In 1986 the Castro regime allowed the Cuban Catholic ecclesiastical community to hold a national conference for the first time in twenty years, and authorized a half-dozen priests and an equal number of nuns to relocate to Cuba. In addition, the last Communist Party Congress softened its attacks on religion and ordered the publication and distribution of a book-length interview with Castro in which the Cuban leader speaks of the compatibility of religion and socialism. More recently, coinciding with the visit to Cuba of John Cardinal O'Connor, the archbishop of New York, the Cuban government restored the church's telex system and authorized the importation of thirty thousand Bibles.

Despite these signs of greater official tolerance, we cannot point to a meaningful Castro-church thaw. Some religious orders are still refused permission to register; others are barred from distributing ecumenical materials. And all Cubans who practice religion, regardless of their faith, continue to be viewed by the government as suspects and are excluded from important positions and denied advancement in many fields.

Intellectual deviationism is today more cruelly punished in Cuba than in most Communist states. This has stifled creativity and dried up the well of nonpolitical literary productions. In the 1960s, poets and writers in Cuba were allowed to depart somewhat from the official Party line and to have their "little heresy." However, since the First Congress of Education and Culture, held in April 1971, arts and letters in Cuba have been Stalinized. The government's position was summarized by Castro: "We, a revolutionary people in a revolutionary process, value cultural and literary creations with only one criterion: their utility to the people. Our valuation is political." The Cuban Socialist Constitution enshrined this principle: no constitutional freedom may be exercised "contrary to the existence and objectives of the Socialist state, or contrary to the decision of the Cuban people to build Socialism and Communism."

Even such a fervent Castroite as the Colombian Nobel Prize–winning author Gabriel García Márquez recognizes that Cuba today is a "cultural catastrophe." As recorded in an interview published in the March 1988 edition of *Vanity Fair*, García Márquez speaks with contempt of the Cuban Communist system. "Some bureaucratic imbecile decides that *this* book is not 'politically positive,' and they don't publish them. But then they *do* publish totally idiotic books." He said of one such tract, "A convict wouldn't read it while taking a shit." García Márquez, who now heads a Havana-based film foundation ostensibly owned by an international trust fund, has no kinder words for the quality of cinematography on the island. He reportedly echoes the local joke that there are three kinds of movies in Cuba: "the good, the bad, and the Soviet."

As the Castro regime tightened its iron grip, non-Communist intellectuals in Cuba, including those who had supported the revolution, were persecuted and arrested. Among them, Heberto Padilla, who in 1968 was awarded a prize for poetry by the government-controlled Union of Writers, was tortured and forced to repent for deviationism. When he finally managed to leave Cuba, he said: "During the last twenty years, I have lived in frightening laboratories of social experimentation, spaces walled by test tubes where the same experiment always ended with the same result: tyranny. I have learned something about the value that is freedom. Perhaps no one in this country [the U.S.] will ever have to go through my kind of apprenticeship, and never have the need to learn the lesson I now know."[4]

The tidal wave of totalitarianism, however, has not totally smothered dissidence in Cuba. The latter still flickers in the clandestine works of defiant intellectuals. One of them, Ernesto Díaz Rodríguez, a poet twice accused of "conspiring against the state" and condemned to an aggregate of sixty years' imprisonment, smuggled out of the island the manuscript of his book, *Un Testimonio Urgente*. When it was published in the United States, he was subjected to reprisals. In a letter received through the underground movement, he recounts his experience: "At midnight . . . I was unexpectedly removed from my cell and taken to the Department of State Security, where I was confined to the torture

chambers for thirty days. During that period I was forced to present myself for numerous interrogatories, all related to my literary
work. Once again I have been threatened. 'Your continuing to
develop a dissident cultural movement, especially abroad, is intolerable, and we will try to prevent it by all the means at our
disposal,' they assured me. For my part, I am not prepared to
give in. . . . To confine a man, to mistreat him, to destroy him
for printing poems, is like destroying a gardener for the horrendous crime of growing roses. . . .'' [5]

The Castro regime cannot point to prosperity to mitigate the
rigors of tyranny. Cuba's economy reportedly shrank 3.5 percent
in 1987 after registering a modest 1.4 percent growth in 1986. The
battered national economy rests solely on subsidized Soviet pur-
chases of Cuban sugar (currently at four times the world market
price) and on subsidized sales to the island of Soviet oil. In 1986,
petroleum exports surpassed sugar as Cuba's leading hard-currency source. The reason for this phenomenon is that the Soviet
Union gives Cuba more than enough crude oil and natural gas for
its domestic needs, and Cuba exports the excess to generate dollars to pay for imports. Soviet subsidies to Cuba, although recently reduced, are still on the order of $12–14 million daily, not
including massive military aid. Even with this extraordinary level
of support, per capita economic growth in Cuba has been among
the lowest in the hemisphere, and its per capita GNP—which in
1952 was the third-highest in Latin America—now ranks fifteenth. [6]

As noted by independent analysts, the Castro regime has been
able to reduce inequalities in urban-rural living standards and in
income distribution (outside the privileged revolutionary clique),
but it has failed to generate new wealth. Weakened by low labor
productivity, inefficiency, absenteeism, a bloated bureaucracy, and
a huge military burden, the Cuban economy has been severely
jolted by the fall in world oil and sugar prices. In July 1986, Cuba
suspended principal and interest payments on its medium- and long-
term indebtedness pending the completion of negotiations to restructure its foreign debts, which have shot up to $6.4 billion. And
in early 1987 Castro declared that to resolve this problem Cuba
will have to cut imports from the West to half of 1986's $1.2 bil-
lion. They actually were reduced to $840 million, according to a
confidential report by the central bank.

These steps, while drastic and painful, are not too uncommon
these days in debt-ridden Latin America. However, what sets Cuba

apart from the rest of the hemisphere is the rationing system instituted in 1962 to allocate scarce supplies of food, clothes, and other consumer goods. While shortages today are perhaps not as acute as in the 1970s, Cubans still line up to receive their quotas of three-quarters of a pound of meat per person each nine to eleven days, two ounces of coffee every fifteen days, one pair of trousers and one shirt every six months, and one pair of shoes per year.

Rationing predictably has created a black market, which in turn has given rise to repressive measures to punish "crimes against the popular economy." In a further attempt to control the black market, the revolution created a parallel market with special stores charging higher prices for rationed goods (up to $120 for a pair of jeans). The consequences of these and other unpopular measures, devoid of incentives, have been deleterious to the country. Anger and discontent have prompted many workers to sabotage production as a form of opposition, and to steal as a means of survival. For example, workers at bakeries steal lard, and shoe factory employees grab the offcuts of hides. This practice is so widespread that Castro declared at a meeting of the Central Committee of the Party that stealing had become an institution and that it was undermining the revolution.

The scarcity of goods and services does not affect, however, the members of Cuba's ruling class, which underpins the revolutionary government. Broadly speaking, the elitists include the occupants of key posts in the Party, state, military, and police apparatus, as well as the top managers of industrial, scientific, and educational institutions. The privileges that accrue to them vary according to their hierarchical position. Most of the elitists have access to well-supplied hard-currency stores for tourists and diplomats, and are entitled to private cars, but the underlings get Ladas and Volvos while the bosses sport Alfa Romeos and Mercedeses.

At the apex of the oligarchical pyramid stands what the Soviets call the *nomenklatura,* the elite within the elite, whose members in Cuba are the Castro brothers and other top party leaders and army chiefs. Not molested by an inquisitive congress or a snooping press, they generously reward themselves with high salaries, trips abroad, beach villas, yachts, videocassette recorders, and access to government satellite dishes to tune in to U.S. televised movies. Such are the powers and the perks of this self-perpetuating elite in Cuba and Soviet-bloc countries that they have confirmed the observation of Friedrich Engels, the German coauthor of the Communist Manifesto, that "once in the saddle" a new ruling class "has never failed to consolidate its rule at the expense of the working class and to transform social leadership into exploitation."[7]

One of the most critical problems facing the Cubans today is the housing shortage, aggravated by a deficient water and power supply. Construction of new houses has significantly lagged behind demographic growth. Large families, including divorced spouses, have had to cram under one roof, frequently with undesirable tenants they cannot evict. This has accentuated the "culture of poverty" found in Castro's Cuba by the well-known social anthropologist Oscar Lewis and his associates. Lewis was surprised to find among poor people so much violence, delinquency, promiscuity, drug trafficking, and escapism into folk religion and the occult.

To alleviate this situation, Castro launched in the mid-1980s a limited private-homeownership program, which included the right to build one's own home. Yearning for a title to their property, handy Cubans embarked on home building and turned it into a thriving cottage industry. This effort helped ease the nation's chronic housing shortage, but Castro, obsessed with creeping capitalism, soon reversed his decision. Accusing some people of "getting rich, buying, selling and trading homes," he terminated the program in early 1987.

Although the Cuban government leaders are aware of the tensions created by housing conditions, they recently received a sobering reminder from the northern Holguín province. As disclosed by Harvard professor Jorge I. Domínguez, seventeen peasant families were evicted and their homes torn down by overzealous officials, allegedly because they were built without state authorization. The victims sought the protection of the local Roman Catholic bishop. Town peasants assembled in front of Party offices to protest. Enraged mothers threw down their children's emblems from the Young Pioneers' Union and stepped on them. Some dared ask how the Batista dictatorship's evictions differed from these. Other officials eventually intervened and promised to give temporary shelter to those who had lost their homes and to build new housing for them.[8]

The government is also wary of the restless youths who often lack private quarters to enjoy a few moments of intimacy with their spouse or companion. To mitigate this problem, the Castro regime has recently increased the number of *albergues* or hourly love nests, which display such suggestive names as El Sport and El Record. But as with almost everything in Cuba today, the romantic couples have to wait in line for a long time, exposed to the knowing glances of passersby. For sensitive girls, this is an ordeal; but for the more seasoned, it's an opportunity to knit or read while they await their turn.

Against this background of political oppression and economic failure, most independent observers point to three areas in which the Cuban revolution has made significant strides: literacy, medical care, and sports.

As part of an all-out educational crusade, the present Cuban government frontally attacked illiteracy in its early years. When Castro rose to power, literacy on the island was close to 80 percent. That placed Cuba in the top quartile of all the nations of the world. Within a few years after the onset of the revolution, the government declared that literacy had reached 97 percent. Subsequent investigations have shown, however, that the national average is closer to the 87–90 percent level if we take into account those more than fifty years old, who apparently were excluded from the government study.

The number of schools throughout the island has sharply increased, and all children have access to education without charge through the sixth grade. Beyond that, schooling is selective and not really free. Students more than cover the cost of education by doing agricultural work without compensation. The right to remain in school after the sixth grade is contingent upon loyalty to the regime. Students must memorize and repeat Communist slogans, perform neighborhood guard duty, join the revolution's Young Pioneers, and meet harvesting goals in the fields. Otherwise their chances of pursuing further studies are practically nil.

After a study of the Cuban educational system in 1983, Richard G. Capen, editor of the *Miami Herald*, commented: "As the father of two teenagers and a nine-year-old daughter, I find these conditions repulsive to any sense of human dignity. The reality of such regimentation and the restrictive power over children overwhelmingly dominated the impressions I gained during my trip to Cuba as part of an Associated Press delegation of news executives."[9] The well-known Spanish socialist professor Martín Segrera, who also visited Cuba that year, noted that all of the school books that were shown to him "falsify history and mutilate geography to an incredible extent: in the world there only appears to be the Soviet Union, which eclipses even Cuba."[10]

It was the fear of Communist brainwashing and militarization that prompted fourteen thousand Cuban parents who could not leave the island in the early 1960s to part with their children and send them off to refugee camps founded by Monsignor Bryan Walsh in Florida, and to orphanages in other parts of the United States. These desperate parents preferred the pain of indefinite separation to the dread of Marxist indoctrination. The daring enterprise, code-named Pedro Pan, was secretly coordinated in Havana by Ramón Grau Alsina and his sister Polita. They processed visas, obtained plane reservations (they blocked ten to twenty seats on every flight), and often accompanied the youngsters to the airport. Shortly after Castro cancelled the "freedom flights," Ramón was arrested and sentenced to thirty years' imprisonment (he served twenty-two) and Polita to fourteen. Upon arriving in Miami, they both were greeted and honored by Thanks, America—a humanitarian institution founded by some of the very same orphans they had shielded and saved.

In the field of medicine, Cuban advances have been widely extolled. The government provides comprehensive services, free of charge, through hospitals and polyclinics that dot the island. Progress has been observed in several areas, including infant mortality, which is reported to have been sharply reduced to nineteen per thousand live births. It should be noted, however, that when Castro came to power, infant mortality in Cuba, at thirty-two per thousand, was already the lowest in Latin America.

From 1960 to 1980, Cuba reportedly increased the number of physicians from one for each 1,060 inhabitants to one for each 700. And life expectancy jumped from sixty-three in 1960 to seventy-three by 1980. This is no mean feat, but severe sanitation problems caused by deficient garbage collection and mosquito control still threaten Cubans' health. In the last few years, the population has been suffering from an increased incidence of such diseases as dengue fever, severe intestinal disorders, malaria, blennorrhagia, and syphilis. Some of these infections have been brought back by troops returning from Africa, but they have spread at home because of inadequate medical treatment, poor nutrition, dirty water, and cramped accommodations.

Despite these hygienic problems, the Castro regime is currently promoting "health tourism" as a tool for selling Cuba's Communist system and earning dollars needed to buy essential goods from Western countries. The services, primarily rendered at the Ciro García Clinic in Havana, range from physical examinations, to kidney-stone removal with laser beam, to open-heart surgery. The U.S. press has reported that foreigners who go there seem generally satisfied with the package deal, which includes free periods for sightseeing. But then they are spared the scarcity of supplies which plagues the nonprivileged sectors of the local population.

Given Castro's recognized ability to distort facts and manipulate statistics, some of the alleged educational and medical achievements in Cuba have been called into question. But even if they are accepted at face value, more schools and hospitals are no substitute for freedom. A modest Cuban sailor who recently defected in Spain said it best. When asked by a reporter why he wanted to leave Cuba, where he had free education and free medical care, he calmly replied: "Because one is not always studying or sick. In life, you know, there is a need for other things. . . ."[11]

Athletics is an area in which Cuba unquestionably excels. It ranks high among the government's priorities and serves as a most effective vehicle to promote the system abroad. Youngsters who have strong athletic skills and are loyal to the revolution have the opportunity to gain national and international prominence. The state cushions them from shortages and discomforts, accords them distinctive privileges, gives them intensive training, and subjects them to rigorous discipline. For the select few, the mastery of sports is not an amateur endeavor, but rather a full-time profession for the greater glory of the regime.

Cuban athletes are among the best in the world. At the Montreal Olympiad in 1976, Cuba, with six gold medals, ranked eighth, ahead of Great Britain, Italy, and France. At the Moscow Olympiad in 1980, the last in which she competed, Cuba's gold medal haul (eight) was the fourth-highest of any nation. And at the Pan American Games in 1987, Cuba finished second, ahead of Canada, with seventy-five gold medals. Although the United States emerged as the undisputed Pan American leader, the Cubans thrashed the Americans in two of the high-profile sports, baseball and boxing.

But despite this enviable string of successes, and despite the special treatment and enticing rewards accorded Cuban athletes, the Castro regime cannot count on their allegiance. Security agents shadow the athletes wherever they go to impede any attempt to defect. In the case of one of my cousins, the former assistant coach of Cuba's Olympic crew team, they were unsuccessful. In the mid-1960s El Tigre Carbonell, as he is nicknamed, seized an opportunity to flee during a crew regatta in Canada. Evading his watchdogs, he hid, then ran and leaped to freedom. Renowned Cuban athletes have done the same.

One of the most spectacular defections was that of Roberto (Tony) Urrutia, Cuba's weight-lifting champion in his 165-pound class. Having won a bronze medal at the 1976 Summer Olympics in Montreal and three consecutive gold medals at the world weight-lifting competitions in '77, '78, and '79, Tony became a national hero in Cuba pampered by the government. Still, he was unhappy living under mounting political pressure and with no individual freedom. As recently recounted in *People* magazine, during the summer of 1980, while training in Mexico, Tony decided to defect. He knotted bedsheets to a window ledge in his hotel room and tossed the sheet out of the window. He climbed down to the street, ran to the U.S. embassy, and requested political asylum. The guards denied him entry, so he ran around to the side of the building, scaled the fence, and rushed inside. He told the stupefied receptionist who he was, and said: "I want protection. I want the marines." He got both. And after several years of arduous work rebuilding his life, Tony also got the opportunity to compete again . . . under the American flag.

These and other defections, along with the continuous exodus of Cubans of all ages, reflect gloom and hopelessness. Castro remains in firm control of Cuba. There is, at present, no broad-scale organized resistance on the island. Militant opposition dwindled following the Kennedy noninvasion pledge in the wake of the Missile Crisis. Those who were born after 1959, or were under twenty-one when Castro seized power, have no knowledge or recollection of personal liberties. Many of them seem conditioned to depend on the government to direct their lives and supply their bare needs for food, clothing, housing, education, medical care, and jobs. Pervasive discontent has been neutralized or muffled. Impotence has given way to resignation.

And yet, despite his apparent strength, Castro needs to apply massive doses of repression and indoctrination to endure. Political transgressions are severely punished, even with the death penalty. Everything the Cubans see on television, hear on radio, or read in the newspaper is larded with Communist slogans and revolutionary verities. Institutions or forums purportedly designed to foster "participatory democracy" carry no weight; the Party leadership wields absolute power. Without facing any serious threat from abroad, the government continues to maintain the population in a constant state of military tension to galvanize support and tighten control. One has to look very hard to find a Cuban between eighteen and fifty years of age who is not involved in some kind of military activity. We cannot, therefore, speak of peace in Cuba today. As postulated by Henry David Thoreau, "A peace which depends upon fear is nothing but suppressed war."

In such a regimented environment, disillusionment and resentment are rarely overt, although the youths these days are more vocal and critical than in the past. To gauge the situation, one has to read intangibles, such as the relative popularity of the *El Líder Máximo*. Castro retains the charisma of power, but not the ebullient, wildly energetic personality that used to spawn waves of enthusiasm across the country. Crowds herded to attend May Day parades and revolutionary rallies continue to break into rhythmic clapping and chant "Fi-del! Fi-del!" But the joyful spontaneity of the earlier stages of the revolution has been replaced by the stern rigidity of party discipline.

Castro no longer embodies the promise of success. After nearly thirty years in power, he himself recited a long litany of failures and mistakes during the 1986 Third Party Congress. But he is still viewed as an invincible force, having overcome innumerable challenges and outlived seven hostile U.S. administrations. Like the awesome Himalayas, his attraction is his endurance; his magic is that he's *there*.

A more poignant sign of desperation is the sharp rise in the rate of suicides in Cuba. According to the 1981 annual report by the Cuban Ministry of Public Health, which was smuggled out of the island, the rate jumped from 17.1 suicides for every 100,000 deaths in 1977 to 27.5 per 100,000 in 1981—one of the highest levels in the world. Many of these suicides, designed to dramatize political protest, suggest a strong disenchantment with the course of the revolution. Members of Castro's inner circle have not been immune to this malaise. Over the last few years, the former President of Cuba appointed by Fidel, Osvaldo Dorticós, four *comandantes*, and a number of lesser officers and associates have killed themselves.

But what perhaps depicts most dramatically the ordeal of the Cuban people is an incident that occurred at the former residence of my wife's great-uncle in Havana, now occupied by the Peruvian embassy. In 1980, Cubans started to break into foreign embassies to try to escape the country. Finally, a handful of people crashed into the Peruvian embassy. Castro exploded and said something like "If you people want to leave, go ahead and leave!

Everyone who wants to leave, go to the Peruvian embassy." Within hours, ten thousand men, women, and children thronged the courtyard and garden of the embassy. Military police had to cordon off the area, because there were tens of thousands more trying to get in.

Then Castro said, "All those who want to leave, go to the docks at Mariel." About 125,000 people, including a few thousand ex-convicts, misfits, and spies planted by Castro, flooded the Mariel area before it was shut off. A "freedom flotilla," composed mainly of small, leaky boats manned by Cuban exiles, came to the rescue of relatives and friends. Most of the refugees belonged to the working class—the poor fisherman, peasant, laborer—the very Cubans Castro had promised to save from "capitalist injustice" and "U.S. imperialism."

By now, more than one million disillusioned Cubans have left their homeland. It is estimated that between one and two million more would like to depart as well. Looking for a social and economic safety valve, Castro recently agreed to reinstate the immigration pact with Washington, which will enable an additional quarter million Cubans to emigrate to the United States by the mid-1990s. As in the past, desperate families will not wait. They will sail on anything that floats—from stolen fishing boats to rafts made of inner tubes and scrap lumber—braving the turbulence of the Gulf and implacable pursuit by Castro's patrol boats and helicopters. They are sailors in despair. Undaunted in their search for freedom, they drift into the darkness and pray for a flare.

CHAPTER 17
The Émigrés

While Cubans on the island were making a Communist state, Cubans in Miami were remaking an American city. Between 1959 and 1988, close to 700,000 (of the million who have left Cuba) settled in Miami and helped transform a January-to-March placid vacation resort into an all-year-round vibrant bilingual metropolis. Thanks, in part, to the $8 billion purchasing power of the Hispanic community in Greater Miami (Dade County), the city has weathered a construction glut and a slack in Latin American tourism and continues to advance as a dynamic business and cultural center.

Since Castro came to power, there have been three major waves of Cuban migration.[1] The first wave began in January 1959 and ended in October 1962 with the Missile Crisis. During this period there were daily flights between Havana and Miami, and the influx of about 250,000 refugees came primarily from the middle, upper-middle, and upper classes. Most of them were well-educated and had considerable professional and managerial experience. This group, which benefited from very generous U.S. government assistance organizations, such as the Cuban Refugee Center and the Cuban Student Loan Program, became the role model for the subsequent migrations.

The second major wave began in December 1965 and ended in April 1973. During this period two daily "freedom flights" airlifted close to 400,000 refugees representing all socioeconomic levels. This massive influx of Cubans, who arrived with "visa waivers" issued pursuant to the 1966 Cuban Preference Law, blended easily with the first-wave refugees.

The third wave was composed of 125,000 refugees who came during the 1980 boatlift from Mariel to Key West. This group suffered serious disadvantages not faced by the first two waves. The "Marielitos," as they were dubbed, were relatively less skilled, and, having lived for twenty years under a totalitarian regime, lacked the individual initiative and drive to cope with the challenges of a free-market society. Moreover, they arrived during a severe recession and without the status required to receive federal government assistance. To compound their problems, their image was tarnished by the 5 percent or so common criminals and mental patients sprinkled among them by Castro. Despite these major handicaps, most of the Marielitos have adjusted well over time, and a good number of them have excelled in their endeavors.

To understand the evolution of the Cubans in the United States, it is important to remember that we did not come as immigrants pulled by the American economic dream, but as refugees pushed by the Cuban political nightmare.[2] During the early stages of exile, the Cubans' zeal for progress was not in evidence. Most of us focused primarily on the liberation of our homeland. There was no thought of permanent U.S. residence, much less of citizenship. Our plans in Miami were tentative, temporary.

Even the small minority of affluent exiles hesitated to buy a house. The fall of Castro was thought imminent. Cubans would gather after Sunday mass to discuss the events of the week, their voices rising to a crescendo with emotional wavings of hands. The usual parting words were "We'll celebrate *La Nochebuena* [Christmas Eve] in Cuba this year," or "We'll soon eat our *lechoncito asado* [the traditional roast suckling pig] in our country." Optimism was often sparked by U.S. policy statements on Cuba, or by epic pronouncements trumpeted by exile leaders with dashes of wishful thinking. The fading lives of the elders added a dramatic sense of urgency. For them, time was of the essence. Every hour of wait could be their last one.

Despite the proliferation of exile groups and their frequent quarrels over turf and tactics, morale was high and *la causa* or *la lucha*—the struggle—remained the focal point of the Cuban community. Professional or business projects, then, did not command a high priority, and public discussions centered on nothing but the impending invasion. With tensions running high, patriotic rallies with flags, hymns, and orations often served as a therapeutic release of emotions.

In describing the psychology of the followers of the Duke of Monmouth, the English statesman and historian Macaulay wrote that "delusion becomes almost a madness when many exiles who suffer in the same cause herd together in a foreign country." This was axiomatic in the case of the Cubans, who clearly preferred consoling illusions to disturbing realities. Craving for upbeat news, they used to accost those who seemed to be on the inside with the lighthearted Cuban saying "Tell me something good, even if it's not true."

The Bay of Pigs was a tremendous setback, but more devastating to the cause was the Kennedy-Khrushchev accord struck during the October 1962 Cuban Missile Crisis. Although Washington denied the existence of a noninvasion pledge that has seemingly frozen the Cuban status quo under Castro, the exile groups soon saw their bellicose activities restrained or barred, and most of their U.S. financial assistance withdrawn.

Following the resignation of Dr. Miró Cardona as president of the Cuban Revolutionary Council in 1963 and the subsequent dissolution of the council, other exile leaders tried sundry approaches to galvanize and unite the splinter forces and renew the struggle. Dr. Carlos Márquez Sterling, the former president of the Cuban Constitutional Assembly of 1940, organized "patriotic clubs" in various cities of the United States with large exile concentrations, as Martí had done prior to the 1895–1898 war of independence against Spain. Dr. Laureano Batista-Falla, the young and talented president of the Cuban Christian Democratic Movement, tried to rally its affiliated parties and groups in Latin America and Europe, while he personally funded and led intelligence and action missions.

To provide a democratic infrastructure, Mr. José "Pepín" Bosch, then chairman of Bacardi, financed a referendum among Cuban exiles designed to underpin a representative coalition against Castro. To gain international legitimacy and backing, the last constitutional President of Cuba, Dr. Carlos Prío, the former president of the Senate, Dr. Eduardo Suárez Rivas, and other dignitaries attempted to form a Cuban government-in-exile. Dr. Enrique Huertas, president of the Cuban Medical Association in exile, sponsored the creation of "Bank José Martí" to fund the war against Castro. And José Elías de la Torriente, with apparent continental endorsement, spearheaded an all-out liberation effort which ended tragically with his assassination in Miami.

These and other well-intentioned initiatives foundered because they lacked unified and sustained exile advocacy, Cuban underground coordination, and U.S.–Latin American support. Unwilling to bow to adversity, Eloy Gutiérrez Menoyo, a *comandante* of the Cuban Rebel Army who had defected, decided to wage an indigenous war without relying on external factors beyond his control. Assisted by Nazario Sargen's Alpha 66 organization, he landed in Cuba in December 1964 with a small group of freedom fighters and headed for the mountains. After having evaded armed helicopters and thousands of troops sent to hunt him down, he was captured and confined twenty-two years in Castro's *gulag*. Released in December 1986, at the urging of Spain's President of the Council of Ministers, Felipe González, Gutiérrez Menoyo left Cuba with deep moral and physical scars, but determined to resume the struggle and lay bare the inhuman plight of his former fellow inmates.

Among the other Cuban exiles who did not renounce their anti-Communist militancy following the Kennedy-Khrushchev accord were a number of staunch Bay of Pigs veterans. After having received special training at Fort Benning, Georgia, more than sixty of them joined the American forces in Vietnam. One of the volunteers, Félix Rodríguez, devised and implemented a system using low-flying helicopters, warplanes, and small airborne squads for destroying entrenched Vietcong positions. Such was his effectiveness and daring in battle that the CIA's chief of operations in Saigon during the period 1970–1972 stated: "Félix knows more about low-intensity insurgency than almost anyone else alive."[3]

Given Félix's unusual expertise, it was not surprising to learn that Lieutenant Colonel Oliver North selected him in 1985 to lead the training and supply missions in Central America. For Félix and other Cuban exile operatives this was no ordinary covert assignment. It was, they thought, the prelude to a much larger and fulfilling undertaking: "Nicaragua today; Cuba tomorrow."

Other Bay of Pigs veterans decided not to engage in irregular warfare and remained in the U.S. armed forces. Among those who have made their mark is Erneido Oliva, the second commander of the Bay of Pigs brigade. He rose through the ranks of the U.S. Army and has earned the grade of brigadier general of the National Guard of the United States.

Not all the Cuban exile militants have followed a law-abiding, conventional path. A few, like the Russian nihilists of the nineteenth century, have engaged in extreme acts of violence directed against those who support and abet the Castro regime. Still others, lured by the riches of the growing drug traffic in Miami, de-

filed their ideals and engaged in crime, which swelled in the early
1980s with the deadbeats and convicts sent by Castro during the
Mariel exodus.

Most Cuban activists, however, have kept the flame of resistance alive without transgressing the law. Tony Varona, the respected democratic warrior from the early days, now heads the
Cuban Patriotic Junta, which embraces a large number of mainstream militant groups. Ably assisted in Washington by the inde-
fatigable Claudio Benedí, they have been denouncing human rights
violations in Cuba and alerting the Latin American republics to
the continued threat of Castro Communism. Another large exile
organization is CID (Cuba Independent and Democratic), led by
a former *comandante* of the Cuban Rebel Army, Huber Matos,
who was jailed by Castro for twenty years. Matos and his colleagues are trying to stimulate dissension within the Cuban regime
in the hope of an eventual break with Castro and his totalitarian
system. And the Cuban-American Foundation, a group of dynamic business and community leaders directed by Jorge Mas
Canosa, has embarked on the most far-reaching educational and
lobbying venture ever launched by anti-Castro exiles to drum up
support for the cause of freedom in Cuba and Central America.

The exiles' strident anticommunism and intransigence have
had some ill effects. Between 1970 and 1980, the non-Hispanic
white population in Dade County dropped 11 percent. Some of
those leaving displayed bumper stickers that read: "Will the last
American out of Miami please bring the flag?" The Cuban exiles
countered with their own stickers, reading: "Don't worry; they're
only 90 miles away." The journalist George F. Will drew a parallel with the American Jews to explain the heat in the heart
of Little Havana: "Imagine the mood of Jews if Israel were
tyrannized and were located 90 miles east of Long Island,"
he mused.[4]

The revolutionary fever of the Cuban Diaspora, while still
high, for years has been on the wane. After the mid-1960s most
of the exiles realized that the liberation of Cuba was not achieva-
ble under prevailing conditions and started to change their status
and mentality, from refugees to immigrants. Spurred by adversity,
a large number of them became overachievers in their relentless
pursuit of success.[5] They did not carry a heavy baggage of resentment, nor did they have a fixation on the past. Quick to learn
new skills or to perfect those they had, they worked extra hours
to excel. Not all became "walking miracles," symbols of afflu-

ence, but many of them have proved (as if further proof were indeed necessary) that refugee-to-millionaire stories are no fiction in this great land of opportunity.

Cuban entrepreneurship has led to the creation of some twenty thousand businesses in Miami and vicinity. And Cuban bilingualism, keenness, and zeal have been a major factor in inducing more than two hundred U.S. corporations to open regional offices in southern Florida, in attracting tourists and businessmen from most of the countries south of our shores, and in transforming Miami into the banking center of Latin America.

There are more than four hundred Cuban-American senior bank executives in the area, several of whom have reached the highest positions, like Raúl Masvidal, Bay of Pigs veteran, former chairman of three Miami banks, and highly successful and influential businessman in South Florida; Carlos Arboleya, vice-chairman of Barnett Bank (South Florida), the largest in the state; and Carlos García Vélez, at the helm of the powerful savings-and-loan group Amerifirst. The dean of the Cuban-American bankers, however, is Dr. Luis Botifoll, chairman of Republic National Bank, under whose leadership RNB surpassed the other thirty Latin banks in Miami and became the largest Hispanic financial institution on the U.S. mainland, with deposits and assets of close to $1 billion each.

One of the most remarkable Cuban-American business success stories of the last three decades is that of Bacardi, a worldwide rum empire composed of thirteen semiautonomous companies controlled by about two hundred Cuban descendants of Don Facundo Bacardí. In 1960, Castro confiscated the properties of the Cuban Bacardi Company, valued at $76 million, and attempted unsuccessfully to seize the trademark. The family went into exile, reincorporated the Cuban company in the Bahamas, and aggressively expanded its then small international operations. Bacardi today, led by Manuel Jorge Cutillas and other young members of the family, is sold in 175 countries, has captured a 60 to 70 percent share of the world rum market, and generates total revenues of close to $2 billion (inclusive of excise tax).

The Americans acquired a taste for Bacardi rum early in the century. In 1896, a U.S. mining engineer named Jennings Cox reportedly invented a refreshing drink by mixing Bacardi and lime juice while on a project near the Cuban town of Daiquirí. Two years after, when the Spanish-American War broke out, the U.S. troops landed there and quenched their thirst with Cox's drink (subsequently known as a daiquiri). Prohibition later exposed more Americans to Bacardi, since it was easier and less expensive to smuggle rum from Cuba than to bring in British whiskies. But it was only after Castro that Bacardi sales soared in the United States. For nearly a decade, Bacardi rum has outsold all other brands of distilled spirits in the huge American market.

Building on their traditional area of expertise, Cuban émigrés also have emerged as sugar potentates. The Fanjul brothers, who recently increased their landholdings and sugar mills by acquiring Gulf & Western's $200 million business in Florida and the Dominican Republic, are probably the largest individual sugar cane magnates in the world, producing a total of about one million tons per year. On the commercial side of the business, Cuban-American sugar brokers hold key positions in major trading firms, including Czarnikow Rionda, which is largely owned by the émigré Leandro Vázquez and presided over by another Cuban, Arturo Sterling.

Tobacco is another field where Cuban-Americans have excelled. Castro was able to confiscate all of the cigar companies on the island, but he could not seize the know-how that had been handed down over the years from father to son. Ramón Cifuentes of Partagás, one of Cuba's former tobacco barons, managed to escape with his family's craftsmanship and trademark. Starting afresh in exile, he went to the Dominican tobacco center of Santiago, taught the growers and workers the uncompromising Partagás techniques, and commenced selling a variety of quasi-Havana which has been rapidly capturing a share of Cuba's traditional markets.

Néstor Plasencia Fernández is another successful tobacco grower, but through the vicissitudes of exile he has had to face anew the flames of revolution. One of the largest cigar producers in Cuba, Plasencia fled the island with his family soon after Castro confiscated their enterprise. To rebuild their shattered lives, they settled in northern Nicaragua and developed a very profitable tobacco business. Seven years ago, they again had to flee. This time they ran from the Sandinistas, who took over their 250-acre tobacco farm, and relocated in Honduras. "That's life, I suppose," Plasencia recently told a reporter while puffing one of the five million cigars that are handmade on his new plantation each year. "But let me tell you, we don't buy land anymore. We only rent."[6]

The émigrés also have fared well in the competitive theater of corporate America. Several hundred Cuban executives and professionals who dealt with U.S. companies in pre-Castro days, as well as an array of up-and-coming Cubans who completed their education in exile, have been able to progress within the Latin American subsidiaries or divisions of U.S. corporations. Given their language proficiency, motivation, and background, their development by and large has been smooth and their level of competence high.

Moving up the corporate ladder, however, has not been easy. As Cuban émigrés have expanded their areas of responsibility beyond the effusive Latin cultures, they have had to learn to economize on words without impairing substance (the gentle art of the crisp memo), to argue a point without piercing the eardrums, to analyze issues without introducing emotions, and to tone down individuality and temper in the supreme interest of efficiency and consensus.

And yet, despite the challenges, Cuban émigrés have risen to multinational line or staff positions of distinction. A few examples will illustrate this point. Antonio Navarro, author of the book *Tocayo,* which recounts his experiences in the Cuban underground, moved from a management post in Peru with W. R. Grace to senior vice-president of the corporation. Emilio Alvarez-Recio, who years ago started with Colgate-Palmolive in Panama, was promoted to positions of increasing importance in Spain and the Philippines, and is now one of Colgate's vice-presidents with worldwide responsibilities. Alvaro Carta, who broadened his sugar expertise, headed the agricultural division of Gulf & Western during the conglomerate era of Charles Bluhdorn. And Enrique Falla, who participated in the Bay of Pigs invasion, completed his studies after his return from prison, acquired operational savvy with Dow Chemical/Latin America, and was recently promoted to vice-president and chief financial officer of the corporation.

Cuban émigrés are also well represented on the executive floors of major U.S. commercial and investment banks, from Chase Manhattan to Continental Illinois, from Merrill Lynch and Shearson Lehman Hutton to PaineWebber. The star of the group is the forty-two-year-old Cuban-born, British-bred Roberto G. Mendoza, executive vice-president of Morgan Guaranty Trust Company in charge of mergers and acquisitions. Displaying a forceful style, exemplified by blitzes of enthusiastic and occasionally abrasive "Mendoza-grams" (as his notes are known in the bank), Roberto is determined to carry out his mandate: to make Morgan a Wall Street power broker. Carving a niche in this crowded and competitive field is no simple task, but Mendoza has the support of an army of analysts (110 before the 1987 market crash) and the depth of Morgan's international presence. He also has a unique opportunity to crown his career. According to a *New York Times* feature article on Mendoza, "Many believe that if he builds his operation into a major force on Wall Street, then he will become Morgan's next chairman, succeeding Lewis T. Preston."[7] Although he allegedly suffered a setback in early 1988 when Morgan's client Hoffman–La Roche failed to consummate the hostile takeover of Sterling Drug, Roberto remains a solid and respected executive with a very bright future.

The Cuban émigrés' most phenomenal executive success story, however, is that of Roberto C. Goizueta, who leaped to the top of a major U.S. company whose name is the most widely recognized American symbol the world over: Coca-Cola. Born in Havana in 1931, he earned a degree in chemical engineering from Yale and went to work for Coke in Cuba. When he fled to Miami in 1960, Coke assigned him to its research division for Latin America, and in 1964 he was transferred to headquarters. Robert Woodruff, Coca-Cola's aging patriarch, was impressed with Goizueta's talent and dynamism and prevailed upon the board in 1981 to name him chief executive over more conventional competitors.

As noted by *Fortune* magazine, "At Coke, the anointing of a Cuban-born chemical engineer rather than a good ol' boy marketer was tantamount to a palace coup. Woodruff may have realized that it would take an outsider to break with the past and get the company moving again."[8] That is precisely what Goizueta did after taking office. He shook up the sleepy giant and its Southern traditions and instilled a new and bold entrepreneurial spirit, with concomitant risks and conspicuous blunders. Roberto's drive has heightened competition between Coke and archrival Pepsi, to the detriment of the lesser brands. And it has added spark and zest to the longest and most exhilarating corporate duel in modern times: the Cola Wars.

Outside the structured environment of large U.S. corporations, Cuban émigrés have earned public recognition as supersalesmen in various fields, from hamburgers to diamond-studded watches to financial services. Gerardo Larrea is a prime example. A Cuban professional, Larrea took up residence in Mexico after he left Cuba and gained experience in the soft-drink-bottling business. In the mid-1970s he was appointed president of Pepsi-Cola Mexicana, PepsiCo's largest franchise operation in the world outside the United States. This challenging post gratified Larrea until an opportunity came to carry out his enterprising dream. In 1976 he left Pepsi and, in partnership with Heinz, acquired the floundering Burger King operation in Puerto Rico, consisting of eighteen fast-food restaurants that were barely breaking even. Larrea revamped the operation, tightened controls, improved quality, and stimulated consumer demand with frequent hard-hitting promotions. Today he dominates 66 percent of the buoyant hamburger market in Puerto Rico, with close to eighty restaurants selling more than $100 million a year.

When the *New York Times* carried a two-page story in 1986 titled "The Art of Selling to the Very Rich," the fifty-four-year-old Cuban émigré Gedalio Grinberg was featured as the epitome of success, promoting a $1 million Piaget 87.87-carat diamond watch. In 1961 Grinberg acquired the American distribution arm of the Swiss-made Piaget watches when the manufacturer was selling no more than a few hundred watches a year. Now his North American Watch Company sells more than five thousand Piagets, along with other costly watches, and does over $120 million in business. Appealing to affluent customers, Grinberg advertised Piaget as the most expensive watch in the world. "The reason has been here since civilization started," he said. "People want to show their station in life. To the Egyptians, station was how many things they put in their tombs. In England in the seventeen hundreds, it was the big castles. Now it's by acquiring products like beautiful watches."[9] Grinberg's current plan is to do for luggage what he did for watches: turn an ordinary commodity into a luxury symbol of status.

Packaging and selling a financial product whose time had come was Jorge H. Coloma's route to national reputation and personal wealth. Born in Cuba in 1944, Jorge arrived in New York with his family and no money in 1961. He worked as a messenger and went to school at night. After a stint in the Republic National Bank in New York (at twenty-six he was already a vice-president), he moved to Miami, where he started his own firm, FAIC Securities Inc. This firm amassed and sold to banks and other institutions blocks of FDIC-insured certificates of deposit for a spread. In only seven years it became the largest brokerage house of that sort in the country. In mid-1987 he sold out to his partners, not to wallow in luxury, but to start another similar enterprise.[10]

Technology is not a Cuban forte, and yet a number of émigrés have attained prominent standing in the field of computers. One of them is Armando Codina, who at age eleven was packed off by

his desperate parents, along with thousands of other unaccompa-
nied Cuban children who were being sent to orphanages and foster homes in the United States. Sheltered until his mother was
able to escape from Cuba, Armando finished high school and took
a job at a bank. There he acquired a passion for computers and
saw the potential for software to deal with the paperwork maze
of doctors. He developed a system, based on a simple database,
and licensed it through seven branch offices across the country.
He sold his multimillion-dollar business several years ago, and is
now patenting other inventions and pursuing major real estate
ventures. "You've heard about the American dream," Codina once
said in a speech, "Well, let me tell you, it is alive and well. . . ."[11]

But in the field of technology no Cuban émigré, to my knowledge, has surpassed Juan Benítez's feat. Having left Cuba in 1965
as a teenager without his parents, he settled in Kansas City and
took no less than three jobs, all at or below minimum wage. By
age nineteen, he managed to finish high school and saved enough
money to make it through college in mechanical engineering. After
graduation, he worked in tooling and process engineering at the
General Motors auto assembly plant in St. Louis, and at the subsidiaries of other major conglomerates. He became an expert in
clean-room/dust-free engineering, essential to fabricating semi-
conductors. Uncomfortable with the rigidities he saw in corporations, Benítez yearned for an opportunity to build a new plant
from scratch.

In the summer of 1980, he joined Micron Technology, a small
start-up semiconductor company in Boise, Idaho, that was looking for someone to be responsible for overall construction of a
semiconductor facility. Benítez's task was daunting. He had to
build a plant capable of producing millions of computer chips every
month in an environment that could admit no hint of dust or vi-
bration. And he had to do so in record time, with a fraction of the
resources Japanese and U.S. corporate giants could devote to
construction in the most rapidly growing industry of our times.
Using largely laminar wood instead of steel and devising a new
atmospheric management system consisting of five huge fans that
impelled the air through some four miles of ducts, Benítez's building process exceeded industry standards and his facility took half
as long to construct as did similar plants in California, and cost
one-quarter as much.

As *Reader's Digest* tells the story, "Scarcely more than two
years later, Micron had managed to produce the smallest 64K

DRAM semiconductor, and had moved into the ranks of the top ten producers in the world. And at the center of this drama was a Cuban refugee named Juan Benítez, who only fifteen years before had been cleaning toilets in Kansas City.'' [12]

Cuban professionals in exile, particularly the lawyers, have had a very rough time. Their law degrees from Cuba were totally useless in the United States. Mario Goderich is one of the many who rose from abject poverty to success. When he arrived in Miami in 1961 with his wife and two children, and saw there was "nothing for lawyers," he got a job as a hotel desk clerk and worked at a factory in his off hours. Searching for broader horizons, he went to New York, where he combined a clerkship at IBM, an evening shift at a Doubleday bookstore, and weekend desk work in a hotel. A very bad cold forced him to return to Miami, where, with part-time jobs as a newsboy, schoolbus driver, and librarian, he finished law school and passed the bar. In 1978, he was appointed circuit court judge, the first Cuban émigré to hold that position. [13]

At present, there are more than five hundred Cuban-Americans practicing law in South Florida. Some of the exiled attorneys settled in Washington, D.C., like Francisco García Amador and José "Pepe" Camacho, who rose to the highest positions within the law departments of the Organization of American States and the International Finance Corporation, respectively. Others, mostly young graduates, joined Wall Street firms and law departments of U.S. corporations. And a few left the United States to pursue their career abroad. Such was the case of the late Manuel Vega Penichet, who, with his wife and fourteen children, relocated to Spain, started afresh in the university, studying side by side with some of his children, and founded one of the top international corporate law firms in Madrid. Joaquín Comella, another Cuban-born attorney with vast banking experience, cofounded a top-notch firm in Mexico and gained considerable prominence despite his handicap of not being a Mexican citizen.

In the field of medicine, Cuban-American doctors (over 4,500 in Miami and other U.S. cities) have distinguished themselves after studying anew to revalidate their degrees. Among those singularly honored in exile is Dr. Agustín J. Castellanos, a revered pediatrician and cardiologist who developed in Havana, in 1934, the angiocardiographic method of visualizing the main blood vessels connected to the heart. In recognition of his discovery, the American Association of Cardiology awarded him in 1962 its coveted gold medal. This was the second time in its history that the award was conferred on a foreign citizen. The first recipient was Madame Curie of France.

Younger Cuban-American doctors also have gained international fame. Dr. Manuel Viamonte, a renowned authority in radiology, is one of them. He pioneered in Florida the cyclotron and the tomograph. In recognition of the high standing he and many other Cuban doctors have achieved in exile, the World Medical Association, the most widely representative medical institution in existence, recently elected as its president the head of the Cuban Medical Association in Exile, Dr. Enrique Huertas. This is the first time in its history that a refugee has been accorded this honor.

In architecture, Cuban émigrés have left their imprints. The Yale-educated Hervin Romney (now working on his own) was one of the founders in 1977 of the Miami firm Arquitectónica, which has revolutionized urban architecture in the United States with its bold geometry and brilliant colors. Winners of prestigious awards, Arquitectónica has erected iconoclastic buildings in various cities, including an ellipse-shaped courthouse with "jazzy blue glass stripes," an ultramodern office building that defies gravity, and a surrealistic condominium notable for its red triangular rooftop prism and a huge cubic hole gouged out of the center. *Esquire* magazine (December 1984) hailed the young partners of Arquitectónica as daring visionaries with a "blueprint for the city of the future."

In academia, Cuban-American professors have earned accolades, not only as scholars, but also as essayists, economists, and historians. They have taught in numerous universities across the United States—from Harvard (Jorge I. Dominguez) to the University of Illinois (Mauricio Solaún); from The City University of New York (Julio Hernández Miyares) to Stanford (Modesto Maidique); from Georgetown (Luis E. Aguilar and José Manuel Hernández) to East Tennessee State University (Eduardo Zayas-Bazán); from Florida International University (Jorge Salazar-Carrillo) to Johns Hopkins University (Alejandro Portes); from the University of Pittsburgh (Carmelo Mesa-Lago) to Yale (the late Carlos Díaz Alejandro).

The most enterprising of the group is perhaps the forty-seven-year-old Cuban-born Modesto Maidique. After earning a Ph.D. in solid-state physics from the Massachusetts Institute of Technology, he cofounded a semiconductor company in Boston that is now a $300 million operation. He subsequently taught at MIT, Harvard, and Stanford, and in 1986 was appointed president of

Florida International University in Miami—the first Cuban-American to head a large U.S. university. The following year, Secretary of Education William Bennett asked Maidique to consider a nomination for the position of Under Secretary—a high honor he had to decline because of his commitment to the university.

Cubans have been prolific writers in exile. During the period 1959–1985 they published more than 750 books just on literature. In the early years, the prevailing nostalgia and cult of the past tended to cloud judgment and limit vision. Thereafter, however, most of the writers have become more open-minded and expansive—their élan not stultified by a ghetto mentality. Venerable Cuban men and women of letters, like Lydia Cabrera, the foremost living authority on Afro-Cuban themes, and Enrique Labrador Ruiz, a towering figure in the contemporary narrative of Latin America, have been a fount of knowledge and of renewed inspiration.

A number of younger novelists have made their mark beyond Latin America. Severo Sarduy was awarded a prize in France for the best foreign novel (*Cobra*). Pedro Entenza, Alvaro Villa, and Ramiro Gómez Kempt were each accorded honors in Europe. Hilda Perera, author of several stories and novels, including *Los Robredal,* has thrice been nominated finalist for Spain's coveted Planeta award.

Within the United States (and Europe), Reinaldo Arenas's recent *Farewell to the Sea: A Novel of Cuba* has elicited very favorable commentaries. *Saturday Review* called it "a stunning literary tour de force . . . a sometimes horrifying, sometimes blackly humorous tale of personal hypocrisy within political duplicity. . . . It will surely excite an array of urgent voices on the strength of its artistic achievement and controversial force."

But the most prominent of Cuban novelists in exile, the one who has garnered the highest praise, is Guillermo Cabrera-Infante. Born in Cuba in 1929, he broke with Castro in the mid-1960s and has since lived in London. Cabrera-Infante has been compared to Nabokov and Beckett because he can write luminous prose in both Spanish and English. According to the *New York Review of Books,* "with *Three Trapped Tigers,* he entered the front rank of Latin American novelists. The book belongs with Cortázar's *Hopscotch,* García Márquez's *One Hundred Years of Solitude,* and Donoso's *The Obscure Bird of Night.*"

In the political, revolutionary genre, in the United States and beyond, plaudits greeted Mario Lazo's *Dagger in the Heart,* Carlos Franqui's *Family Portrait with Fidel,* and José Luis Llovio-Menéndez's *Insider,* but the laurels went to Armando Valladares for his trenchant memoir of twenty-two years in Castro's prisons, *Against All Hope.* Ronald Radosh wrote about Valladares's revelations in the *New York Times Book Review* (June 8, 1986): "It has taken us twenty-five years to find out the terrible reality—Mr. Castro has created a new despotism that has institutionalized torture as a mechanism of social control." George F. Will commented in *Newsweek:* "There are words and deeds and words that are mighty deeds. You have rarely read words mightier than those of Armando Valladares's *Against All Hope.*" Mary McGrory of the *Washington Post* called the book "the shocker of the year." And *Time* magazine ranked it first among the nonfiction "Best of '86."

Among the émigrés who have left their imprints in journalism are Guillermo Martínez Márquez, a well-known veteran who was one of the founders of the Inter-American Press Society, and Carlos Alberto Montaner, one of the most incisive syndicated columnists in Spain and Latin America today. And in the field of literary prose, Luis E. Aguilar shines with his thoughtful essays and riveting stories, and Carlos Ripoll and Octavio Costa excel with their historical vistas and biographical portraits.

In the realm of poetry, many Cuban émigrés have been lauded for their compositions, which cover the gamut from the mystical to the romantic to the patriotic. To name but a few would be risky, if not deadly—such is the passion and the controversy that poetry arouses among Cubans. Perhaps it is safe to say that of the living poets in exile, the doyen is Eugenio Florit, who for years has enriched Latin American literature with his crystalline and melancholy verse.

The younger bards who have captured the limelight in the last few years are those who, like Angel Cuadra, Heberto Padilla, Armando Valladares, and Jorge Valls, have experienced the horrors of Castro's *gulag.* Most of their celebrated literary works—representing the "poetry of protest"—were smuggled out of Cuba when they were in prison and published in several languages. The following verses of Valls reflect the pain and love with which they withstood their plight:

Damn, Cuba, you have nailed me!
I burst into flower for you
with the passion of my life,

denying myself over and over . . .
I embraced your children and I was set ablaze with them
(my brothers, my beloved brothers,
my painful, hurtful, harsh brothers).
I suffered their pain and the pain that they did not suffer . . .
I have been your living verse.
You have been my cross, and I have loved you,
for what is better to love
than a cross for reaching from the earth to the sky? . . .[14]

In the arts, Cuban exiles also have excelled. Fernando Bujones, who left Cuba when he was four, ranks today among the most accomplished ballet dancers in the world, and Lourdes López gained recognition and fame after she joined the late George Balanchine's dance company in 1974. Painters and sculptors of note abound. José Gómez-Sicre, the Cuban-born founder and first director of the Museum of Modern Art of Latin America in Washington, D.C., lists sixty-nine prominent artists in his newly published anthology *Art of Cuba in Exile*. They include consummate masters of the past (apart from the internationally acclaimed Wilfredo Lam) whose works have graced the leading museums of the Americas, like Mario Carreño and Cundo Bermúdez; representatives of the subsequent group of Cuban modernists, such as Emilio Sánchez, Rolando López Dirube, Roberto Estopiñan, and José Mijares; and exponents of the "Miami generation" of Cuban artists, from Humberto Calzada to Pablo Cano. The last were uprooted from Cuba when they were very young. The angst of acculturation and exile have led them to "more introspective, wistful, and even tormented imagery," but most of them have retained elements of the Cuban character, pronounced in its vitality of light and color.

Cuban music, which gained universal acclaim thanks to Ernesto Lecuona and other gifted composers of the pre-Castro era, continues to enthrall the world. The fiery black singer Celia Cruz has been hailed as the foremost interpreter of the *son* and a precursor of salsa music. Having conquered Latin America with her Afro-Cuban rhythms, she took Europe by storm. This is how London's *Observer* magazine described her: "For more than thirty years, her rich, versatile contralto and infinite powers of improvisation have defined the style of female singer in this infectious music. Every generation produces its rivals, but Celia, now in her sixties, shows no signs of relinquishing her throne."[15]

The "crossover dream," the perennial aspiration of many Hispanic musicians to score a hit in the U.S. market, was achieved by Gloria Estefan and her compatriots from the Miami Sound Machine. Cuban-born children of refugees, they formed a band twelve years ago and started practicing in a Miami garage. With their refined, upbeat blend of contemporary pop and Cuban rhythms, they soon cracked the American market. "Dr. Beat," from their bilingual album *Eyes of Innocence,* became an international dance hit. And their next album, *Primitive Love,* yielded three Top Ten singles, including the burning Afro-Cuban dance hit "Conga." With their current "Rhythm Is Gonna Get You" and "Anything for You," which climbed to No. 1 on the *Billboard* pop chart, the Miami Sound Machine has become a stunning success.

The tiny but effervescent Gloria commented to reporters: "We're the first generation to grow up in the U.S., having been born in Cuba, but even with all its U.S. influence, I think our music remains close to the source." Thinking about the future, she sadly remarked: "I suspect that the music of our children will probably not have that influence, except for what is handed down to them through us." [16]

Sax player Paquito D'Rivera is another Cuban-born artist whose crossover dream came true. He remained in Havana until 1980, playing a tropical version of jazz. Since American jazz is considered subversive by the Castro regime, Paquito cunningly termed it "progressive Cuban socialist music." Despite this ingenious cover, he became suspect and decided to escape when he passed through Spain on a band tour. By the time D'Rivera's bag was stashed on the plane, he had dodged his watchman at the Madrid airport and was on his way to the American embassy, carrying his most precious possession—his sax. Based in Manhattan, he has risen to fame in less than eight years, playing his bopped-up, salty, sensuous jazz with strong Afro-Cuban inflections. [17]

Although Cuban musicians are best known for their percussive multirhythms, their fame is not limited to popular music. Manuel Barruecos, a Cuban-born classical guitarist, has gained international stature in his genre interpreting Mozart, Granados, and De Falla. The noted Cuban soprano Virginia Alonso has sung various operas with Plácido Domingo to positive reviews. And Horacio Gutiérrez, who at age eleven made his debut with the Havana Symphony and in 1971 was a medalist in the Tchaikowsky Competition, is regarded by critics as one of the most accomplished concert pianists in America today. According to *Connoisseur* magazine, "One virtuosic gift apparent in all of Gutiérrez's playing is his ability to make the wooden, hammer-struck, steel-strung modern grand sing—and cry, buzz, glitter, hum, as well as produce a dozen other effects of keyboard articulation." [18]

Eduardo Machado, at thirty-five, who left Cuba at age eight, speaking no English, was hailed by *Time* (July 11, 1988) as perhaps the most gifted playwright among all the Hispanics. Eduardo began writing plays when a therapist suggested he compose an imaginary letter of forgiveness to his mother. One of his best works is *Once Removed*, which captures the perplexity and determination of a family uprooted by the Castro revolution.

Cuban émigrés have also made their mark as actors, directors, and artistic producers. María Conchita Alonso, raised in Caracas by her Cuban-born parents, has starred with distinction in several films, including *Moscow on the Hudson* with Robin Williams and *The Running Man* with Arnold Schwarzenegger. And the suave, Cuban-born Andy García, who caught the critics' attention as a bad guy in *8 Million Ways to Die* and switched sides to play the Italian George Stone in *The Untouchables,* was hailed in 1987 as "one of the year's hottest discoveries," according to *Newsweek.* In the field of production, *Improper Conduct,* the creative work of the world-renowned Spanish-Cuban photographic director Néstor Almendros and of his colleague Orlando Jiménez-Leal, depicting persecution under the Castro regime, was considered by Vincent Canby of the *New York Times* one of the finest documentaries in 1984. And in 1988, the thirty-eight-year-old Cuban-born writer-director Ramón Menéndez produced *Stand and Deliver,* described by *Newsweek* as a "tremendously compelling" film about the learning experience of Hispanics who refuse to "succumb to the inertias of system and stereotype."

In the glittering world of fashion, the Cuban-born Adolfo ranks among the leading designers in America today. After a brief stint with Balenciaga in Spain, he started designing hats on Seventh Avenue and became New York's most renowned milliner. Then in the 1960s, he plunged into clothes and started making Chanel-like dresses. Adolfo's success is highlighted today by his exclusive "club" of admirers and clients. According to *Women's Wear Daily,* the supreme arbiter of American fashion, if the Adolfo club had officers, "it would boast Nancy Reagan as president and Betsy Bloomingdale as secretary."

And in the arena of competitive sports, the feats of Cuban

athletes in exile rival the achievements of their counterparts on the island. In boxing, the exiles have produced three world welterweight champions—Luis Manuel Rodríguez, Kid Paret, and José Mantequilla Nápoles—and two featherweight champions—Ultimio Ramos and José Legra. Four other Cuban émigrés fought for the crowns in the lightweight and middleweight divisions. In baseball, more than twenty-five Cuban exile players have established records in the major leagues, including Tony Oliva, Luis Tiant, and, most recently, José Canseco. And in the New York Marathons of 1980 and 1984, Cuban-born Alberto Salazar finished first among three thousand competitors.

Few emigrations have left such an indelible mark in so many fields in such a short period of time. These success stories, and many others worthy of note, are not limited to Cuba's former intelligentsia or affluent elite. They cut across all socioeconomic strata. The outstanding results achieved reflect special talents or skills, motivation, and tenacity. They also point to the Cubans' ability to adapt to a new environment, to turn adversity into opportunity, to look ahead and start anew.

As the Cuban émigrés progressed with their work, they became conscious of their potential political clout, notably in South Florida. The need to protect their interests and assert their rights, particularly in light of occasional ethnic flare-ups, prompted Cuban-Americans to join forces and play a more active public role in Miami and neighboring counties. This has not been easy, given the historical rivalries among Cubans and their individualistic bent. Nevertheless, they have managed to wield their influence and elect twenty Cuban-born government officials in southern Florida, including four mayors and seven state representatives.

The most encouraging note of the 1987 electoral campaign in Miami was that it was conducted without the rancor that had divided the community in the past. The candidates did not whip up racial and ethnic fears and prejudices, and the incumbent mayor of Miami, the Cuban-born, Harvard-educated Xavier Suárez, won a second term in a runoff vote backed by a majority in each of the three segments of the population.

A further indication of the Cuban-Americans' weight and prestige in South Florida is the fact that five of their business and community leaders, Luis Botifoll, Raúl Masvidal, Armando Codina, José Hernández, and Carlos Arboleya, have been invited to join "the Non-Group," an unofficial and very private organization which is reputed to be the shadow government of southern Florida. Among its close to forty members are the owners or chief executive officers of Knight-Ridder, Arvida Disney, Eastern Airlines, Burdines, the Miami Dolphins, and the major banks, insurance companies, and utilities.

In Hudson County, New Jersey, a Cuban-American was able to sway local politics under most unusual circumstances. Octavio J. Alfonso, a sixty-year-old former Cuban labor activist, was elected in 1984 to the nine-member governing board of that county. Campaigning door-to-door in the state's most ethnic district, which holds a large concentration of Cuban exiles, Alfonso unseated the incumbent Democrat by nearly 1,500 of the 24,069 votes cast. It was a stunning victory, but what made it so unusual was that the winner could not speak English. The stout, graying Alfonso explained in Spanish: "To see the needs of the community one does not need the language if one has the heart and courage." Although fluency in English was not a legal prerequisite for office, Alfonso immediately began studying English five days a week with a tutor. Alfonso said, *"Yo soy el pequeño"*—the underdog. "I have to work the hardest." [19]

Cuban migration also was responsible for a dramatic social, economic, and political turnaround in another area of New Jersey. The *New York Times* summarized it thus: "A touch of Havana brings life to Union City." There, less than three decades ago, crime was rising, income was declining, and the people were leaving. A wave of Hispanic immigrants, mostly Cubans, bought decaying businesses and homes and halted the downturn. Having revitalized and gained virtual control of Union City, the émigrés recently elected a son of Cuban immigrants, Robert Menéndez, mayor of that community.

The political salience and influence of Cuban émigrés are also manifest in Washington, D.C., and other centers of power. José Sorzano, who was a law student when he left Cuba in 1961, graduated from Georgetown University in Washington, D.C., was appointed principal deputy U.S. ambassador to the United Nations under Jeane Kirkpatrick, and was later named the National Security Council's chief Latin American specialist at the White House. Three other Cuban émigrés have served as U.S. ambassadors as well: Mauricio Solaún (Nicaragua), Alberto Martínez Piedra (Guatemala), and Otto Juan Reich (Venezuela).

More than fifteen other Cuban-Americans have been honored with presidential appointments, including the poet Armando Valladares, U.S. representative to the Human Rights Commission of the United Nations, with ambassadorial rank; the former sugar magnate José Manuel Casanova, U.S. delegate to the Inter-American Development Bank; the former professor Rita Rodríguez, member of the board of directors of the U.S. Export-Import Bank; the businessman Alberto Cárdenas, chairman of the President's Advisory Committee on Small and Minority Business Ownership; the attorney Juan del Real, general counsel of the Department of Health and Human Services; and the real estate developer Carlos Salmán, member of the board of directors of the Overseas Private Investment Corporation.

The presidential appointee who has been most active politically is a forty-eight-year-old veteran of the Bay of Pigs invasion force, Jorge Mas Canosa. He was appointed chairman of the advisory board of Radio Martí, which beams news, editorial comment, and entertainment to Cuba under the able stewardship of Ernesto F. Betancourt. Backed by the Cuban-American National Foundation, Jorge is now seeking congressional approval to launch Television Martí, a Florida-based TV station to transmit news, information, and films to Cuba.

The group led in Miami by the former Speaker of the House of Representatives of Cuba, Lincoln Rodón, has a more targeted mission: to rescind the so-called Kennedy-Khrushchev accord on Cuba, which seemingly inhibits the United States and Cuban exiles from stimulating and supporting internal resistance against Castro. This group is marshaling its arguments and publicizing its case through a well-documented book titled *Cuba and Its Right to Freedom*.

Alex Castellanos, a Cuban-born refugee who arrived with his family in Miami at age six, has a somewhat different agenda. Having cofounded the political advertising firm Murphy & Castellanos in Alexandria, Virginia, he wants to become a media guru, a powerful TV image-builder and shaper of elections. Alex and his partner gained prominence in the 1988 campaign and were featured in *Fortune* magazine as "new-style media masters" in the selling of the President.[20]

Wooing Cuban-American political activists and voters started in earnest several years ago. During the 1984 presidential campaign, Cuban émigrés played a major role within the Hispanic communities. In recognition of their soaring influence, Tirso del Junco, a Cuban-American doctor from California, was elected chairman of the Republic National Hispanic Assembly. And during the 1988 campaign, all of the Republican presidential candidates made every effort to capture the Cuban-American conservative-leaning votes in the fourth-most-populous state of the Union: Florida.

The Cuban émigrés are politically active, but most of them are no longer absorbed in the thought of an eventual return to their homeland. They have happily settled in this country and currently enjoy the satisfaction of achievement and the blessings of freedom and prosperity. They do not currently have a transient, exile mentality. Even the elders, who occasionally feel the nostalgia of Cuba, already have roots in this country: children born in Cuba but raised and educated in the United States who call themselves YUCAS (young, upwardly mobile Cuban-Americans), and grandchildren born and brought up in the United States who can barely speak Spanish.

And yet, a large number of Cuban-American families retain their cultural, religious, and national traditions. Relatives, including distant cousins, and friends still gather to celebrate a joyful event or to mourn a common grief. Despite the external pressures of the environment, most of the families manage to support and care for the aged and the handicapped at home. Emotions, although more subdued than in the past, tend to fluctuate between euphoria and melancholy. Life is lived to the fullest—with verve and style. There is music in the blood and drama in the speech. People are considered important, but issues are not taken too seriously. There is no problem that the imagination and hard work cannot conquer and that laughter cannot cure. There is a light side to everything except God, family, honor, and heritage.

These traits have survived, to a certain degree, even among Cuban-Americans who do not reside in Florida. The annual pilgrimage to Miami serves to reinforce their idiosyncrasies. Emigrés from all walks of life regularly visit the exile mecca. The frugal and the needy in the Northeast who wish to pay less than the $100-plus one-way Greyhound fare and enjoy "a Latin home on the road" can ride on La Cubana—a double-decker bus on the New York–Miami route, complete with Spanish-speaking stewardess, television set, and thimble-size doses of strong Cuban coffee. Owned and run by émigrés, this bus service, founded in 1978, carries about 25,000 passengers a year, primarily Cubans visiting relatives.[21]

The "Cubanization" of Miami, which undoubtedly attracts many of the émigrés, has often been reduced to stereotyped descriptions of the 3.5-mile stretch known as Little Havana. There, it is reported, you can hear the clinking of dominoes and the firing of oaths and salty repartee, or smell the old-style Cuban cooking of spicy roast pig and black bean soup, or pulse to the Latin salsa beat, or listen to the boasts of noisy raconteurs.

This colorful but somewhat disparaging portrayal, coupled with negative allusions to the Marielitos jail riots, ethnic disputes, and *Miami Vice,* tends to besmirch the public image of the émigrés in Miami and to belittle their manifold contributions to the community. For apart from their undeniable economic impact, Cuban-Americans, led by Alberto Vadía and other philanthropists, have inspired many major programs in Dade County, from the United Way to the Miami Opera Society, from the County School Board to the League Against Cancer, from the Miami book and film festivals to Miami Citizens Against Crime.

Their immersion in community affairs, however, has not led to the demise of their cultural heritage. Keeping the flame of Cuba alive are several publishers, like Juan Manuel Salvat's Ediciones Universal and La Moderna Poesía, eight Spanish-language radio stations, two television stations, and twenty newspapers and magazines, including Horacio Aguirre's *Diario Las Américas,* probably the most widely read Hispanic newspaper in the country. *The Miami Herald,* which is keenly aware of the growing Latin influence in the area, has recently revamped its Spanish supplement, *El Nuevo Herald.* In addition, distinguished intellectuals, like José Ignacio Rasco, offer history-oriented programs to their compatriots, and a number of scholars from the University of Miami and Florida International University, among them Jaime Suchlicki, Enrique Baloyra, Antonio Jorge, José Ignacio Lasaga, and other Latin American specialists, issue numerous writings on Cuba.

Back in the 1960s, an illustrious Cuban statesman and master of letters, Juan J. Remos, launched what he called an "educational crusade" designed to salvage the Spanish language within the exile community, reaffirm Cuban traditions, and foster unity through culture. He died shortly after having spearheaded the program, but two women known for their intellectual acumen and patriotic zeal, María Gómez Carbonell and Mercedes García-Tudurí, along with other colleagues, carried out his noble project. They have issued numerous publications, held periodic cultural events, and conferred awards on the émigrés who have shined in the fields of arts, letters, and science.

The climate created by them has stimulated other cultural and patriotic initiatives, like the Congress of Intellectual Dissidents, the Cuban-American National Council, and the Cuban Museum of Art and Culture. Although not many of the émigrés are actively involved in these endeavors, there is a resurgence of interest in family roots and Cuban mores. Indeed, several of the current civic leaders are carrying the baton symbolically passed on to them by their elders. Ariel Remos, the son of Juan J. Remos, is a highly respected columnist in Miami and now heads the educational crusade spurred by his father. And Uva Clavijo, the granddaughter of Cuba's foremost story writer, Alfonso Hernández Cata, is an essayist and poet of the first rank and an enthusiastic community leader.

Even the second-generation Cuban-American architects, who have no memory of Cuba, are looking into their cultural background and drawing inspiration from the Spanish and Mediterranean architectural legacy of the Caribbean. Although their styles differ, they share an affinity for the colonial traditions found in Cuba, including spacious courtyards with fountains, sheltered porches, and graceful verandas.

Social activities in Miami, from the traditional fifteenth-birthday balls (*los quince*) to the multitudinous Calle Ocho Carnival Miami, exude Cuban flair. The Carnival—a felicitious initiative of Leslie Pantín, Jr., and the Kiwanis Club—started a decade ago as an "open-house party" offered by Cuban-Americans to the rest of the community to celebrate life together in Miami. Last year, the police estimated that some one million people of all ages and ethnic backgrounds gathered to partake in the festivities, which included the world's longest conga line, stretching twenty-four blocks in Little Havana.

Club life, involving competitive sports and multiple social events, is another tradition the Cubans have nurtured in Miami through the "Big Five" (as Havana's pre-Castro leading clubs were called) and other similar associations. The most recent and distinctive of the lot is the Miami Rowing Club, whose facilities were partly funded by José María Arellano. A forty-four-year-old oil broker whose grandfather had founded one of the Big Five clubs in Havana and whose father had coached its Olympic crew, José María, along with his cousin Agustín and several friends, pledged funds to carry out the project.

"What was a boat shed on scrubland ten years ago . . . ," the *Miami Herald* noted, "has evolved into a high-profile 400-member family sport and exercise group."[22] The organization now has a two-story clubhouse with meeting rooms, a dance floor, an

Olympic-size swimming pool, and basketball and volleyball courts. They have been so successful that they have been able to sponsor rowing programs for inner-city children, give financial support to the University of Miami's new rowing team, and attract prestigious national and international rowing events to Miami.

The founders are not out to make money, but to exercise, foster friendships, and kindle remembrances. One of the club's major events each summer is the Varadero Regatta, a replica of the old Cuban national crew competition held at Varadero Beach. Teams wearing the colors of the historic clubs race each August. Veteran oarsmen from the old clubs turn out, as do younger generations of rowers. "It's very exhilarating," Arellano told me, beaming with satisfaction. "We have had three generations of Cuban athletes here in one spot!"

These and other communal events tend to strengthen national ties. But it's within the families that traditions and values are truly enhanced. This is particularly so in the case of my wife's prolific family, the Mendozas, whose seven branches have grown to almost 1,300 living members. Founded in 1855 by Don Antonio González de Mendoza y Bonilla, a renowned lawyer who became the first president of the Supreme Court of Cuba after the Spaniards left, the entire family used to get together in Havana every twenty-five years to celebrate their relationship. (As the Mendozas will tell you themselves, they are pretty much just like everybody else on earth, only more so.)

Despite the dispersion and hardships of exile, the respective core groups of the Mendoza family gather frequently, but only twice since 1959 have representatives of the seven branches assembled *en masse*. The last full reunion took place at the Miami Rowing Club in August 1988. More than seven hundred relatives from all over the world came to the party, each wearing a T-shirt with a distinctive color representing his or her branch. As an in-law, I attended the memorable celebration.

At first, many felt like strangers, particularly the youngsters who didn't know each other. After a while, however, they were all commingling, cheering, and dancing. Torrential weather conditions marred the field day, but did not deter most of the participants from posing for a family picture in the rain. The organizers distributed a 103-page history of the Mendoza family, including a genealogical tree that spans seven generations.

In a spacious salon of the rowing club, a museum of the family was set up. There I heard a senior member speak with devotion of their national heritage and ancestral ties. Everybody around him listened closely, even those who could not follow well in Spanish. The words did not matter. There was a feeling of allegiance, a spirit of identity, a sense of belonging. The family hearth was still burning; the Cuban bonds remained strong. One of the elder Mendoza ladies looked at the young ones with pride. Misty-eyed, she turned to her husband and whispered: "There is hope. There is hope."

CHAPTER 18

Looking Ahead

Influential scholars, journalists, and congressmen view Castro's recent conciliatory tone—indeed, his peaceful overtures—as an opportunity to ease tension in the Caribbean. Some believe that Castro has mellowed with age. Others feel that mounting economic pressure and declining Soviet aid have prompted Castro to explore a rapprochement with the United States. The time has come, they contend, for broad or phased negotiations with the Cuban ruler.

Since Castro came to power, the United States has attempted on numerous occasions to reach an accommodation with him—not always, I might add, with consistency and vision. During the period 1959–1960, Washington made several formal and informal offers to negotiate all differences with Cuba. Most of these offers were channeled through Ambassador Philip Bonsal, a polished diplomat with inexhaustible reserves of patience and optimism. Unable to mollify Castro, the White House secretly requested in early 1960 the mediation of the Argentine ambassador to Havana, Julio Amoedo. None of these efforts reached fruition.

In the fall of 1963, William Atwood, special adviser to the United States delegation to the United Nations, held a series of talks with the Cuban ambassador to the United Nations to discuss the possibility of a rapprochement. McGeorge Bundy, head of the National Security Council, reportedly told Atwood that President Kennedy was in favor of "pushing towards an opening toward Cuba" to take Castro "out of the Soviet fold and perhaps wiping out the Bay of Pigs and maybe getting back to normal.''[1] These exploratory talks, however, occurred at the same time the CIA offered a Cuban *comandante* a poison pen device for Castro's assassination (Operation AM/LASH). With the change of administration following President Kennedy's tragic death, Atwood's talks with the Cubans became less frequent, and they eventually ceased early in 1964.

On March 1, 1975, Secretary of State Henry Kissinger declared: ''We see no virtue in perpetual antagonism between the U.S. and Cuba. . . . We are prepared to move in a new direction if Cuba will.'' Castro expressed interest in normalizing relations, and the Ford administration eased the economic embargo and dropped the demand that Cuba sever its ties with the USSR as a precondition for negotiations. Secret talks between U.S. and Cuban envoys went on for a year, but Castro's vision of a new direction—airlift of eighteen thousand Cuban troops into Angola—later increased to 50,000, was not exactly what Kissinger had in mind. The talks broke off.

The Carter administration considered that a free and powerful nation like the United States had nothing to fear, and perhaps something to gain, in opening communications with Cuba. White House and State Department officials privately met with Fidel. ''Interests Sections'' were subsequently created as a device for resuming direct diplomatic contacts without reestablishing formal relations. Carter was encouraged by Castro's response to his 1977 initiative. Fidel released 3,900 political prisoners and most U.S. citizens detained on the island. In addition, he allowed Americans living in Cuba and dual nationals to come to the United States, and he authorized Cuban-Americans to visit Cuba. More than 100,000 exiles flew to the economically depressed island with money, gifts, and amazing stories of affluence in freedom. Their impact on the islanders exacerbated prevailing unrest, which in turn led to the massive Mariel exodus in 1980. Castro, though, had the last laugh in this episode. After ordering a security crackdown in Cuba, he shipped to Florida several thousand common criminals, spies, and social misfits.

Prior to the Mariel migration, while the Carter administration was negotiating in good faith with Cuba, Castro sent seventeen thousand soldiers to fight in Ethiopia under Soviet command. Russian pilots replaced them in Cuba. Fidel also exploited ''targets of opportunity'' in the Caribbean Basin, particularly in Nicaragua. He engineered the merger of three factions into the

Sandinista National Liberation Front (FSLN) and provided military training and arms to the local guerrillas. Castro's duplicity finally wore out Carter's patience, and the negotiations ended.[2]

The Reagan administration also explored ways of improving relations with Castro. In November 1981, Secretary of State Alexander Haig secretly conversed in Mexico with Cuba's Vice Prime Minister and leader of the old guard of the Communist Party, Carlos Rafael Rodríguez, and in March 1982, General Vernon Walters met in Havana with Fidel. None of these talks progressed because of Cuba's continued involvement in Africa and Central America.

In 1984, Castro started to send fresh signals suggesting he would like to ease tensions with the United States. Wayne S. Smith, who headed the U.S. Interests Section in Havana from 1979 to 1982, affirmed after a meeting with Castro that he was "a man with whom we might deal." While still a formidable adversary, he showed, according to Smith, signs of a new patience and a disposition toward accommodation.[3] The journalist Tad Szulc also reported that Castro believed that a partial improvement in relations with the United States was possible. During Szulc's interview, Fidel pledged that "feelings of hostility and hatred toward the North American people would never be sown in Cuba."[4]

In early 1985, Castro hosted three American congressmen—Leland, Leach, and Alexander—at a retreat off the Bay of Pigs. Mornings devoted to swimming and spearfishing were followed by rounds of intense discussions. The congressmen were impressed not only by Castro's snorkeling skills, but also by his professed desire to negotiate with the United States. According to Alexander, "President Reagan would make a serious mistake if he rejected the conciliatory offer tendered this month by Fidel Castro. The Cuban leader's message is clear: he wants to lessen the tensions between Cuba and the United States. This, he hopes, will give Cuba access to United States markets. . . ."

Castro's conception of a deal, however, was rather one-sided. As reported in the January 9, 1984, edition of *Newsweek,* a journalist asked him: "Suppose the U.S. says to you: Let's make a deal. We will open up diplomatic, economic and technical links with Cuba. But in return, you will have to stop supporting Nicaragua, Angola, and revolutionary movements such as SWAPO." Castro answered thus: "They would be asking a price too high for our honor and for our principles in exchange for material benefits that we are not too interested in. But even if we were interested in those benefits, we would not be willing. We could never pay such a price." Fidel's curt response dashed all hopes for a quid pro quo.

Following the signing of an immigration agreement in December 1984, there was a warming in the U.S.-Cuba relationship. But this came to an abrupt halt in May 1985 when Washington inaugurated its broadcast service to Cuba, Radio Martí. Castro denounced this service as a cynical and provocative attempt at subversion, and suspended the five-month-old immigration agreement with the United States. In early July, Castro traded insults with President Reagan when the latter included Cuba in a list of five countries that he said formed a "confederation of terrorist states." Castro countered by calling President Reagan "a big liar" and "a madman, an imbecile, and a bum" who was "saying a bunch of stupidities and lunacies."

Since Castro's outburst was, in part, provoked by Washington, we have to look at his actions to determine the sincerity of his overture. Unfortunately, these actions did not suggest peaceful inclinations. Soviet arms deliveries to Cuba grew from an average of 15,000 tons a year in the 1970s to over 66,000 tons in the mid-1980s—about ten times more than U.S. military assistance to *all* of Latin America. Cuba's armed forces surpassed the two hundred and fifty thousand mark, a fivefold increase over 1960, without including paramilitary and reserve organizations of over a million strong. And the Castro regime expanded its sophisticated military bases in several parts of the country, and continued to train and arm Marxist guerrillas and agitprop agents.

Still, with the revival of the immigration accord in November 1987 (following secret parleys with U.S. representatives in Canada and Mexico), Castro reportedly has sent new signals to Washington for a fuller dialogue involving Central America, Africa, the base at Guantánamo, and economic and trade relations. As in the past, these overtures raise critical questions. Is the Cuban ruler honestly determined to bury the hatchet and settle his differences with the United States? Could and should Washington embark on a negotiation course with Castro under current conditions?

These questions are expected to generate controversy. The debate on Cuba today is by no means quiet and dispassionate. Opinions differ sharply on the present direction of the Castro regime and the outlook for improved U.S.-Cuban relations. Total objectivity seems impossible. The issues are still too sensitive for detached, academic discourse. Cuba remains, to a large degree, intertwined with politics, tinged with biases, and imbued with emotions.

On the one side, skeptics opposing negotiations opine that Castro is just posturing, staging a deceptive peace offensive, diverting attention from the violence he continues to spread. On the other side, proponents of full-scale diplomacy believe that Castro needs U.S. trade and aid, and that economic incentives would induce him to liberalize his regime, stop subversion, and break or loosen his ties with the Soviet bloc. Both of these extreme positions appear to be partially flawed. The record shows that limited agreements with Castro, like the recent immigration accord and the promised withdrawal from Angola, may be possible, particularly if they offer the Cuban regime a safety valve or an opportunity to balk or renege. But beyond that, would a visceral anti-American and messianic tyrant like Castro transform totalitarianism, renounce agitation, and abandon the world center stage to become simply a Latin *caudillo* lured by U.S. dollars into a neutral, insular role? Based on everything we know about Castro, this would seem highly improbable.

But Fidel's inclinations aside, Cuba is not truly the arbiter of her future and Castro is not really the master of his destiny, protestations of autonomy notwithstanding. The island is almost totally dependent on the Soviet bloc, which buys Cuba's sugar currently at four times the world market price, and supplies its oil requirements, for both internal use and export, at highly subsidized levels. Without these subsidies and other forms of aid, which account for about one-quarter of Cuba's gross national product, the Cuban economy would grind to a halt. As for Castro himself, he could not remain in the limelight boasting eighty thousand activists in thirty countries and defying the "Colossus of the North" without the support and protection of the "Red Bear."[5]

Given these realities, would the USSR, without considerable pressure, relinquish control over Cuba or refrain from using the island as a launch pad for espionage and subversion? From a Western pragmatic perspective, a strong case could be made in the affirmative. After all, Cuba does not lie within Russia's sphere of influence; the carrying costs of the island are very high, and Soviet tangible gains to date have not been commensurate with investment. Cuba currently receives more than half of all Soviet foreign aid. From a $1 million daily level in 1975, Russian assistance to Cuba jumped to $8 million in 1979 and to about $16–18 million at present, including arms and trade subsidies.

Why would the Soviets continue to pump so much money into a collapsing economy five thousand miles away? A *Forbes* magazine article gave a simple but illuminating response: "Because they know it is their best buy when it comes to making trouble for the U.S. For less than the annual cost of supporting a single aircraft carrier task force, the Soviet Union has developed a wondrous weapon.''[6] Stated another way, from the standpoint of Russia's geopolitical interests, the domination of Cuba has major political, psychological, and strategic significance. It has enabled the Soviet Union to bypass NATO, jump the Atlantic, bury the Monroe Doctrine, flout the inter-American defense treaty, and establish a stronghold for expansion in an area that is of crucial importance to the security and well-being of the United States and its allies. Control of the island has also permitted the Russians to use, as surrogates, phalanxes of intrepid Cubans who have become the vanguard of the Communist offensive in Africa, Latin America, and other parts of the world.

Glasnost and *perestroika* (the current winds of openness and restructuring in the USSR), while encouraging, offer no guarantee that the Kremlin will curl up comfortably and forgo its hegemonic goals. History suggests it will not. Lenin's New Economic Policy, which introduced free-market variants in the Soviet economy, and Khrushchev's reforms, did not essentially alter the totalitarian system, nor slow down the gargantuan growth of the Communist party and its international network of sympathizers and fanatics. And Brezhnev's détente, which arguably improved relations with the West, did not prevent Moscow from embarking on the most phenomenal military buildup in modern times, and from eventually extending its power or influence to Laos, Vietnam, Cambodia, Angola, Ethiopia, Mozambique, South Yemen, Afghanistan, and Nicaragua.

Admittedly, the internal crisis faced by the Soviet Union today is more acute than in the recent past. The Russian economy is a shambles; it has shown no growth for years. Marxist-Leninist ideology is losing its cutting edge and luster, even among young militants. From Soviet Central Asia to the Baltic states, minority populations are openly challenging Russian rule. Technological backwardness is undermining the big power status that gives the Bolshevik regime its legitimacy and appeal. These manifestations of rot and decay, and the ensuing reforms announced at the Communist Party Conference in Moscow, have prompted some U.S. journalists and scholars to announce the end of the Cold War and to scoff at those who allegedly still hold on to a ''Manichean view of the world.''

There is no doubt that Gorbachev is trying to decentralize

and energize the Soviet economy while pursuing certain military cuts. But a number of well-known experts in foreign affairs question his willingness or ability to make the critical jump from economic to political decentralization in Russia, and from adventurism to nonintervention abroad. Based on past experiences, these pundits urge Washington not to engage in superpower negotiations without linkage; not to shower Moscow with untied loans, transfers of technology, subsidized trade, and uneven concessions in arms control agreements. As the *Economist* of London in its refreshingly witty style reminded us, "a fat bear is not necessarily cuddly." Absent a dramatic and lasting change in the Kremlin's militaristic and expansionist behavior, the British periodical warned, "a richer Russia will simply be a fitter fighter."[7]

While Soviet agreement to withdraw from Afghanistan is heartening (if indeed this permits the Afghan people to determine their own fate), other developments are disturbing, to say the least. After the United States stopped all military aid to the contras, the Russians continued delivering arms to Nicaragua. As disclosed by Washington, Soviet shipments exceeded $500 million in the twelve months following the end of U.S. aid. And despite talk of disarmament, the USSR has significantly strengthened its installations in the eastern Mediterranean, has increased its ground forces in the Far East to 390,000, or forty-three divisions, and is rapidly expanding its Pacific fleet and operational aircraft.

These unsettling actions notwithstanding, the West has enabled the Soviet Union and its client states to step up their activities in international capital markets. By now, the actual debt incurred by the Soviet bloc has reportedly reached $125 billion, a jump of 55 percent in the last three years alone.[8]

With respect to Cuba, a senior official of the Castro regime who recently defected, Gustavo Pérez Cott, disputed widespread speculation of friction between Moscow and Havana over conflicting economic policies. He explained that the Russians had delivered less equipment and supplies to Cuba than scheduled in 1987, but that the deficit had been caused by production problems and was being made up. According to Pérez Cott, Moscow promised to increase its level of support in 1988 by about 10 percent, assuring Castro that "aid to Cuba would not be lessened because of any of the reforms taking place in the Soviet Union."[9]

Against this backdrop, the question remains, what to do about Cuba? U.S. diplomatic isolation and economic embargo have not resulted in the removal or liberalization of the Castro regime, nor in the withdrawal of Soviet forces and "technical" advisers from the island nation. The sanctions have weakened the Cuban economy and shown a measure of resolve and moral outrage, but they have not subdued the regime or modified its practices. Why, then, people ask, don't we negotiate with Castro? What is there to lose by trying? Pressure on the White House to commence the dialogue is mounting. It is fueled by the hope of disengagement and peace raised by Costa Rica's President Arias's settlement proposal for Central America, and by the new spirit of détente emanating from the Reagan-Gorbachev summit meetings.

But opening broad-scale negotiations on Cuba is not a win-win proposition. History has taught us that negotiations with an expansive totalitarian regime, unless preceded by or combined with the exercise of power, smack of appeasement. Moreover, dealing with Castro, without meaningful changes beyond grandstand plays, would create false expectations and invite scorn and disdain. The onus to prove sincerity would not necessarily fall on Castro. A master propagandist, he could place the United States on the defensive and emerge unscathed. Through the skillful use of deception, he could walk away with concessions based on assurances he might not fulfill. This would induce potential Castros in this hemisphere to secure Soviet-backed political longevity, knowing that they could eventually count on the United States to dignify them with diplomatic recognition and bail them out with economic aid.

Castro has not ceased to engage in Potemkin-type duplicity to mask embarrassing realities. In response to the United States campaign that has portrayed Cuban prisons as dungeons and torture chambers, Castro finally permitted human rights experts to visit the largest penitentiaries and to communicate with some of the inmates. Except for a dreadful section in Combinado del Este known as the Rectangle of Death, the experts reported that conditions seemed "within the range of the tolerable and within the range of what large prisons tend to be like in the United States." They apparently were not aware that just a few days before their visit, forty-four political prisoners were severely beaten because they refused to be moved to newly renovated cells in an attempt by Castro to mislead human rights experts from the International Committee of the Red Cross and the United Nations.[10]

Under prevailing conditions, there is no short-term, risk-free formula to resolve the Cuban quagmire. There is not even a consensus on how to grapple with the festering problem. Yet there is a U.S. legal instrument that sets the course and lays the foundation for action—a bipartisan covenant which was adopted by almost unanimous vote in 1962, was ratified by the Senate in 1982, and remains the law of the land: the Joint Resolution on Cuba (Public Law 87-733). Despite its explicit and mandatory terms, the resolution has been largely ignored. This explains, in part, why U.S. credibility and influence in Latin America have ebbed, while Soviet-Cuban presence and intrusion have grown. And so today we face not only an expansionist Cuba, but also a threatening Nicaragua, a defiant Panama, and a besieged El Salvador.

Under the joint resolution, the United States is obligated "to prevent by whatever means may be necessary, including the use of arms, the Marxist-Leninist regime in Cuba from extending by force or threat of force its aggressive or subversive activities to any part of this Hemisphere." Washington has made genuine efforts to shield some of the Central American countries from Castro Communist subversion through economic aid, social reforms, and military assistance. But this emergency program, often blocked or whittled down by Congress, has been reactive and has left Cuba—the principal source of external intervention—unperturbed and untouched. Castro has therefore remained free to recruit, train, arm, and finance Marxist insurgents in the Caribbean and beyond. Impunity has maintained his appeal despite failures at home; relentless aggressiveness has glorified his image.

As noted by the journalist Charles Krauthammer in a pithy essay, "The authority of the charismatic despot . . . rests largely on a myth of invincibility. . . . So long as the outside world cowers, accommodates and appeases, that authority grows unchallenged. Munich is the model. Once the outside world returns fire, that shock alone can be enough to shake the foundations of the despot's power. The American air raid on Libya is the model. Its military significance was minimal. Its psychological significance was enormous."[11]

The joint resolution also obligates the United States "to prevent in Cuba the creation or use of any externally supported military capability endangering the security of the United States." Despite the tenor of this precept, Washington has not fully leveraged its dominant position in the Caribbean, which peaked during the 1962 blockade of Cuba, to press or induce the Soviets to withdraw their military presence from the island, or at least to stop the progressive buildup. U.S. warnings and threats have produced no lasting impact. The Russians have kept close to fifteen thousand crack troops and military and civilian advisers in Cuba, enlarged huge underground installations that may contain strategic arms, and built their most sophisticated offshore facilities for bombers, nuclear submarines, and electronic equipment.

Despite the Soviets' repeated violations of the Kennedy-Khrushchev accord barring the introduction in Cuba of offensive weapons systems, Washington has not officially rescinded its pledge not to invade the island, nor has it applied all possible diplomatic linkages, tradeoffs, and other pressures, short of war, to remove the threat.

The January 1984 report of the Kissinger Commission on Central America underscored the strategic implications for the United States: "The Soviets have already achieved a greater capability to interdict shipping than the Nazis had during World War II, when 50 percent of U.S. supplies to Europe and Africa were shipped from the Gulf [of Mexico] ports. German U-boats then sank two hundred and sixty merchant ships in just six months, despite the fact that Allied forces enjoyed many advantages, including a two-to-one edge in submarines and the use of Cuba for resupply and basing operations. Today this is reversed. The Soviets now have a two-to-one edge overall in submarines and can operate and receive aircover from Cuba, a point from which all thirteen Caribbean sea lanes passing through four chokepoints are vulnerable to interdiction."

The Kissinger Commission report also stressed: "The Soviet ability to carry out a strategy of 'strategic denial' is further enhanced by the presence near Havana of the largest Soviet-managed electronic monitoring complex outside the Soviet Union, as well as by the regular deployment of TU-95 Bear naval reconnaissance aircraft."

Finally, the joint resolution commits the United States to working "with the Organization of the American States and with freedom-loving Cubans to support the aspirations of the Cuban people for self-determination." In the past, Washington had sufficient OAS votes to condemn and ostracize the Castro regime, to institute a blockade on Cuba, and even to send troops into the Dominican Republic. But today, in the absence of a consistent, bipartisan U.S. policy toward Cuba and Nicaragua, even Caribbean nations, which traditionally have sided with Washington on security issues, hesitate to antagonize Castro and the Sandinistas for fear of being left alone. They have seen the pendulum in the

United States move from activism to isolationism; from White House supremacy to Congressional encroachment; from the arrogance of power to the paralysis of might.

Perplexed and contemptuous of a preeminent Uncle Sam lacking the will to exercise leadership, the presidents of the largest Latin American countries are openly courting Castro, excluding the United States from their meetings, and eagerly awaiting the projected grand tour of Gorbachev.

U.S.-pledged support to freedom-loving Cubans has dwindled away since the mid-1960s. Today, limited resources are available only for intelligence missions, radio broadcasts to Cuba, and propaganda efforts to improve human rights conditions on the island. Exile militants are kept on a short leash, and no arms shipments to spark resistance inside Cuba are permitted. While the rebels in Afghanistan, Angola, Cambodia, and Nicaragua have received U.S. military assistance, albeit with frustrating irregularity, the remnants of the Cuban underground have been left without stimulus and without aid.

For more than twenty years, Castro has not faced any significant military actions or threats from abroad. This has enabled the Cuban leader to step up his "internationalist" activities without worrying too much about the home front. Yet, for the first time since the creation of the Cuban Politburo, a major shake up has taken place. During the Third Party Congress held in Havana in 1986, nearly half of the alternate Central Committee members were dropped, as were over one-third of the full members. These dismissals were preceded by the removal of the Interior Minister, Ramiro Valdés; the president of the Central Planning Board, Humberto Pérez; and the Party Secretary for Ideology, Antonio Pérez Herrero. Although these purges did not trigger violent clashes or acrimonious debates, they do reflect frictions and tensions within the system.

Moreover, a large number of young soldiers are weary of their "internationalist" missions and of the irritating contrast between the privileges enjoyed by the Castro clique and the austerity imposed on the rest of the population. According to Brigadier General Rafael del Pino, the deputy commander of the Cuban air force who defected in May 1987, corruption in Cuba starts at the very top, with Fidel. He currently leads a less than Spartan life, having access to various mansions with bowling alleys and heated pools installed specially for him. When he and his brother Raúl go hunting on their estates, they usually ask the air force to send them an AW-2 or a helicopter to skim the mangroves and scare up the ducks so they can shoot them. "This is unthinkable," declared General del Pino. "It's like something the Tsars of Russia might do." [12]

Mounting restlessness and dissension have prompted the Cuban regime to create the "Purple Berets," a full corps specifically designed to catch army deserters (more than fifty thousand in the last three years, according to General del Pino). Anticipating further unrest, Castro has started to buy riot helicopters (the Polish-made MI-2) painted gray and equipped with paralyzing gas, tear gas, nets, and different types of flares.

These internal developments, in and of themselves, are not sufficient to spur instant and dramatic changes in Cuba, but they reflect underlying weaknesses of the Castro regime which could be turned to advantage if we do not shore up the battered tyranny but instead stimulate the latent forces of dissent. The objective is to generate enough pressure over time to detach the Soviets from the island and restore self-determination to the Cuban people under a freely elected government.

Diplomacy alone, even if we could resurrect Prince Metternich, could not deliver these long-term (most likely post-Castro) results. To achieve them, the United States would probably require a sustained and integrated strategy, pursuant to the Joint Resolution on Cuba, encompassing economic, political, psychological, and military pressures on Cuba; a strategy that would not only protect the countries beset by Castro Communist subversion but also retaliate at the source; a strategy that would involve both the Soviet proxy in Havana and its principal in Moscow.

In pursuing this integrated approach, the United States need not, and should not, act alone. If freedom-loving Cubans are convinced that Castro is no longer shielded and that they are no longer abandoned, they would rebuild the resistance movement and press for Soviet withdrawal and political change, as the Afghanistan rebels have done with American aid. OAS support under the Rio Treaty could also be obtained, but only after the United States has revamped its erratic policies toward Latin America and addressed the security issues and the broader socioeconomic problems, exacerbated by the debt crisis.

Despite the clear mandate of the joint resolution, a proactive strategy designed to build pressure and support dissent within Cuba would most likely encounter strong opposition in the United States at the present time. With high hopes for a new détente with the

Soviets and their protégés in the Caribbean, not many wish to rock the boat or even be reminded of our cyclical experiences with the Russians in the past—from elation to shock; from thaw to freeze. This could be dangerous, for if we are lulled into complacency during the current peace offensive, we might not be willing or able to meet additional challenges from Castro and the Sandinistas, or to respond to an eventual flare-up of hostilities inside Cuba.

The latter contingency could well occur, particularly when Castro goes. Although he has lost considerable prestige and influence, he still remains the absolute leader with an aura of invincibility. There is no successor in sight, however, with comparable charisma and power to prevent possible feuds or rifts. Fidel's brother, Raúl, head of the armed forces, is being groomed for Fidel's post. He is already acting as a sort of Deputy Prime Minister in charge of administration and taking a bigger hand in the economy and political affairs. While more disciplined than Fidel, he has clashed with the Ministry of the Interior and left some open wounds. As a ruler, he is likely to face violent resistance, which could result in another Hungary if we allow the Russian tanks to crush the burst of freedom.

Much of this is conjecture, but one thing seems certain: the continued strategic importance of Cuba and its disproportionate influence beyond its shores. If the past is prologue, if geography has any relevance, and if the Soviet presence in this hemisphere has any purpose, a Communist-controlled Cuba, if not confronted and stopped, will maintain its expansionist trajectory—a trajectory that has repeatedly placed the island in the eye of international storms, at the center of major world events fraught with danger.

The USSR is well aware of the United States' predominance in the Caribbean and fears the day when Washington might conclude that the permanent presence in Cuba of a Soviet forward base bristling with sophisticated weaponry is incompatible with the peace and security of the Americas. That is why the Russians have greatly increased the cost of Cuba's liberation, but not to the point of incorporating the island into the Warsaw Pact. The Soviets will do everything in their power to keep their prized possession—except go to war over it.

Cuba's future hangs to a large extent in the balance of geopolitics. This is not a new phenomenon; it has been Cuba's fate. Viewed from inside the island, from the standpoint of the Cuban people, geopolitics has meant the move from Spanish colonial rule (coupled with the British conquest of Havana), to American occupation, to independence under U.S. tutelage or influence, to Soviet subjugation—all in the last two centuries. This has some of the makings of another Poland, perennially subjected to superpower interventions and pacts, denied by geography the right to live without external interference, and, in its endless quest for the stable freedom that eludes its people, prepared to suffer, dare, conquer, and try anew.

Cuba's agenda, as and when it regains its right to self-determination, is indeed monumental: reconciliation of families torn by internecine feuds and hatred; political moderation to avoid all forms of extremism and vengeance; revitalization of the economy with fresh infusion of capital and talent; diversification of exports to stave off dependence on a single product and reliance on a single market. This and more will be required to rebuild the country. But while this agenda is awesome, it pales compared to the preceding task of removing the Soviets and their totalitarian infrastructure from the Caribbean island. That is the Gordian knot that eventually will have to be cut if the Americas are to remain the hemisphere of freedom and if Cuba is to become again the Pearl of the Antilles.

This, in essence, is the Cuban saga—a saga that was kept alive in my family through most of the decade of the 1960s primarily by my two grandfathers exiled in Miami: José Manuel Carbonell and José Manuel Cortina. They both evoked history without bitterness and conjured up memories with emotion.

Carbonell had great difficulty leaving Cuba. When he finally received the required government permit, he flew to Mexico, where his daughter Lydia lives and where he had many dear friends from his days as Cuban ambassador and dean of the diplomatic corps. Three former presidents of Mexico, from the leftist Lázaro Cárdenas to the conservative Miguel Alemán, tried to convince him to remain in that country. He gratefully declined their hospitality and generous offer of financial assistance because he felt that the pro-Castro policies of Mexico were contrary to the interests of Cuba.

He settled in Miami, where he often regaled us with poetry, his silvery-white hair undulating like a lion's mane and his warm, vibrating voice shaping the words. Most cherished were the concluding verses of a poem in Spanish he had dedicated to my father when the latter was a young boy:

Honor and love your country above all;
Respect, bless, and defend your family.
On everything else, do as you please;
I'm feeling old watching you grow.

He hung on to life until he was almost ninety, hoping to spend his last days in a free Cuba. When he was hospitalized in Florida just before he died, the return to his homeland became a burning obsession. In his hours of delirium he recited poems and dictated proclamations, all on Cuba. Toward the end, he thought he heard the call to arms and asked for his uniform—the same one he had worn during the war of independence. He died in bliss, clutching the flag in his epic dream.

My other grandfather, Cortina, also remained devoted to Cuba. I visited him a few months before he passed away in Miami. The old tribune's health was rapidly deteriorating. He had lost much weight. His magnetic eyes seemed like two sunken lakes glistening with sadness. Yet he was incredibly articulate, and displayed flashes of the same eloquence that had captivated the League of Nations in Geneva and the Cuban Senate. Although I was not able to record all of the conversation, I managed to retain his most salient remarks.

Our dialogue inevitably centered on Cuba. Cortina noted that "in just over fifty years, we were able to build a republic, which, despite its drawbacks and defects, was the envy of Latin America. But," he added, "we did not have the discipline and foresight to guard it against our own passions. And our ally, who for so many years prevented the domination of the island by a hostile power, ignored history, disregarded geography, and underestimated the Russian threat. This incredible myopia has turned a local problem, which could have had a local solution, into an international crisis stymied by the fear of a U.S.-Soviet confrontation."

When I asked my grandfather whether he saw any light ahead, he stated with conviction: "The situation is complex and risky, but not insoluble. I don't anticipate any significant liberalization of the regime, because Castro knows that it could precipitate his own downfall, given the Cubans' bent for extreme reactions. Nor do I expect the government to cease its subversive activities, for that is the *raison d'être* of a highly subsidized Soviet satellite so far away from Moscow."

Trying not to sound too pessimistic, he predicted, "The day will come when the United States will wake up and respond to the threat, and when the Cubans will touch off the upheaval, as they did under brutal colonial rule, despite the concentration on the island of Spain's formidable armies. Appearances led the Spaniards to believe that Cuba would be their 'ever-faithful' possession. They did not perceive the Cubans' ability to mask their rebelliousness.''

To underscore this point, Cortina added: ''When our foremost hero, José Martí, was twitted by skeptics who contended that the atmosphere in Cuba was not conducive to liberation, he calmly responded: 'You see the atmosphere; I see the subsoil.' And in the subsoil of Cuba today there is unreleased tension; there is contained indignation. The island is a volcano which someday will erupt with the intensity of the Cubans' passion for freedom. It will take time,'' he warned me, ''much longer than in the past, for never before has Cuba been subjected to such total regimentation under such a cunning and resourceful ruler.''

With resignation, he said, ''I will not see the day, and perhaps you won't either. But it will come. And when it does,'' he affirmed with pride, ''Cuba will be the first Soviet satellite to rise and roll back the Iron Curtain. And to vindicate the honor of the republic tarnished by those who today serve as legionnaires of Marxism-Leninism, the Cuban leaders who emerge will tour the world as champions of democracy and missionaries of freedom. Never underestimate the Cubans!''

Cortina paused after the peroration, his bony hands shaking with emotion. It was late, and I decided to leave. My grandfather painfully walked with me to the door. He embraced me for a long time, knowing perhaps that his end was near. Just before I entered the car, I turned around to bid him farewell, but he did not see me. His eyes were gone, adrift in the horizon, possibly searching for the island he loved—so close, yet ever so far.

Almost twenty years have elapsed since the passing of my two grandfathers. Their stirring words still ring in my ears, but not with the same intensity as in the early 1970s. The raising of a family, the pursuit of professional goals, and the ineluctable transit of time have tempered my fervor and placated my longings. Extended stays in Europe and Latin America have added perspective to my insular vista. And a strong attachment to the United States, my wife's and my own country of adoption, where two of our three children were born, has quelled the anguish of exile and afforded us a new beginning with the incentives of freedom and a feeling of home.

Our country of birth is today very distant—removed from the mainstream of our lives, lost to an ideology of hatred and violence that is alien to us. My wife and I have no urge, no desire, to return to that environment. And yet . . . the blood calls, the memories arouse, the heritage commits. We have not reneged on our roots; we have not forgotten Cuba. Our children are eager to learn about the family background. Proud of their ancestry, they ask us to recount the tales of the past. We do so with a sense of history, harboring no illusions of resurrecting times long dead and gone.

Just before the end of 1987, when we were preparing for the holidays, the press reported that two Cubans, a father and his seventeen-year-old son, had sneaked out of Cuba on inner tubes tied together to ride the waves of the stormy sea. Suffering from exposure, dehydration, and severe sunburn, they drifted some 250 miles and were finally rescued off the coast of Florida. To break with Castro Communism and gain freedom, they risked their own lives.

Our children were deeply moved by their ordeal. They asked us many questions about the captive island, and wondered whether someday the suffering would end and liberty would dawn. Their queries reflected more than a passing interest. They were prompted by genuine yearnings and concern. The family roots are alive. The Cuban saga still continues.

Notes

CHAPTER 1

1. See International Commission of Jurists, "The Case of the Airmen," in *Cuba and the Rule of Law* (Geneva: 1962), pp. 181–91.
2. Fidel Castro, *Discursos para la Historia,* compilation of speeches (Havana: 1959), Vol. 2, pp. 75–76.
3. Daniel James, *Cuba: The First Soviet Satellite in the Americas* (New York: Avon 1962), pp. 225–26.

CHAPTER 2

1. This incident occurred in January 1960, when in the course of a television interview Castro made some offensive remarks about Spain and Spanish priests. The Spanish ambassador, Juan Pablo de Lojendio, was so incensed that he rose from bed where he was recovering from a minor illness and rushed to the studio to confront Fidel. The television viewers saw the Spanish ambassador appear on the stage shouting: "They have insulted me! They have insulted me! I demand the right to reply!" Castro was visibly shaken, and only recovered after the ambassador was physically ejected from the studio.
2. Hugh Thomas, *Cuba: The Pursuit of Freedom* (New York: Harper & Row, 1971), p. 803, n. 3.
3. Luis Conte Agüero, *Los Dos Rostros de Fidel Castro* (Mexico: Editorial Jus, 1960), p. 22.
4. Quoted in Jules Dubois, *Fidel Castro* (Indianapolis: Bobbs-Merrill, 1959), p. 15.

348

5. U.S. Senate Internal Security Subcommittee, hearings, *Communist Threat to the United States Through the Caribbean,* July 17, 1960, Part 5, p. 284.

6. Revelations published in the newspaper *El Mundo* (in exile, Wilmington, Delaware), October 19, 1960.

7. U.S. Senate Internal Security Subcommittee, op. cit., May 2, 1960, Part 7, p. 353.

8. Juan Vivés, *Los Amos de Cuba* (Buenos Aires: Emecé, 1982), pp. 51, 73.

9. See Alberto Niño H., *Antecedentes y Secretos del 9 de Abril* (Bogotá: Editorial Pax, 1949); and Angel Aparicio Laurencio, *Antecedentes Desconocidos del Nueve de Abril* (Madrid: Ediciones Universal, 1973).

10. Quoted in Carlos Franqui, *Family Portrait with Fidel* (New York: Random House, 1984), p. 226.

11. U.S. Senate Internal Security Subcommittee, op. cit., September 2, 1960, Part 10, p. 725.

12. Quoted in Aparicio Laurencio, p. 39.

13. See Thomas, pp. 815–16.

14. Salvador Díaz-Versón, *El Zarismo Rojo* (Havana: Impresora Mundial, 1958), p. 28.

15. According to Dr. Juan Antonio Rubio Padilla, a leader of the Auténtico Party who attended the Montreal Conference, Castro visited him just before the meeting was held to inquire whether the Cuban Communist Party would be allowed to join the anti-Batista front. When Rubio Padilla told Castro that the conference would not only not invite the Communists but would take the affirmative step of denouncing Marxism-Leninism, Fidel became very angry and sputtered: "In that case, I will break with the Ortodoxo Party and go to war myself." The conference did not invite the Communists but refrained from denouncing Marxism-Leninism. See Dr. Rubio Padilla's testimony in Nathaniel Weyl, *Red Star over Cuba* (Greenwich, Conn.: Devin-Adair, 1960), pp. 113–14.

CHAPTER 3

1. Lionel Martín, *El Joven Fidel* (Barcelona: Grijalbo, 1982), p. 163.

2. Carlos Franqui, *Family Portrait with Fidel* (New York: Random House, 1984), p. 241.

3. Ibid., p. 248.

4. Ibid., p. 241.

5. See Carlos Franqui, *Diario de la Revolución Cubana* (Barcelona: Ediciones R. Torres, 1976).

6. Martín, pp. 194–95.

7. José Suárez Núñez, *El Gran Culpable* (Caracas: 1963), p. 79.

8. Ibid., p. 84.
9. Theodore Draper, *Castro's Revolution: Myths and Realities* (New York: Praeger, 1962), p. 191.
10. See País's letter to Castro of July 7, 1957, in which he opposes Fidel's "capricious and unipersonal action in certain fields." Quoted in Lucas Morán Arce, *La Revolución Cubana* (Ponce, Puerto Rico: Imprenta Universitaria, 1980), p. 135.
11. *Verde Olivo,* July 30, 1961. See Draper, p. 22.
12. Adolfo Merino, *Nacimiento de un Estado Vasallo* (Mexico City: B. Costa-Amic, 1966), p. 89.
13. Dr. Carlos Márquez Sterling, interview by author, Miami, August 1986.
14. Morán Arce, pp. 238–39.
15. Tad Szulc, *Fidel: A Critical Portrait* (New York: Morrow, 1986), pp. 427–28.
16. Morán Arce, p. 203.
17. Paul D. Bethel, *The Losers* (New York: Arlington House, 1969), p. 60.
18. See Earl E. T. Smith, *The Fourth Floor* (New York: Random House, 1962), p. 37.
19. Wayne S. Smith, then a young officer at the State Department, has written extensively on this subject. Although he is highly critical of Ambassador Earl E. T. Smith, he acknowledged in his recent book on Cuba that the United States should have sought a "middle way," i.e., moderate forces to fill the vacuum, and "even in retrospect, it is difficult to understand why we did not." See Wayne S. Smith, *The Closest of Enemies* (New York: W. W. Norton, 1987), p. 20.
20. Morán Arce, pp. 240–43.
21. Franqui, *Family Portrait,* p. 243.
22. Quoted in Nathaniel Weyl, *Red Star over Cuba* (Greenwich, Conn.: Devin-Adair, 1960), p. 158.
23. Earl E. T. Smith, p. 159.
24. During the September 2, 1960, hearings before the U.S. Senate Internal Security Subcommittee, Ambassador Pawley declared: "I was unsuccessful in my effort, but had [Assistant Secretary Roy] Rubottom permitted me to say [to Batista] that 'What I am offering you has tacit approval, sufficient government backing,' I think Batista may have accepted it."
25. Toward the end of December 1958, a few days before the Batista regime fell, Washington decided to support a "third force" represented by the Cuban exile leaders Tony Varona and Justo Carrillo. The offer, however, came too late. See John Dohn Dorschner and Roberto Fabricio, *The Winds of December* (New York: Coward, McCann & Geoghegan, 1980), pp. 285–86.
26. Earl E. T. Smith, pp. 229–30. The other five U.S. ambassadors who basically concurred with Smith were Spruille Braden,

Arthur Gardner, William D. Pawley, Robert C. Hill, and Whiting Willauer.

CHAPTER 4

1. Juan Vivés, *Los Amos de Cuba,* (Buenos Aires: Emecé, 1982), p. 34.
2. According to Vivés, on March 6, 1959, Carlos Rafael Rodríguez and Flavio Bravo flew to Moscow via Madrid, and Severo Aguirre, Max Figueroa, and César Escalante went to Red China. To ensure the secrecy of their mission, Castro's Ministry of Foreign Relations gave them passports with false identities. Ibid., pp. 34–35.
3. This important episode was recounted in Daniel James, *Cuba: The First Soviet Satellite in the Americas* (New York: Avon, 1962), pp. 234–37.
4. U.S. Senate Internal Security Subcommittee, hearings, *Communist Threat to the United States Through the Caribbean,* June 12, 1961, p. 803.
5. *Times of Havana* (Miami), September 15–17, 1961.
6. Dr. Luis Botifoll, interviewed by author, Miami, August 1986.
7. Richard Nixon, *Six Crises* (London: 1962), pp. 351–52.
8. Morgan and Carreras turned against Castro in 1961 and were shot, and Eloy Gutiérrez Menoyo subsequently tried to overthrow the regime and was captured. He remained in prison for over twenty years stoically withstanding degrading conditions. Thanks to the personal intervention of the President of the Council of Ministers of Spain, Menoyo was released and allowed to leave Cuba in December 1986.
9. The Platt Amendment was introduced by U.S. Senator Orville Platt as a rider to the U.S. Army appropriations bill of March 2, 1901. Incorporated as an appendix to Cuba's 1902 Constitution (under strong pressure from Washington) and ratified by treaty in 1903, the Platt Amendment governed U.S. relations with Cuba until 1934, when it was formally abrogated. The most controversial clauses were those that recognized the United States' right to limit Cuba's financial transactions, intervene in the internal affairs of the island, and buy or lease lands for naval or coaling stations.

CHAPTER 5

1. Manuel F. Artime, *Traición!* (Mexico City: Editorial Jus, 1960), pp. 53–72.

2. The term actually used was *caballería,* a land measure equivalent to about 33.5 acres.
3. Hugh Thomas, *Cuba: The Pursuit of Freedom* (New York: Harper & Row, 1971), p. 1282.
4. U.S. Senate Internal Security Subcommittee, hearings, November 5, 1959, Part 3, p. 163.
5. Philip W. Bonsal, *Cuba, Castro, and the United States* (Pittsburgh: University of Pittsburgh Press, 1971), p. 109.
6. Ambassador Julio Amoedo, interview by author, New York, September 1985. According to the records of the Argentine chancellery, the U.S. ambassador to Buenos Aires, William Beauliac, and President Eisenhower himself expressed appreciation for Ambassador Amoedo's mediation effort. See Juan Archibaldo Lanús, *De Chapultepec al Beagle: Política Exterior Argentina, 1945–1980* (Buenos Aires: Emecé, 1984), p. 347.
7. Mario Lazo, *Daga en el Corazón* (New York: Minerva, 1972), p. 219.
8. Thomas, p. 1264.
9. Bonsal, p. 132.
10. Juan Vivés, *Los Amos de Cuba* (Buenos Aires: Emecé, 1982), p. 81.
11. The term "revolution betrayed" has frequently sparked heated debates. In reality, Castro did not betray his own revolution, which he unveiled only after the totalitarian controls were in place. However, he deceived the people with false promises and betrayed their trust.

CHAPTER 6

1. International Commission of Jurists, *Cuba and the Rule of Law* (Geneva: 1962), p. 79.
2. Theodore Draper, *Castro's Revolution: Myths and Realities* (New York: Praeger, 1962), p. 106.
3. Carlos Franqui, *Family Portrait with Fidel* (New York: Random House, 1984), pp. 247–48.
4. Arthur Krock, "The Lively Issue of Castro's Justification," *New York Times,* May 18, 1961.
5. Refers to periods of great wealth, particularly in 1920 when the world sugar price rose from 7 cents per pound to 22½ cents and turned Cuba into a new tropical El Dorado.
6. Ortiz is quoted in Erna Fergusson, *Cuba* (New York: Knopf, 1946), pp. 245–46.
7. Howard Hunt, *Give Us This Day* (New York: Arlington House, 1973), p. 39.
8. U.S. Department of State, *Current Documents,* July 9, 1960, Document 78, p. 207.

9. Ibid., Document 79, pp. 207–8.
10. Chairman Nikita Khrushchev, as quoted in the *New York Times*, July 13, 1960.

CHAPTER 7

1. For further background, see Germán Arciniegas, *Biografía del Caribe* (Buenos Aires: Editorial Sudamericana, 1973).
2. Stephen Bonsal, *When the French Were Here* (New York: Doubleday, 1945), p. 120. See additional details in José I. Lasaga, *Cuban Lives* (Miami: Revista Ideal, 1984), pp. 105–21.
3. W. C. Ford, *Writings of John Q. Adams* (New York, 1917), Vol. 7, pp. 372, 373, 379, as quoted in Harry Frank Guggenheim, *The United States and Cuba: A Study in International Relations* (Salem, N.H.: Ayer, 1970), pp. 3–4.
4. Ibid.
5. A. A. Ettinger, *The Mission to Spain of Pierre Soulé* (1932), pp. 363–64, as quoted in Harry Frank Guggenheim, *The United States and Cuba*, p. 19.
6. G. J. A. O'Toole, *The Spanish War* (New York: W. W. Norton, 1984), p. 44.
7. Horatio S. Rubens, *Libertad, Cuba y su Apóstol* (Havana: La Rosa Blanca, 1956), pp. 192–93.
8. Erna Fergusson, *Cuba* (New York: Knopf, 1946), p. 217.
9. See reference to Mahan in the address by Spruille Braden, former U.S. ambassador to Cuba, before the Cuban Chamber of Commerce in the United States on May 17, 1961.
10. José Manuel Cortina, *Caracteres de Cuba* (Havana: Editorial Lex, 1945), p. 209.
11. Guggenheim, pp. 156–57.
12. See U.S. Department of Commerce, *Investment in Cuba* (Washington, D.C.: 1956), pp. 62–64.
13. See Norberto Fuentes, *Hemingway in Cuba* (Secaucus, N.J.: Lyle Stuart, 1984), pp. 191–92.
14. Admiral Arleigh Burke, in *Congressional Record*, A4880, July 3, 1963.
15. Eddy Bauer, *History of World War* (New York: Galahad Books, 1979), p. 258.
16. Maurice Zeitlin and Robert Scheer, *Cuba: Tragedy in Our Hemisphere* (New York: Grove Press, 1963), p. 192.

CHAPTER 8

1. Juan Vivés, *Los Amos de Cuba* (Buenos Aires: Emecé, 1982), pp. 98–100.

2. Edward B. Ferrer, *Operation Puma: The Air Battle of the Bay of Pigs* (Miami: International Aviation Consultants, 1982), p. 70.
3. Ibid., pp. 82–83.
4. Ibid., p. 77.
5. Paul D. Bethel, *The Losers* (New York: Arlington House, 1969), p. 244.
6. Armando Valladares, *Against All Hope* (New York: Knopf, 1986), p. 17.

CHAPTER 9

1. Maxwell D. Taylor et al., *Operation Zapata: The "Ultrasensitive" Report and Testimony of the Board of Inquiry on the Bay of Pigs* (Frederick, Md.: Aletheia Books University Publications of America, 1981), p. 7.
2. Haynes Johnson, *The Bay of Pigs* (New York: Dell, 1964), p. 61.
3. *U.S. News & World Report,* February 4, 1963, p. 33. This quotation was confirmed by Dr. Varona in conversation with the author in August 1986.
4. Howard Hunt, *Give Us This Day* (New York: Arlington House, 1973), p. 158.
5. Peter Wyden, *Bay of Pigs* (New York: Simon & Schuster, 1979), p. 21.
6. Hunt, p. 182.
7. Juan Archibaldo Lanús, *De Chapultepec al Beagle: Política Exterior Argentina, 1945–1980* (Buenos Aires: Emecé, 1984), p. 248.
8. U.S. House Internal Security Subcommittee, hearings, *Communist Threat to the United States Through the Caribbean,* July 27, 1961, pp. 874–75.
9. Arthur M. Schlesinger, Jr., *A Thousand Days: John F. Kennedy in the White House* (New York: Fawcett, 1965), p. 238.
10. U.S. Senate Foreign Relations Committee, Exécutive Sessions, Vol. 13, Part I (1961), p. 341.
11. Hunt, p. 107.
12. Taylor, introduction by Luis E. Aguilar, p. xiii.
13. According to the testimony of General Lemnitzer, chairman of the Joint Chiefs of Staff, "the plan as it was originally evaluated by the JCS did have the D-1 strike in the morning and in the evening. . . . Now on April 12th . . . this plan was changed so that the full weight of the attack would be on the morning of D-Day." (Thereafter the attack was cancelled.) See U.S. Senate Foreign Relations Committee, op. cit., p. 601.
14. Schlesinger, p. 241.
15. Charles J. V. Murphy, "Cuba: The Record Set Straight," *Fortune,* September 1961, p. 224.

16. Schlesinger, p. 248.
17. Admiral Arleigh Burke told Captain Edward B. Ferrer of the brigade's air force that "he had ordered this display of force in the hope that, at the last moment, Kennedy would change his mind about U.S. involvement at the Bay of Pigs." See Edward B. Ferrer, *Operation Puma: The Air Battle of the Bay of Pigs* (Miami: International Aviation Consultants, 1982), p. 144. According to most historians, however, the naval deployment consisted only of the seven destroyers that accompanied the aircraft carrier *Essex*.

CHAPTER 10

1. Haynes Johnson, *The Bay of Pigs: The Leaders' Story of Brigade 2506* (New York: Dell, 1964), p. 74.
2. Ibid., p. 83.
3. Edward B. Ferrer, *Operation Puma: The Air Battle of the Bay of Pigs* (Miami: International Aviation Consultants, 1982), p. 145.
4. Ibid., p. 139.
5. Peter Wyden, *Bay of Pigs: The Untold Story* (New York: Simon & Schuster, 1979), p. 170.
6. Ferrer, p. 162.
7. Wyden, p. 246.
8. Johnson, p. 134.
9. Ibid., p. 139.
10. Ferrer, p. 210; Wyden, p. 270.
11. Maxwell D. Taylor et al., *Operation Zapata: The "Ultrasensitive" Report and Testimony of the Board of Inquiry on the Bay of Pigs* (Frederick, Md.: Aletheia Books/University Publications of America, 1981) p. 28.
12. Johnson, p. 155.
13. Ibid., p. 162.
14. During the Bay of Pigs postmortem (the Taylor Investigation), Admiral Burke and Allen Dulles gave the opinion that if the men of the brigade had had sufficient ammunition and air cover, they could have held the beachhead for a much longer time and could well have caused a chain reaction of success throughout Cuba, with resultant defection of some of the militia and increasing support from the populace. This is difficult to prove, but one thing is certain: the invasion as ultimately stifled and cut back was doomed from inception. See Taylor, pp. 29–30.

CHAPTER 11

1. Haynes Johnson, *The Bay of Pigs: The Leaders' Story of Brigade 2506* (New York: Dell, 1964), p. 201.

2. Ibid., p. 202.
3. Arthur M. Schlesinger, Jr., *A Thousand Days: John F. Kennedy in the White House* (New York: Fawcett, 1965), p. 264.
4. See Armando Valladares, *Against All Hope,* (New York: Knopf, 1968), pp. 67–74.
5. Ernesto Aragón, who sat in an adjacent room and overheard the conversation, reported it to author.
6. Author did not find the original document in Miró's personal files, but he saw an unsigned summary in Spanish titled "Main Points of the Agreement of October 31, 1961." Aragón confirmed to the author that the summary served as the basis for all subsequent discussions with the White House on Cuba.
7. Schlesinger, p. 267.
8. Johnson, p. 233.
9. Ibid., pp. 323, 327.
10. Dissatisfied with the fate of the flag, and disappointed that even the post-Kennedy Republican administrations had decided to coexist with a Communist Cuba, the men of the brigade tried to retrieve their emblem. Faced with bureaucratic delays, they hired a lawyer to expedite the process. They finally got their flag back in April 1976. It had been kept crated in a museum basement.

CHAPTER 12

1. *Miami Herald,* August 17, 1960.
2. Juan Archibaldo Lanús, *De Chapultepec al Beagle: Política Exterior Argentina, 1945–1980* (Buenos Aires: Emecé, 1984), pp. 250–51.
3. Ibid., p. 260.
4. Ibid.
5. José Joaquín Caicedo Castilla, *El Derecho Internacional en el Sistema Interamericano* (Ediciones Cultura Hispánica, 1970), pp. 296–307.
6. To secure the Haiti vote, the U.S. delegation reluctantly agreed to resume aid to the airport at Port au Prince. See Arthur M. Schlesinger, Jr., *A Thousand Days: John F. Kennedy in the White House* (New York: Fawcett, 1965), p. 717.

CHAPTER 13

1. James Reston, *New York Times Magazine,* November 15, 1964.
2. U.S. Senate Committee on Foreign Relations and Committee on Armed Services, hearings, *Situation in Cuba,* September 17, 1962, pp. 70–72.

3. Theodore C. Sorensen, *Kennedy* (New York: Harper & Row, 1965), pp. 677–78.

4. James Daniel and John G. Hubbell, *Strike in the West: The Complete Story of the Cuban Crisis* (New York: Holt, Rinehart & Winston, 1963), pp. 92–93.

5. As a result of the negotiations conducted by John J. McCloy at President Kennedy's request, Khrushchev declared on November 20, 1962, that the Ilyushins would be withdrawn.

6. Henry M. Pachter, *Collision Course: The Cuban Missile Crisis and Coexistence* (New York: Praeger, 1963), pp. 230–34.

7. UPI dispatch by John Callcott, Bonn, November 13, 1962.

8. Roswell L. Gilpatric, Deputy Secretary of Defense, interviewed by Bob Clark, ABC correspondent, and John Scali, ABC correspondent, on *Issues and Answers,* November 11, 1962.

9. See Senator Strom Thurmond's press release of February 2, 1962, and his detailed intelligence report of February 4, 1963, titled "Behind the Brush Curtain."

10. *Bohemia,* Vol. 51, No. 38 (September 20, 1959), p. 109.

11. Paul D. Bethel, *The Losers* (New York: Arlington House, 1969), pp. 362–63.

12. See David Lawrence, "Blockade," *U.S. News & World Report,* March 18, 1963.

13. U.S. Senate Preparedness Investigating Subcommittee, *The Cuban Military Buildup,* May 1963, p. 15.

14. Ibid., p. 3.

15. See *Diario Las Américas,* Miami, December 18, 1962.

16. Luis V. Manrara, *Russian Missiles in Red Cuba* (Truth About Cuba Committee, 1968), pp. 59–60.

17. Ibid., pp. 55–56.

18. Relying on his own intelligence sources, Senator Strom Thurmond announced on the Senate floor on January 15, 1962, that missile bases were being constructed in Cuba.

19. According to the reports rendered in 1961–1962 by Colonel Oleg Penkovsky, senior officer in the Chief Intelligence Directorate of the Soviet General Staff, many of the Soviet big missiles were still then on the drawing boards, in the prototype stage or undergoing tests. "Right now," Penkovsky affirmed, "we have a certain number of missiles with nuclear warheads capable of reaching the United States or South America; but these are single missiles, not in mass production, and they are far from accurate." See Oleg Penkovsky, *The Penkovsky Papers,* translated by Peter Deryaben (New York: Doubleday, 1965), pp. 327–28.

Peter Wright, a former senior British intelligence officer, has recently challenged the Penkovsky report as a Soviet disinformation ploy. According to Wright, Moscow was intent on convincing the United States that the missile gap was an illusion, and that, if anything, the Soviets lagged behind the West. See Peter Wright, *Spy Catcher* (New York: Dell, 1987), pp. 266–67.

20. According to Raymond L. Garthoff, "the United States did not in 1962–63 formalize a commitment assuring against possible invasion of Cuba." But he noted: "Without making the unequivocal commitment the Soviets wanted, Kennedy did state that if the Soviet Union abided by the exchange of correspondence, so would the United States." On August 7, 1970, then National Security Adviser Henry Kissinger assured the Russian chargé Yuli M. Vorontsov that the United States regarded the understanding as in effect, and "noted with satisfaction" that the Soviet Union also regarded it as "still in full force." See Raymond L. Garthoff, *Reflections on the Cuban Missile Crisis* (Washington, D.C.: Brookings Institution, 1987), pp. 81, 83, 95.

CHAPTER 14

1. Concerning the noninvasion pledge, Kennedy actually stated that he was "confident that other nations of the Western Hemisphere would be prepared to do likewise."

2. *Miami News,* March 19, 1963.

3. *Miami Herald,* March 18, 1963.

4. Paul D. Bethel, *The Losers* (New York: Arlington House, 1969), p. 379.

5. Ibid., pp. 379–80.

6. Andrew St. George, "The Tension Is Already Gnawing at All of Us," *Life,* April 12, 1963. In May 1966, Tony Cuesta was captured by Castro forces when he tried to infiltrate several operatives into Havana. Vowing never to be taken alive, he tried to kill himself by detonating a grenade. He was blinded by the explosion and suffered serious injuries, but he survived and served twelve years in prison. Released in late 1978, Tony arrived in Miami to a hero's welcome.

7. Statement issued by the Departments of State and Justice, March 30, 1963.

8. See David Lawrence, "The New 'Neutralism'," *U.S. News & World Report,* April 15, 1963.

9. Roscoe Drummond, "Cuban Issue Has Two Sides," *The Washington Post,* April 7, 1963.

10. Roscoe Drummond, "Exile Raids Good Beginning," *Miami News,* April 1, 1963.

11. Henry J. Taylor, "Our Cuban Policy's a Leaky Bean Bag," *Miami Herald,* April 5, 1963.

12. Ibid.

13. *Miami Herald,* April 29, 1963.

14. *Miami News,* April 4, 1963. As noted by the *Economist* (March 7–13, 1987), "After President Kennedy took his Thor [Jupiter] missiles out of Italy and Turkey, the Soviets started to deploy their SS-20s. Before the SS-20s the Russians had in service an earlier generation of medium-range missiles, clumsy brutes but capable of doing huge damage to Western Europe, and the Americans had nothing of the sort in Europe at all."

15. C. L. Sulzberger, in *International Herald Tribune,* March 3, 1986.

16. See U.S. Senate Select Committee to Study Governmental Operations with Respect to Intelligence Activities, *Interim Report* (Washington, D.C.: U.S. Government Printing Office, November 20, 1975).

17. In 1983, the Soviets began also to send flights to Cuba of two Tu-142 antisubmarine warfare (ASW) versions of the Bear (the Bear F). Since there reportedly was no solid basis for a challenge under the 1962 and 1970 understandings, Washington accepted the new Soviet escalation. See Raymond L. Garthoff, *Reflections on the Cuban Missile Crisis* (Washington, D.C.: Brookings Institution, 1987), pp. 102–3.

18. *Russia in the Caribbean,* Part 2, Special Report issued by the Center for Strategic and International Studies of Georgetown University (Washington, D.C.: 1973), p. 108.

19. *Robert Kennedy in His Own Words,* ed. Edwin O. Guthman and Jeffrey Shulman (New York: Bantam, 1988), p. 379.

CHAPTER 15

1. A detailed list of Castro's foreign service officers expelled from Latin American republics during the first half of 1961 is contained in the report submitted by the Cuban Revolutionary Council to the Inter-American Peace Committee of the OAS on December 26, 1961.

2. See *U.S. News & World Report,* March 11, 1963, p. 69.

3. Ibid.

4. Paul D. Bethel, *The Losers* (New York: Arlington House, 1969), p. 131.

5. For an account of the Castro-Betancourt meeting, see Jay Mallin, *Fortress Cuba* (Chicago: Regnery, 1965), pp. 73–74.

6. *Congressional Record,* Senate, August 23, 1965, p. 20505.

7. Paul Charles Ehrlich, *"M" Magazine,* September 1987, p. 112.

8. *New York Times,* July 1, 1987, p. A7.

9. Pamela S. Falk, "Cuba in Africa," *Foreign Affairs,* Summer 1987, p. 1091.

10. Shirley Christian, *Nicaragua: Revolution in the Family* (New York: Random House, 1985), p. 90.

11. Ibid., p. 103.

12. Robert A. Pastor, *Condemned to Repetition: United States and Nicaragua* (Princeton, N.J.: Princeton University Press, 1987), pp. 147–48.
13. "Insight," *Washington Times,* November 2, 1987, p. 7.
14. *Economist,* March 26, 1988, p. 13.

CHAPTER 16

1. Since then, the United Nations Educational, Scientific, and Cultural Organization has started to restore the historic center of Havana, and other parts of the city have undergone a facelift with fresh coats of paint. Yet despite the improvements, the Cuban capital is but a dingy shadow of what it once was.
2. The name is fictitious, to protect Pedro's relatives in Cuba.
3. U.S. Department of State, *Country Reports on Human Rights Practices for 1986,* February 1987, p. 460.
4. *New York Times,* September 17, 1981.
5. Carlos Ripoll, *The Cuban Scene: Censors-Dissenters* (Washington, D.C.: Cuban-American National Foundation, 1982), p. 14.
6. Hugh S. Thomas, George A. Fauriol, and Juan Carlos Weiss, *The Cuban Revolution 25 Years Later* (Boulder, Colo.: Westview Press, 1984), pp. 29–30.
7. For historical perspective see Michael Voslensky, *Nomenklatura: The Soviet Ruling Class* (New York: Doubleday, 1987).
8. Jorge I. Domínguez, "Cuba in the 1980s," *Foreign Affairs,* Fall 1986, pp. 125–26.
9. Richard G. Capen, Jr., *Miami Herald,* July 3, 1983.
10. Martín Segrera, *Un Testimonio Socialista sobre Cuba, La Prensa Española en el 25 Aniversario de la Revolución Cubana* (Washington, D.C.: Cuban-American National Foundation, 1984), p. 27.
11. Manuel Sánchez Pérez, "El Fin del Castrismo," *Diario Las Américas,* October 21, 1987.

CHAPTER 17

1. Luis J. Botifoll, *Cómo se Creó La Nueva Imagen de Miami* (Miami: Consejo Nacional de Planificación, 1984).
2. See Manuel G. Mendoza's publications on Cuban migrations. He has taught social sciences at Miami Dade Community College.
3. See article by R. W. Apple, Jr., "Aide to Bush Says Neither Knew of Friend's Link to Contra Arms," *New York Times,* December 13, 1986.
4. George F. Will, "The First Contras," *Newsweek,* March 31, 1986.
5. Family income within Dade County's Latin community, while still

below national level, grew from an average of $10,000 in 1975 to $27,500 in 1984. This contrasts with the median family income for Latins in the thirteen Southwestern states of $24,100 per annum. See Carlos J. Arboleya, *La Comunidad Cubana de Miami (25 años después). Diario Las Américas,* May 5, 1985.

6. See article by Lindsey Gruson, "Flames of Revolution Keep a Family on the Run," *New York Times,* October 21, 1987.

7. Robert A. Bennett, "Restoring Morgan to Its Original Role," *New York Times,* October 19, 1986, p. 8F.

8. *Fortune,* October 26, 1987, p. 47.

9. N. R. Kleinfield, *New York Times,* June 15, 1986.

10. Robert Sherrill, "Can Miami Save Itself?" *New York Times Magazine,* July 19, 1987, p. 68.

11. See George Gilder, *The Spirit of Enterprise* (New York: Simon & Schuster, 1984).

12. "Behind the Cuban-American Miracle," condensed by *Reader's Digest,* December 1985, from George Gilder, *The Spirit of Enterprise.*

13. Guy Guglotta and Guillermo Martínez, "The Exiles Create a New World," *Miami Herald,* December 11, 1983, p. 8M.

14. Carlos Ripoll's translation of Jorge Valls's verses is to be published in a bilingual anthology, "Caged Voices: Poetry from Cuban Jails."

15. *Observer* Sunday magazine, July 12, 1987, p. 18.

16. Stephen Holden, "The Pop Life," *New York Times,* September 2, 1987.

17. "Hot Bop from a Tropical Gent—Sax Player Paquito D'Rivera Soars High on an Expatriate Dream," *Time,* February 6, 1984, p. 68.

18. Lesley Valdes, "Phenomenon—Horacio Gutiérrez—He Makes the Piano Sing," *Connoisseur,* January 1985, pp. 38–39.

19. Frank Bayak, "Cuban-Born Official Causes Language Flap," Associated Press, North Bergen, N.J., July 8, 1985.

20. Patricia Sellers, "The Selling of the President in '88," *Fortune,* December 21, 1987, pp. 131–32.

21. Lydia Chavez, "A Ride on *La Cubana*: Latin Home on the Road," *New York Times,* August 21, 1986, p. B-1.

22. John Arnold, "What's This Row All About?" *Miami Herald,* June 23, 1987.

CHAPTER 18

1. Senate Select Committee on Intelligence Activities Interim Report, *Alleged Assassination Plots Involving Foreign Leaders,* November 20, 1975, pp. 173–74.

2. See Robert A. Pastor, "What to Do About Cuba?" *Miami Herald,* December 27, 1981, Section E; and "Revolutionary Cuba—Toward

Accommodation or Conflict?'' Foreign Policy Association—Great Decisions '85, pp. 6–13.

3. Wayne S. Smith, "Cuba—Time for a Thaw?" *New York Times Magazine,* July 29, 1984.

4. Tad Szulc, "Friendship Is Possible, But . . . ," *Parade,* April 1, 1984.

5. At least since 1968, when Castro endorsed the Warsaw Pact invasion of Czechoslovakia, Cuba has dutifully followed most of Moscow's foreign policy dictates.

6. Jerry Flint, "Cuba: Russia's Wondrous Weapon," *Forbes,* March 28, 1983, p. 39.

7. *Economist,* February 14, 1987, p. 13.

8. See Alain Besançon, "Gorbachev Without Illusions," *Commentary,* April 1988, p. 55.

9. Joseph B. Treaster, "No Cuba-Soviet Strain, Defector Says," *New York Times,* May 12, 1988.

10. Joseph B. Treaster, "3 Ex-Cuban Prisoners Tell of Beatings and Protests," *New York Times,* June 4, 1988.

11. Charles Krauthammer, "How to Deal with Countries Gone Mad," *Time,* September 21, 1987, p. 82.

12. *General del Pino Speaks: An Insight into Elite Corruption and Military Dissension in Castro's Cuba* (Washington, D.C.: Cuban-American National Foundation, 1987), p. 44.

Historical Chronology
of Cuba

1492	October 27: Christopher Columbus discovers the island of Cuba.
1511–1524	Diego Velázquez undertakes the colonization of Cuba, which was to serve as a Spanish base for the conquest of nearly half the continent.
1538–1700	French, English, and Dutch pirates, corsairs, and buccaneers frequently attack Cuba, the meeting place of the Spanish fleets.
1762	British occupation of Havana, ending in 1763.
1809–1825	Wars against the Spanish crown for the independence of its colonies in South America. Early conspiracies and rebellions in Cuba founder.
1823	U.S. President James Monroe lays down the Monroe Doctrine, whereby the United States considers any attempt by European powers to extend their "system" to the Western Hemisphere as dangerous to peace and to the security of the United States. The doctrine does not apply to the then existing colonies, such as Cuba. Unable to acquire the strategic island (despite repeated efforts), Washington prefers to freeze the status quo and leave Cuba under the control of a weakened Spain.
1868–1878	The Ten Years War between Cuba and Spain. It ends with a peace treaty and promises by Spain, largely unfulfilled, to liberalize the Cuban regime.
1895	Beginning of the final war of independence. Death in combat of Cuba's foremost hero, poet, and visionary, José Martí.

1898	February: The U.S. battleship *Maine,* anchored in Havana harbor, blows up. April: The U.S. declares war on Spain. December: End of Spanish-American War and beginning of a U.S. military government in Cuba committed to consolidating peace and leaving the control of the island in Cuban hands.
1901	March: The U.S. President signs the amendment to the U.S. Army appropriations bill proposed by Senator Orville H. Platt. Pursuant to the "Platt Amendment," the U.S. retains the right to intervene in Cuba to preserve its independence and maintain adequate government for the protection of life, property, and individual freedom. June: Under considerable U.S. pressure, the Cuban Constitutional Assembly adopts the Platt Amendment as an appendix to the Cuban Constitution.
1902	May 20: End of U.S. military government in Cuba. Inaugural of the Cuban republic and of its first elected President, Tomás Estrada Palma.
1903	Cuba agrees to lease the United States military bases in the port cities of Guantánamo and Bahía Honda for an indefinite period. (Bahía Honda was later excluded.)
1906	Estrada Palma's fraudulent reelection sets off armed insurrection. At the behest of Estrada Palma, the United States intervenes and appoints Charles Magoon governor of the island for the period 1906–1909.
1909	The republic is restored. José Miguel Gómez is elected President.
1912	A minor racist uprising prompts U.S. President Taft to dispatch U.S. Marines to Cuba. Strong protest and energetic action by President Gómez and his Foreign Minister, Manuel Sanguily, avoid another U.S. occupation of the island.
1913	Beginning of the constitutional government of Mario García Menocal.
1917	Reelection of Menocal, charged with fraud, triggers armed uprising. U.S. statement that no government resulting from a revolution will be recognized helps Menocal quell the revolt.
1921–1925	Constitutional government of Alfredo Zayas. U.S. President Harding sends special envoy, General Enoch Crowder, who meddles in the internal affairs of Cuba in an attempt to stamp out corruption.
1925	The Cuban Communist Party is founded and promptly joins Moscow's Comintern. General Gerardo Machado is elected President.

1928–1933	Extension of Machado's mandate through a fascist-type arrangement and repressive measures sets off armed resistance. Mediation by U.S. Ambassador Sumner Welles fails. Army deposes Machado on August 12, 1933.
1933–1939	A period of turmoil ensues with provisional governments largely controlled by Fulgencio Batista, a sergeant who rose to army chief on the crest of a populist movement. In May 1934 the United States abrogates the Platt Amendment, but retains the naval base of Guantánamo and considerable influence in Cuba.
1940	A progressive Constitution is promulgated with the participation of all the political parties and sectors of the population.
1940–1952	This period encompasses three constitutional governments: Fulgencio Batista (1940–1944), Ramón Grau San Martín (1944–1948), and Carlos Prío Socarrás (1948–1952). Despite the lingering twin evils of corruption and political violence, representative democracy survives, and the republic achieves a relatively high level of social, economic, and cultural development.
1952	March 10: Just a few weeks before general elections, a military coup d'état derails the constitutional process and ushers in the dictatorship of Fulgencio Batista.
1953	July 26: Fidel Castro leads the attack on the Moncada barracks at Santiago de Cuba. Castro is arrested, tried, and sentenced to prison. His defense before the court is subsequently published under the title *History Will Absolve Me*.
1954	November 1: General Batista is "elected" President (most of the opposition groups abstain).
1955	Fidel Castro is released from prison, under a general amnesty, and departs for Mexico to launch an armed expedition against Batista. Cuban exile leaders, including former President Carlos Prío, return to Havana and press for a democratic opening under the aegis of the Society of Friends of the Republic, headed by the patriot Cosme de la Torriente.
1956	The "Civic Dialogue" between representatives of the nonviolent opposition and Batista delegates collapses. Terror and counterterror spread. December: Castro lands in Cuba from Mexico with eighty-two followers and establishes himself in the Sierra Maestra.
1958	March: The United States orders an embargo on arms to Batista. November: Batista thwarts final attempt to find constitutional solution by rigging general elections.

December: U.S. Ambassador Smith informs Batista that the United States would not support his government nor that of his successor, and that it would be advisable for him to leave Cuba.

1959   January 1: Batista resigns and flees by plane to the Dominican Republic. Castro declares national strike to force resignation of all government officials and surrender of the army.

January 5: Castro's designee, Dr. Manuel Urrutia, assumes post as provisional President of Cuba and appoints Dr. José Miró Cardona Prime Minister. Castro becomes commander-in-chief of the armed forces.

January 7: United States recognizes the Cuban provisional government.

January 21: U.S. names Philip Bonsal ambassador to Cuba.

February 16: Castro takes over the post of Prime Minister, replacing Miró Cardona, and steps up summary execution of Batista "war criminals."

April 16–17: Castro on U.S. visit denies Communist influence in his regime, states that Cuba will not confiscate property belonging to foreign-owned private firms, and reiterates promise of free elections.

Late April: Eighty-four Cubans and Panamanians set sail from Cuba to "liberate" Panama. During the following four months, similar attacks are launched against the dictatorships of Nicaragua, the Dominican Republic, and Haiti.

May 17: Cuban government passes Agrarian Reform Law and creates the National Agrarian Reform Institute, with broad powers to spur collectivization.

July 17–18: Castro forces President Urrutia out of office and appoints the Marxist lawyer Osvaldo Dorticós as new President.

1960   February 4–13: Soviet First Deputy Premier Anastas Mikoyan, on visit to Cuba, concludes agreement for USSR to buy five million tons of sugar over five years, and extends credit.

April–May: The Cuban government assumes full control of the press.

June 23: Castro threatens U.S. with seizure of all American-owned property and business interests in Cuba if U.S. cuts sugar quota.

June 29–July 1: Castro confiscates U.S.- and British-owned oil refineries because they refuse to refine Soviet oil.

July 6: President Eisenhower cuts back Cuba's assigned share of U.S. sugar market in 1960 by 700,000 tons.

The Cuban government orders the expropriation of all U.S.-owned property in Cuba. (By October 1960, American businesses worth nearly $1 billion had been seized.)

July 9: Soviet Prime Minister Nikita Khrushchev threatens to give Cuba military protection if the U.S. intervenes in the island.

President Eisenhower warns that U.S. would never permit "the establishment of a regime dominated by international communism in the Western Hemisphere."

August 28: OAS passes Declaration of San José condemning threats of extracontinental intervention in the Americas. A few days later, Castro derides the OAS and tears the declaration into shreds at a public rally.

October 13: The Castro regime, in one sweep, takes over 380 all-Cuban enterprises and accelerates expropriations without compensation.

October 19: U.S. imposes embargo on exported goods to Cuba, except for medical supplies and most foodstuffs.

1961   January 2–3: Castro orders U.S. embassy to reduce staff to eleven people.

U.S. severs diplomatic relations with Cuba.

February 3: The Cuban government completes the purge of the judiciary by ordering the dismissal of 120 judges.

March–April: Major anti-Castro exile groups in Miami form the Cuban Revolutionary Council, headed by Dr. Miró Cardona.

April 17–19: Bay of Pigs invasion fails.

May 1: Castro declares that Cuba is a socialist state and that there will be no elections because his government is based on the direct support of the people.

June 7: The Cuban government decrees the nationalization of education and intensifies Marxist indoctrination.

July 26: Castro announces that all political parties in Cuba must be integrated into the United Socialist Revolutionary Party.

September 17: The Cuban government deports 136 Catholic priests.

December 1: Castro proclaims himself to be a Marxist-Leninist since his university years.

1962   January 31: The OAS conference of foreign ministers held in Punta del Este declares Marxism-Leninism incompatible with the inter-American system and excludes the Castro regime.

March 12: Castro institutes nationwide food and soap rationing.

August 20: Press reports state that between July 27 and

July 31, twenty Soviet ships arrived at four ports in Cuba with three to five thousand Soviet-bloc technicians and large quantities of arms.

October 3: President Kennedy signs Congressional joint resolution empowering the President to use force if necessary to oppose Communist aggression or subversion from Cuba, and to prevent externally backed military capability on the island.

October 22: President Kennedy discloses the construction of missile launching pads and the presence of offensive rockets in Cuba. The U.S. imposes a quarantine to stop deliveries of such weapons by the Soviet Union.

October 28: Soviet Premier Khrushchev agrees to dismantle Soviet bases and to ship offensive weapons back to the USSR against U.S. assurances that it will not invade Cuba or allow others to do so.

November 12: U.S. Defense Department announces that forty-two missiles have been removed from Cuba, but Castro does not allow on-site inspection.

November 20: Chairman Khrushchev announces that USSR will withdraw IL-28 bombers from Cuba in thirty days. President Kennedy lifts naval quarantine.

December 24: 1,113 Bay of Pigs prisoners arrive in Miami. Castro agreed to the release in exchange for $53 million worth of medicines, drugs, and baby food.

December 29: President Kennedy, in Miami, speaking before thirty thousand Cubans, receives the flag of the Cuban Brigade and promises that "this flag will be returned to this Brigade in a free Havana."

1963   February 28: U.S. State Department issues statement that USSR has "advised the U.S. that it intends to retain indefinitely in Cuba a 'residual' military force after the early withdrawal of several thousand troops."

March 1: John A. McCone, Director of Central Intelligence, reports that Cuba in 1962 trained 1,000–1,500 Latin Americans for sabotage.

March 30: U.S. State Department issues statement that "hit-and-run attacks by Cuban refugee groups against Soviet ships and other targets in Cuba . . . are neither supported nor condoned by this Government." Militant exiles are quarantined and their speedboats impounded, and Washington enlists the support of the British authorities in the Bahamas to patrol adjoining seas.

April 28: Dr. Miró Cardona resigns from the Cuban Revolutionary Council and charges President Kennedy and his administration with breaking promises and agreements made with exile leaders for the liberation of Cuba.

Washington rejects these charges and gradually ends economic support to the council and other militant groups.

November 22: The CIA reportedly gives one of Castro's *comandantes* a ballpoint pen rigged with a very fine hypodermic needle to kill the Cuban ruler (Operation AM/LASH). President Kennedy is assassinated in Dallas the same day.

1964   July: Following the discovery in Venezuela of three tons of war equipment shipped by Castro to foment revolution, the OAS condemns and penalizes his regime. All member states, except Mexico, sever diplomatic and economic relations with Cuba.

December: The conference of Latin American Communist parties held in Cuba endorses the guerrilla struggles in Colombia, Guatemala, Honduras, Haiti, Paraguay, and Venezuela.

1965   April: President Lyndon B. Johnson orders the landing of 23,000 U.S. troops in the Dominican Republic to "prevent the establishment of another Cuba in this hemisphere." The OAS provides multilateral support under the Rio Treaty and paves the way for free elections.

1966   January: The Tricontinental Conference of African, Asian, and Latin American Peoples is held in Havana. The U.S. Senate Internal Security Subcommittee describes it as "the most powerful gathering of pro-Communist, anti-American forces in the history of the Western Hemisphere."

1967   March: Castro splits with the Venezuelan Communist Party, reportedly opposed to Havana's strategy of armed struggle.

August: The Latin American Solidarity Organization (OLAS) holds its first meeting in Havana. Most delegates favor the Castroite guerrilla movements.

October: Che Guevara is killed in Bolivia, trying to create several Vietnams in Latin America.

1968   January: Havana announces the arrest of a "microfaction" of forty-three state officials and party members headed by Aníbal Escalante, a leader of the old Cuban Communist Party. They are charged with treason to the revolution.

August: Castro signals new Cuban-Soviet accommodation by endorsing the Warsaw Pact invasion of Czechoslovakia.

1969   July: The arrival in Cuba of a seven-ship Soviet naval squadron, including a guided-missile carrier, marks the renewal of Russian expansionism in the Caribbean.

1970   July: Castro admits that the ten-million-ton sugar crop was a fiasco and promises to overhaul the Cuban economy.

September: Salvador Allende's electoral victory in Chile, with a 36 percent plurality, ushers in a pro-Marxist government. Although wary of the existing democratic institutions, Castro lends Allende his full support and tours Chile the following year.

The Nixon administration warns Moscow that the servicing of nuclear submarines either in or from Cuba would be considered a violation of Kennedy-Khrushchev accord of 1962. (The Soviets backed down and withdrew their subtender. But their retreat was only temporary. The submarine base in Cienfuegos was completed and remains operational.)

1971   The Congress of Education and Culture held in Cuba officially endorses Stalinism. In his closing speech, Castro condemns any artistic or literary creation contrary to the revolution. "Our valuation is political," he says.

1972   Cuba is admitted to the Soviet-controlled Council of Mutual Economic Assistance (COMECON). The establishment of an intergovernmental coordinating committee increases Moscow's influence on Cuban economic policy-making.

1973   A Cuban-American anti-hijacking agreement is signed.

1974   Secretary of State Henry Kissinger sends a message to Castro suggesting secret talks to explore the possibilities of improving relations on a broad basis. (The talks went on for almost a year.)

1975   The U.S. votes with the majority in the OAS to allow member governments to maintain diplomatic relations with Cuba if they wish.

Following the landing of some eighteen thousand Cuban combat troops in Angola, Washington ends the talks with Castro's emissaries.

1976   Cuba adopts new Constitution, which institutionalizes Communist Party control.

1977   Pursuant to President Carter's instructions, White House and State Department officials privately meet with Castro to seek a rapprochement. Interest Sections are established in Havana and Washington. Castro subsequently releases 3,900 political prisoners and most U.S. citizens detained on the island, and allows Cuban-Americans to visit relatives in Cuba.

Castro sends seventeen thousand troops into Ethiopia to crush the Somali invasion of Ogaden.

1978   Two squadrons of Russian MiG 23/27 fighter-bombers arrive in Cuba. Both are far superior to the IL-28s President Kennedy had forced the Soviets to remove from Cuba in 1962.

	Cuban radio announces that the three factions of the San-dinista Front fighting the Somoza dictatorship in Nicara-gua had agreed to merge their forces. Castro makes military assistance conditional on unification under the hard-line Marxist militant Tomás Borge (coordinator of the group).
1979	Somoza resigns and leaves Nicaragua. A provisional gov-ernment is established in Managua effectively controlled by the Sandinistas.

Senator Richard Stone of Florida discloses at a Foreign Relations Committee hearing on SALT II that there is a Soviet brigade in Cuba. Pressed by Senator Frank Church, chairman of the committee, President Carter affirms that the "status quo is unacceptable." Moscow's unwilling-ness to withdraw the brigade deals a mortal blow to dé-tente. SALT II is shelved.

Castro chairs a Non-aligned Summit in Havana and promises not to impose Cuba's radicalism on anyone. (Cuba had been one of the few "nonaligned" nations which refused to condemn the Soviet invasion of Afghanistan.)

Castro engineers the unification of Marxist guerrilla groups in El Salvador under the Farabundo Martí Front.

1980   About 125,000 Mariel boatlift refugees arrive in the United States along with several thousand common criminals, spies, and social misfits infiltrated by Castro.

1981   U.S. Secretary of State Alexander Haig meets in Mexico with Cuban Vice-Premier Carlos Rafael Rodríguez to ex-plore a possible settlement. Talks lead to naught.

1982   General Vernon Walters meets in Havana with Castro in a further attempt to improve relations. No tangible prog-ress is made.

1983   The U.S. launches invasion of Grenada to stop reign of terror and Cuban-backed military buildup.

1984   U.S.-Cuban agreement is reached involving the return to the island of the Mariel excludables and the issuance of U.S. visas to Cuban immigrants, including former politi-cal prisoners.

1985   Radio Martí is approved by Washington and starts trans-mitting to Cuba. The Castro regime views this as a hostile act and suspends the execution of the immigration agree-ment.

1986   Chilean security forces discover a huge arsenal brought to the country on Cuban trawlers as part of a major of-fensive to bolster the local Marxist guerrilla group Ma-nuel Rodríguez Patriotic Front.

Cuba suspends principal and interest payments on its me-dium- and long-term debt pending the completion of ne-gotiations to restructure its $3.5 billion indebtedness.

During the Third Party Congress held in Havana, Castro recites litany of failures and mistakes. Numerous members of the Central Committee are dismissed.

1987   Castro agrees to reinstate the immigration pact with Washington, which will enable an additonal 250,000 Cubans to emigrate to the U.S. by the mid-1990s.

Castro orders a crackdown on "capitalists in disguise": private homeowners, small farmers, and artisans and craftsmen engaged in moonlighting.

1988   Two U.S. federal indictments charge seventeen people with smuggling Colombian cocaine into Florida through a Cuban military base.

Castro sends arms and security officers to Panama to shore up besieged ruler Manuel Antonio Noriega.

Castro promises New York Cardinal O'Connor that he will release 385 political prisoners and agrees to let UN Commission on Human Rights and other agencies inspect prisons.

Former Cuban prisoners arrive in Miami with reports of continued beatings and denounce Castro's efforts to mislead human rights inspectors.

Cuba and South Africa agree to withdraw their troops from Angola and from Namibia. No accord yet reached, however, on Jonas Savimbi's participation in an Angolan government of national reconciliation.

Index